CU01083878

The Arab Spring Abroad

The Arab Spring revolutions of 2011 sent shockwaves across the globe, mobilizing diaspora communities to organize forcefully against authoritarian regimes. Despite the important role that diasporas can play in influencing affairs in their countries of origin, little is known about when diaspora actors mobilize, how they intervene, or what makes them effective. This book addresses these questions, drawing on more than 230 original interviews, fieldwork, and comparative analysis. Examining Libyan, Syrian, and Yemeni mobilization from the United States and Great Britain before and during the revolutions, Dana M. Moss presents a new framework for understanding the transnational dynamics of contention and the social forces that either enable or suppress transnational activism. This title is also available as Open Access on Cambridge Core.

DANA M. MOSS is Assistant Professor of Sociology at the University of Notre Dame. Her research investigates how authoritarian forces repress their critics and how social movements resist this repression in a globalized world. Her work has been published in top sociology venues, and has received several awards from the American Sociological Association. This is her first book.

Cambridge Studies in Contentious Politics

General Editor

Doug McAdam *Stanford University and Center for Advanced Study in the Behavioral Sciences*

Editors

Mark Beissinger *Princeton University*
Donatella della Porta *Scuola Normale Superiore*
Jack A. Goldstone *George Mason University*
Michael Hanagan *Vassar College*
Holly J. McCammon *Vanderbilt University*
David S. Meyer *University of California, Irvine*
Sarah Soule *Stanford University*
Suzanne Staggenborg *University of Pittsburgh*
Sidney Tarrow *Cornell University*
Charles Tilly (d. 2008) *Columbia University*
Elisabeth J. Wood *Yale University*
Deborah Yashar *Princeton University*

Rina Agarwala, *Informal Labor, Formal Politics, and Dignified Discontent in India*
Ronald Aminzade, *Race, Nation, and Citizenship in Post-Colonial Africa: The Case of Tanzania*
Ronald Aminzade et al., *Silence and Voice in the Study of Contentious Politics*
Javier Auyero, *Routine Politics and Violence in Argentina: The Gray Zone of State Power*
Phillip M. Ayoub, *When States Come Out: Europe's Sexual Minorities and the Politics of Visibility*
Amrita Basu, *Violent Conjunctures in Democratic India*
W. Lance Bennett and Alexandra Segerberg, *The Logic of Connective Action: Digital Media and the Personalization of Contentious Politics*
Nancy Bermeo and Deborah J. Yashar, editors, *Parties, Movements, and Democracy in the Developing World*
Clifford Bob, *The Global Right Wing and the Clash of World Politics*
Clifford Bob, *The Marketing of Rebellion: Insurgents, Media, and International Activism*
Robert Braun, *Protectors of Pluralism: Religious Minorities and the Rescue of Jews in the Low Countries during the Holocaust*
Charles Brockett, *Political Movements and Violence in Central America*
Marisa von Bülow, *Building Transnational Networks: Civil Society and the Politics of Trade in the Americas*
Valerie Bunce and Sharon Wolchik, *Defeating Authoritarian Leaders in Postcommunist Countries*
Teri L. Caraway and Michele Ford, *Labor and Politics in Indonesia*

(continued after index)

The Arab Spring Abroad

Diaspora Activism against Authoritarian Regimes

DANA M. MOSS
University of Notre Dame

CAMBRIDGE
UNIVERSITY PRESS

University Printing House, Cambridge CB2 8BS, United Kingdom

One Liberty Plaza, 20th Floor, New York, NY 10006, USA

477 Williamstown Road, Port Melbourne, VIC 3207, Australia

314–321, 3rd Floor, Plot 3, Splendor Forum, Jasola District Centre, New Delhi – 110025, India

103 Penang Road, #05–06/07, Visioncrest Commercial, Singapore 238467

Cambridge University Press is part of the University of Cambridge.

It furthers the University's mission by disseminating knowledge in the pursuit of
education, learning, and research at the highest international levels of excellence.

www.cambridge.org
Information on this title: www.cambridge.org/9781009272155
DOI: 10.1017/9781009272148

© Dana M. Moss 2022
Reissued as Open Access, 2022

This work is in copyright. It is subject to statutory exceptions and to the provisions of relevant licensing
agreements; with the exception of the Creative Commons version the link for which is provided below, no
reproduction of any part of this work may take place without the written permission of Cambridge University
Press.

An online version of this work is published at doi.org/10.1017/9781009272148 under a Creative Commons
Open Access license CC-BY-NC-ND 4.0 which permits re-use, distribution and reproduction in any medium for
non-commercial purposes providing appropriate credit to the original work is given. You may not distribute
derivative works without permission. To view a copy of this license, visit https://creativecommons.org/licenses/by-
nc-nd/4.0

All versions of this work may contain content reproduced under license from third parties. Permission to
reproduce this third-party content must be obtained from these third-parties directly.

When citing this work, please include a reference to the DOI 10.1017/9781009272148

First published 2022

A catalogue record for this publication is available from the British Library.

Library of Congress Cataloging-in-Publication Data

Names: Moss, Dana M., author.
Title: The Arab Spring abroad : diaspora activism against authoritarian regimes / Dana M. Moss.
Description: Cambridge, United Kingdom ; New York, NY : Cambridge University Press, 2021. | Series:
Cambridge studies in contentious politics | Includes bibliographical references and index.
Identifiers: LCCN 2021014186 (print) | LCCN 2021014187 (ebook) | ISBN 9781108845533 (hardback) |
ISBN 9781009272155 (paperback) | ISBN 9781009272148 (epub)
Subjects: LCSH: Arab Spring, 2010- | Arabs–Foreign countries. | Arab countries–Politics and
government–21st century. | BISAC: SOCIAL SCIENCE / Sociology / General
Classification: LCC JQ1850.A91 M68 2021 (print) | LCC JQ1850.A91 (ebook) |
DDC 909/.097492708312–dc23
LC record available at https://lccn.loc.gov/2021014186
LC ebook record available at https://lccn.loc.gov/2021014187

ISBN 978-1-009-27215-5 Paperback

Cambridge University Press has no responsibility for the persistence or accuracy
of URLs for external or third-party internet websites referred to in this publication
and does not guarantee that any content on such websites is, or will remain,
accurate or appropriate.

Contents

Figures

Tables

Acknowledgments

This project has incurred many debts over the years. It would not have been possible without funding from the National Science Foundation's Doctoral Dissertation Research Improvement Grant (#1433642), the American Institute for Yemeni Studies' Pre-Dissertation Fellowship, several Kugelman Citizen Peacebuilding Research Fellowships, the Center for Global Peace and Conflict Studies' Research Award, funding from the Center for the Study of Democracy and the Department of Sociology at University of California, Irvine (UCI), and a Type I Faculty Research Grant from the University of Pittsburgh. I am especially grateful to all of the members of UCI's Center for Citizen Peacebuilding – and especially Larry and Dulcie Kugelman – for their exemplary enthusiasm for graduate student research. Parts of this book have appeared previously in *Social Forces* (Moss 2020) and *Social Problems* (Moss 2016b). I thank the editors at Oxford University Press for permission to reprint parts of these articles here.

I do not have the words to adequately thank the activists and organizers who spent many precious hours speaking with me about their experiences. Many went out of their way to facilitate my fieldwork, host me in their homes, share meals, and help me find my way, literally and figuratively. Special thanks are due (in no particular order) to Rabyaah Althaibani and her family, Ibrahim Al Qataby, Mazen Obaid, Safa Mubgar and the girls, Adel Aulaqi, Shaima Saif, the Al-Hakimi family, the Mashjari family, Ilham Ali, Khaled Ahmed, Ayat Mneina, Abdallah Omeish, Rihab Elhaj, Walid Raghei and his parents, and Gihan Badi and her family for their gracious assistance and overwhelming hospitality. I certainly would not have made it to Libya and back, given the timing of my trip after the 2013 attack on the US consulate in Benghazi, without Abdallah, Rihab, and Walid. Thanks also to the many organizers I met along the way who invited and welcomed me to their events.

I am deeply indebted to the many scholars who have commented on this work in part and in full. David Snow, my exceptional advisor and mentor of many years, has always counseled me with wisdom and patience; I have been beyond lucky to have him as a guide and dear friend. Yang Su's candid insights, belief in my abilities, and coaching make me a better scholar; I continue to strive to "have more swagger" (but also not too much). David Meyer is a tireless guide who never neglects to ask how I am doing; thank you for helping to shepherd this book into reality. A debt is also owed to David J. Frank for being such a wonderfully wise and positive mentor over these many years.

Many others lent their labor to making this book better, suffering through early drafts of the manuscript and its article-length components to help me get out of my own way. These individuals include the participants of my book workshop in 2018 – Sidney Tarrow, Roger Waldinger, Wendy Pearlman, and Clifford Bob – as well as Lauren Duquette-Rury, Charles Kurzman, Rory McVeigh, Josh Bloom, Suzanne Staggenborg, Phillip Ayoub, Andy Andrews, John Markoff, Jackie Smith, Alejandro Portes, Colin Beck, John McCarthy, Jack Delehanty, Gerasimos Tsourapas, Ali Chaudhary, Kim Ebert, Marcus Michaelsen, Maria Koinova, Marlies Glasius, Fiona Adamson, Bahar Baser, L. E. Picard, Mohammed Bamyeh, Judy Stepan-Norris, and Charles Ragin. The participants of the 2020 Culture and Politics Workshop at the University of North Carolina at Chapel Hill and the 2019 New York University Abu Dhabi conference on "Theorizing Social Change, Institutions, and Culture," especially Zeynep Ozgen, Edward Kiser, Elisabeth Anderson, and Michelle O'Brien, all provided extremely helpful comments on different drafts. I am also deeply appreciative of the research assistance of Mark Robison and Eli Williams at the University of Notre Dame. The ever-cheerful John Ewing did an exceptional job helping me to edit the manuscript, and Trent Hancock produced a masterfully digitized index with grace and patience. Thank you both for your efforts on my behalf. I also thank the anonymous reviewers who provided feedback on an earlier version of the manuscript.

Many friends, mentors, and colleagues – including Ali Kadivar, Aliza Luft, Ann Hironaka, Ann Mische, Atef Said, Brandon Gorman, David Cunningham, Diana Fu, Edelina Burciaga, Edward Lemon, Eric Schoon, Francesca Polletta, Gillian Kennedy, Hank Johnston, Irene Bloemraad, Jaime Kucinskas, Jean Beaman, Jeffrey Lane, Junia Howell, Katie Bolzendahl, Karida Brown, Kraig Beyerlein, Maria Abascal, Mark Paterson, Michael Goodhart, Nina Bandelj, Pamela Oliver, Roberta Lessor, Roger Rouse, Saipira Furstenberg, Sharon Quinsaat, Tarun Banerjee, William Carbonaro, and Waverly Duck – have been sources of invaluable advice and support. Melanie Hughes and her spouse, Britton, made Pittsburgh feel like home for us. Our years spent in California would have been deeply impoverished without the friendships of Beth Gardner, Amber Tierney, Savannah Steele, Zaib Tufail, Matt Rafalow, Mariam Ashtiani, Josh and Laina Malnight, Sahar Khan, Burrel Vann, Martín Jacinto, and many others. I will never forget the generosity of Hibba Abugideiri, Catherine

Warrick, Barbara Romaine, Brian Jones, and Rick Eckstein of Villanova University, and of Jane Satterfield, Ned Balbo, Barbara Vann, and Lovell Smith at Loyola University in Maryland. Thank you for seeing me and appreciating my efforts; I will forever appreciate yours.

I spent almost every day revising this book with the brilliant sociologist Jessica Simes and the most incredible group of scholar-writer friends, including Cati Connell, Sultan Doughan, Merav Shohet, Jackie Jahn, Ana Villarreal, Paula Austin, Sarah Miller, and Saida Grundy. Thank you all for your encouragement and commiseration this year and beyond; your unwavering comradeship has made my heart full. The final months of revising this book amid a global pandemic, the 2020 US presidential election, and a move to the Midwest would have been overwhelming without the unconditional love and laughter from Sarah Gregory, my oldest friend from across the pond.

My penchant for asking questions and challenging the answers is owed to my parents, Nancy and John. Thank you for always being so enthusiastic and understanding about my plans. All of my family members have been tremendous sources of encouragement and support during this project. Special thanks are also due to Kate and Don Picard for helping to make this work possible. To anyone I may have forgotten, please know that I value you beyond words.

In closing, this book is dedicated to Layla Picard. She has been my daily source of inspiration to keep this project going. I am beyond lucky to have such a brilliant and all-around wonderful person as my wife and best friend.

A Note on Transliteration

This book uses a simplified version of the 2012 Library of Congress style of transliteration for Arabic (www.loc.gov/catdir/cpso/roman.html). Diacritical marks, such as macrons and underdots, have been omitted except for 'ayn (') and hamza (') when they appear in the middle of a word, e.g., Sana'a, Aden (rather than 'Aden), Tha'er. Arabic plurals, both irregular and sound, are rendered simply with an "s." Proper nouns with universally accepted English spellings are rendered accordingly.

Abbreviations

CT	conflict transmission
FSA	Free Syrian Army
ICC	International Criminal Court
ICG	International Crisis Group
ISIS	Islamic State of Iraq and Al-Sham
LCC	Local Coordination Committees (in Syria)
LETF	Libyan Emergency Task Force
MENA	Middle East and North Africa
NATO	North Atlantic Treaty Organization
NFSL	National Front for the Salvation of Libya
NGO	nongovernmental organization
SAC	Syrian American Council
SNC	Syrian National Council
TR	transnational repression
UCI	University of California, Irvine
UN	United Nations
YCA	Yemeni Community Association

This title is part of the Cambridge University Press *Flip it Open* Open Access Books program and has been "flipped" from a traditional book to an Open Access book through the program.

Flip it Open sells books through regular channels, treating them at the outset in the same way as any other book; they are part of our library collections for Cambridge Core, and sell as hardbacks and ebooks. The one crucial difference is that we make an upfront commitment that when each of these books meets a set revenue threshold we make them available to everyone Open Access via Cambridge Core.

This paperback edition has been released as part of our Open Access commitment and we would like to use this as an opportunity to thank the libraries and other buyers who have helped us flip this and the other titles in the program to Open Access.

To see the full list of libraries that we know have contributed to *Flip it Open*, as well as the other titles in the program please visit https://www.cambridge.org/core/services/open-research/open-access/oa-book-pilot-flip-it-open/flip-it-open-acknowledgements

Introduction

The Middle East and North Africa (MENA) has long fascinated Western observers, more often than not out of a sense of misguided curiosity. Owing to imperialism, Orientalism, and enduring stereotypes, commentary has revolved around a central query: Why is the region and its people so "backward"? The social sciences have remained focused on this question, albeit in a modified form, since the fall of the Soviet Union (Bayat 2013; Munif 2020). As researchers looked optimistically to a post-1989 future that appeared to be liberalizing, they asked why the wave of democracy sweeping the formerly colonized world had bypassed the MENA region. The answer provided, in one form or another, was that regimes led by autocrats, kings, and presidents-for-life were too powerful and the people too weak – too loyal, apathetic, divided, and tribal – to mount a credible challenge to authoritarian rule.[1]

Such a view errs, of course, by overlooking how countries across the MENA region have given rise to social movements for liberation, equality, and human rights throughout modern history (Bayat 2017; Gerges 2015). Whether emerging from the gilded elite or the grassroots, its people have always fought against foreign rule and domestic tyranny (Bayat 2013). Even so, mass mobilization against enduring dictatorships seemed unlikely after the "Global War on Terror," launched by the United States and its allies after the terrorist attacks of September 11, 2001, made friends out of former enemies. Foreign powers fed dictatorships in places such as Egypt, Libya, and Yemen billions of dollars' worth of aid and weapons. They also cooperated with so-called enemies, such as the Assad regime in Syria, to render and torture suspects of

---

[1] See Brownlee et al. (2015: Introduction, ch. 1) for a comprehensive overview of the literature oriented around democratization and authoritarianism in the MENA region.

terrorism. By 2010, autocrats augmented by oil wealth had Western nations so cozily in their pockets that their confidence in perpetual rule was sky high.

With so much attention focused on authoritarian durability, it is little wonder that the revolutions to follow caught scholars and governments by surprise (Bamyeh and Hanafi 2015). This new era of revolt began in Tunisia in December 2010; within weeks, demonstrations against corruption and repression had spread to Egypt, Yemen, Libya, Syria, and Bahrain. These uprisings, which have become known as the "Arab Spring,"[2] spanned from the sapphire-blue waters of the Mediterranean coast to the green highlands of the Arabian Peninsula. As tens of thousands of ordinary people demanded their dignity by marching in the streets against corruption and abuse, popular movements and insurgencies destabilized regimes thought to be unshakable. The conflicts that ensued produced both improbable triumphs through selfless heroism and devastating losses through abject slaughter. But well before this wave gave rise to resurgent dictatorships and civil wars (Lynch 2016), the masses shook the earth with rage and made dictators quake with fear.

Revolutions are rarely neatly confined to their places of origin, however. They also galvanize anti-regime activists in the diaspora around the globe, and the Arab Spring was no exception. Diaspora mobilization for the Arab Spring was no trivial matter. Long before foreign governments and international organizations jumped in to support revolutionaries, ordinary emigrants, refugees, and their children protested in Washington, DC, London, and New York City against their home-country regimes; channeled millions of dollars' worth of aid to poorly equipped insurgencies and beleaguered refugees; and traveled homeward to join the revolutions as rescue workers, interpreters, and fighters. Diaspora activists' efforts to help their compatriots under siege not only heralded a new wave of transnational activism, but exposed regimes' crimes against humanity and saved lives on the ground. Their mobilization against authoritarianism also signified a new phase in community empowerment and collective action, particularly among those who had grown up in places where speaking out against ruling dictatorships could get a person imprisoned, tortured, or killed.

---

[2] As scholars such as Holmes (2019) have rightly pointed out, the Arab Spring is a misnomer since many non-Arabs participated in revolts and protests, from the Nubians of Egypt to the Kurds of Syria. I use this label intentionally, however, because it commonly refers to the protest wave initiated in Tunisia in 2011 and carried on by protesters in Yemen, Egypt, Libya, Syria, and Bahrain in 2011 (and beyond in some cases). In contrast to Bayat (2017), I characterize these movements as *revolutionary* (rather than "refolutionary") due to the fact that they demanded the fall of dictatorships, not reforms, and new social, economic, and political arrangements to ensure justice and equity (see also Brownlee et al. 2015; Holmes 2019). Of course, what these demands actually meant to participants in practice depended on who or what movements within the revolutionary coalitions one is referring to (e.g., the Muslim Brotherhood versus secular feminists).

Although the Arab Spring uprisings are well-known, the role that diaspora movements played in this revolutionary wave is not. This is not surprising, given the guiding assumption among social scientists that protesters must be present – proximate, in person, and ready to storm the gates – to challenge authoritarians.[3] As economist Albert Hirschman (1970) describes in his hallmark work *Exit, Voice, and Loyalty,* populations aggrieved with their governments can do one of three things. They can either remain *loyal* and hope for the best, *voice* their dissent at home through protest – a high-risk strategy in authoritarian contexts – or *exit*, thereby voting against authorities with their feet. Hirschman argues that exit in the form of emigration, whether forced or voluntary, decimates the potential for voice and social change.[4] By breaking up dissident networks and separating leaders from their adherents, exit acts as a safety valve for regimes by releasing pressure from below, thereby reducing "the prospects for advance, reform, or revolution" (Hirschman 1986: 90).

Yet, as the case of the Arab Spring abroad demonstrates, dissidents who travel abroad have the potential to induce change from without. In fact, those who remain loyal to the people and places left behind can use voice *after* exit to demand change at home (Glasius 2018; Hirschman 1993; Hoffmann 2010; Mueller 1999; Newland 2010; Pfaff 2006; Pfaff and Kim 2003). Members of diasporas – a term used here to refer to the exiles, émigrés, expatriates, refugees, and emigrants of different generations who attribute their origins to a common place – do so for many reasons.[5] Memories of their lives before displacement,

---

[3] For notable exceptions, see works by Amarsaringham (2015) and Quinsaat (2013, 2019).

[4] This is why regimes "behead opposition groups by allowing, encouraging, and forcing exit" (Hirschman 1993: 84) and cast their opponents into exile. Authorities also discredit exiles by slandering them as traitors and outlaws (Glasius 2018).

[5] Here, "diaspora" is a descriptor used akin to the way sociologists use the term "emigrant" – a person who has exited from a country where they no longer reside – but it is also preferable to using the latter term since many diaspora activists have never themselves emigrated, being of the second or third generation, and because many of my respondents called themselves diaspora members. By using "diaspora" to describe activists and their movements and organizations (which is a synonym of diasporic, but less awkward), I refer to the biographical, cognitive, and structural orientations of persons and their social, political, and economic practices vis-à-vis a shared place of origin, that is, a "home-country." While many diasporas speak of a "homeland" instead of a home-country – as in the case of the Palestinians or Kurds – the actual places where diaspora members are rooted tend to fall within the jurisdictions of states. I thus use home-country and homeland interchangeably in some parts of this book for practical and stylistic reasons.

In order to distinguish the attributed place of origin from the place of residence, I use "host-country" as a synonym of "receiving country" or "country of settlement." This does not mean that the persons in this study only consider their place of origin as "home" and their place of residence as temporary. I found that many interviewees consider the United States or Britain more so their "home" than anywhere else; for others, they felt belonging to (and rejection from) more than one country as well. In a world where persons are increasingly embracing hybrid identities (Hall 2016) and may attribute their belonging to multiple locations and communities, the distinctions here are made for the purposes of analysis and are not intended to essentialize

connections to grandparents and friends from home, summertime visits to their hometowns, annual picnics and flag-flying parades, religious gatherings and diaspora associations, grief and nostalgia over childhoods spent in the homeland, and foreign business dealings all serve to bind members of national and ethnic groups to a home-country (Guarnizo et al. 2003; R. Smith 2006). So too do experiences of marginalization in the host-country make them feel more at home in their places of origin. Consequently, diaspora members' "ways of being and ways of belonging" can bind them to the homeland and become transnational in character (Levitt and Glick Schiller 2004: 1002), rather than bound within their place of settlement.[6]

History shows that exile has long served as an incubator for diaspora voice. While traumatic for its victims, banishment enables dissidents to survive abroad during periods of repressive crackdown at home (Gualtieri 2009; He 2014; Ma 1993; Shain 2005[1989], 2007; Taylor 1989). Many nation-states have been founded by exiles, including China's Sun Yat-sen, Poland's Tadeusz Kościuszko, and Vietnam's Ho Chi Minh. Others have captured revolutions already underway, as when Vladimir Lenin returned by German train to lead the Bolshevik coup d'état in Russia and Ruhollah Khomeini arrived by plane from France to forge the Islamic Republic of Iran. Diaspora members from the Balkans, Ireland, Sri Lanka, and Eritrea have bankrolled wars and funded

---

persons' experiences or felt sense of belonging, which are subject to change over time. As scholars such as Anthias (1998: 563–64), Brubaker (2005, 2015), and Wald (2008, 2009) argue, we should not assume that diaspora members experience "some kind of primordial bond" because "there may be as much difference and division as commonality and solidarity." This is why this study treats collective action by diaspora members as a dependent variable, as per the calls of Brubaker (2015) and Waldinger (2015).

[6] Diasporas need not be organized into a bounded, distinct group to retain loyalties to people and places in the homeland and take up voice on their behalf. Because diaspora members do not constitute naturally occurring groups, scholars have increasingly refuted the notion that their members form pre-configured communities through trauma and displacement (Cohen 1996). Instead, the term "diaspora" is used increasingly to designate persons with a common tie to a foreign place of origin, as in the case of refugees and expatriates, immigrants, and economic migrants (Safran 1991; on the use of the term, see also Anderson 1998, 2006[1983]; Appadurai 1997; Butler 2001; Clifford 1994; Tölölyan 1996). Diaspora members' transnational ties to the homeland and to one other are often forged through the conscientious mobilization strategies by exiles, emigrants, and states (Abramson 2017; Ragazzi 2014; Sökefeld 2006). Their members may, for instance, form social and political associations in order to foster membership in a community, whether real or "imagined," and to inculcate a sense of shared history and interests (Anderson 2006[1983]). In these ways, second and later emigrant generations can retain transnational membership and feel deep affection for foreign locales, even if they themselves do not remember their early years in the homeland or have never visited it themselves. These efforts also reinforce loyalties and obligations to the home-country by drawing members' attention to the realities of home-country conflicts and crises and suggesting what kinds of interventions are needed (Duquette-Rury 2020; Shain 2007: 5). As Shain (2007: 106) argues, transnational connections may be social, psychological, economic, or all of the above; when kin are threatened by home-country crises, these attachments have high stakes and real-life consequences.

nation-building projects from afar by channeling cash and matériel to their homelands (Hirt 2014; Hockenos 2003; Lainer-Vos 2013; Ma 1990; Maney 2000). In a world where having a nation-state grants ethnic groups protection (Mann 2005), minority movements among Tibetans, Palestinians, Basques, and Kurds have demanded sovereignty and ethno-religious rights in their homelands (Adamson 2019; Bamyeh 2014; Baser 2015; J. Hess 2009). Expatriates with axes to grind, such as anti-communist Cubans and Iraqis opposing Saddam Hussein, have also forged powerful lobbies to challenge home-country governments and shape host-country foreign policy (Ambrosio 2002; Mearsheimer and Walt 2007; T. Smith 2000; Vertovec 2005). In these cases and many others, exiles and diaspora movements have become what Yossi Shain (2005[1989]: xv) describes as "some of the most prominent harbingers of regime change" in the world (see also Field 1971).

As authoritarianism resurges across the globe today and in the foreseeable future (Repucci 2020), diaspora movements will undoubtedly continue to play a central role in an increasingly urgent fight against dictatorships. But although they have played a notable role in fomenting change in their homelands for centuries, surprisingly little attention has been paid to explaining their interventions. To fill this gap, I address two central questions: When do diaspora movements emerge to contest authoritarianism in their places of origin? How, and under what conditions, do activists fuel rebellions therein? By systematically investigating how revolutions ricocheted from Libya, Syria, and Yemen to the United States and Great Britain, this book provides interesting new answers.

The central contribution of *The Arab Spring Abroad* is the provision of a set of conditions explaining when, how, and the extent to which diasporas wield voice after exit against authoritarian regimes. In so doing, the book demonstrates that exit neither *undermines* voice, as Hirschman (1970) suggests, nor does it necessarily *foster* voice, as historical examples of exile mobilization illustrate. Instead, I argue that while *some* exiles use exit as an opportunity for voice, diaspora members' ties to an authoritarian home-country are more likely to *suppress* voice after exit within the wider anti-regime community for at least one of two reasons.

The first is that *home-country regimes may actively repress voice* in the diaspora using violence and threats. When they do, non-exiles are likely to remain silent in order to protect themselves and their relatives in the home-country. The second reason is that *home-country ties can entangle diaspora members in divisive, partisan conflicts rooted in the home-country.* When these home-country rifts travel abroad through members' transnational ties, they can factionalize regime opponents and make anti-regime solidarity practically impossible. I find that these two transnational forces – what I term *transnational repression* and *conflict transmission*, respectively – largely deterred anti-regime diaspora members from Libya, Syria, and Yemen from coming out and coming together against authoritarianism before the revolutions in 2011.

This book then demonstrates how and why this situation can change. Specifically, I show how major disruptions to politics-as-usual in the home-country can give rise to voice abroad. As regimes massacred demonstrators, prompted the formation of revolutionary coalitions, and led to major humanitarian crises during the Arab Spring, they induced what sociologist David Snow et al. (1998) call *quotidian disruptions* to everyday life and regime control. The revolutions therefore not only produced civil insurgencies and wars at home, but also traveled through diaspora members' ties to produce quotidian disruptions abroad. As I detail further below, as the Arab Spring undermined the *efficacy* of regimes' long-distance threats and *united* previously fragmented groups, outspoken exiles and silent regime opponents decided to come out and come together to wield voice to an unprecedented degree.

At the same time, the final chapters of the book argue that even after diaspora members take up voice in unprecedented ways, they only come to make impactful *interventions* in anti-authoritarian rebellions if two additive factors come into play. Drawing from the comparative analysis, I show that they must (1) gain the capacity to *convert resources* to a shared cause, and (2) gain *geopolitical support* from states and other powerholders in order to become auxiliary forces for anti-authoritarianism. When they do, they can channel cash to their allies, mobilize policymakers, and facilitate humanitarian aid delivery on the front lines. Otherwise, activists may voice their demands on the street, but they will not become empowered to fuel rebellion and relief when their help is needed most. Taken together, by bringing attention to the important, but dynamic and highly contingent, roles that diaspora movements play in contentious politics, this study demonstrates when voice after exit emerges, how it matters, and the conditions giving rise to diaspora movement interventions for rebellion and relief.

Before elaborating these claims, this chapter summarizes the events of the Arab Spring, explains the puzzles that motivated this research, and justifies the comparisons that form the basis of my analysis.

1.1 THE ARAB SPRING UPRISINGS

The Arab Spring began with a lone spark of discontent on December 17, 2010, when a young Tunisian named Mohammed Bouazizi set himself on fire to protest police harassment. This act of despair galvanized demonstrations, and after a police crackdown, protests escalated into a nationwide rebellion against the twenty-three-year dictatorship of Zine El Abidine Ben Ali. After labor strikes crippled the country and the military refused to shoot into the crowds, Ben Ali and his family fled Tunisia to Saudi Arabia, stunning global audiences on January 14, 2011. Just days later, activists in Egypt followed suit. On January 25, protesters in Cairo broke through police cordons to occupy a central downtown location called Tahrir Square. After setting up an encampment, snipers and thugs attacked the sit-in movement in full view of the international media.

Protesters stood their ground in Cairo and beyond, set police stations ablaze, pleaded with the military to defect, and spurred a nationwide labor strike. After failing to quell the protesters with force, Egypt's pharaoh-president Hosni Mubarak resigned days later, on February 11.

As rumors circulated as to which regime would be next, activists and ordinary people in the region's poorest country, the Republic of Yemen, came out in force. From the dusty, cobblestoned roads of the capital Sana'a to the humidity-soaked lowlands of the south, citizens of one of the world's most heavily armed nations marched peacefully to demand the resignation of their longtime president, Ali Abdullah Saleh. Vowing to stay on, it did not take long before Saleh unleashed gunmen to clear the streets. The brazen murders of unarmed protesters, including a massacre on March 18, dubbed the Friday of Dignity (*Jumaat al-Karamah*), led to the defection of military, government, and tribal elites. After pitched battles with loyalists in the summer, Saleh remained dug in – that is, until a bomb planted in the presidential palace sent him to a hospital in Saudi Arabia. Facing pressures at home and sanctions from the United Nations, he eventually signed a deal, brokered by the members of the Gulf Cooperation Council, to step down in November 2011 in exchange for legal immunity.

While Egyptians battled regime loyalists back in February, rumors circulated online that Libya was planning its own "Day of Rage." The regime of Colonel Muammar al-Gaddafi attempted to preempt protests by arresting a well-known lawyer, Fathi Terbil, in Libya's eastern city of Benghazi. Instead of preventing protests, however, the arrest of this local hero did the opposite. Benghazians had long suffered at the hand of Gaddafi, who had come to power in 1969, and Terbil's arrest provoked a riot. As the military in Benghazi defected or fled, protests spread westward all the way to the capital of Tripoli. In response, Gaddafi promised to cleanse the streets of "rats" and "cockroaches" (Bassiouni 2013). After the United Nations Security Council approved intervention against his onslaught, a nascent insurgency of military defectors and volunteers became embroiled in a revolutionary war backed by global powers. But intervention by NATO was no guarantee of success. A terrible siege against the port city of Misrata and a stalemate along the Nafusa Mountains dragged on into the summer. In August, however, the forces of the Free Libyan Army (also known as the National Liberation Army) broke the impasse and marched on Tripoli, prompting Gaddafi and his loyalists to flee into the desert. By November, the self-proclaimed "King of Africa" was captured and killed, signifying the end of a forty-two-year-long nightmare.

In February, once-unthinkable forms of public criticism began to emerge in Syria, which had been kept under the thumb of a totalitarian family dynasty for more than forty years. As demonstrators in Damascus were beaten and incarcerated for holding peaceful vigils, protests erupted in outlying cities such as Dara'a against local corruption and daily indignities. The response of Bashar al-Assad's regime was murderous, and the imprisonment of children who had scrawled Arab Spring slogans in graffiti only stoked more outrage. While the growing protest movement initially called for reform, repression turned protesters into full-scale revolutionaries. Bashar al-Assad unleashed the full power of the military and loyalists against civilians according to the creed "Bashar, or we burn the country," and revolutionaries were left with little choice but to defend themselves from being massacred. Facing barrel bombs, Scud missiles, and chemical weapons, entire towns and cities were decimated by Assad and his backers (including Hezbollah, Russia, and Iran) in the following months and years. The ensuing war also enabled foreign extremists, from Ahrar al-Sham to the so-called Islamic State (ISIS), to flood in from Iraq, which Assad used to further justify mass destruction. As hundreds of thousands were killed and millions fled, the violence produced the world's worst refugee crisis since World War II. Ten years later, pockets of resistance remained active, but the regime's allies had enabled its survival. However, it should not be forgotten that for a time, the Syrian people had brought it to the brink.

More to the point: In the early days of the Arab Spring in 2011, the fate of these movements was far from certain; as spring turned into summer, people across the world tuned in day and night on their laptops and televisions to watch the uprisings unfold. Stomach-churning reports detailed the exceedingly high price that ordinary people in the region were paying for speaking out. Victims included defenseless youth in Yemen, mowed down by snipers; video footage displayed their lifeless bodies lying side by side, wrapped in white sheets stained with blood. Libya's most beloved citizen-journalist with a kind smile, Mohammed Nabbous, was shot and killed in March during Gaddafi's attack on Benghazi. In May, global audiences learned that a thirteen-year-old boy named Hamza al-Khateeb had been tortured to death by Syrian forces for smuggling food to protesters under siege. Nevertheless, the people persisted. Libyans rallied around the slogan "we win or we die" of famed freedom fighter Omar al-Mukhtar, a martyr of the resistance against Italian colonizers. Syrian men carried their children on their shoulders to the city of Homs's iconic New Clock Tower to chant "al-sha'ab yurid isqat al-nitham!" (the people demand the fall of the regime!). Tens of thousands of Yemeni women and men occupied the highways of Sana'a, the sloping streets of Ta'iz, and the lowlands of Aden in the south to demand liberty, bread, and dignity.

Further afield, other movements were crushed or quelled. Bahrain's sit-in movement in Manama was swiftly suppressed under the weight of Saudi tanks, while protesters in Morocco and Jordan struck a tacit détente with their kings. Meanwhile, the masses in Libya, Syria, and Yemen faced prolonged and bloody standoffs over the course of 2011 and beyond that would forever change the region. It would also have an indelible impact on anti-regime diasporas across the world.

1.2 THE ARAB SPRING ABROAD

As the Arab Spring spread across the region, so too did it activate supporters in the Libyan, Syrian, and Yemeni diasporas. Over steaming teacups in a crowded London tea shop, a young professional named Sarah recalled how the Arab Spring marked her entrée into the anti-regime struggle. After Gaddafi's forces had fired on unarmed protesters in February, she told me, Sarah's aunt rang her from Benghazi to report that her young cousin had been killed. Sarah was stunned. She had not even been following the news that day, much less anticipating an open revolt that would impact her family so deeply. After a shocked pause, Sarah urged her aunt to stay indoors. But her aunt had refused, declaring, "Sarah, it's either him or us." In the words of Omar al-Mukhtar, the time had come to win against their oppressor or die trying. Gunfire rattled in the background as Sarah hung up the phone.

The following day, Sarah continued, she met her Libyan friends at a cafe. Usually, they chatted about work or played squash. Today, clasping their hands around ceramic cups, the mood was sullen. Sarah's friend finally spoke up. He proposed that they go protest at the Libyan embassy. They agreed, but Sarah was nervous. Despite having attended demonstrations for other causes in the past, she had never done anything political for Libya before. Sarah pulled the hood of her sweatshirt tightly around her face as they waited for a bus to Knightsbridge in central London. Libya's uprising had just begun and the consequences were uncertain, but it had suddenly become unthinkable to stay at home and do nothing.

For Libyans forced into exile, on the other hand, the Arab Spring was the moment that they had been waiting for their entire lives. Thousands of miles away, in the trimmed suburbs of Los Angeles, a young couple named Hamid and Dina told me their story. Like Sarah, Dina's activism for regime change was new; Hamid, on the other hand, was a seasoned veteran. His uncles had been killed fighting Gaddafi in the 1980s, and the family had been forced to flee after his birth. This dislocation bonded Hamid to fellow exiles – lifelong friends such as Ahmed and Abdullah, Hibba and M.[7] – whose hatred of Gaddafi smoldered like a burn on their guts. From these friendships they forged *Gaddafi Khalas!* (Enough Gaddafi!), an organization dedicated to publicizing the regime's atrocities and organizing a protest against Gaddafi's 2009 visit to the United Nations in New York. With regime change looking evermore hopeless by this time, the members of Enough Gaddafi! felt a responsibility to keep the torch of resistance alive. "We had no money and no experience," Hamid told me, "but we had heart. Besides, who else was going to do the job of reminding the world

---

[7] Some names are pseudonyms, or have been shortened to first names or a first initial, according to the preferences of the interviewees and Institutional Review Board-mandated procedures from the University of California, Irvine when these data were collected. Names reported to me second-hand during interviews have also been anonymized.

what a monster Gaddafi really was?" In the years before the revolution, however, their movement was a lonely one. Libyans abroad generally avoided uttering Gaddafi's name, much less broaching the subject of regime change.

In the early days of 2011, Hamid followed the riotous protests underway in Tunisia and Egypt with a fastidious obsession, staying up nights to watch the rebellions unfold on his computer. Once rumors circulated that Libya was going to have an uprising of its own, the Enough Gaddafi! network was ready. If the Libyan people were brave enough to speak out from behind a thick wall of censorship and isolation, he and his colleagues told me, outsiders needed to take notice. Armed with little more than their laptops, Hamid and his friends transformed instantly into the revolution's public relations team. They exposed regime violence unfolding beyond the view of the international media, posted recordings of Libyans' testimonies on Twitter, and documented the death toll in real time. Once at the very fringe of global politics, Hamid and his friends were catapulted overnight into its center by the Arab Spring.

As anti-regime activists like Hamid launched an all-out information war against Gaddafi using the Internet, newcomers like Sarah amassed donations for places like Misrata, a city that became known as Libya's Stalingrad after relentless shelling by the regime. Dina, who met Hamid over the course of the war, traveled from California to Doha and into Libya's liberated territory to coordinate media for the revolution's government-in-waiting. They were joined by many others. Surgeons and students booked tickets to Cairo, driving for hours to volunteer in Libya's field hospitals, remote battlefields, rebel media centers, and tented refugee camps. Businessmen, bureaucrats, and teachers who had previously given up hope of a future without Gaddafi transformed into lobbyists, imploring outside powers to stop the regime's slaughter of civilians. From the first hours of Libya's uprising in February to the fall of Tripoli in August, activists from the diaspora mobilized to lend their labor and their voices to the revolution. Determined not to let their conationals suffer in silence, the anti-regime diaspora joined the struggle in every way imaginable as an auxiliary force against authoritarianism.

Likewise, Syrians in the diaspora intervened for rebellion and relief as the uprising escalated from isolated pockets of resistance to a war that engulfed their homeland. Syrian youth in Chicago and London helped protesters in Damascus to coordinate flash mobs using their MacBooks. White-collar professionals from Arkansas and Florida ushered reporters and politicos, such as US Senator John McCain, into liberated territories while guarded by grim-faced men carrying automatic rifles. Longtime exiles introduced revolutionaries in Syria to US Ambassador Samantha Power at the United Nations and spoke with Jon Stewart on *The Daily Show*. Volunteers from Bristol and Manchester drove ambulances and delivered trauma kits to hospitals in the liberated province of Idlib. Activists also flooded into Turkey to join the revolutionary government-in-waiting, send aid across the border, and hold trainings on how to document war crimes. Long before pundits claimed that the Syrian revolution was doomed to fail, Syrians at home and abroad joined forces to rebel against iron-fisted totalitarianism and support the victims of Assad's scorched-earth response.

Yemenis abroad also mobilized to support the thousands of protesters who poured onto the streets over the course of 2011. Self-appointed lobbyists in Washington, DC, and London demanded that world powers and the United Nations force president Saleh to resign. Activists demonstrated outside the Saudi and Yemeni embassies to demand an end to violence against civilians. Activists held photography exhibitions to educate the public about the uprising and organized fundraising banquets for Islamic Relief's aid work in Yemen. Local leaders also challenged the inertia of their community organizations by demanding that regime sympathizers vacate their posts and make way for new leadership. From her university's cafeteria in Birmingham, a young organizer named Shaima exalted that the Arab Spring had induced "a revolution in the UK, without a doubt!" by bringing community members together for hope, democracy, and dignity as never before.

1.3 THE ROLE OF DIASPORA MOVEMENTS IN CONTENTIOUS POLITICS

Not all emigrants "keep a foot in two worlds" and retain ties to people and places at home (Levitt 2003; Levitt and Glick Schiller 2004; Waldinger and Fitzgerald 2004). The feeling of belonging to the country of origin, as sociologist Roger Waldinger (2015) argues, is subject to fray as later generations become incorporated into their receiving society. Transnational practices may also be "blocked" by home-country conflict and inaccessibility (Huynh and Yiu 2015). Yet, as Waldinger and other social scientists such as Peggy Levitt and Nina Glick Schiller (2004) have demonstrated, first-, 1.5-,[8] and second-generation cohorts often retain some meaningful connection to their places of origin, whether through video chats with their relatives or through their self-professed identities (Brinkerhoff 2009). Equipped with insider knowledge, multilingualism, and a personalized stake in home-country politics, these ties become even more precious when the home-country is insulated from the global media and caged by a repressive regime. Under such circumstances, personalized connections to loved ones at home may be the only way to gather reliable information that circumvents state propaganda and international isolation.

Diaspora members influence homeland affairs by transferring a myriad of resources homeward. Not all diasporas are equally wealthy, but even poor migrants from countries such as Haiti, Tajikistan, and Honduras send millions of dollars homeward every year. In 2017, migrants sent an astounding $613

---

[8] Members of a 1.5 generation typically refer to those who emigrate to a new country by the age of fourteen and come of age in another territory.

billion to their home-countries by air, sea, and wire, 76 percent of which went to low- and middle-income countries (World Bank 2018). These remittances vastly outnumber official aid to these countries by a factor of three (Ratha et al. 2019). Even then, these figures do not account for the millions of dollars that move through informal channels, such as local agents and wire services, to the most remote locales (Horst 2008b, 2008c; Laakso and Hautaniemi 2014; Lyons and Mandaville 2012; Orjuela 2008).

Remittances tie diaspora members to their homelands by reinforcing a sense of obligation to those left behind (Glick Schiller and Fouron 2001). They also grant diasporas a disproportionate influence in home-country politics (Kapur 2010; Lainer-Vos 2013; Shain 2007). While most are used to support family members, remittances are also channeled into public works, charity, and political parties (Bada 2014; Duquette-Rury 2020; Horst 2008a, 2008b, 2008c; Portes and Fernández-Kelly 2015; R. Smith 2006). For these reasons, sending-state governments are increasingly wooing their diasporas by granting national members dual citizenship, out-of-country voting rights, and congressional seats, as well as by forming institutions to foment connectivity (Brand 2014; Gamlen 2014; Gamlen et al. 2017; Harpaz 2019; Ragazzi 2017). Their remittances can also make or break the peace by extending the duration of civil wars, funding reconstruction efforts, or both (Adamson 2013; Brinkerhoff 2011; Byman et al. 2001; Cederman et al. 2009; Collier and Hoeffler 2000; Collier et al. 2003; Orjuela 2008; Shain 2002; H. Smith and Stares 2007).

Diasporas are further primed to become transnational political players because of their privileged "positionality" (Koinova 2012) vis-à-vis those left behind (Germano 2009). Their members often include wealthy, well-educated, and highly skilled activists who go abroad to study at globally ranked universities. Equipped with multilingualism and multiculturalism, "cosmopolitan patriots" (Appiah 1997) and second-generation youth often literally speak the languages of insiders and outsiders alike (M. Hess and Korf 2014). They send what Levitt (1998) calls "social remittances" homeward in the form of foreign cultural practices, knowledge, and skills (Wescott and Brinkerhoff 2006). By circulating ideas that promote civil, political, and human rights, these members enact transnational citizenship and diffuse liberal norms (Boccagni et al. 2016; Finn and Momani 2017; Lacroix et al. 2016). Phillip Ayoub's (2016: 34) study of Polish activism in Germany from 1990 through the 2000s, for instance, shows that expatriates engage in "norm brokerage" by translating international norms to audiences at home and, in turn, connecting outside supporters with home-country activists. Their positioning between social worlds makes them powerful proponents of liberal change (Brinkerhoff 2016; McAdam et al. 2001). It follows that diaspora activists have access to the rhetoric, tactical adaptations, and strategical savvy to remake the homeland in their image (Shain 1999). Researchers also argue that elites are especially primed to become powerful influencers at home (Guarnizo et al. 2003) because their privileges enable them to participate in public affairs and circulate between two or more worlds.

Diaspora groups who settle in countries that purport to uphold political rights and civil liberties are further advantaged by what social movement scholars call "political opportunities" for transnational action (McAdam et al. 1996; Meyer 2004; Tarrow 1998, 2005). These opportunities include the rights to hold peaceful protests, establish social movement organizations, and lobby for political causes at the domestic and international levels (Bauböck 2008; Brubaker and Laitin 1998; Cohen 2008; Eccarius-Kelly 2002; Fair 2007; Orjuela 2018; Østergaard-Nielsen 2003; Wayland 2004). Not all diasporas settle in places that protect the right of assembly or the free flow of information, but those who do are especially well-positioned to disseminate their grievances online, in their communities, and through protests (Amarsaringham 2015; Bernal 2014; Betts and Jones 2016; Brinkerhoff 2005; Quinsaat 2019). Exiles find themselves gaining added opportunities for voice when their aims align with the agendas of host-country policymakers (DeWind and Segura 2014), as in the cases of anti-regime Russians, Cubans, and Iranians in the United States. Iraqi exiles like Ahmad Chalabi, who was on the Central Intelligence Agency's and State Department's payroll for decades, became infamous for helping the administration of president George W. Bush justify the occupation of Iraq (Roston 2008). In this way, as political scientists Alexander Betts and Will Jones (2016: 9) argue, outside patronage "animates" diaspora elites and their movements.

Taken together, research on transnational movements, migration, and diasporas illustrate how contentious politics are not contained within the borders of the nation-state. As national groups and belonging become increasingly "unbound" across state borders (Basch et al. 1994; Harpaz 2019) and transnational practices become easier and cheaper to undertake (Vertovec 2004), so too do diaspora actors appear to wield disproportionate influence in homeland affairs. Equipped with the ties, resources, and political opportunities needed to act on their anti-regime grievances, their actions can create a "serious politics that is at the same time radically unaccountable" (Anderson 1998: 78; see also Adamson 2004; T. Smith 2000). It is for these reasons that scholars such as Benedict Anderson (1998) and Samuel Huntington (1997, 2004) have expressed alarm at the ways in which diaspora movements instigate insurgencies and influence policy in pursuit of sectarian self-interests. Such "unencumbered long-distance nationalists," Anderson (1998: 78) warns, "well and safely positioned in the First World, ... send money and guns, circulate propaganda, and build intercontinental computer information circuits, all of which have incalculable consequences in the zones of their ultimate destinations." For better and for worse, anti-regime diasporas appear well-poised to wield, in Hirschman's terminology (1970), loyalty and voice *after* exit as weapons for change at home.

1.4 EMERGENT PUZZLES FROM THE ARAB SPRING ABROAD

Studies of diaspora and emigrant mobilization have advanced our understanding of contentious politics by demonstrating that their transnational practices shape home-country politics, conflicts, and international relations (Adamson 2006). In light of their home-country loyalties and members' relatively privileged "positionality" abroad (Koinova 2012), it is not especially surprising that diaspora members mobilized to help their compatriots under siege during the Arab Spring. As I set out to investigate this phenomenon by undertaking fieldwork across the United States and Great Britain, I found that Libyans, Syrians, and Yemenis had played up to five major roles in the uprisings. First, they *broadcasted* information about events on the ground and revolutionaries' demands to outside audiences through protests, lobbying, and by publicizing information. Second, they *represented* the revolution to their host-country governments and the media, whether formally or informally, and served in its various organizations and governments-in-waiting. Third, they *brokered* for the rebellions and relief efforts by connecting their allies on the ground with outsiders in politics, the media, and civil society. Fourth, they *remitted* their skills, material aid, and cash to the cause. Lastly, they *volunteered* in the home-country and immediately outside its borders to help their conationals in every way imaginable. While my interviewees firmly asserted that revolutionaries at home were the real heroes, they nevertheless became a collective transnational auxiliary force against authoritarian regimes in 2011 and beyond.

Yet, much of what I learned and observed about diaspora mobilization over the course of my research was downright puzzling – and not only to me, but to many of my respondents as well. For instance, beginning in the fall of 2011, I witnessed hundreds of Syrian Americans come out to support the revolution by demonstrating on the streets of Southern California. During these events, participants raised their voices to demand dignity and freedom for Syria through chants, public appeals, and in song. However, their efforts to engage in what social scientists call public, collective claims-making (Koopmans and Statham 1999; McAdam et al. 2001) by criticizing the Assad regime and demanding international support also had a protective, private quality to it. On the street corners of Anaheim, for instance, demonstrators often hid their faces behind scarves and sunglasses. At a community meeting hosted by the Syrian American Council of Los Angeles in December 2011, I was explicitly instructed not to photograph the audience even though an organizer declared that "the wall of fear has been broken!" Even more confusingly, some activists showed their faces in their communities, but not online; others created pro-revolution Facebook pages, but then quickly made them secret or closed groups. And until I became a familiar face, my presence at protests was also viewed with suspicion. As I observed, the Syrian community was coming out on the streets in greater numbers each week to condemn the Assad regime. However, despite being thousands of miles from the front lines, many seemed deeply reluctant to lend their faces and names to the cause, sometimes even month or years after the revolt's inception.

I was also perplexed by the content of my conversations with Yemeni activists, which often went on for hours over steaming bowls of *ful*, a delicious bean stew that bubbled in blackened bowls, and rice heaping with a traditional salsa-like condiment called *sahawag*. During these extended interviews, I learned that anti-regime mobilization was a deeply unifying *and* fragmenting experience for Yemenis in the diaspora. For instance, from a Yemeni cafe in Birmingham, England, a beaming man named Ali in dark-rimmed glasses described how the Arab Spring had made him feel marginalized and maligned in his own community. Ali described how his writings about the Yemeni revolution were being criticized and censored by his conationals on Facebook, how he and his friends had been shut out of protests, and how hurt they felt by others' efforts to shut them up. Ali had been a longtime supporter of change in Yemen, but as a result of these experiences, he had withdrawn his support shortly after the uprising began. Many other Yemenis echoed a version of his story.

Syrian activists were also deeply divided, and often preoccupied with perceived power grabs and accusations of co-optation in their movements abroad. The transcripts of our conversations read as venting sessions against other like-minded activists and movements *within* the opposition who, as several British respondents put it, spent as much time "slagging each other off" as actually helping their compatriots at home. As a result, many of the most ardent anti-regime exiles and community figures ended up withdrawing their support for the revolution as time wore on. I also learned that diaspora activists' actual interventions in the rebellions and for badly needed humanitarian relief varied considerably. Syrians in Britain, for instance, reported numerous obstacles to supporting the Arab Spring, from the costs of continuously volunteering their time and labor to being left out of the policymaking process. Syrians in the United States, while certainly reporting fatigue and burnout, instead forged a robust set of advocacy and relief organizations and continued lobbying over the course of the revolution and subsequent war.

Furthermore, although Yemenis hailed the Arab Spring as a turning point in their communities, they also detailed their incapacity to help revolutionaries in a tangible way. As Yemen's dissidents were gunned down in city squares and field hospitals were overrun with casualties in 2011, organizers like Shaima found their activist groups unable to do much more than voice their solidarity on the streets from a distance. Shaima and I spent hours together on buses and sipping teas in Birmingham's Bull Ring discussing this paradox. "Here, we're educated," she mused. "We have activist resources .... Even if you're not educated to a certain level, there's opportunities here. It's about just being able to pick it up and move it. But *how do you do that?*" Others across the United States and Britain echoed her befuddlement. The Arab Spring was a remarkable time for the anti-regime diaspora, signifying a new phase in community empowerment and collective action. But activists like Shaima had wanted to do more. As I scrawled notes on planes, trains, and at protest events, so too were my jottings filled with question marks.

The emergence of activism for the Arab Spring abroad clearly illustrates how diaspora movements can matter. Yet, four years of fieldwork on Arab Spring-inspired mobilization left me with a series of questions that needed answering. Why did so few diaspora members openly criticize home-country regimes, as Libyan American Hamid's Enough Gaddafi! network had done, before 2011? Why did it take so long for many of them, especially in the Syrian community, to declare their allegiance to the Arab Spring openly in public? Why did many longtime anti-regime activists withdraw their support for the revolutions in Syria and Yemen? And why did many more conclude that their mobilization potential remained unfulfilled, despite an unprecedented showing of support in 2011?

The more I immersed myself in the existing literature to find answers, the broader my questions became. In the parlance of social movement scholars, why would anti-regime diaspora members with political opportunities, resources, and network ties strategically *refrain* from speaking out against regimes? Why would collective action fragment and die off during a period of acute conflict and need in the home-country? Why do only some diaspora movements with significant privileges vis-à-vis their home-country counterparts succeed in fulfilling their goals? With the potential of transnational activism to make or break the peace at home, inattention to these questions is a serious lacuna. By investigating how these uprisings reached from the global periphery to diaspora communities at the world's "center," this book provides some interesting new insights. The next section elaborates why a comparison of Libyan, Syrian, and Yemeni diaspora activism for the Arab Spring from the United States and Britain provides a useful set of answers. Following this, this book presents a new framework for explaining voice after exit against authoritarian regimes.

1.5 INVESTIGATING LIBYAN, SYRIAN, AND YEMENI ACTIVISM FROM THE UNITED STATES AND BRITAIN

It is sometimes hard to recall what the uprisings meant to those of us who watched them unfold on our screens in real time. I began graduate school just a few months prior to the uprisings with a plan to study social movements in the Middle East. Having spent time in Yemen, studying and volunteering for a local rights organization, I was intrigued by how social movements managed to exist at all, much less pursue human rights, in authoritarian contexts. To some, my topic came off as a curiosity. Responses by US-focused scholars along the lines of *"are* there social movements in the Middle East?" were not uncommon. These reactions changed after the Arab Spring uprisings emerged and inspired the Occupy Wall Street movement, which diffused from New York all the way to Tel Aviv. All of a sudden, my generation was witnessing a global outpouring of rage against authoritarianism and economic austerity on a scale that we had never before witnessed in person.

As the revolutions dethroned dictatorships and shut down city streets, my plans to return to Yemen were undone by the revolution itself. My detour to Jordan that summer was productive, but I felt as if I was missing all the action. Upon returning home to California that fall, however, I discovered that the Arab Spring had emigrated practically to my backyard. Protest movements in support of the uprisings had been popping up in places such as Mile Square Park near my apartment in Orange County, California, to Dearborn, New York, Liverpool, and London, and I wanted to learn more about them. My spouse and I, along with several friends, had co-founded a small nonprofit organization called The Yemen Peace Project in 2010. While we initially worked to criticize the devastating impacts of US drone warfare in the country and to celebrate Yemeni filmmaking and art, many Yemenis became aware of our organization because of our director's tireless work on social media during the 2011 revolution. By the fall of 2011, when I sent inquiries to our Yemeni contacts asking for information about diaspora activism, many responded by inviting me to learn about their work in concentrated communities such as those in Brooklyn, Liverpool, and Birmingham.[9] After doing fieldwork across different cities and spending countless hours in Yemenis' homes, cafes, and in their community associations in 2012, I conducted a total of ninety-two interviews with Yemenis (and one non-Yemeni stakeholder) who had participated in activism for the Yemeni Arab Spring.

While I had refined my questions and learned a great deal during this trip, I had still returned home with more questions than answers. As a result, I made the decision to expand my comparison to include Syrian and Libyan mobilization in the United States and Britain for several reasons. First, while few Yemenis called Southern California home, the region was inhabited by a notable number of Libyans and Syrians who mobilized in response to the Arab Spring as well. Thanks to the kind reception I received from organizers, I joined social media groups and listservs advertising local awareness-raising events, fundraisers, and demonstrations for Libya and Syria. While attending community picnics, fundraising banquets, protests, and awareness-raising forums, their testimonies raised additional questions about diaspora

---

[9] During our preliminary conversations to coordinate the logistics of my trip, several of my key respondents mentioned two things that piqued my curiosity. First, they reported that the effects of the Arab Spring on these communities' voice and visibility were unprecedented. I wanted to know how so and why. Second, Yemenis from both sides of the "pond" claimed that the *other* group had mobilized more effectively than they had. In other words, Yemenis in Britain praised Yemeni-American efforts as being more effective than theirs, and vice versa. This led me to ask if and why this was the case. See the Methodological Appendix for more information.

mobilization. Furthermore, because the Syrian revolution was still unfolding over the course of 2011 and 2012, this gave me an opportunity to see how the Arab Spring was impacting mobilization efforts in real time.

But given the fact that the Arab Spring also occurred in other countries such as Tunisia, Egypt, and Bahrain in 2011, why compare diaspora movements from Syria, Libya, and Yemen? Examining the anti-regime activism of these groups in the United States and Britain made sense on other grounds beyond my newfound access to community events. Out of the six MENA countries that gave rise to revolutionary movements during the Arab Spring,[10] all had been ruled by authoritarian regimes for decades prior to the Arab Spring; undoubtedly, diaspora members from all of these countries were moved by the revolutions.[11] However, only Libya, Syria, and Yemen produced *initial* struggles to upend dictatorships that were sustained over the course of months or longer. For Libyans, this occurred from the uprising's emergence in February to August 2011 when Gaddafi was overrun; the Syrian uprising began in February 2011 and continues at the time of this writing; for Yemenis, the revolution emerged in January 2011 and continued until Saleh agreed to step down that November. In contrast, Tunisia, Egypt, and Bahrain's initial uprisings averaged approximately one month each in duration.

This is not to say that the revolutions were identical in duration or character – far from it.[12] As I elaborate in the chapters to come, variation in the uprisings had important impacts on diaspora activism. Nevertheless, the Libyan, Syrian, and Yemeni rebellions took place in contexts that were highly repressive and resource-poor, and they required outside assistance, including international publicity, political leverage, and humanitarian aid, to survive. As a result, each revolution was prolonged enough to give diaspora members the

---

[10] Tunisia and Egypt's initial revolutionary uprisings against dictatorships took a matter of days, and Bahrain's protest movement in Manama was crushed by Saudi intervention in March 2011. Jordan and Morocco's uprisings did not escalate into revolutionary movements demanding the fall of their sovereigns, despite the emergence of protests; see Moss (2014) for an analysis on why Jordan's movement remained reformist. Subsequent years have seen additional protests, counter-revolutions, and revolutionary uprisings in Egypt, Sudan, Algeria, and elsewhere (e.g., Holmes 2019). The comparison I make here is about the initial phase of revolutionary mobilization to oust longtime autocrats and change governmental leadership (Brownlee et al. 2015).

[11] For research on sustained and episodic diaspora activism for Egypt, see Kennedy (2019); on Bahraini exile mobilization, see Beaugrand and Geisser (2016).

[12] Libya's uprising escalated quickly into a zero-sum nationwide revolutionary war intent on overthrowing the Gaddafi regime by force. Syria's Arab Spring began as a disparate protest movement that evolved into a revolutionary war as regime brutality provoked a backlash; by 2014, violence from the regime, its allies, and extremists had produced the world's worst refugee crisis since World War II (Chatty 2018). Yemen's revolution involved primarily peaceful, long-term protest encampments in urban centers; despite attacks against protesters and battles between defected armed factions and regime forces in the summer, regime violence did not succeed in stoking a nationwide war in 2011.

opportunity to forge popular movements intent on intervening on behalf of rebellion and relief.

The US-Britain comparison was useful for several reasons as well. First, these two host-countries contained many of the most consequential diaspora communities from Libya, Syria, and Yemen in 2011. Britain hosted the largest community of Libyans outside of their home-country in the city of Manchester at this time due to chain migration and state-sponsored scholarships to its universities. Both host-countries granted refuge to many prominent anti-Gaddafi figures owing to their opposition to his international acts of terrorism in the 1980s and 1990s. Syrians are the oldest and one of the largest Arab immigrant communities in the United States, home to many upper- and middle-class professionals. Syrians in Britain are a smaller community in size (see Table 1.1) but nevertheless home to students and professionals, as well as refugees persecuted by the Assad regime. Yemenis were Britain's "first Muslims" (Halliday 2010[1992]) owing to South Yemen's colonial ties with Britain and their employment on British coal ships. Outside of Saudi Arabia and the UAE, Yemenis in the United States and Britain send more remittances homeward than from any other country. Taken together, on the eve of the Arab Spring, each group had significant numbers of first- and 1.5-generation residents in the United States and Britain.[13]

Furthermore, the United States and Britain are geopolitical powerholders with permanent positions on the UN Security Council. Their international influence grants anti-regime diasporas political opportunities to lobby policymakers in London and Washington, DC, and at the United Nations headquarters in New York, on matters of the homeland. Both are wealthy democratic states that attract emigrants by virtue of their opportunities for political freedom and social mobility, real and perceived. At the same time, each has subjected groups from the MENA region to discriminatory and Islamophobic policies, immigrant quotas and refugee bans, and rhetoric that paints their members as threats to national (read: white, Anglo-Christian) culture, security,

---

[13] These ties keep immigrants embedded in two worlds simultaneously and connected to political events at home (Levitt 2003; Levitt and Glick Schiller 2004). At the same time, I am not claiming that diaspora activism from the United States and Britain was the only kind that mattered in the Arab Spring. On the contrary, diaspora members and newly minted refugees mobilized from places such as Stockholm, Beirut, and Abu Dhabi for the home-country revolutions (Dickinson 2015). However, the US-Britain comparison provides an opportunity to explain why diaspora mobilization varies in spite of their relative advantages and political opportunities for transnational mobilization – especially given anti-regime diaspora members' English-language capabilities, the *lingua franca* of global communication and expertise, necessary to talk to and through mainstream media; as well as their proximity to the governments of two major world powers and permanent members of the UN Security Council, and their relative economic and social capital vis-à-vis their counterparts at home.

TABLE I.I. *Estimated number of persons identified as Libyan, Syrian, and Yemeni in the host-country*

	Self-Identified Ancestry, US[a]	Foreign Born, England and Wales[c]
Yemenis	29,358	15,046[d]
Libyans	~9,000[b]	17,774
Syrians	147,426	8,848

[a] Data from the 2010 American Community Survey, country of ancestry. These figures are the combined totals of persons who listed Yemeni or Syrian as a first or second entry.
[b] This figure was quoted to me by an advocate for the Libyan American community, but a survey-derived estimate is unavailable. The ancestry data for the 2000 census and the 2010 American Community Survey contain no data on the Libyan-American population.[14]
[c] Data from the 2011 Ethnic Group census for England and Wales, Office of National Statistics (www.nomisweb.co.uk/census/2011/QS211EW/view/2092957703?rows=cell&cols=rural_urban).
[d] The BBC writes that there are "an estimated 70–80,000 Yemenis living in Britain, who form the longest-established Muslim group in Britain" but does not cite a source for these figures (www.bbc.co.uk/religion/religions/islam/history/uk_1.shtml).

and interests for over a century.[15] The terrorist attacks of September 11, 2001, led policymakers in both the United States and Britain to instigate a global war on terror that turned inward, increasing community-wide profiling, surveillance, detention, and deportation of Arabs and Muslims (Brighton 2007). Because these host-countries provide similar "contexts of reception" for Middle Easterners (Bloemraad 2006), they provide contextual similarities that can help clarify why diaspora mobilization varies in substantive ways for the same national group across host-countries.

I was able to conduct interviews with Yemeni and Libyan activists after their heads of state had been deposed and the revolutionary movements ostensibly ended in 2012 and 2013, respectively. I conducted a total of sixty-eight interviews for the Libyan case during the post-Gaddafi transition period, which led me to Tripoli in pursuit of the repatriated. I had hoped to do the same with Syrian activists, but the uprising in Syria never reached the same stage. After conducting fieldwork with this community since 2011, I made the strategic decision to conduct interviews in 2014, seventy-nine in total, as the uprising turned into a multisided internationalized civil war and produced a major

---

[14] According to Neal Conon, host of *Talk of the Nation* on National Public Radio, "We don't really know how many Libyans live in the US because there aren't enough to be classified in the census" (National Public Radio 2011).
[15] Despite their categorization as white in the United States, Middle Easterners have often been treated as second-class citizens and lumped together as Arab-Muslim Others despite their ethnic, religious, and linguistic diversity (Cainkar 2009, 2018; Maghbouleh 2017; Naber 2012).

humanitarian disaster. Despite this variation in timing,[16] this research design enabled me to compare how diaspora mobilization had emerged and changed within and across groups over time.

In total, I conducted 239 in-depth interviews among the diaspora communities listed in Table 1.2.[17] Our extended conversations addressed their migration histories and activist backgrounds, their involvement in social movements before and during the Arab Spring, and perceived failures and successes of their collective efforts. In all, their ranks represented a total of sixty-one groups and organizations, both formal and informal, spread across the United States and Britain.[18] Activists working for relief warranted inclusion because their home-country regimes viewed independent humanitarian work as traitorous. In fact, those working to deliver charity to the needy incurred as much risk as freedom fighters themselves, as numerous aid workers disappeared into prisons and have been subjected to bombings, torture, and state-sanctioned murder. Many activists engaged in both overtly political and humanitarian work, or switched from one to the other when political work became too fractious.

Because my resources did not allow me to visit every interviewee in person, I relied on media like Skype and Viber to reach participants in Cardiff, Wales, and Bradford, England; those who were working at the time in Turkey and Qatar; and those who were residing across Michigan (Dearborn, Flint, and Ann Arbor) and in Boston, Chicago, Austin, Houston, Miami, and the San Francisco Bay area. I conducted all interviews in English, though respondents and I frequently used Arabic terms, and no interviewees were excluded from the study on the basis of language. Activists' abilities in English and Arabic varied, though many were proficient in both.

Finally, I undertook ethnographic observations (and sometimes participant observations) of thirty events related to the revolutions and relief efforts from 2011 until 2014. Most of these events took place with Syrian activists in the Greater Los Angeles area where I was studying and living at the time, though

---

[16] Some degree of case-based unevenness is inevitable when studying real-world events due to the researcher's inability to control conditions as they would in a lab experiment; this does not, however, negate the validity of comparative research or the comparisons of countries within geopolitical regions (Brownlee et al. 2015; see also Goodwin 2001).

[17] Among these respondents, 231 were members of the 3 national identity groups. Eight others worked closely with activists in the American and British diasporas, but did not fit precisely into these categories. These respondents included a Lebanese-British head of a Syrian humanitarian organization, an Anglo-British member of the Yemen desk at Chatham House in London, and two Libyan-Canadian activists who worked with conationals from the United States and Britain during the 2011 revolution.

[18] Research procedures followed Institutional Review Board protocols. Because political conditions in activists' home- and host-countries have worsened at the time of this writing (see Meek et al. 2017; Sengupta 2017), I refrain from specifying identifying information when it could be of potential risk to them. However, many of these activists have "gone public" with their claims in the media and are widely known in diaspora movement communities (and to regimes) already, regardless of conflict dynamics at home. See also the Methodological Appendix.

TABLE 1.2. *Metropolitan areas visited for data collection*

Libyan Case	Syrian Case	Yemeni Case
Leeds, Britain	Bristol, Britain	Birmingham, Britain
London, Britain	London, Britain	Liverpool, Britain
Manchester, Britain	Manchester, Britain	London, Britain
Southern CA, USA	Southern CA, USA	Sheffield, Britain
Washington, DC, USA	Washington, DC, USA	New York, USA
Tripoli, Libya		Washington, DC, USA

they frequently brought together a range of Arab Spring supporters from different national communities (For readers interested in the analytical approaches and strategies used for verifying and triangulating the data, please see the Methodological Appendix).

In all, what began as a curiosity about diaspora activism led to fieldwork spanning several years and three continents. Thanks to the generosity of my respondents, it produced hundreds of conversations, over three hundred hours of voice recordings, and about two thousand single-spaced pages of transcripts and field notes. These data were analyzed to answer two questions: When do diaspora members engage in public, collective claims-making against authoritarian regimes? How and why do their mobilizations vary over time?

1.6 THE CONDITIONS SHAPING VOICE AFTER EXIT

In answering these questions, the book's central contribution is the provision of a set of conditions explaining when, how, and to what extent diasporas wield voice against authoritarian regimes. My argument, in brief, is that when home-country ties subject diaspora members to regime threats and violence (*transnational repression*) and divisive political disputes (*conflict transmission*), anti-regime voice will be weak. When *quotidian disruptions* at home upend these transnational deterrents abroad, diaspora members become empowered to capitalize on host-country political opportunities and express voice against regimes in word and deed. However, the extent to which they then intervene on behalf of rebellion and relief will be mitigated by two additional additive forces – that of *resource conversion* and *geopolitical support* by states and other international powerholders. When either or both of these forces are lacking, activists may be free to voice their claims on the street, but diaspora mobilization will do little to fuel rebellions and help their allies at home.

The theoretical framework is detailed in Chapter 1. This chapter grounds my arguments in existing research and elaborates how the book's theoretical contributions advance our understanding of transnational activism and voice-after-exit among diasporas. Readers uninterested in theory may choose to skip directly to Chapter 2, which describes how the rise of authoritarian-nationalist regimes in Libya, Syria, and Yemen in the 1960s and 1970s pushed emigrants abroad. Owing to the additional "pull" factors of host-countries with democratic freedoms and educational opportunities, the United States and Britain came to host a range of anti-regime members, exiles, and well-resourced professionals with the requisite grievances to form opposition movements abroad. First- and second-generation regime opponents also retained ties to their home-countries in the form of familial connections, experiences and memories, self-professed identities, and – for those not in exile – regular trips to visit the home-country. Nevertheless, anti-regime movements were small, atomized, and considered partisan by their conationals before the Arab Spring. Neither Libyan and Syrian exiles nor well-resourced white-collar professionals were able to forge public member-based associations or initiate mass protest events until well into the Arab Spring. Yemeni movements, meanwhile, focused on supporting southern separation from the Yemeni state, rather than on the reform or liberalization of the central government.

Chapter 3 then demonstrates why this was the case, illustrating how two transnational social forces depressed and deterred anti-regime mobilization before the Arab Spring. They did so by embedding diaspora members in authoritarian systems of state control and sociopolitical antagonisms through individuals' home-country ties. As the third column in Table 1.3 describes, each of these transnational forces was sufficient to suppress diaspora mobilization, but they often operated conjointly before the Arab Spring.

The first mechanism, which I call *transnational repression*, refers to how regimes exert authoritarian forms of control and repress dissent in their diasporas. Regime agents and loyalists from Libya and Syria in particular did so in numerous ways, including by surveilling nationals living abroad, making threats against them, and by punishing regime critics and their family members in the homeland. I find that transnational repression by the Libyan and Syrian regimes made most non-exiles far too mistrustful and fearful to join the exiles who dared to speak out against the regimes before the Arab Spring. As Chapter 3 details, decades of transnational repression among these groups, which included the assassinations of Libyans in London in the 1980s and 1990s and the surveillance of Syrians as far afield as California, deterred the diaspora's collective ability to speak out and organize against their tormentors. Plagued by widespread suspicion and paralyzing fears of conationals, neither diaspora produced a public membership-based anti-regime association or mass protest in the United States or Britain before 2011. The Yemeni regime, in contrast, attempted to repress its diaspora, but did not have the capacity to silence anti-regime members to the same degree due to its relatively weak governance at home and abroad.

The second mechanism that deterred diaspora mobilization before the Arab Spring is what I call *conflict transmission*, which refers to the ways in which political conflicts and identity-based divisions travel from the home-country through members' ties to the diaspora. I find that conflict transmission divided

TABLE 1.3. *Summary of findings*

National Group	Host Country	Deterrents to Voice before 2011	Quotidian Disruption during the Arab Spring	Resource Conversion to Rebellion and Relief	Geopolitical Support by (a) Host-Country (b) Third Parties	Interventions in the Arab Spring
Libyan	US	Transnational repression (TR) + Conflict transmission (CT)	Nationwide revolution rapidly disrupted TR and CT.	Sufficient	(a) Strong	Full-spectrum
	Britain				(b) Strong	
Syrian	US	Transnational repression + Conflict transmission	Slowly escalating revolution gradually disrupted TR and CT through 2014. Factionalism, competition in the anti-Assad opposition revived CT by 2014.	Sufficient → Insufficient	(a) Moderate → Weak	Full-spectrum → Muted
					(b) Moderate	
	Britain				(a) Weak	Constrained → Muted
					(b) Moderate	
Yemeni	US	Conflict transmission	Revolutionary north-south coalition-building undermined CT. Breakup of this coalition revived CT.	Insufficient	(a) Weak	Selective
	Britain				(b) Weak	

anti-regime diasporas and undermined their mobilization before the 2011 revolutionary wave in several ways. Cleavages among Libyan regime opponents stemmed primarily from the Gaddafi regime's efforts to rehabilitate itself in the 2000s, which divided hardline regime opponents from reformers. For Syrians, competition and mistrust between anti-regime groups, including between Syrian Kurds, secular liberals, and various factions of the Muslim Brotherhood, reproduced destructive fissures among anti-regime members before the uprisings. For Yemenis, the resurgence of a southern secessionist movement in Yemen around 2007 pitted southern separatists against pro-unity northerners at home *and* abroad by tying anti-regime activism to Yemen's fate as a unified republic. This conflict transmission led to avoidance of politics, censorship, and fights over communal resources in Yemeni communities on both sides of the Atlantic Ocean. In each case, the transmission of home-country conflicts to the diaspora inhibited the capacity of conationals to work collectively for regime change before 2011.

Given the deterrent effects of transnational repression and conflict transmission, what brought Libyans, Syrians, and Yemenis together for the Arab Spring? Chapter 4 describes how the Arab Spring mobilized members of the anti-regime diaspora not only by stirring grievances and inducing new hopes for change at home, but by disrupting the normative operation and effects of transnational repression and conflict transmission in the diaspora. The Arab Spring induced what David Snow and his collaborators (1998) call a "quotidian disruption" abroad for several reasons. First, the Arab Spring upended the silence-inducing effects of transnational repression in the diaspora as regime repression engulfed members' loved ones at home. After members' relatives were killed, detained, and forced to fight or flee, diaspora members felt released from the obligation to keep quiet in order to protect their loved ones from the threat of repression – what I call "proxy punishment" – in Libya and Syria. Activists also decided to come out publicly for the uprisings when they perceived that the home-country regime's use of repression escalated into collective, arbitrary violence. To them, this escalation signified that going public no longer posed *additional* risks to their significant others, thus transforming public activism from a high-risk activity into a low-risk one.

The risks and sacrifices undertaken by vanguard activists – such as Hamza al-Khateeb, the Syrian boy who was tortured to death by regime forces for smuggling food to protesters under siege in early 2011 – also led respondents to come out against the regimes in public for moral reasons. Such incidents broadened diaspora members' sense of moral obligation from their immediate families to the national community as a whole. Diaspora members also went public when they perceived that the regimes were unable to deliver on the threat of transnational repression. After witnessing the defections of students and officials abroad, Libyans felt empowered to come out in public. Furthermore, by 2012, some Syrian respondents came to believe that the regime was too consumed by war at home to sanction them individually. Perceived changes in the regimes' capacities for repression, therefore, rendered high-risk activism as low-risk (McAdam 1986) and signaled openings in activists' opportunities for dissent (McAdam 1999[1982]; Tarrow 2005).

The Arab Spring likewise disrupted the deterrent effects of conflict transmission by rallying anti-regime diaspora members around a common enemy. Anti-regime Libyans abroad experienced a relatively high degree of cohesion as rebels at home launched a zero-sum war against Gaddafi. By uniting these individuals around the slogan "the regime must go," boundaries within diaspora groups were reconfigured (Wimmer 2013) and organizers gained the capacity to instigate mass protests.

At the same time, as Table 1.3 summarizes in the column on Quotidian Disruptions, the Arab Spring's effects on public mobilization and anti-regime solidarity did not unfold at the same pace or endure equally across national groups. While Libyans in the United States and Britain came out rapidly as regime control at home and abroad collapsed, the Syrian revolution emerged gradually. Accordingly, the *pace* at which activists went public abroad in both host-countries was staggered because regime agents and loyalists continued to threaten and sanction activists abroad during the revolution's first year. The continuous threats posed by transnational repression led some activists to engage in what I call "guarded advocacy" by covering their faces during protests, posting anonymously online or not at all, and refusing invitations to speak to the media. It was only late in 2012 when most of the Syrians I interviewed made the decision to "come out," but many knew of others who had not yet, and never would.

The quotidian disruption of conflict transmission also changed over time. Syrian unity across their places of residence splintered as the revolution at home became more internally divided, competitive, and morally compromised. Likewise, once southern Yemenis split from the revolution a few months into the uprising at home, so too did most South Yemeni activists in the diaspora follow suit. The resurgence of conflict transmission from the Arab Spring itself, therefore, undermined the abilities of Syrian and Yemeni organizers to express unified claims to outsiders and led to personalized conflicts, withdrawals, and a shift away from overtly politicized activism among many participants.

After explaining the initial emergence of diaspora movements for the Arab Spring, Chapter 5 then describes differences in activists' collective interventions for rebellion and relief. As summarized in the far-right column of Table 1.3, the analysis finds that Libyan activists and their movements across the United States and Britain performed what I call a *full-spectrum* role in the revolutions by undertaking five major strategies for the revolution's duration. First, they *broadcasted* their allies' claims to outside audiences through the Internet, protests, and awareness-raising events in person and online. Second, they *represented* the cause by joining the revolution's cadre and media teams, and by lobbying on its behalf. Third, they *brokered* between parties to the conflict, including between revolutionaries, the media, and policymakers. Fourth, they *remitted* resources homeward, from their expertise and skills to cash and medical supplies. Fifth, they *volunteered on the ground*, venturing home to deliver aid, perform surgeries, become interpreters, assist refugees, and even fight with groups known as the Free Libya Army.

In contrast, the responses of the Syrian anti-regime diaspora varied by host-country and over time. While Syrian American movements initially played a full-spectrum role along with their Libyan counterparts, activists in Britain were significantly *constrained* in attempting to broker for and represent the revolution. Eventually, both movements were *muted* by the time I conducted interviews in 2014. Yemenis in both the United States and Britain, on the other hand, played a far more *selective* role in the Arab Spring than either the Libyan or Syrian groups, focusing primarily on broadcasting the aims of the independent youth-led movement and representing the cause to policymakers. Activists recognized that the anti-regime diaspora needed to do more to help their compatriots; yet, most felt blocked from doing more than expressing their solidarity in symbolic ways, such as by holding demonstrations.

The final chapters explain this variation, arguing how two mechanisms shown in the remaining columns of Table 1.3 – *resource conversion* and *geopolitical support* – transformed some, but not all, diaspora movements into auxiliaries for the Arab Spring. Chapter 6 demonstrates how the varied conversion of diaspora resources to the cause – their home-country network ties, social capital, and fungible resources – mitigated their movements' interventions. Libyans' resources in the United States and Britain were sufficient to address their allies' needs over time, and Syrians initially had sufficient resources to do the same. However, overwhelming regime repression and growing unease with a fractious rebellion damaged activist-beneficiary networks as the revolution wore on. Furthermore, as Syria's humanitarian crisis escalated, diaspora resources were drained or diverted from the anti-regime cause. As a result, Syrians' collective roles in the Arab Spring were drastically reduced.

While Yemen's largely peaceful revolution did not require the full range of resources needed by Libyans and Syrians entangled in zero-sum wars, activists' abilities to channel support homeward were hindered by insufficient network ties to protest encampments. This made resource transfers dependent on the existence of personal connections, which were sparse across their movements. Yemenis' abilities to launch and sustain protest movements also suffered over time as participants' resources were exhausted. Yemenis in the diaspora poured an exhaustive amount of labor and resources into the effort, but their resources were insufficient to turn them into transnational auxiliaries for the Arab Spring.

Chapter 7 shows how diaspora activists' interventions were also shaped by the degree of *geopolitical support* that their allies at home received from their host-country governments and influential third parties, including states bordering the home-country, international institutions, and the media. Support for the Libyan cause was high and consistent as foreign powers, the international media, and relief agencies intervened on behalf of the revolution. Strong geopolitical support gave activists opportunities to broker between parties, represent the revolution to outsiders, and remit their labor, cash, and material aid to the front lines. Support for the Syrian cause, on the other hand, varied between US and British governments. This difference gave Syrian *Americans* an elevated role to play as brokers and representatives, while Syrians in Britain were largely shut out of policymaking.[19] Once geopolitical support for the anti-Assad effort waned across the board by 2014, however, most activists' roles in policymaking were muted in both host-countries. Finally, geopolitical support for the Yemeni revolution was weak in light of Western powers' backing of an agreement drawn up by members of the Gulf Cooperation Council to supposedly stabilize Yemen (which backfired spectacularly). As a result, Yemenis in the United States and Britain were invited to meetings, but not incorporated into policymaking. This left them hopeful but frustrated with their inability to do more for their compatriots.

1.7 CONCLUSION

By bringing attention to the conditions that shape diaspora mobilization over time, this study adds an important chapter to a growing literature on revolutions and the Arab Spring. While much work focuses on the dynamics of contention that unfold within nations, revolutions are not contained events within national territories. Instead, mass revolts against regimes are fundamentally "transboundary" phenomena, as George Lawson describes (2019), that send shock waves across oceans, galvanize extra-national forces, and mobilize activists across borders (Beck 2014; Bell 1972; Berberian 2019). Diaspora participation in the Arab Spring did not, by itself, determine whether the revolutions would win or lose. But given activists' roles as the revolutions' publicists, lobbyists, funders, rescue workers, and fighters, explaining diaspora mobilization is essential for understanding one of the most consequential protest waves in modern history, as well as for explaining how contentious events unfold more generally (Abdelrahman 2011; Adamson 2016; Beaugrand and Geisser 2016; Seddon 2014).

This book also fills a significant empirical gap in the study of transnational movements, migration, and ethnic studies. Increasing focus on the experience of Arabs and Muslims in the West has brought notable attention to the ways in which opportunities in the *mahjar*, or diaspora, have been undermined by marginalization in the receiving-country. Arabs and Middle Eastern Muslims have certainly experienced widespread discrimination across the West for well

---

[19] For more information on Syrian cultural brokerage with mainstream media, see also Andén-Papadopoulos and Pantti (2013).

over a century, and studies are beginning to bring needed attention to the ways in which Arabic-speaking immigrants have worked together to contest host-country discrimination, racism, and violence (Gualtieri 2009, 2020; Pennock 2017; Yadav 2016). At the same time, lumping these minority groups together as Arabs and Muslims (Brubaker 2004, 2013) glosses over the differences in voice *within* and *between* community members. For example, Libyan Americans gained a much broader and more influential voice in foreign policy-making during the Arab Spring than did Yemenis, even though both Muammar al-Gaddafi and Ali Abdullah Saleh were treated as allies in the war on terror in the years immediately preceding the revolutions. By examining these variations, we gain needed insights into how diaspora and emigrant groups are treated differently by their host-country governments according to their national identities. This book therefore provides new insights for understanding how diasporas' "contexts of reception" respond unevenly to their calls for liberal change, human rights, and democracy at home depending on their varied identities (Bloemraad 2006, 2013).

The chapters that follow also suggest the importance of moving beyond characterizations of MENA communities as "Arab" or "Muslim" by address-ing the experiences of minority groups during episodes of contention. As demonstrated in the pages that follow, repressed minorities such as the Libyan Amazigh, Syrian Kurds, and South Yemenis sometimes merge their claims with the majority. However, the conditions under which they join with long-distance nationalists should not be taken for granted. As sociologist Rogers Brubaker (2015) argues, individuals with shared characteristics do not necessarily experience solidarity, trust, or a sense of "groupness." Rather, such groupness may be the invention of the outside observer. It is for this reason that treating diaspora solidarity as a dependent variable is warranted.

I

Diaspora Activism and the Dynamics of Voice

The fact that social movements reach across state borders to instigate change in places where their members do not reside is not a new phenomenon (Foner 1997; Maney 2000). As Karl Marx, a founder of sociology and an émigré himself, argued in *The Communist Manifesto*, international solidarity has always been necessary to combat authorities who abuse their populations behind a shield of state sovereignty (Marx 1978[1872]). Even so, the fruits of global capitalism have made cross-border connectivity faster and cheaper in recent years. During the Beijing student movement in 1989, democracy advocates had to fax missives, page by page, to their Chinese compatriots in California.[1] Today, video footage of Black Americans being killed at the hands of police and attacks against democracy protesters in Hong Kong travel instantaneously through internet-based media to portable, super-computing smartphones. Likewise, activists disseminate movement names, slogans, and hashtags across these media, bringing recognition to movements such as Black Lives Matter and #MeToo and inspiring others to follow suit. Equipped with these tools, even Luddites can become whistleblowers by spreading information on a global scale.

This chapter draws on advances in the study of transnational movements and migration to illustrate how activists reach beyond their proximate contexts to advocate for change across borders. While diaspora activism is centuries old (Green and Waldinger 2016; Moya 2005), globalization has enabled dispersed populations to forge and sustain transnational communities, both real and imagined (Anderson 2006[1983]), and contest authoritarian regimes more easily than ever before (Bauböck 2008; Østergaard-Nielsen 2001; Vertovec 2005).

[1] I thank Dr. Yang Su, Associate Professor of Sociology, University of California, Irvine, for pointing this out.

Yet, relatively little is known about how diaspora movements emerge or why their transnational political practices change over time. This chapter presents a framework to help fill these gaps by drawing inductively on the Arab Spring abroad. Adopting Albert Hirschman's (1970) heuristic vocabulary of *exit*, *voice*, and *loyalty*, I propose the conditions under which diaspora movements become empowered to act on their loyalties and wield voice after exit against authoritarianism. Specifically, I show how *transnational repression* and *conflict transmission* suppress voice; how *quotidian disruptions* give rise to it; and how *resource conversion* and *geopolitical support* transform voice into the means of contentious political action. In so doing, this book demonstrates why anti-authoritarian diaspora mobilization is a contingent, and even fragile, force for change in a highly globalized world. The conceptual and theoretical warrants for these arguments are elaborated below.

1.1 THE TRANSNATIONAL TURN IN MOBILIZATION AND MIGRATION STUDIES

The study of how contentious politics operate transnationally has expanded rapidly in the decades since Joseph Nye and Robert Keohane (1971, 1972) declared that the cross-border interactions of non-state actors are an essential dimension of contemporary politics. Since that time, the transnational turn in the study of social movements has demonstrated that activists mobilize transnationally in different ways.[2] Local movements savvy to the need for international support do so by engaging in "scale shift" (Tarrow 2005), by redirecting their claims from the local arena to supranational, state-regulating actors. The purpose of scale shift is to mobilize international institutions and agencies to come to the defense of movements and their constituents (Tarrow 2005). As Keck and Sikkink's (1998) landmark research demonstrates, the ties between local movements, nongovernmental organizations (NGOs), and international bodies such as the United Nations can grant activists important forms of leverage. By "naming and shaming" relevant authorities, activists persuade human rights organizations such as Human Rights Watch and Amnesty International to take up their claims and condemn regime crimes (Hafner-Burton and Tsutsui 2007). They also lobby governments and international bodies to exert corresponding pressure on offending authorities to change their practices and policies (Brysk 2000; Carpenter 2010; Hafner-Burton and Tsutsui 2007; Keck 1995; Tsutsui 2004, 2006, 2018). Bestowed with an internationalized set of "political opportunities" (Kay 2011; Tarrow 2001) – a relatively stable set of conditions that facilitate activism – transnational

---

[2] For related works on the interactive dynamics of transnational social movements, international organizations, and state-regulating institutions, see Boli and Thomas (1999), Della Porta and Tarrow (2005), Keck and Sikkink (1998), McCarthy (1997), Risse et al. (2013), Risse-Kappen (1995), Ron et al. (2005), J. Smith (2008), J. Smith and Johnston (2002), and Tsutsui (2018).

practices help activists overcome domestic political constraints. In this way, besieged movements can gain life-saving forms of attention and build cross-national alliances that address local problems (Bob 2001, 2005; Keck and Sikkink 1998).

Movements also become transnational by forming networks and coalitions with other grassroots actors dedicated to addressing a common cause (Ayoub 2013, 2016; Kay 2011; von Bülow 2010). Social movement groups sharing feminist, LGBTQ+, labor, environmental, and religious values and missions, to name just a few examples, join forces to increase their numbers and commitment (Tilly 2004). They also form coalitions to contest harmful practices, such as austerity policies imposed by the World Bank and International Monetary Fund, the use of sweatshops by Google and Nike, imperialistic wars waged by the United States in Vietnam and Iraq, and the corporate and state-fueled practices driving climate change (Meyer and Corrigall-Brown 2005; J. Smith 2008). So too do activists join forces at international conferences, from those sponsored by the United Nations to the World Social Forum, in order to exchange stories and tactics. By building cross-border alliances, activists demonstrate the moral imperative of working collectively on the basis of human beings' shared fate (Russo 2018; C. Smith 1996). Studies of movement diffusion and spillover demonstrate that the spread of social movement campaigns can grant vulnerable allies attention and leverage in a highly stratified world system (J. Smith 2008; Soule 2004, 2013).

Diaspora movements who mobilize transnationally in order to induce changes in their places of origin play an important role in this internationalized civic realm (Adamson 2002; Al-Ali and Koser 2002; Fadlalla 2019; Rudolph and Piscatori 1997; Wald 2009). They pose formidable challenges to home-country regimes by naming and shaming immoral and illegal practices, remitting cash to freedom fights, lobbying for intervention, and disrupting regimes' monopolies on information and public goods. They also articulate alternative loyalties to the homeland in ways that challenge regimes' monopolies over the *meaning* of loyalty to the nation.[3] When operating "in the relatively free environment of democratic host states with much better forms of communication and international recognition," Shain argues that diasporas do not just

---

[3] As Shain (2005[1989]: 164) writes,

Political exiles often find themselves in a uniquely difficult posture, because they are removed from the domestic political order from which they must draw their loyalists, and also because they are vulnerable to charges of disloyalty. An important part of the exiles' struggle is therefore to challenge the home regime's attempts to impose its own interpretation of national loyalty both at home and abroad. In Albert Hirschman's schema, the home regime maintains that "exit" from the national soil, especially when followed by "voice" against the existing authorities in the state, is an expression of national "disloyalty." Exiles contest this view, maintaining that their "exit" was not an alternative to internal "voice" (opposition) against the regime, but indeed a sine qua non for the exercise of "voice."

act as the homeland's "tail" but "may dominate the wagging" (2005[1989]: xv; 2007: 125). Accordingly, their movements can stoke sectarianism and prolong civil wars, as well as contribute to conflict resolution and reconstruction (Chalk 2008; Cochrane et al. 2009; Davis and Moore 1997; Fair 2005; van Hear and Cohen 2017). Thus, despite their displacement – and indeed because of it – diaspora members' enduring loyalties reshape the political terrain at home and the international responses to conflicts therein.[4]

1.2 EXIT AND VOICE: UNPACKED

As the transnational turn in the mobilization and migration literature makes clear, exit can facilitate voice against abusive regimes when diaspora members' transnational ties promote loyalty to the people and places left behind (Duquette-Rury 2020; Hoffmann 2010). By voice, Hirschman means the literal words and actions that express discontent, from grumblings to violent protest (1970: 15). For diaspora members, voice can take many forms, including postings on social media, public protests that call for host-country governments to intercede, and direct interventions in home-country wars and charity.

Writing on voice against authoritarian regimes, political scientist Guillermo O'Donnell (1986) usefully suggests that voice varies according to whom it is directed. The first dimension is what he calls "horizontal voice," which signifies the ability to express dissent *within* one's community without the fear of sanctions. One expresses horizontal voice when Tweeting complaints about the majority political party and when expressing a political preference to a friend or neighbor. Horizontal voice is premised on what scholar Phillip Ayoub (2016: 23) calls interpersonal *and* public visibility. Visibility is required so that aggrieved persons can locate each other, communicate with one another, and forge social movements based on common grievances and aims. In other words, visibility enables persons with common grievances to rally around shared identities and claims without repercussions and be recognized by the wider society and the state. Perhaps there are some exceptions to this rule, as in the case of online anonymous groups that hack corporations. Nevertheless, without horizontal voice, collective action on behalf of shared causes becomes unlikely.

The second dimension is "vertical" voice (O'Donnell 1986). Vertical voice is directed toward authorities and powerholders through actions such as protest and lobbying. By mobilizing to gain the attention of policymakers, the media, NGOs, and other influential actors, activists work to "draw in the crowd" into the fight (Gamson and Wolfsfeld 1983; Lipsky 1968; Schattschneider 1960).

---

[4] The struggle for "freedom, self-determination, and national identity" has been "paradoxically" transnational (Field 1971: 5) owing to the opportunities that activists gain in advocating for change from afar and owing to the role that exiles play in long-distance nationalism (Anderson 1998; Hockenos 2003).

They also indirectly wield vertical voice against authoritarian regimes by launching insurgencies and undermining regimes' attempts to control information and resource distribution. In these ways, movement actors talk back to regimes through their actions.

By emigrating to freer societies, exit facilitates the survival of movements in the wake of repressive crackdowns in the home-country and allows movements to survive in "abeyance" (Taylor 1989). Exit to democracies also presents "political opportunities" for activists to engage in new types of resistance (Quinsaat 2013; Sökefeld 2006; Tarrow 2005). Political opportunities signify changes to actors' contexts that make them more inclined to enact voice, whether owing to the reduction in risks or because of their potential to make alliances with decision-makers, or both (McAdam 1999[1982]; McAdam et al. 1996; Meyer 2004; Tarrow 2011). Diaspora members who settle in democratic contexts should therefore gain political opportunities to engage in both horizontal voice (among each other) and vertical voice (to authorities).

At the same time, as scholars have recently come to point out, transnational activism is not a consistent feature of diaspora life (Betts and Jones 2016; Chaudhary and Moss 2019; Duquette-Rury 2016; Guarnizo et al. 2003; Koinova 2011, 2018; Levitt and Glick Schiller 2004; Waldinger 2008, 2015). Their movements can certainly be efficacious in shaping the homeland in their image (Hockenos 2003). But although "ethnic" lobbies have incurred a reputation as influencers in home-country and international affairs (e.g., Huntington 2004), diaspora members' public, collective claims-making activities are episodic, and even downright rare in some communities. Yet, relatively little is known about how their collective efforts for change in the homeland come about in the first place, or why their mobilization dynamics vary within and across national groups.

Because diaspora movements can potentially build nations and tear them down, understanding when, how, and the extent to which diaspora members' loyalties transform into voice against illiberal regimes remains an important topic of inquiry. Under what conditions, then, do diaspora members wield voice after exit against dictatorships? By treating anti-regime collective action as a phenomenon warranting explanation – that is, taking up voice as a dependent variable – this study shows why diaspora mobilization against authoritarian regimes is a highly contingent phenomenon.

1.3 DETERRENTS TO VOICE AFTER EXIT

Building inductively on the comparison of Arab Spring movements abroad, I argue that diaspora movements' shared origins, grievances, and political opportunities are insufficient for explaining voice after exit for several reasons. Chief among them is the fact that, as Levitt and Glick Schiller (2004) argue, diaspora members who retain transnational ties to a country of origin are "simultaneously" embedded in political, social, and economic conditions in that place of origin. As a result of their biographical, familial, and identity-based ties across borders, conditions "over there" in the home-country impact persons living "here" in the diaspora (Waldinger 2008, 2015). This simultaneity, I assert, means that diaspora members are not only transnational *actors* but also transnational *subjects*. Their capacities for mobilization are therefore impacted by their embeddedness in, and relational ties to, the home-country.

Accordingly, diasporas do not simply act on, or in response to, conditions in the home-country according to their advantages abroad. Rather, home-country conditions *act back on them* through their transnational ties in an interactive fashion. This means that exit is a relative, rather than absolute, phenomenon (Hoffmann 2010) precisely because diaspora members maintain "ways of being and ways of belonging" (Levitt and Glick Schiller 2004: 1002) that keep them tied to authoritarian home-country contexts. Ties to the home-country may therefore just as likely *depress* the members' willingness and capacity to work together for regime change as *fuel* transnational activism (Duquette-Rury 2016, 2020).

Building on this, I argue that two deterrents stemming from the home-country – *transnational repression* and *conflict transmission* – suppress transnational activism for liberal change by subjecting diaspora members to authoritarian systems of social control and divisive home-country conflicts. By transnational repression, I mean the ways in which home-country regimes work to silence and punish dissenters abroad through tactics such as surveillance, threats, and harming their family members at home. By conflict transmission, I mean the ways in which divisive home-country politics are reproduced in diaspora communities through members' biographical and identity-based ties. Such ties can "produce conflicting views" among diaspora members that "mirror debates in the homeland rather than dictate them" (Shain 2007: 126). By making it difficult for exiles to garner community support or form robust civil society organizations, I find that each of these conditions, which can also work in tandem, was sufficient to constrain anti-regime diaspora mobilization before the Arab Spring (see also Chaudhary and Moss 2019).

1.3.1 Transnational Repression

The borders of the given nation-state delimit a regime's power and jurisdiction in important ways (Mann 1984; Weber 1978). As discussed above, the movement of populations from authoritarian contexts to relatively liberal ones presents political opportunities for voice. But despite the importance of the host-country in shaping these opportunities (Bob 2002; Tarrow 2005), authoritarian regimes often permeate state borders to pursue their enemies and control their diasporas in "blatantly progovernmental and policelike" ways (Bauböck 2003; Délano and Gamlen 2014; Miller 1981: 401; Shain 2005[1989]: ch. 8). A growing number of studies on *transnational repression* demonstrate that regimes do so by surveilling diaspora communities in person and online; by threatening activists; and even by assassinating dissidents abroad and harming their family members at home.[5] As the 2018 murder of Saudi dissident and journalist Jamal Khashoggi in Istanbul[6] gruesomely illustrated, regimes undertake these acts precisely because diaspora members have the potential to discredit dictators from abroad. The threats posed by transnational repression do not preclude voice entirely, as many of those in exile will have already incurred the costs of activism and accept the risks of continuing to speak out. However, the operation of transnational repression can effectively isolate these exiles in their communities, instill widespread fear and mistrust, and render popular mobilization a practical impossibility. This, in turn, dampens horizontal voice within communities in spite of their shared identities and anti-regime grievances.

The exercise of "extra-territorial authoritarianism" and "counter-exile strategies" is not a new practice (Dalmasso et al. 2017; Shain 2005[1989]). France's Bonapartist dictatorship suppressed subversive acts among exiles in England in the 1850s (Shain 2005[1989]); Mussolini's regime hunted anti-fascist Italians abroad during its reign of terror (Cannistraro 1985); and countless opposition figures have been murdered, from Leon Trotsky, who was assassinated in Mexico on Stalin's orders in 1940, to Orlando Letelier, a former diplomat who was killed via car bomb in Washington, DC, in 1976 by Chilean dictator Augusto Pinochet.[7] Today, the technologies that make transnational activism ever easier also facilitate transnational repression, as when regimes use spyware to hack dissidents' cell phones and social media accounts (Al-Jizawi et al. 2020; Michaelsen 2017; Moss 2018). What this means is that the diaspora members who are most likely to be aggrieved by abuses taking place in the home-country are also those most strongly subjected to disincentives to speak out. The operation of transnational repression can therefore mute horizontal voice between diaspora members and hinder efforts to project vertical voice toward authorities.

---

[5] For academic studies, see Adamson and Tsourapas (2020); Cooley and Heathershaw (2017); Glasius (2018); Lemon (2019); Lewis (2015); Michaelsen (2017, 2018); Moss (2016b, 2018); Shain (2005[1989]); Tsourapas (2020a, 2020b). See these studies for additional references of reports by NGOs such as Amnesty International and Human Rights Watch on transnational repression.

[6] Jamal Khashoggi (1958–2018) was a journalist, author, and dissident from Saudi Arabia who was lured to the Saudi Arabian consulate in Istanbul, Turkey, under the pretense that he would be allowed to obtain a marriage license. Instead, he was strangled to death by agents of Saudi Crown Prince Mohammed bin Salman, dismembered with a bone saw, and disappeared. The following year, the Office of the United Nations High Commissioner for Human Rights issued a report holding the Saudi regime responsible for this premediated, extrajudicial, and extraterritorial execution.

[7] I am grateful to my colleague Dr. Samuel Valenzuela, Kellogg Professor of Sociology at the University of Notre Dame, for alerting me to this important example of transnational repression.

1.3.2 Conflict Transmission

Social movements are fundamentally shaped by whether individuals come together on the basis of shared grievances and interests (Curtis and Zurcher 1973; Rucht 2004), and diaspora members' propensities to express voice are likewise shaped by their shared origins and identities. Collective identities forged by common emigration circumstances and characteristics, whether real or imagined, can facilitate mobilization by producing common enemies, shared reasons for collective action, and sentiments of solidarity between participants (Polletta and Jasper 2001).[8] Nationalist identities based on diasporas' country of origin, for example, can unite otherwise heterogeneous populations during periods of crisis or celebration and promote "long-distance nationalism" (Anderson 1998). Diaspora members' willingness to work together is further influenced by the historical circumstances that create particular cohorts of emigrants (Eckstein 2009; Guarnizo et al. 2003; Masud-Piloto 1996; Pedraza-Bailey 1985), particularly when authoritarianism creates waves of politically and economically motivated migrations.

A diaspora is not a naturally bounded or preconfigured group, however, and the same characteristics that bind persons from the same home-country together can just as easily split them apart (Brubaker 2004, 2015; Wimmer 2013). As Rogers Brubaker (2005, 2015) argues, shared identities, cultures, and practices do not automatically create the "we-ness" necessary to forge solidarities or sustain social movements. Not all members' national origins may be equally salient or important to them at a given point in time, and divisions based on conflicts around race and ethnicity, religion, region, social class, and other factors can divide their members in significant ways (Anthias 1998: 570, 577–78; Guarnizo and Díaz 1999; Pupcenoks 2012, 2016). As a result, emigrants may express stronger loyalties to region, religion, ideology, political party, or ethnic group than they do to the nation. In fact, political opportunities provided by the host-country may facilitate the assertion of *alternative* loyalties that have been suppressed in the homeland, such as Kurdish Syrian (rather than Arab Syrian) and South Yemeni (as opposed to Yemeni) demands for territorial autonomy.

Accordingly, the willingness of diaspora members to work together for a given home-country's causes cannot be assumed even when they have shared origins, grievances, and opportunities. As scholars studying Colombian immigrants and refugees have shown, shared ties that embroil emigrants in histories of war and violent trauma undermine nationalistic solidarity and trust between conationals (Bermudez 2010; Guarnizo and Díaz 1999). Likewise, research on Somali communities demonstrates that racial, ethnic, and class antagonisms

---

[8] Sociologist David A. Snow defines a collective identity as a shared attribution that distinguishes a collective from one or more sets of others (Snow 2013).

travel with refugees from the home-country to their places of refuge, reprodu-
cing caste-like stratifications and intra-community conflicts after settlement
(Besteman 2016; Rawlence 2016). Varied migration circumstances can also
fracture diaspora members over their transnational home-country bonds, as in
the cases of generational divides between emigrant cohorts from Vietnam and
Cuba (Huynh and Yiu 2015; Pedraza 2007). The transmission of conflicts to
the diaspora through members' cross-border ties is also likely to create disagreements over the use of organizations for activism. Literature on mobilization suggests that activists can grow their movements by appropriating
"indigenous" structures in minority communities, such as ethnic or religious
organizations, and converting their participants, resources, and legitimacy to
the movement (Andrews 2004; McAdam 1999[1982]). This form of resource
conversion provides movements with legitimacy and a base of adherents and
potential participants. However, what I call *conflict transmission* can render
such resources a major site of contention over who has the right to command
them (Besteman 2016). Members' common ties to a home-country can therefore *undermine* their willingness and capacity to work together when shared
origins embed them in partisan homeland politics, stigmatized identities, and
intra-opposition cleavages.

1.4 HOW QUOTIDIAN DISRUPTIONS FACILITATE VOICE

Given that transnational repression and conflict transmission deter voice, under
what conditions do diaspora members come out and come together for change
at home? The answer, detailed in Chapter 4, is once again rooted in their ties to
the homeland. I argue that just as authoritarianism and conflict travel abroad,
so too do *disruptions* to these normative conditions. During episodes of turmoil
and contestation, changes to regime control and power relations in the home-
country travel abroad through members' ties. Thus, diaspora voice against
authoritarianism can result from what David Snow et al. (1998) call a "quotidian disruption." This theory suggests that groups suffering from previously low
degrees of political empowerment and high degrees of alienation are likely to
require a major disruption to the norms and routines of everyday life to
mobilize them for change. For diaspora members, disruptive changes that travel
abroad have the potential to *activate* horizontal voice between diaspora
members and motivate action aimed at expressing collective, vertical voice
(Wald 2008).

Building on this concept, I argue that heightened mobilization and repression
in the home-country will not only disrupt the quotidian at home, but also
promote voice abroad by *undermining the normative operation and effects of
transnational repression and conflict transmission.* In the case of the Arab
Spring, this occurred when escalating regime repression engulfed diaspora
members' loved ones in the home-country (as when their relatives became
pro-revolution in orientation or action, were forced to flee from violence, or

were detained or killed by the regime). These changes released diaspora members from the obligation to keep silent in order to protect their loved ones by undermining the relational mechanisms that made transnational repression an effective deterrent. The risks and sacrifices undertaken by vanguard activists for the Arab Spring also disrupted the normative effects of transnational repression by broadening diaspora members' objects of obligation and their sense of shared fate with the national community (Moss 2016b: 493; Mueller 1992). When peaceful protesters were slaughtered, participants came to "believe the costs of protest should be collectively shared" (Hirsch 1990: 245) and felt called to mobilize openly for moral and emotional reasons (White 1989).

Diaspora activists also embraced voice when they perceived that the regimes were unable to deliver on the threat of transnational repression. Libyans abroad felt empowered to come out when the defections of students and officials signified the collapse of regime control abroad. Syrians did so when escalations in violence at home posed imminent or arbitrary threats to their loved ones in Syria, leading respondents to perceive that coming out would not incur additional costs on their significant others. Both situations suggest that regimes facing insurgencies and zero-sum threats to their survival may be unable to repress-as-usual abroad. Perceived changes in the regimes' capacities for repression, therefore, rendered high-risk activism as low-risk (McAdam 1986) and signaled openings in activists' opportunities for dissent (McAdam 1982; Tarrow 2005).

Diaspora members overcame the effects of conflict transmission when previously factionalized groups and individuals in the home-country joined popular anti-regime coalitions. When the formation of revolutionary coalitions at home brought together formerly atomized and divided groups for regime change, these solidarities also traveled abroad to soften divisions between anti-regime diaspora members. Accordingly, the formation of mass movements in the home-country made anti-regime diaspora members more willing to work together for both strategic and emotional reasons. However, once opposition groups at home became embroiled in internal power struggles and splintered once again, so too did diaspora activists re-fragment abroad. The extent to which diaspora members came out and came together for the Arab Spring, therefore, was contingent on the degree to which disruptions to conflict transmission endured.

1.5 WHEN DIASPORA MOVEMENTS MAKE A DIFFERENCE

After diaspora members come out and come together, they have the potential to undermine authoritarian regimes in different ways. They can do so indirectly by lodging claims to their host-country governments, third-party states, the media, and to international bodies in order to persuade these powerholders to grant their allies attention and support (Bob 2005; Brysk 2000; Kay 2011; Keck 1995;

Keck and Sikkink 1998; Lipsky 1968). Diaspora members violate regimes' monopolies on information and diffuse conflicts to the international arena by "drawing in the crowd" (Schattschneider 1960). They also work directly with their allies in the home-country to channel their allies' claims outward and channel resources inward, including cash, material aid, and themselves as volunteers (Hockenos 2003). In these ways, diaspora members become impactful interventionists by engaging in partnerships across different arenas of civil society and governance, as well as by moving tangible and intangible resources across borders. But under what conditions do they become empowered to undertake and sustain these actions and sustain these forms of voice?

Below, I argue that diaspora movements' abilities to intervene in meaningful ways for rebellion and relief are dependent on two additive, conjoined conditions: (1) their capacities to *convert resources* to a shared politicized cause, and (2) the extent to which they gain *geopolitical support* from outside power-holders.[9] When resource conversion and geopolitical support are sustained over time, diaspora activists gain the capacity to become auxiliary forces against authoritarianism by channeling voice and resources across different fields of action, for example, from the halls of the US Congress to the front lines in Benghazi, Libya. Without resource conversion and geopolitical support, diaspora activists will lack the relationships and structural conditions necessary to channel resources homeward. In cases such as these, their voice will be limited to demonstrating their solidarity from a distance.

1.5.1 Resource Conversion

Studies of social movements have long argued that resources fundamentally shape activists' capacities for action (Cress and Snow 2000; Jenkins and Eckert 1986; McAdam et al. 2001; McCarthy and Zald 1977). Within diasporas, loyalty to causes and conationals in the home-country can motivate members to allocate fungible and material resources to an insurgency. Activists may also convert their social capital to politicized causes, turning skills and knowledge into "social remittances" (Ayoub 2016; Levitt 1998), as when doctors volunteer in field hospitals and bilingual activists use their skills to broker between home-country dissidents and international donors (Adamson 2002, 2005; Guarnizo et al. 2003; Koinova 2012; Levitt 1998). Diaspora members' network ties to persons on the ground are also vital, as these ties form the basis of working partnerships that enable the transfer of information, remittances, and mutual support (Moss 2020).

While diaspora movements are often well-resourced compared to their home-country counterparts, not all are equally endowed to meet their allies' needs.

---

[9] For additional work that draws attention to the importance of immigrant cohesion and host-country political institutions, see Ögelman et al. (2002).

Relatively poor migrants do indeed transfer billions of dollars to their families, and as data from the World Bank illustrate, these amounts appear to be growing every year (Ratha et al. 2019). However, remittances are not as free-flowing as they may appear from these data (Faist 2000). The allocation of resources to a political movement in the home-country depends on a number of factors, including diaspora members' migration histories and collective wealth. Immigrants from the professional, middle, and upper classes in the home-country are more likely to enter the professional sector, less likely to be tasked with supporting family members at home, and less likely to arrive to the host-country with significant debts. Those from refugee and working-class communities often face the opposite situation, finding themselves burdened with settling debts and sending remittances homeward, paying the way for family members to join them, and working long hours in jobs without benefits. Diaspora members with socioeconomic privilege are therefore more likely to allocate their time and resources to social movements and have the capacity to convert resources to political causes.

Furthermore, as Lauren Duquette-Rury (2020) finds in her study of exit and voice, US-based migrants' interventions for development in Mexico are constituted not only by members' willingness to help the people and places left behind, but also by the conditions in their home-countries. Mistrust between insiders and outsiders, the absence of partners to receive and distribute resources on the ground, and violence undermine their abilities to remit homeward. Even the wealthy will have their fungible resources drained when causes and crises become prolonged. In these ways, resource conversion depends on the continuous availability of resources and active, networked relations with insiders. Without these, diaspora members will lack resources to give or persons to receive them. Furthermore, during periods when remittances are needed most, diaspora members may face legal and territorial blockages that prevent them from moving resources to the front lines. This leads us to the importance of geopolitical support, explained below.

1.5.2 Geopolitical Support

Social movements are embedded in historically situated political environments that bestow some movements with advantages and others with disadvantages, and these environments shape whether movements are likely to achieve their goals (Amenta 2006; Eisinger 1973; Kitschelt 1986; McAdam 1999[1982]; Tilly 1978). Such factors include whether governments are receptive to movements' demands and whether movements have or gain allies over the course of their campaigns (McAdam et al. 1999; Meyer 2004). As case studies of pro-Israel Jewish American and anti-Castro Cubans suggest, diaspora lobbies become powerful when their interests and ideologies are shared with policymakers (Haney and Vanderbush 1999; Quinsaat 2013, 2019; T. Smith 2000). Studies of transnational movements also widely support the notion that external attention grants activists leverage and influence (Bob 2005; J. Smith 2004; Tsutsui 2018). When diaspora movements receive what Betts and Jones (2016: 9) call "external animation," they become activated and encouraged by these powerholders to express voice.

Extending these claims, I argue that diaspora interventions are shaped by the degree of *geopolitical support* they receive from their host-country governments, states bordering the home-country, international institutions, and the media. Whether these geopolitical powerholders support diaspora activists depends on a range of factors, including officials' security and economic interests, their ideologies and professed values, and institutional missions. Outside actors are also more likely to incorporate diaspora movements into their policy-making and practices when activists can fill in gaps in outsiders' knowledge about their homelands. Western journalists seeking to report from the front lines, for instance, may rely on diaspora brokers for access and language interpretation; state actors similarly rely on activists to provide intelligence and the legal and moral justifications for foreign intervention (Moss 2020).

The geopolitical support of states is especially important when diasporas seek to transfer resources across national borders. Diaspora members from conflict zones face hurdles in sending remittances when banks seek to "de-risk" their dealings and governments block remittances, citing reasons of counter-terrorism (Fadlalla 2019; Gordon and El Taraboulsi-McCarthy 2018). Just as Palestinian Americans have been accused of supporting terrorism abroad for their charitable efforts (Pennock 2017), the current war on terror poses significant obstacles to organizing even for basic humanitarian relief among South Asian, Middle Eastern, African, and Muslim communities (Chaudhary 2021; Horst and van Hear 2002). Because transnational ties embed diaspora members in geopolitical conflicts, persons accused of channeling remittances to the so-called wrong cause can face severe penalties. Accordingly, diaspora members' abilities to move resources homeward – particularly to isolated places in the world's periphery – will be severely compromised unless they gain the geopolitical support of gatekeepers.

1.6 CONCLUSION

In closing, the primary contribution of this book is a process-driven framework for explaining anti-authoritarian voice after exit. My argument, in summary, is that when home-country ties subject diaspora members to *transnational repression* and *conflict transmission*, anti-regime voice will be weak. When *quotidian disruptions* upend these transnational deterrents, diaspora members will become empowered to capitalize on host-country political opportunities and express voice against regimes in word and deed. The extent to which they intervene on behalf of rebellion and relief is then mitigated by two additional additive forces of *resource conversion* and *geopolitical support*.

The chapters to follow elaborate the empirical evidence for these claims based on a comparison of activism among Libyans, Syrians, and Yemenis in the United States and Britain before and during the Arab Spring. Chapter 2 begins by discussing their emigration histories and contexts of reception in the host-countries. I then explain the weakness of anti-regime voice in the period immediately preceding the Arab Spring, which provides a basis for comparing the effects of the 2011 revolutions on the diaspora mobilization to follow.

2

Exit from Authoritarianism

While Middle Easterners have been depicted as recent arrivals to the West, the United States and Britain have served as notable receiving countries for these populations for well over a century (Cainkar 2013). Factors pulling emigrants to these countries have included educational and employment opportunities, labor recruitment, and colonial ties between the United Kingdom and southern Yemen. The first major wave of emigrants – consisting primarily of Christians from greater Syria and sailors from British-held parts of Yemen – began in the 1880s. While some of these immigrants experienced newfound peace and prosperity in their host-societies, they were also subjected to ghettoization, nativist violence, and discrimination. Their arrival to port cities such as New York and South Shields in England continued until restrictive immigration quotas and travel bans were imposed in the aftermath of World War I (Bozorgmehr et al. 1996; Gualtieri 2020; Hooglund 1987; Jacobs 2015). By virtually banning migration from Asian countries and the former Ottoman Empire, migration slowed to a trickle.[1]

The United States and Britain provided similar "contexts of reception" for emigrants from the region for much of this period. Although persons from the Middle East and North Africa have been classified in the US Census as "white" – and one had to be white in order to naturalize in the United States from the Naturalization Act of 1790 until 1952 – their whiteness has been marginal and probationary at best across the western world (Maghbouleh 2017).

---

[1] As migration expert Sarah Gualtieri (2020: 146) writes, the first wave of emigrants from greater Syria to the United States began in the 1800s and continued until the US Immigration Act of 1924; the second wave occurred during the interwar period but was hampered by quotas and restrictions; and the third was marked by major wars in the region, especially over the state of Israel and the subsequent Palestinian refugee crisis.

As a matter of practice, Middle Easterners have been treated as racially and culturally inferior – as "yellow" Asians, morally and politically suspect Turks, or as members of the "brown" race – throughout their history (Cainkar 2018; Jamal and Naber 2008; Naber 2014). Because the ability to naturalize was tied to being white, Syrian Christians in the United States fought for this recognition, eventually gaining permission to naturalize and vote in the 1910s. After extensive battles in the courts, Yemenis were not granted permission to do the same until the 1940s. In 1965, governments in the United States and Britain struck down overly restrictive migration policies and readjusted country-specific quotas. In combination with push factors – political instability, stifling economic immobility, and state-sponsored scholarships – Libyans joined their counterparts from Yemen and a recently independent Syrian nation during this period in search of opportunities abroad.

As is the case for any diaspora, the political voice and visibility of these national groups was indelibly shaped by geopolitical circumstances. After the 1967 Arab–Israeli war and amid the tumult of global protests in the 1960s, members of these communities joined labor movements and pan-Arab associations to contest Zionism, imperialism, and discrimination (Shain 1996). Likewise, they also became subjected to heightened degrees of surveillance and persecution as potential Palestinian insurgents and communists for decades afterward (Pennock 2017). Following the terrorist attacks of September 11, 2001, Arab and Muslim immigrants were further subjected to mandatory special registration, mass arrests, secret and indefinite detentions, wiretapping, and visits by the Federal Bureau of Investigation (Cainkar 2009; Howell and Shryock 2003; Naber 2006; Staeheli and Nagel 2008). Taken together, these populations' transnational ties have been used to indict them as enemies of the state and as potential terrorists (Nagel 2002).

In light of these historical circumstances, this chapter investigates how emigrants and refugees from Libya, Syria, and Yemen mobilized for change in their home-countries from the United States and Britain before the 2011 Arab Spring uprisings. After providing the requisite contextual background, I focus in depth on their anti-regime mobilizations during the periods of authoritarian rule that became the impetus for the 2011 uprisings. For Libyans, this began in 1969 after Muammar al-Gaddafi overthrew Libya's King Idris. In Syria, Hafez al-Assad came to power in 1970, with his son Bashar appointed through manipulated elections after Hafez's death in 2000. In Yemen, Ali Abdullah Saleh came to power in 1978, first in North Yemen (the Yemen Arab Republic, YAR) before becoming president of the modern-day Republic of Yemen that joined north and south (formerly the People's Democratic Republic of Yemen, PDRY).

As this chapter illustrates, repression and economic hardship in their home-countries had forced many regime opponents into exile from authoritarian rule. The dislocation of varied oppositionists, from political elites to grassroots revolutionaries, civil society actors, and student activists, gave rise to new anti-regime networks abroad. Members of these diaspora networks and groups would play an important role in auxiliary activism for the Arab Spring in 2011 and beyond. I also find that Libyan, Syrian, and Yemeni immigrants in the United States and Britain established groups dedicated to the empowerment and socialization of the diaspora community itself. According to respondents who had been involved directly in the founding and operations of these associations, such groups were intended to be strictly apolitical, focusing instead on meeting the professional, economic, and social needs of the national immigrant community. However, as I elaborate later in Chapter 3, the conversion of these organizations – what social movement scholars call "indigenous organizations" (McAdam 1999[1982]) – into politicized "mobilizing structures" (McAdam et al. 1996) enabled them to channel significant resources to Arab Spring allies in 2011 and beyond.[2]

This chapter also sets up the puzzles that I address in Chapter 3. First, in spite of their relative opportunities for voice, the political initiatives of anti-regime diaspora members from Libya and Syria remained relatively small, informal, or underground. The data demonstrate that attempts to broaden the scope and publicity of their claims to mobilize the wider anti-regime community in the open were largely unsuccessful. Meanwhile, Yemenis had several groups dedicated to political change, but these groups called for the autonomy or secession of southern Yemen from the north, rather than for regime change of the central government. Second, although emigrant communities often work collectively to support development and charity in their places of origin through fundraising and hometown associations (Moya 2005), *no* Libyan or Syrian groups were dedicated to development or aid in the home-country. Only in the Yemeni case did a few organizations undertake some charitable efforts; these were, however, exceedingly small and not the primary purpose of the associations that spearheaded these campaigns. Taken together, organizations dedicated to home-country development or charity were notice-ably *lacking* in all three national communities prior to the Arab Spring. Chapter 2 explains these missing mobilizations as the result of transnational deterrents that have been largely overlooked in studies of transnational move-ments and diasporas to date.

---

[2] McAdam et al. (2001: 45) argue that "Mobilizing structures can be preexisting or created in the course of contention but in any case need to be appropriated as vehicles of struggle." While I do not disagree, I contend that there is an important significance to the *conversion* of preexisting organizations to political causes; these organizations bring their own set of constituencies and resources to a movement and lend it legitimacy. Furthermore, creating new structures also takes significant resources, which can place an undue burden on activists. See Chapter 6 of this book on resource conversion for details.

2.1 LIBYA: FROM COLONY TO NATION

The modern nation-state of Libya is situated in the Maghreb of northern Africa between Tunisia and Egypt, along the Mediterranean Sea. It is comprised of three regions: Tripolitania in the northwest, which encompasses the capital city of Tripoli; Fezzan in the southwest; and Cyrenaica in the east, which includes Libya's second-largest city of Benghazi. Captured by the Ottomans in the sixteenth century, Libya remained part of the Turkish empire until it was taken by the Italians in 1912. Between the World War I and World War II, Libyans resisted colonial rule via insurgency led by Omar al-Mukhtar of Cyrenaica. The Italians responded without mercy to popular demands by the indigenous communities, including the Amazigh, for their rights.[3] By imprisoning and starving the population in concentration camps, their efforts to keep control ended up imprisoning more than 110,000 civilians and murdering forty to seventy thousand (Ahmida 2006; St. John 2017).

After the Allied powers captured Libya from the Italian fascist regime in 1942 during World War II, Britain and France split the country and governed different regions. Libya's King Idris returned from exile in Egypt, and the United Nations declared the country independent by 1951. The constitution, drawn up under the auspices of a black, red, and green flag, was modeled on the West and instituted a respectively liberal state guaranteeing many civil rights. Idris was a weak king, however, and perceived by many as a stooge for Western powers, which profited greatly from economic trade and the use of its coastal ground as a base for American military forces. At this time, Libya's population was only about three million people, despite residing in the fourth-largest nation in Africa.

On September 1, 1969, a cabal of military men calling themselves the Free Officers Movement overthrew King Idris in a bloodless coup d'état. They were led by a twenty-seven-year-old captain named Muammar al-Gaddafi. Sporting a starched beige uniform and a gold-threaded officer's cap, Gaddafi was virtually unknown at the time, but it would not take long for his name to become synonymous with Libya itself. After expelling Western powers, the political elite, and banning the Latin script, Gaddafi was hailed by many outsiders as an anti-imperialist hero. Over the course of his forty-two-year rule, however, the Libyan people became the subjects of a brutal political experiment requiring total acquiescence. The regime constructed numerous internal security forces dedicated to coup-proofing the regime. As in other totalitarian societies of the twentieth century, a huge percentage of the population was incorporated into

---

[3] Libyan tribes include Arab, Tuareg, and Tabu, the latter of which dominate the southern Fezzan region. The Tabu were historically "a clan-based society of camel herders, speaking a language of Nilo-Saharan origin," while the Tuareg are originally pastoral nomads whose populations span "the Sahara and the Sahel in southern Libya and parts of Algeria, Burkina Faso, Mali, and Niger" who speak "a dialect of Amazigh (or Berber) known as Tamasheq" (Wehrey 2017).

the state's security apparatus and conscripted into the military. Under the guise of erecting a socialist republic for the masses, Gaddafi created Revolutionary Committees[4] to enforce loyalty and root out dissenters. Anyone suspected of doubting their leader was branded a traitor and convicted without a trial. Ordinary Libyans, students, communists, and Islamists did not take this treatment lying down, and protested vehemently through marches, petitions, and strikes. The Revolutionary Committees reacted with a vengeance, beating, imprisoning, and hanging organizers in grotesque public executions. Early resistance suffered further as students and activists were conscripted and forced to die in a pointless war with neighboring Chad between 1978 and 1987.

In 1973, Gaddafi dissolved all preexisting laws, placing the nation under a brand of Islamic *shariah* law, and eliminated the private sector. In 1975, he published the first of his three-part *Green Book* outlining his vision of social revolution, which children were forced to study in schools. In 1977, he dubbed Libya the *Jamahiriyya*, and claimed to serve as Libya's figurehead under popular rule, led by the General People's Committees. Claiming that Libya's Amazigh and Tuareg ethnic populations (sometimes referred to as Berbers) were a colonial invention, he instituted an Arabization program that outlawed their distinct identities and cultural symbols.[5] And despite his brash talk against Western powers and capitalism, Gaddafi was deeply reliant on foreign weaponry, trade, and technologies to enforce totalitarian power (Bassiouni 2013; Wright 2012: 206). In turn, the Gaddafi family amassed extraordinary wealth and absolute power for itself.

2.2 EXITING GADDAFI'S *JAMAHIRIYYA*

By expelling foreign powers, nationalizing industry, and routing out government officials who had served King Idris, Gaddafi created a wave of exiles and emigration of businessmen, doctors, and technocrats in the 1970s. At the same time, the regime also needed to equip and train its own nationals to run the oil sector. For this, the regime sent people abroad, particularly to the United States

---

[4] Due to his concerns about coup-proofing his regime, Gaddafi's bloated military apparatus was generally underequipped and undermined by the deliberate rotations in leadership; meanwhile, the best equipped forces, such as the Military Intelligence, the 32nd Brigade (*katiba*) led by Gaddafi's son Khamis, the Revolutionary Guard (*al-Hiras al-Thawri*), and the Jamahiriyya Security Organization (*Hayat Amn al-Jamahiriyya*), were dedicated to rooting out domestic dissent and protecting the Gaddafi family (Bassiouni 2013: 133–42).

[5] The Tuareg and Tabu have been subjected to neglect, coercion, and cooptation by Gaddafi, as well as the suppression of their culture, for decades. As Wehrey (2017) writes, the regime imposed the "systematic marginalization of two major non-Arab communities in the south, the Tabu and the Tuareg, to whom the Libyan dictator promised full citizenship rights in return for service in his security forces, particularly in the case of the Tuareg. These promises never materialized...." In 1994 he revoked the Tabu people's citizenship, denying them basic access to employment and healthcare, and the Tuareg were routinely conscripted by Gaddafi for use in his security forces.

and Britain, on student scholarships. The English city of Manchester, due in part to its clustering of prestigious universities and the process of chain migration, became home to the largest concentration of Libyans outside Libya.[6] By 2011, national statistics reported 15,046 Libyan nationals residing in Britain, with two-thirds of them living in Manchester (El-Abani et al. 2020). Libyans also came abroad to the United States as refugees and students after 1965. Students were expected to return in order to bring their skills back to the homeland, though many remained abroad to escape repression and conscription into the Libyan military.

In the face of such extreme brutality, survivors had little choice but to go underground or flee the country. In 1981, the National Front for the Salvation of Libya (NFSL), founded by an ambassador-turned-defector named Dr. Mohamed Yusuf al-Magariaf, plotted from Sudan to overthrow Gaddafi by force.[7] After the NFSL's CIA-backed assault on Gaddafi's compound was exposed by informants in 1984, key leaders were captured and executed, and the group never recovered. Survivors fled into neighboring states, traveling with their families from one country to the next using forged passports. Due in large part to Western governments' growing animus toward Gaddafi and his links with international terrorist attacks, some NFSL fighters and their families were granted asylum in Britain and the United States.

As Libyan dissidents escaped Gaddafi's dystopia, their aspirations for a freer Libya traveled with them. By the 1970s, approximately one hundred thousand Libyans had left their homeland, and those who gained asylum in the United States and Britain used this opportunity to continue their activism and to recruit new members. Ahmed, who grew up in exile with other NFSL families in Lexington, Kentucky, recalled,

My father came to the United States on a scholarship from the Libyan government to study engineering. He became politically active, was opposed to some of the activities of the regime, and was pretty vocal about it. Eventually that led to participation and involvement with the National Front for the Salvation of Libya – the *Jebha*, as we affectionately call it. That became a major part of the community that grew up in exile. Many of our social functions [and] formative experiences were really brought about by this network of individuals who made the principled decision to stand up against the regime and were paying the consequences for those decisions abroad.

Others formed smaller groups congruent to the NFSL, such as Mahmud, an activist-turned-businessman. "Some of the students who had been harassed – I was one of them – had to leave to go to UK," he explained.

---

[6] See Othman (2011) for more information about Libyan education in the Manchester community before the 2011 revolution.

[7] Sudanese president Gaafar Nimeiry, irked by Gaddafi's adventurism in Africa, provided refuge to NFSL insurgents until he was overthrown in 1985.

Others like myself kept gathering together outside, and we had a political movement. I was a joint member of the National Democratic Party, which was active for a long time since 1970. [It was] a mixture of Libyan intellectuals, students, and civil societists. We gathered to collect information and talk about human rights issues. We had a newspaper called the Voice of Libya, *Sawt Libya*, as a privately funded organization. Our members were across London, Egypt, and Switzerland.

As opposition to Gaddafi took an increasingly Islamist turn in the 1980s, dissidents in the diaspora mobilized in the spirit of a religiously oriented vision of liberation. According to Pargeter (2008: 87), Libyan students who were attracted to the ideology of the Muslim Brotherhood movement originating in Egypt "formed their own *Ikhwani* [Brotherhood] groups in the United States and the United Kingdom and, in 1979, began referring to themselves as the Libyan Islamic Group, *Jama'a Islamiyya Libiya*." Others sharpened their fighting skills in the internationalist brigades of anti-Soviet fighters in Afghanistan. According to Middle East expert Alison Pargeter (2008), between eight hundred and one thousand Libyans joined the international struggle, with about three hundred returning to launch the Libyan Islamic Fighting Group against Gaddafi.

Another dissident named Dr. Mohamed Abdul Malek joined the European Muslim Brotherhood after his emigration to Manchester. He founded an initiative called Libya Watch, a one-man organization dedicated to raising awareness about imprisoned Brotherhood members in Libya. Dr. Abdul Malek explained,

As part of Libya Watch, we would support asylum seekers from Libya. I remember there was one incident in which we showed this [British] judge the public hanging of individuals in Libya in Ramadan. You know what he said? "This is a fabricated tape. This cannot be true." It was very difficult for Westerners to appreciate what was going on because it simply does not happen here. But it was real. It was *very* much real.

Political activism before the Arab Spring also focused on one of the regime's most egregious crimes. During the region-wide crackdown on the Muslim Brotherhood in the 1980s, Libyan Brothers and other dissidents were imprisoned in the regime's hellish Abu Salim prison. After prisoners organized a strike in 1996 against increasingly inhumane conditions, approximately twelve hundred inmates – many of them gravely crippled by disease and torture – were gunned down en masse. Information in Libya was so tightly controlled that the victims' families and the outside world remained unaware of the massacre for years. In the early 2000s, the regime began to send notices to the families that their loved ones had died. Grieving relatives and lawyers in Benghazi started calling on the regime to acknowledge the Abu Salim Massacre. To support their demands, dissidents in Britain organized demonstrations. "The anniversary of the Abu Salim prison massacre was a day that we would not miss," Dr. Abdul Malek of Libya Watch attested. Nagi, a former British emigrant who I interviewed in Tripoli, recalled,

The Abu Salim prison massacre demonstrations [happened] in Manchester and in London, but mainly Manchester, in support of their demands. We did a lot of activities, displaying posters and things, trying to raise the awareness of these issues.

Along with these efforts, a small group called the Libyan Human Rights Commission was founded in the United States in 1995 by émigré activists, with at least one member being formerly affiliated with the NFSL, to criticize the regime over its abysmal human rights record. In 2002, a small but significant number of websites emerged to publicize information about the country and to post the writings of Libyans, usually under pseudonyms. Ashur Shamis, who was exiled in 1969 after Gaddafi's coup, established a political organization called the Libya Human and Political Development Forum in London. As part of this initiative, he founded an online newspaper called *Akhbar Libya* that would often broach sensitive subjects, such as corruption among Libyan elites, using information gleaned from insider contacts. According to Gazzini (2007), *Akbar Libya* started as a four-page newspaper in the 1980s before going online in the early 2000s. Sites such as Libya Watanona (Our Homeland Libya), run by Dr. Ibrahim Ighneiwa, posted articles, histories, and letters in English and Arabic and was a hub for remembrances and grievances, but it did not have a specific political agenda. Other sites, such as Justice4Libya, were dedicated to remembering those who had been imprisoned and killed in the 1996 Abu Salim Massacre. A community leader who came up numerous times in my interviews, Ali Kamadan Abuzaakik, founder of the American Libyan Freedom Alliance (ALFA) in Washington, DC, also held meetings to evaluate the state of the opposition and consider their future course of action (Bugaighis and Buisier 2003). Exile organizations such as these were scattered and small, however, and generally lacked non-exile membership.

In 2005, members of the American and British NFSL, the Libyan Human Rights Commission, and other dissident groups such as the Libyan Constitutional Union and the Libyan League for Human Rights met in London to declare themselves a coalition called the National Conference for the Libyan Opposition. According to scholar Alice Alunni's (2019, 2020) extensive research on this conference, their members attempted to transcend ideology and Islamism to unite under a nationalist agenda. As part of this effort, they referenced the 1951 constitution and came together under the flag of King Idris's rule. Covered by the BBC and Al Jazeera, the Libyan regime condemned the conference. In doing so, however, the regime incidentally raised awareness of the opposition abroad and the 1951 governmental framework inside of Libya (Alunni 2019: 251).

In the 2000s, a number of websites were created from abroad in order to promote Amazigh culture and identity. In the 1970s, Libya's Amazigh association, the *Rabita Shamal Afriqiya*, was forcibly closed and its members arrested on charges of creating an illegal political party (Al-Rumi 2009). Because the heritage and language of this ethnic group had been repressed for decades in

Libya, some diaspora members only learned about their people's history after going abroad to study; according to Al-Rumi (2009), "A number of activists have attempted to use the web to reconnect Libyan Berbers with their language." One such website called Tawalt, which opened in 2001 from California (Alunni 2020: 143) and closed without explanation in 2009, "was the richest such cultural website, offering not only downloadable grammar books but also audio recordings of grammar classes of Tarifit, Tashalhit, and Nafusa, different branches of the Tmazight language. Unlike Tawalt, which is in Arabic (they claim to be the first ever Amazigh website in Arabic), two other Berber cultural websites, Libyaimal.com and Adrar.5u.com, are exclusively in Tmazight." According to Al-Rumi (2009), a UK-based organization called the Libyan Tamazight Congress (*Agraw a'Libi n'Tmazight*, ALT), founded in 2000, also demanded that the Gaddafi regime make official reference to the Tmazight language in the constitution and recognize the presence and legitimacy of the Amazigh people in Libya.

By the early 2000s, interviewees who had grown up in political exile attested that their parents' generation had given up hope or had spent a lot of time "discussing but not enough time doing, or reaching out," as M., a Libyan American activist, recalled. Their hopes for change at home were further dampened as Gaddafi's relations with the West improved. Gaddafi had been isolated in the global community for decades for sponsoring international acts of terrorism, including most infamously the 1988 Lockerbie airplane bombing.[8] In December 2003, following the US-led occupation of Iraq, Gaddafi agreed to give up Libya's weapons of mass destruction and settle his foreign debts. His son and heir apparent, Saif al-Islam, also sought to repair Libya's international reputation as a pariah state by releasing some political prisoners and opening an investigation into the Abu Salim Massacre.

This rapprochement was bad news for many of Libya's former freedom fighters. In addition to being persecuted by Gaddafi, members of the Libyan Islamic Fighting Group also became caught in the post-2001 war-on-terror dragnet. Under President George W. Bush, the United States began helping Gaddafi capture former fighters in 2004 and rendered them back to Tripoli for interrogation and torture. Britain also signed a rendition agreement with Gaddafi in a memorandum of understanding in 2005 (Human Rights Watch 2011b). Warming relations also made British officials more hesitant to accept refugees from Libya (Blitz 2009).

After 2004, the diaspora itself became a key component of the regime's plan to reestablish ties with the international community. In order to improve

---

[8] The Lockerbie bombing refers to the bombing of Pan Am Flight 103, which – on its way from Frankfurt to New York (John F. Kennedy International Airport) and Detroit via London – exploded over Lockerbie, Scotland, killing a total of 270 people. While Gaddafi publicly denied responsibility, an investigation by British and American authorities found two of his agents to be responsible; while he paid compensation to the families, many of whom were American, in 2003.

Libya's legitimacy, many exiles received assurances by regime officials that they could return safely home. Saif al-Islam also coaxed the youth to reestablish ties with their homeland by sponsoring luxurious group trips to Libya, akin to Israel's birthright trips for Jewish Americans. In 2007, during Gaddafi's and Saif al-Islam's campaign to reintegrate themselves into the world community, a law banning Amazigh names was struck down, and the government hosted the Paris-based World Amazigh Conference for the first time (Alunni 2020). However, this was accompanied by subsequent mob violence and attacks against Amazigh figures inside of Libya and the mysterious closing of the Tawalt website in 2009, most likely due to regime intimidation and pressure.

In response to Gaddafi's reintegration into the global community, Hamid and fellow exile Abdullah established a social movement network called *Gaddafi Khalas!*, or Enough Gaddafi, in 2008. M., a member of the Enough Gaddafi network, explained that they used their English-language skills and technological savvy to launch a website and a "new form of opposition, the next wave of opposition."

We staged protests, and [published] different reports on violations going on, in particular focused on Abu Salim victims and the massacre and the families of those individuals on social media, bringing up the violations of the past forty-two years. We tried to bring that to light, to look back at a lot of the violations that happened in the 1980s against college students, and put it into the foreground the international community should not be dealing with Gaddafi because he's a criminal.

This group also held a protest against Gaddafi's 2009 visit to the UN headquarters in New York. By this time, Gaddafi had turned into a bloated, incoherent megalomaniac. Sashaying in *jird* cloaks in front of the camera, his rambling speeches and eccentricities appeared laughable to outside observers. But his buffoonery masked a poignant cruelty that lay hidden behind a thick curtain of censorship. Regime control over the media and the Internet was hugely effective in isolating Libya from the rest of the world. Assuming that the Libyan people were too complacent, cowed, or brainwashed to resist Gaddafi, it seemed during my early graduate studies as though pundits had written Libya off as an example of unshakable authoritarian entrenchment. But although violence seemed to have succeeded in stamping out mortal threats to Gaddafi's rule within the nation's borders, the repression that had forced many of Libya's bravest and brightest abroad had also produced an anti-regime diaspora that remained steadfastly loyal to the homeland. It was these dissidents and professionals who would come together and help to bring about his downfall in 2011.

At the same time, public efforts to condemn Gaddafi in the years preceding the Arab Spring were rare. Protests, such as those initiated by Enough Gaddafi and Libya Watch, were small and led by a minority of exiles. Furthermore, in spite of the notable presence of anti-regime members in the United States and Britain, neither host-country diaspora produced civic membership-based associations dedicated to ousting Gaddafi. In summary, the Libya anti-regime movement abroad, while noteworthy and important, was exceedingly small, lacked cohesion, and rarely involved non-exiles before the 2011 revolution.

2.3 LIBYAN SOCIALIZING AND EMPOWERMENT INITIATIVES

Respondents who grew up in exile reported that their parents never intended to remain apart from Libya for long. Khaled, a second-generation Libyan American and the son of an NFSL activist who had grown up in Lexington, Kentucky, recalled, "We always thought that next year, next year, we're going to go home. We used to say, *lan nahruhu*: 'when we will return.'" But as repeated attempts to overthrow Gaddafi failed, interviewees like Khaled reported that their parents began to accept the fact that their exile might be permanent. Recognizing that youth like Khaled risked becoming estranged from their Libyan identity and culture, activist Dr. Gaddor Saidi founded the Libyan Association of Southern California in 1986 in Orange County as a way to organize regular community gatherings for families across the region. Gaddor reported that the association was apolitical even though many of those who founded it were in exile and involved in some kind of opposition activity, as he had been himself. He recalled,

Myself and others who organized it, we always made sure that it's open, that we don't get into the politics so that we at least give the young people some kind of platform to have some connection to their country. Hoping that one day they will go back. [But] we were thinking that it's not going to happen in our lifetime, especially when Gaddafi's children started taking hold of the country.

From Manchester, Zakia, who was forced to escape Libya with her husband and seek refuge in Britain in 1998, formed the Libya Women's Association in 2003. Her group, which intentionally avoided any involvement with home-country politics, was founded to promote the social development of "Libyan women, and make them more active in the UK – to study, go out, and meet people. We did many activities for kids to push them to get all the positive things in the UK." In the United States, members of the diaspora established a camp for youth called Amal, which means "hope" in Arabic. Adam of Virginia, a former participant in Amal and a second-generation exile, recalled fondly that because Libyans were scattered across the United States, the camp provided "an opportunity for everybody to come together, for families to meet up again. This is like our Libyan family. Of course, our immediate cousins are overseas in Libya. [But] these [people] are our surrogate cousins, mothers, fathers." Initiatives like Amal were critical in fostering strong social and cultural ties for second-generation exiles who never knew, or who barely remembered, their homeland. As Abdullah, who grew up in the NFSL-Lexington community with Khaled, recalled,

[The adults] had schools on Sundays that taught us Arabic; we had young people who annually would rent a theater and put on shows. As much as we were a product of America, there was always a really strong bond between us and Libya, even just culturally, despite the fact that most of us had never been or would [not] go back and forth.

While I found no other named community associations during my research, respondents across various cities reported regularly hosting informal social events, such as religious *Eid* celebrations and annual community picnics. Respondents reported that these initiatives fostered their heritage and home-country connections, thereby inculcating loyalty to Libya among the younger generations. These ties would come to fruition and become conduits for activism during the 2011 revolution, as subsequent chapters explain.

2.4 THE RISE OF THE ASSAD REGIME

The modern-day state of Syria, like Libya, was once part of the Ottoman Empire. It was ensconced in a territory known as "greater Syria," which included Lebanon, Jordan, Israel, the Palestinian Territories, and parts of contemporary Iraq. As emigrants fled war, religious persecution, and political violence, Syrians reached both the United States and Britain by the 1860s, settling in a larger wave than began in the 1880s (Gualtieri 2009, 2020; Seddon 2014). Muslims, however, were largely blocked from emigrating because of their forced conscription into the Ottoman military. Under the Ottomans, Syrians were considered part of the "yellow race" in the West and were associated with anarchists, papists, barbarism, and "Moslem" threats (Younis 1995). Thus, the majority of early Syrian emigration to the United States and Britain was comprised of Christians (Orthodox, Maronite, Melkite, and Protestant) who attained social mobility as peddlers, traders, and merchants (Younis 1995: 233).

Syrians became categorically distinguished from Turks in 1899 in the United States, though they were also suspect due to their Orthodox, non-Anglo origins (Jamal and Naber 2008). Through forming robust civic organizations, including the Federation of Syrian American Societies, they contested racial discrimination in the courts (Bragdon 1989; Gualtieri 2009, 2020; Younis 1995). By 1915, Syrians came to be considered white, and therefore able to naturalize, after a Syrian Christian named George Dow won his third appeal in court (Jamal and Naber 2008). By 1920, no Syrians were refused citizenship on the basis of their supposed race.

From the 1880s until the more restrictive quotas of the 1920s, Syrians emigrated to New York, New Orleans, into Texas and California through Mexico, and eventually spread to most states; about one hundred thousand Syrians entered the United States during this period (Gualtieri 2020). While they continued to face discrimination and racism, they also mobilized to improve their collective treatment. When US Senator David Reed called them "Mediterranean trash," Syrian American clubs pressured Reed to walk back his comments (Younis 1995: 216). So too did the Syrian American Federation of New York defend the naturalization rights of Syrians and lobby President William Taft for citizenship (Gualtieri 2009: 110–11). And although Syrians' allies in the white Protestant church argued that "they do not carry revolutionary theories or propensities" (Younis 1995: 123), Syrians did mobilize from the United States on matters of national independence. The *Suriya el-Fetat* (Young Syria Party) was founded in 1899 to support a free homeland and recruit fighters in the struggle. During the turn of the twentieth century, media reports described how "revolutionists on lower Washington Street" in Manhattan plotted against Ottoman power (Younis 1995: 140). According to historian Adele Younis, they also lobbied the US government to help free Syria from the "Mohammodan [*sic*] Government of Damascus" (1995: 385). Syrian American organizations from states such as Massachusetts and Oklahoma also participated in the first Arab Congress, which convened in Paris in 1913 (Gualtieri 2009: 88).

Elites in the community sparred in the press about whether the immigrant community was really "for" or "against" the Turkish Sultan (Fahrenthold 2013), but they nevertheless professed a kind of long-distance nationalism that bridged sectarian labels (Fahrenthold 2019; Gualtieri 2009: 83–84). Later, Syrians in New York formed the National Independence Party of Syria to inspire resistance to French occupation, and the New Syria Party (Gualtieri 2009; Pennock 2017). Syrian presses also highlighted attacks, including the bombing of a Syrian's home in Georgia in 1923 (Younis 1995: 245) and the lynching of a Syrian man in Florida and the killing of his wife by a police chief (Gualtieri 2020: 27). They advertised the community's achievements, campaigns by elite women's groups for charity, and assimilation-related activities such as literacy classes. Federations in the 1950s also agitated on behalf of the Palestinian refugee issue, as when the National Association of Syrian and Lebanese American Federations met with US President Truman in 1951 to convince him to attend to the problem (Gualtieri 2020: 83).

During World War I, a secretive accord between Britain and France called the Sykes–Picot Agreement was drawn up in 1916 and forged the modern-day boundaries of Syria. At the end of the war in 1918, Syria came under French control as per this arrangement and, as sanctioned by the League of Nations, became a mandated protectorate of the French. Battles for territorial control continued, which prompted the emigration of Christians in large numbers to the West. Battles also ensued against French rule, after which Syrians and the French agreed upon a treaty of independence in 1936. Hashim al-Atassi became Syria's first president under the new constitution. After France fell to the Nazis in 1940, Syria came under the rule of the Vichy regime. Later, the Free French and the British regained territory, but this did not upend colonial control until 1946. At this time, Syrians came to be distinguished from the Lebanese and

Palestinians in the United States and Britain. Syria's independence was also followed by years of constant turmoil. Many Syrian Jews fled to the emergent state of Israel after Syria's loss in the 1948 Arab–Israeli war. Coup after coup ensued by colonels as different military factions vied for control. An alignment between Syria and the USSR pitted them against Turkey, leading to a cold-war era conflict that continues to influence Syrian politics today.

In 1958, Syria merged with Egypt, under President Gamal Abdel Nasser, to form the United Arab Republic, but Syria experienced another coup and withdrew from the union. In 1962, the government continued to discriminate against Kurds as so-called foreign agitators by stripping citizenship from some 120,000 of them (roughly 20 percent of this minority group). This policy trapped them in a country that had rendered them stateless as part of a vicious Arabization campaign (Chatty 2010; Human Rights Watch 1996).

In 1963, a group of officers launched a coup d'état against Syria's government that would eventually bring its Ba'ath Party members to power. During this time, a young officer named Hafez al-Assad was promoted to Minister of Defense. By November 1970, Hafez launched a so-called corrective revolution that made him prime minister. In 1971, President Hafez ushered in an iron-fisted dynasty that would last decades, enforcing total control over Syria's diverse population by forming a powerful coalition of Alawis (a minority sect of Shi'a Islam of which Hafez was a member), Sunni military men, and the business class. The regime also deployed a whopping twelve security agencies to surveil the population, subjecting regime critics, leftists, Islamists, and minorities to totalitarian state terror (Ziadeh 2011). As Syria expert Lisa Wedeen (2015[1999]) argues, Hafez built himself into a cult personality, and people were forced to perform "as if" they loved him unconditionally in elaborate public rituals. As the regime came to employ at least one person in every five, intelligence agents of *al-Mukhabarat* were literally everywhere. Activists and everyday people were detained without charge, and prisons were rife with unspeakable acts of torture, from the "German chair," designed to induce unconsciousness and break detainees' backs, to rapes and beatings with iron rods (Paul 1990).

As is often the case, extreme repression provoked a backlash,[9] particularly by groups suffering from the brunt of regime repression, such as the Kurds and the outlawed Muslim Brotherhood. The regime and the Brotherhood's radical flank waged war on each other until Hafez al-Assad dealt the group a decisive blow in 1982. After a Brotherhood cell in Hama reacted against a regime ambush in the early hours of February 2, Hafez responded by deploying at least ten thousand troops to seal off the city and destroy the resistance once and for all. Within a week, it was reported that "Syrian tanks are methodically

[9] For superb demonstrations of severe repression's backlash effect, I recommend works by Goodwin (2001), Hess and Martin (2006), and Rasler (1996).

leveling vast areas of Hama."[10] The entire city was cut off from electricity, telephone communications, food, and water; regime soldiers looted people's homes and raped inhabitants. Residents succumbed to starvation and death from otherwise treatable injuries. Those who tried to flee were often caught at military checkpoints, and the highways running through the city remained under lockdown.[11]

The press blackout during this period was highly effective as the city remained officially sealed off from outsiders for months. By May, reports were circulating figures of ten, twenty-five, and fifty thousand civilian casualties. Even Assad's biographer, Patrick Seale (1982), reported in the British press that "refugees from Hama claim that 'at least 25,000 people' were slaughtered and whole neighborhoods devastated in a two-week orgy of killing, destruction and looting." What became known as the Hama Massacre would foreshadow the regime's merciless reaction to the 2011 uprisings and the many massacres to come during the Arab Spring.

2.5 ESCAPE FROM THE CULT OF ASSAD

After the United States and Britain changed entry rules for immigrants from the Middle East and Asia in 1965, Syrian immigrant communities began to settle in Britain and became far more diverse in the United States. They came to include non-Christians, political refugees, students on state-sponsored scholarships, and businessmen. Survivors of the Hama Massacre of 1982, for instance, and many Muslim Brothers were forced abroad in the wake of this atrocity. One survivor of the crackdown named Walid Saffour formed the oldest known anti-regime group in either the United States or Britain in the late 1980s. This London-based organization was called the Syrian Human Rights Committee. This organization was dedicated to publicizing atrocities committed by the regime during and since the Hama Massacre. Dr. Saffour and other exiles also held periodic protests outside the Syrian embassy in London to commemorate these events. When I met his daughter Razan in Manchester, she told me,

---

[10] Reports circulated that some army units defected within the first week of the assault, which were difficult to verify. The loyalty of the security forces most certainly came under significant stress during this period, as in Dara'a and elsewhere (Abdulhamid 2011). Out of a quarter of a million members, more than half are conscripts (see Heydemann 1999; Ziadeh 2011). The massacre of primarily Sunni civilians by Sunni army conscripts on behalf of the Alawite-dominated government caused a significant rupture in the regime's offensive. While few details are known and it is not clear how many soldiers defected, this likely prolonged the conflict significantly.

[11] Responding in an Orwellian fashion, the Syrian government denied anything unusual was happening in Hama. Ahmed Iskander, Minister of Information, described reports of mass murder as the "stuff of dreams"; other officials went further, dismissing accusations of "serious disturbances" as "lies" and "a flagrant intervention" in Syria's affairs (Seale 1982).

When we were born, we grew up very much in this opposition atmosphere. I had an uncle who was tortured to death in Tadmor Prison. My father, he was also tortured in the '80s. He refused to go out and protest for [the regime], so they took him and they broke his nose, broke his back. They put him in a wheel and they pushed him down a very steep staircase. Usually people die, but he survived to tell the tale. So when he came here, he was very, very active.

Another anti-regime organization, the Western Kurdistan Association, was founded by Dr. Jawad Mella. Dr. Mella was a Peshmerga fighter in Syria and exiled to London in 1984. He established the association to serve as a government-in-exile for Syrian Kurds and to lobby the British government to support the secession of a Kurdish-dominated region of his homeland, dubbed Western Kurdistan. Dr. Mella also attested to assisting Kurdish Syrian refugees in Britain through charitable works, bringing members of the community together to form a Kurdish football team, and housing a small Kurdish library, museum, and archive in the London neighborhood of Hammersmith that had recently closed at the time of our interview. Dr. Mella also maintained ties to the broader transnational Kurdish movement by representing Kurdish Syrians in the Kurdish National Congress and by displaying the Kurdish national flag at the Western Kurdistan Association's headquarters. Dr. Mella and his activist colleagues also held periodic protests outside the London embassy and took every opportunity to speak to the media about the need for independence from the Syrian Arab Republic.

Political activism increased ever so slightly in the 2000s at home and abroad during a brief and tenuous opening in autocratic rule. Hafez died in 2000 and his youngest son, Bashar, was recalled from his medical practice in London to take the throne. Despite coming to power through a sham election and hastily rewritten constitutional rules, the transition was an initial cause for hope. Bashar had been relatively distant from regime politics for some time, and as an ophthalmologist, he and his glamorous wife, Asma, appeared young and cosmopolitan. Bashar was credited with bringing the Internet to Syria, and pro-democracy activists took advantage of the thaw in illiberalism to push for reforms. Prominent intellectuals and reform-minded Ba'ath Party members led the charge, organizing informal meetings to discuss their demands. In a "Statement of the 99," they called for an end to the permanent state of martial law, the release of all political prisoners, the safe return of political exiles, and the right to form civic associations and political parties. In 2001, a bolder "Statement of the 1,000" called for expanded rights and constitutional reforms. Kurdish leaders, who had long been stripped of their citizenship in Syria, mobilized to press for rights and recognition. Outsiders declared that a Damascus Spring was underway. But while Bashar initially closed the regime's notorious Mezzeh prison, released some political prisoners, and allowed some civil society groups to come above ground, these openings slammed shut in 2001 after the regime arrested many organizers and increased internet censorship.

During the false promise of Bashar's reforms in the early 2000s, second-generation exiles came of age in the West and joined their elders to advocate for democracy at home. Malik had been in exile since his birth in Jordan because of his father's oppositional activities. Growing up in London, he and others in the global anti-regime diaspora communicated through "Paltalk," a precursor to Skype, to discuss political change back home.

You had chatrooms where people get the mic and they talk. You had a Syrian group there, which was the opposition; the room was called Syria Justice and Freedom. I was there every night – I was basically *hooked* on this – from 8 p.m. to 11 or so. That was the peak. People would join to talk about issues related to Syria, some of whom lived in the US, some in the Gulf, some in Jordan. It was all anonymous, so no one quite knew who you were. This is how I got to know politics.

By 2006, Malik, his brother Anas, and their friends sought to forge an alternative to what he described as the two "classic" options in the exiled opposition: the Muslim Brotherhood and the communists. He went on to co-found a network of second-generation British Syrian exiles called the Syrian Exiles League. This group, which they later dubbed the Syrian Justice and Development Party, lobbied on behalf of exiled and stateless Syrians in the international community and founded a satellite channel called Barada TV. From London, Malik and his colleagues broadcast pre-recorded anti-regime programs with the intention of reaching audiences in Syria. Barada TV also provided fellow exiles with a unique platform to discuss the need for regime change in Syria and its atrocities against minorities, including against a Kurdish uprising in Al-Qamishli in 2004.

In 2005, the assassination of Lebanese Prime Minister Rafik al-Hariri stoked an uprising that led to the withdrawal of Syria's occupation of Lebanon. Reformers seized upon this opportunity to publish the Damascus Declaration in 2005, which called for constitutional reforms, the recognition of Kurdish rights, and gradual political liberalization. (Muslim Brothers chose instead to form a National Salvation Front with the former vice president Abdul Halim Khaddam when he defected in 2006; see Conduit 2019.) The surge in hope for change and the newfound audacity of civil society leaders in Syria inspired the formation of new groups abroad as well. This included the Syrian American Council (SAC) in 2005, established by several first-generation immigrants in Burr Ridge, Illinois. The purpose of SAC was to support the burgeoning civil society movement in Syria and promote a general dialogue about civil liberties, but without explicitly mentioning or criticizing the regime by name. Its founding members also attempted to set up chapters in other US cities and invited well-known activists from Syria to attend their inaugural event in Chicago.

Movements-in-exile, including the Muslim Brotherhood and the Syrian Justice and Development Party, joined activists in Syria to sign the Damascus Declaration in 2005. However, the proponents of the Damascus Declaration were arrested, leading to a new wave of exile. Activists Ammar Abdulhamid and Khawla Yusuf, a married couple, moved to the suburbs of Washington, DC in 2005 after being threatened by the regime during this crackdown. They continued their activities abroad by establishing the Tharwa Foundation in 2007. They dedicated this organization to promoting democratic change, nonviolent resistance, and minority rights in Syria. Ammar also produced a six-part series titled *FirstStep*, broadcast through the Syrian Justice and Development Party's Barada TV channel out of London, to advocate for a nonviolent revolution in Syria.

Dr. Radwan Ziadeh, who had been an invited guest of the SAC inaugural event in Chicago a few years earlier, was forced into exile in 2007. He established the Syrian Center for Political and Strategic Studies in Washington, DC, as an outspoken regime critic and academic. In a related case, Ayman Abdel Nour, a former Christian member of the Syrian Ba'ath Party had been forced to join his extended family in California after demanding reform. From exile he established a website called All4Syria in Arabic as a place to discuss political change at home. Artist-activists in exile like Marah Bukai, who settled in northern Virginia, remained an outspoken critic of the regime. Another figure named Rami Abdulrahman (born Ossama Suleiman), forced to leave Syria in 2000 (MacFarquhar 2013), founded the Syrian Observatory for Human Rights from his new home in Coventry, England, in 2006. This one-man operation, much like Dr. Abdul Malek's Libya Watch, was dedicated to drawing attention to human rights abuses and the plight of political prisoners.[12] All of these individuals, in conjunction with their contacts on the ground, would come to play important roles in the 2011 revolution.

Overall, the United States and Britain came to host several anti-regime organizations in the 2000s that were primarily headed by individual exiles. The formation of the Syrian American Council was the only attempt to establish a *membership*-based advocacy organization during this period. However, as Chapter 3 explains, SAC organizers remained unable to recruit members

---

[12] Unfortunately, Mr. Abdulrahman did not respond to my requests for an interview in 2014 – however, this was likely because he was simply too busy, running an organization and a private business full time during this period. *The New York Times* reported in 2013 that

> Mr. Abdul Rahman spends virtually every waking minute tracking the war in Syria, disseminating bursts of information about the fighting and the death toll. What began as sporadic, rudimentary e-mails about protests early in the uprising has swelled into a torrent of statistics and details ... Mr. Abdul Rahman rarely sleeps. He gets up around 5:30 a.m., calling Syria to awaken his team. First, they tally the previous day's casualty reports and release a bulletin. Then he alternates between taking news media calls – 10 on a slow day, 15 an hour for breaking news – and contacting activists. (MacFarquhar 2013)

> since the onset of the Syrian revolution, the Syrian Observatory for Human Rights has played a leading role in broadcasting work during the uprising and subsequent war, and has generally earned a reputation as being a trustworthy source of information among NGOs (MacFarquhar 2013).

until the revolution, and anti-regime efforts by individual exiles lacked community support.

2.6 SYRIAN SOCIALIZATION AND EMPOWERMENT ORGANIZING

Like their Libyan counterparts, Syrian respondents reported that periodic gatherings took place across their concentrated communities in the United States and Britain. Since their emigration, Syrians have often maintained their heritage and transnational ties through social events, including outdoor picnics featuring celebrities (*mahrajans*), festivals, conventions, *haflas* (large indoor parties), and events held in Syrian and Syrian Lebanese clubs (Bragdon 1989; Gualtieri 2020; Younis 1995). These occasions brought together Syrians speaking English, Arabic, and Spanish in "spaces that renewed their Syrianness" (Gualtieri 2020: 72–76). The diaspora also gave rise to brick-and-mortar professional associations for doctors and new social clubs in the 2000s. These organizations were made possible by the Syrian community's relatively high degree of wealth, as well as by regime sponsorship. I return to these issues in depth in Chapters 3 and 6.

From the United States, clubs included the Syrian American Club of Houston, founded in 1991. According to board member Omar Shishakly, the club was founded to promote Syrian culture and education by offering Arabic classes and student scholarships. He explained, "It's a cultural club. We're basically non-political in any way or form. We don't support any sides. We also provide scholarships to about twenty students each year." Former member Belal Delati of Southern California also reported that their local Syrian American Association was dedicated to celebrating Syrian national holidays and to helping Syrians "remember their heritage." Parallel organizations operated in Britain; the British Syrian Society was founded in 2003 as a social club, although no Syrians I interviewed for their Arab Spring activism participated in it. Syrians, many of whom received state scholarships to study medicine and science in the West, also produced several professional organizations. Both the Syrian American Medical Association and the Syrian British Medical Society were founded in 2007. After the Arab Spring, these associations played a significant role in addressing the humanitarian crisis caused by regime repression and Syria's ensuing war.

2.7 THE TWO YEMENS BECOME ONE

The Republic of Yemen is a stunning country of lowland deserts, high mountain ranges, and plateaus on the heel of the Arabian Peninsula. One of the poorest countries in the world, Yemen began the twentieth century as two nations: the north, an imamate, and the south, a British protectorate. Prior to the formation of Yemen as the republic we know today, Zaydi tribes fiercely resisted Ottoman invasions from the north, which was key to Turkish trade with India. The Ottomans eventually conquered southern Yemen and the Tihama area along the Red Sea in the late 1530s, but Yemen proved to be a bloodbath for Ottoman soldiers sent in from Egypt. After a series of battles, territories traded hands many times between the Turks and various Yemeni forces, including Zaydi tribesmen of the northern highlands. By the mid-nineteenth century, Ottoman forces and the Zaydis, among other groups, were still battling for control.

As the British Empire expanded its reach across the Asian continent, forces captured the southern port city of Aden, where they enforced a protectorate colonial status and signed treaties with local tribes. In 1892, the Ottomans again sent forces to conquer Yemen's northern capital of Sana'a, which became the administrative capital of the Ottoman's territory in Yemen. However, constant rebellions by Zaydi Imams, such as Yahya Hamidaddin, made imperialistic governance largely impossible. As a result, a treaty with the Ottomans in 1911 made Imam Yahya governor of the Zaydi northern highlands. Meanwhile, Imam Yahya did not recognize the British-Ottoman border agreement that divided Yemen into north and south. Fighting continued between the two sides over Yemen's middle ground as Yahya himself sought to capture Aden. Eventually, a 1934 treaty between the Imam and the British recognized the latter's authority over the "Aden protectorate" for forty years. During this period, Yemen became host to regional and internationalized mobilization by the Muslim Brotherhood and nationalists with competing visions for Yemen's future. In 1948, a Zaydi prince named Abdullah bin Ahmad al-Wazir assassinated Imam Yahya, but Yahya's son, the crown prince Ahmad, was able to regain control. Up until that point, Yahya had largely succeeded in sequestering Yemen from outside influences. At this time, Ahmad opened Yemen to foreign trade through an agreement with the USSR. When Imam Ahmad of the north died in 1962, a terrible civil war ensued in the northern Yemen Arab Republic that pushed out many Yemenis in search of sanctuary.

An uprising in the south by Marxist republicans and a nationalist military organization, who would later turn on each other, ousted the British in 1967 and gave rise to the People's Democratic Republic of Yemen, the region's only socialist republic. The north and south then proceeded to fight each other on and off again in the 1970s. In the midst of this turmoil, Ali Abdullah Saleh came to power in the north in 1978.

In 1986, an internal civil war in the south killed thousands, weakening the state considerably. By 1990, amid the fall of the Soviet Union, the two governments agreed to merge into the Republic of Yemen. However, a civil war broke out between them due to southern grievances about being marginalized under the new elected government. In 1994, Saleh triumphed and became the first elected president of Yemen in 1999. The reunification of Yemen's two halves subjected the south to heavy repression, corruption, and neglect. Saleh relied heavily on northern elites like his longtime ally and cousin, General Ali Mohsen al-Ahmar, commander of the First Armored Division, to repress uprisings in the south (and in the far north, he launched wars against a Zaydi revival movement known as the Houthis). When a peaceful protest movement of unpaid southern pensioners arose in 2007, regime forces cracked down on the demonstrators with lethal force. This escalated long-simmering grievances over the south's repressive occupation by northern elites, and the south has since witnessed the mobilization of various factions for southern autonomy and independence under the banner of the old blue, red, white, and black socialist flag. Saleh's regime may have been Yemen's internationally recognized authority, but its legitimacy remained highly contested across its territory (Day 2012).

2.8 YEMENI EMIGRATION HISTORY AND POLITICAL ACTIVISM

Yemenis were the first Muslims to emigrate to Britain, according to historian Fred Halliday (2010[1992]), due to their recruitment as laborers in the coal furnaces of British naval ships. From port cities like South Shields, they established the first mosques, Islamic schools, and the first Arabic-language newspaper in western Europe called *Al Salaam* (Halliday 2010[1992]).[13] Many of these ships also headed to the United States, and especially New York, beginning in the early 1900s. In both receiving countries, restrictive immigration controls enacted between 1917 and 1924 limited Yemeni emigration. Nativism stoked riots against the hiring of so-called colored seamen, who were already underpaid and working in miserable conditions, in England and Wales. Many of their communities were additionally segregated in the slums of port cities due to racism and nativism.

As Yemenis emigrated, so did their loyalties. In 1936, for example, a leader named Sheikh Abdullah al-Hakimi came to Britain as a sailor and worked to mobilize the community of South Shields to support the Free Yemen Movement in North Yemen. He formed the Committee for the Defense of Yemen in partnership with the Aden-based Grand Yemeni Association and lobbied the British Foreign Secretary Ernest Bevin for assistance (Seddon 2014: 143–44). His paper, *Al-Salaam*, published criticisms of the northern Imam as well, criticizing the leader in an open letter for making the Yemeni people poor and forcing them abroad to survive. His mobilizing efforts faced a number of challenges, not the least of which was competition from community members who supported the Imam. One such member, Hassan Ismail, rallied the community around the Imamate and set up a rival mosque.[14]

---

[13] In Britain, these communities were initially (and erroneously) referred to as *lascars*, an anglicized word from the Arabic term for soldier, *al-askari* (Seddon 2014).

[14] Seddon (2014: 145) writes that "With most of their families and tribesmen still living in the Yemen and under the direct rule of the Imam, it would not make good political sense to offer any

After World War II, the demand for Yemeni labor on ships decreased due to the changeover to oil-based fuel; in both the United States and Britain, Yemenis were compelled to transition to the service sector and industrial manufacturing. In the mid-nineteenth century, Yemenis in both host-countries moved to industrial cities such as Birmingham, Sheffield, Manchester, Toledo, and Detroit through chain migration to factories, where men often lived and worked together. Yemenis also worked in California, with as many as one hundred thousand men working as seasonal labor in the fields (Friedlander 1988). These groupings also corresponded with region and tribe much of the time and made social spaces, such as Yemeni cafes, primarily male spaces. These labor sectors often kept them socially isolated, with limited abilities to attain upward mobility and improve their English skills.[15] Later on, Britain's migration controls of 1962 also constricted Yemenis' abilities to move back and forth between their places of residence in Britain and the South Yemen protectorate, which meant that they had to remain abroad in order to continue making wages. This separated many families, as wives and children were forced to remain at home as anchors to keep remittances flowing to extended families in Yemen (Halliday 2010[1992]). It is estimated that these men sent home $1,000 to $1,500 per year in the 1970s (Halliday 2010[1992]: 14).

Inspired by the torrent of nationalism sweeping the Global South, Birmingham workers formed an organization called the Arab Workers Union to reflect popular support for Nasserism and nationalism. As themes of Arab nationalism circulated around the *mahjar* (Gualtieri 2009: 16), so too did Yemeni Ba'athist supporters compete internally with Nasserists. With the onset of the civil war in North Yemen in 1962, Yemenis mobilized in the community, keeping informed through letters exchanged with family members, the international circulation of Yemeni newspapers, and a radio station from the central Yemeni city of Ta'iz. According to Halliday (2010[1992]: 88), exiles in the British community contributed part of their earnings (totaling sixty thousand pounds) to the new Yemeni National Development Bank, which was risky due to Britain's involvement in a war in the South. Halliday (2010[1992]: 88) also notes that a British news organization accused Yemenis of channeling funds to an insurgency in the South that had killed British forces in the Radfan uprising of 1963, leading to raids. Nevertheless, as workers donated about a pound a week to the effort, the Arab Workers Union collected donations to the National Liberation Front in the South "and transmitted the funds either through the NLF's offices in Cairo or through individual couriers who returned home on temporary visits" (Halliday 2010[1992]).

---

hostile opposition to the Imam that might result in remittances not reaching dependants [*sic*] and also possible reprisals against relatives back home."

[15] Yemeni workers did, however, participate in the US Farmworkers' Movement. See Gualtieri (2020: 65–66).

The Arab Workers Union was also impacted, however, by tensions within Yemen's anti-British coalition following the ousting of British forces from Aden in 1967. Members eventually split off to form the Yemeni Workers' Union, which was founded specifically to "forge a link between the workers here and the workers' movement and the revolutionary socialist movement in the homeland, and therefore to transform work within the ranks of the workers and to increase their understanding of our Yemeni homeland" (Halliday 2010[1992]: 91). Organizers also formed the Arab Workers League in Birmingham and the Yemeni Welfare Association of Manchester in response to these developments, which helped local migrants with passports, taxation, and other issues related to their sojourns. The Yemeni Workers' Union, with chapters across different cities in England and Wales, faced a number of challenges, however, due to workers' intense schedules, geographical spread across different locales, and illiteracy. The lack of full-time middle-class professionals to organize this work also impacted mobilization for the Arab Spring, which I address further in Chapter 6.

Interestingly, while some Yemenis did mobilize as part of the Farmworkers' Movement in California in the 1970s, Yemeni unions were not keen to strike, as this would impact their remittances; they did not possess strike funds (Halliday 2010[1992]: 103). Yemeni unions were also significantly marginalized within white-dominated unions. Rather than focus on workplace issues, they formed these organizations to help with home-country state building, including appeals by Yemen's postcolonial southern government to help build a new nation. They also fundraised for development projects such as water infrastructure, mobilized to support Palestinians, promoted literacy classes, and held community meetings. Literacy in Arabic and English was especially important, given that about two-thirds of Yemenis from South Yemen were illiterate (Halliday 2010[1992]: 98). In 1973, the Yemeni Workers' Union funded a hospital in South Yemen along with migrants in the Gulf region, and other medical aid from Birmingham in 1975, as well as roads, schools, and cultural centers, with most of the funds coming from workers in Birmingham and Sheffield (Halliday 2010[1992]: 94). They also sent funds to the Palestinian resistance and the Omani resistance against the British. According to Pennock (2017: 71), "Yemenis who supported the Omani rebels against the British held political events in the Southend [of Detroit/Dearborn], mainly *haflas* (parties) that incorporated lectures and poetry about the rebellion." According to Seddon (2014), these organizations declined in the 1980s as a recession led many Yemenis to return home or to find work in the Gulf region. In Britain, the community was roughly halved from about fifteen to eight thousand by the 1980s.

Detroit and Dearborn, Michigan attracted many North Yemenis for work via chain migration to the automobile industry. Historian Pamela Pennock (2017: 180) reports that their communities, while often unwilling to strike, did "remain engaged in the political conflicts brewing in Yemen ... and some of them were intensely active on Yemeni political issues through their involvement in the Southend-based Yemeni Arab Association and Yemeni Benevolent Society." Community members included supporters of leftist and rightist political factions within Yemen itself, which caused intra-diaspora conflicts (Pennock 2017: 270–71).[16] North–South tensions dominated activism as well. According to Halliday (2010[1992]: 108), as the governments of North and South Yemen fought wars internally and with one another, this "made North-South collaborations difficult, and the two unions ceased to operate" in the diaspora thereafter. They also faced the problem of home-country officials who demanded bribes in order to renew migrants' paperwork and came to Britain demanding gifts (Halliday 2010[1992]: 77–78). This likely exacerbated grievances and mistrust of home-country ruling elites.

In the 1980s, funding from municipalities in Britain enabled community figures to set up community associations from each country: for North Yemenis, the Yemeni Immigrants General Union, and from the South, Yemeni Community Associations (Halliday 2010[1992]: 108). These organizations were primarily dedicated to promoting the Yemeni community's abilities to navigate British society and achieve social mobility, though historian Fred Halliday (2010[1992]) mentions that they did raise several thousand pounds for a flooding emergency in South Yemen in 1989. In the 1990s, members of the Sheffield community reported establishing several organizations to help their fellow migrants and refugees.

In the years preceding the Arab Spring, anti-regime activism in both host-countries was dominated by calls for southern secession. One former southern politburo member I interviewed in Sheffield named Abdo Naqeeb, for instance, fled the sacking of Aden in 1994 by boat with other members of the defeated government. After settling in Sheffield, he and his colleagues engaged in lobbying efforts in 2004 and 2005, meeting with officials in the British Foreign and Commonwealth Office, as well as with members of Congress in the United States. He was also a proud member of the pro-secessionist "TAJ," or the Southern Democratic Assembly, which established a headquarters-in-exile in London in 2004.[17] Abdo and his colleague Dr. Mohammed al-Nomani explained that they were part of a specific "current" within the former

---

[16] Despite conflicts between Yemeni emigrants owing to conflict transmission, as I explain in detail in Chapter 3, the community would at times mobilize when directly threatened, as in the aftermath of a robbery and murder of Yemeni immigrant Ahmed Ali Almulaiki in Detroit (Pennock 2017). Leaders of an informal organization called the Detroit Yemen Society organized hundreds in a demonstration in front of the Detroit police headquarters in order to demand improved police protection. These "incidents likely facilitated the capacity of Yemenis for major political and labor activity in the fall of 1973" (Pennock 2017: 180).

[17] A week before our meeting in an Indian restaurant in Sheffield in 2012, Abdo Naqeeb and fellow TAJ member Dr. Mohammed al-Nomani had been in Cairo attending a conference of Yemeni southern secessionists led by Ali Naser Mohammed, a former southern elite. Ali Naser Mohammed lost the southern civil war of 1986 against another faction in the Yemeni Socialist

Yemeni Socialist Party, translated somewhat awkwardly into English as the "Party to Reform the Path of Unity [with the North]." This organization was a part of a transnational coalition of separatists with ties to specific factions in the former southern leadership.

Other pro-secession groups were founded independently of the old political establishment entirely. The National Board of South Yemen, also located in Sheffield, was established by secessionist supporters in 2007 to lobby and protest on behalf of popular movements in south Yemen. After being invited to attend one of their meetings during a gray, raining evening in the fall of 2012, I observed their members – men of various ages and political backgrounds, some communists, others unaffiliated with any particular faction – debating amicably in Arabic around a long table about how to plan a protest during an upcoming visit of Yemen's president to London. This group also participated in pro-South rallies in London on several occasions, including in 2009 and 2010, to correspond with diplomatic visits by regime officials. A parallel organization in the United States was founded in response to the 2007 pensioners' crisis in South Yemen to work on a similar set of actions. This group, called the South Yemeni American Association, was formed in New York to lobby the UN on behalf of the southern pro-secessionist movement and held demonstrations publicizing the South's plight.[18]

After the 2006 presidential elections in Yemen, President Saleh indefinitely postponed future elections and sought to amend the constitution in order to abolish presidential term limits. On the eve of the 2011 revolution, the regime faced mounting international pressure to resume elections. However, no movements that I could locate in the diaspora were active in supporting democratic change in Yemen at this time. Rather, the only known anti-regime Yemeni groups operating in the US and British diasporas before the Arab Spring were dedicated to advocating for the cause of South Yemen autonomy and independence specifically.

2.9 YEMENI SOCIALIZATION AND EMPOWERMENT ORGANIZING

Yemenis have long socialized together in mosques, community holiday celebrations, and in Yemeni cafes. However, in terms of their formal socialization and empowerment efforts, I located only one organization dedicated to this effort before the Arab Spring in the United States. The American Association for

Party led by Ali Salem al-Baydh. See Steven Day's (2012) excellent book on these dynamics, *Regionalism and Rebellion in Yemen*.

[18] I contacted supporters of the South Yemeni movement with several interview requests in the New York area, but I never received a response. Because this group had no public online profile or official status that I could find, it remains unknown whether this group's informal membership extended beyond the New York area.

Yemeni Scientists and Professionals, founded in 2004 in Rhode Island, was established to promote education and the professional class among Yemeni immigrants. Other chapters were later formed by community leaders among large Yemeni populations in Michigan and California. This was the most cited organization among the Yemeni Americans interviewed, and according to its website as of 2012, its leaders have worked to deliver education-related aid to Yemen. I also discovered the existence of a group called Yemeni American Association of Bay Ridge, founded in New York in 2010. Little is known about this group and its activities, however, and it appears to have become defunct relatively shortly thereafter.

The Yemeni community in Britain, on the other hand, hosts a greater number of community organizations owing to a legacy of immigrant incorporation policies and government subsidies targeting populous minority communities. This was made possible in part by support for ethnic associations from British local councils in the 1980s (Halliday 2010[1992]: 142). These conditions led to the establishment of Yemeni Community Associations (YCAs) by community leaders in four English cities – Birmingham, Sandwell, Liverpool, and Sheffield – to provide educational and social services to local Yemeni immigrants and their children. While these organizations were intended to be divorced from home-country politics, the merging of the two Yemens in 1990 led to the merger of the YCAs as well. Saleh Alnood, the former elected head of the Sheffield Yemeni Community Association, emigrated from the South in 1989 at the age of thirteen. He explained that

Up till 1990, we had two Yemeni community associations in Sheffield.[19] Unity took place, and we assumed that we had to get unified as well. So we did. It was almost like we were [part of] the establishment in Yemen, when in fact we were independent bodies. We had no connection in terms of an organization of structure or anything to do with [the government in Yemen]. But we assumed: unity in Yemen, we have to unite here.

Organizers also established groups to assist migrants and refugees. Several residents in Liverpool formed the Yemeni Migrant Workers Organization to negotiate with the Yemeni government about making the process of emigration to Britain easier and more transparent. The Yemen Refugee Organization, which was founded by southern secessionist Abdo Naqeeb, also assisted with emigrant and refugee resettlement in Sheffield.

In 2010, a handful of Yemeni youth from London formed two groups aimed at community-building within the diaspora. The three youth founders of the Yemen Forum Foundation, established in 2010, traveled to various Yemeni communities with the intention of forming a UK-wide network dedicated to community development. Awssan Kamal, one of the organizers, explained that

---

[19] Saleh reported that the names of the two former YCAs in Sheffield were the Yemeni Workers Union, which represented the northern Yemeni diaspora, and the Yemeni Community Association, which represented the South.

the initial purpose was to first connect and mobilize the Yemeni diaspora, and in time to develop the capacity to help Yemen as well. The second group, led by a university-age youth named Maha, was called the Yemeni Youth Association. This informal group was founded in 2010 as an apolitical social club for London-based Yemenis. Maha was motivated to form this group in order to help her younger sister remain close to Yemen and to meet other Yemenis. She did so because London, in her estimation, did not have a "proper" Yemeni community at that time. Overall, while these organizations varied in size and scope, the British Yemeni diaspora nevertheless had a relatively robust domestic empowerment sector, while the American Yemeni diaspora was represented by one professional association.

2.10 CONCLUSION

After exiles and émigrés found refuge in the United States and Britain, they appeared to have gained what social movement scholars call the "political opportunities" necessary for activism and social initiatives. As Zakia of the Libyan community in Manchester told me with a wide grin and open palms, "The first time I feel that I'm free, that I'm *safe*, was when I came to England." By keeping hope for change alive, reaching out to their community members, and participating in events for the national community, exiles and youth activists fostered transnational "ways of being and ways of belonging" in their home-countries (Levitt and Glick Schiller 2004: 1002) and laid the groundwork for the building of social movements for the Arab Spring in 2011.

However, I also find that Libyan, Syrian, and Yemeni activists were hardly the "unencumbered" long-distance nationalists envisioned by Benedict Anderson (1998: 74). Despite their opportunities to voice grievances against home-country regimes from abroad, movements for regime change in Libya and Syria remained small and exile-driven, and those for Yemen remained focused on southern independence. And although these diaspora communities hosted nonpolitical empowerment and socialization initiatives for the diaspora itself, less than a handful of Yemeni groups were engaged in charitable efforts of any kind, and no Libyan or Syrian groups were established for this purpose. Despite the fact that the diaspora communities contained exiles and well-educated professionals who were eager to see democratic change and development at home, transnational activism of any kind for democratic change immediately preceding the Arab Spring was weak. What accounts for the character of voice in these anti-regime diaspora communities prior to the 2011 revolutions? Chapter 3 provides the answers, demonstrating how political conditions in the homeland cast a shadow over diaspora mobilization.

3

Silenced and Split

This chapter explains how two transnational forces suppressed voice after exit in the Libyan, Syrian, and Yemeni diasporas before the Arab Spring. The first mechanism is what I call *transnational repression*, meaning attempts by regimes to punish, deter, undermine, and silence activism in the diaspora. While Yemenis reported some fears of transnational repression in their communities, the analysis shows that this phenomenon most forcefully impacted the Libyan and Syrian diasporas. This was because as dissidents escaped the totalitarian terror wrought by Gaddafi and the Assads, regime assassins and informants followed closely behind. Diaspora members learned through their personal experiences, observations, and rumors that regimes had the capacity to inflict real harm on activists and their relatives at home. Corresponding fears of being surveilled, threatened, and punished for using voice had detrimental effects on transnational activism. Although a small group of exiles made their grievances public, as Chapter 2 describes, transnational repression made activism for the home-country a high-risk endeavor for ordinary diaspora members. Because similar repertoires of transnational repression produced congruent effects in the Libyan and Syrian diasporas, this chapter discusses these cases together.

The second factor hindering transnational activism is what I call *conflict transmission*, meaning the reproduction of home-country conflicts within diaspora groups through emigrants' biographical and identity-based ties. The transmission of conflicts to the diaspora reproduced sociopolitical fault lines within all three national communities abroad, creating tensions and factionalism. In particular, conflict transmission split anti-regime members, drawing lines between anti-Gaddafi reformers and hardline revolutionaries, Syrian Kurds and the Syrian Muslim Brotherhood members, and secessionist and pro-unity Yemenis. In addition to hampering solidarity, it also depressed initiatives for charity and development because efforts to distribute resources at home were perceived as tainted by parochialism and corruption. In short, conflict transmission, working in tandem with transnational repression in some cases, undermined anti-regime diasporas' capacities to mobilize for political change before the Arab Spring.

3.1 TRANSNATIONAL REPRESSION

The Gaddafi and Assad regimes deterred dissent in the diaspora through their institutions, agents, and informant networks in different ways (see Table 3.1). By imposing costs on activists abroad and on relatives at home, the threats posed by transnational repression had numerous, interrelated effects. First, they propagated fear, mistrust, and division between conationals in the wider diaspora community. Second, they limited or foreclosed individuals' abilities to speak openly about home-country politics. Third, they relegated public anti-regime mobilization to what were considered to be "fringe" exile groups. Individuals seeking to protect their loved ones in, or their access to, the home-country were thereby obliged to abstain from criticizing the regime in word and deed. These effects significantly constrained Libyans' and Syrians' transnational activism and shaped the character of their organizations and associations abroad.

The most direct form of transnational repression – lethal retribution and attempted assassinations – impacted the Libyan diaspora in the United States and Britain the most. For Gaddafi, dissidents abroad were enemies of the state warranting elimination, and characteristic of his braggadocio, he did not keep

TABLE 3.1. *Typology of transnational repression*

Lethal retribution	The actual or attempted assassinations of dissidents abroad by regime agents or proxies.
Proxy punishment	The harassment, physical confinement, and/or bodily harm of diaspora members' relatives in the home-country as a means of information-gathering and retribution against dissidents abroad.
Threats	Verbal or written warnings directed at diaspora members, including the summoning of individuals by regime officials to their institutions for this purpose.
Surveillance	The gathering and sending of information about conationals to the state security apparatus by informant networks comprised of regime agents, loyalists, and coerced individuals.
Exile	The direct and indirect banishment of dissidents (or suspected dissidents) from the home-country, including when the threat of harm and imprisonment prevents activists from returning.
Withdrawing scholarships	The rescinding of students' state benefits for refusing to participate in regime-mandated actions or organizations abroad.

his violent intentions toward Libya's "stray dogs" a secret (Bassiouni 2013; Pargeter 2012). Vowing that the regime would "follow these people even if they go to the North Pole" (Hilsum 2012: 81), revolutionary committee thugs "were hunting down and killing 'enemies of revolution' at home and abroad" by 1980 (Wright 2012: 208). Moussa Koussa, Libya's Intelligence chief and ambassador in London at the time, was expelled that year by British authorities after telling *The Times of London* that two dissidents had been murdered in the United Kingdom and that more killings were planned. By 1984, the regime was planting bombs at London shops run by Libyans who were "selling newspapers critical of the Qaddafi government" (Nordheimer 1984). Even after Libyan activism for groups like the NFSL died down over time, retribution remained a constant threat. As Mohamed of London recounted, the murder of former NFSL activist Ali Abuzaid in 1995 shook the community to its core. Ali's daughter Huda found her father's body in the early morning in the family's grocery store, where he had been stabbed and mutilated. "He was killed in the most gruesome way," Mohamed winced.

It was obvious the murder was to send out a message. It wasn't a robbery because nothing was stolen. It wasn't a shooting because that would be too clean [for Gaddafi]. We realized in the community, it was an assassination. Because similar murders happened in Malta where somebody would be killed and pretty much decapitated and left in the street. To make a show of it, a bit like the Mexican cartels.

In the United States, at least one murder was attempted in Colorado by a hired gun. Interviewees also attributed a second murder of a Libyan American dissident in California to Gaddafi's henchmen (Hilsum 2012). Speaking of his longtime friend who was killed in mysterious circumstances while working at the gas station, Gaddor recalled, "The word among Libyans here is that Gaddafi killed him." The incident was intended to look like a robbery, but nothing was stolen. "That story is well-known here," Gaddor told me with a grimace.

The Gaddafi regime also reacted violently to protest events abroad. On April 17, 1984, a group of peaceful demonstrators gathered outside the Libyan embassy in London, dubbed the "People's Bureau," to protest the hangings of students back home. These protesters, numbering seventy-two individuals according to *The New York Times*, wore masks to protect their identities (Nordheimer 1984). Suddenly, at least one official from inside the embassy leaned out of the window and shot at the demonstrators in broad daylight, killing a policewoman named Yvonne Fletcher and injuring almost a dozen protesters. Mahmud, who had become active in the anti-Gaddafi National Democratic Party after coming to Britain, was shot in the leg, and the few photographs I could locate of this shocking event show him being carted off into an ambulance while hiding his face under a mask. After a days-long standoff between the Bureau and British forces, Libyan officials were expelled and the embassy was closed. The incident severed diplomatic ties between the regime

and the British government for fifteen years. At the same time, even the closure
of the embassy did not end Gaddafi's campaign of assassinations; as journalist
Lindsey Hilsum writes, "As many as thirty-five Libyans were murdered in
Europe over the next few years" (2012: 81).

This incident had a chilling effect on the diaspora across Britain. *The New
York Times* reported after that incident, demonstrators "scattered" and broke off
contact with everyone except their most trusted friends. Hashem Benghalboun, a
member of the Manchester-based anti-regime group the Libyan Constitutional
Union, summed up the grim situation by stating, "Since the Qaddafi regime
moved terrorism outside of Libya and to the streets of Europe, the dissidents
have endured a life of tension" (Nordheimer 1984). He reported that his brother,
Muhamad, survived three attempts on his life by Gaddafi's agents and remained
under police protection. Because the Gaddafi regime was keeping tabs on students, the Libyan government also proceeded to cut off scholarship funds for any
persons believed to be working against the regime.

The costs of speaking out against Gaddafi for high-profile dissidents were
particularly high, and émigrés' stories resembled Hollywood thrillers.
Renowned Libyan writer Hisham Matar describes in his award-winning
memoir *The Return* (2016) how not even children were exempt from the
regime's hunt for its enemies. After Matar's father, a member of the NFSL
insurgent group, escaped from Libya, Hisham's younger brother Ziad was sent
to study at a remote boarding school in the Swiss Alps. Matar writes, "For two
days running, Ziad noticed a car parked on the path outside the school's main
gate. It had in it four men. They had the long hair so typical of members of
Qaddafi's Revolutionary Committees" (2016: 7–8). Ziad received a phone call
from a friend of his father's warning him to flee. After convincing a teacher to
drive him to the train station, the men trailed in pursuit. Following him onto the
train, they threatened him in Arabic laced with a Tripolitanian accent, "Kid,
you think you are a man? Then come here and show us" (Matar 2016: 9).
Thankfully, Ziad made it home to Cairo with the help of a sympathetic
conductor and his father's colleagues. On another occasion, Matar met his
father, Jaballa, at the airport in Geneva. They passed "two men speaking
Arabic with a perfect Libyan accent: 'So what does this Jaballa Matar look
like anyway?' one of them asked the other" (Matar 2016: 10). Again, they
evaded Gaddafi's men. But in March 1990, his father was kidnapped in Egypt
by local authorities and rendered back to Libya. He spent years in Abu Salim
prison before disappearing from the face of the earth.

Syrians did not report being threatened with violence in the United States or
Britain, although assassinations occurred elsewhere. As Paul (1990: 5) writes,
"The Syrian government has almost certainly been responsible for killing,
injuring, restricting free speech, and otherwise violating the rights of persons
outside of territory it directly controls" in the Middle East. According to
Conduit (2019), the regime attempted to murder dissidents hiding in Iraq in
the 1980s, but they were protected by the Iraqi *Mukhabarat* (Intelligence).

However, the Assad regime succeeded in killing several dissidents in Germany and Spain, as well as thirteen persons in Jordan in 1981 (Conduit 2019). In light of these murders, respondents attested to the terror they felt when embassy officials summoned them and verbally threatened them and their families. For these reasons, interviewees reported avoiding regime institutions whenever possible. A common sentiment expressed in our conversations was that being inside the embassy to renew one's passport or conduct some other business felt like being back home in Syria. Worried about being interrogated and kidnapped from the embassy, Tha'er, a Kurdish Syrian youth activist, reported that he even told his family to call the police if he did not contact them within two hours of his appointment.[1]

In addition to being at risk themselves, activism abroad put both Libyans' and Syrians' relatives at home in danger. While some families had already made the moral and strategic choice to mobilize openly in spite of these costs, the *proxy punishment* of loved ones typically remained a constant source of anxiety for exiles and non-exiles alike. Respondents who were active before the Arab Spring explained that their relatives had been summoned by the dreaded Intelligence and threatened because of their opposition activities in the diaspora. Monem, a Libyan American from California, attested that "My father was harassed consistently while I was abroad." Sondes, whose father founded the one-man anti-regime group Libya Watch in Manchester, recalled, "We'd get calls from my grandfather through the government, who were pressuring him 'tell your son to stop it.'" Others were punished through imposed separations, as when the Assad regime "issued a travel ban on all my family members," according to Dr. Ziadeh, who escaped persecution during the Damascus Spring by gaining refuge in the United States. Those who were not already "on the radar" of regimes had to keep it that way, as a British Libyan named Sarah recalled, or else their parents, grandparents, siblings, and cousins might suffer in their stead.

Libyan and Syrian respondents on both sides of the Atlantic widely also reported that informants were embedded in their communities for the purposes of surveillance; some were known regime loyalists, while others were perceived as having been coerced to inform in exchange for scholarships to study abroad. Tamim Baiou, a Libyan American who was not politically active before the revolution, attested that "we knew that we were being watched and reports were sent on us." When Gaddafi's security apparatus was raided during the fall of Tripoli in 2011, this was confirmed; Tamim obtained his Intelligence file from a friend and recalled that it included "a report about all the details about my wedding" that had taken place years before in California. It was incidents

---

[1] Gualtieri (2009: 162) mentions in her work on Syrian immigration that "under the current president of Syria, Bashar al-Asad, there is a new Ministry of Expatriates." Given that infiltration and repressive social controls permeated every aspect of Syrian governance at home and in the *mahjar*, this ministry undoubtedly took up surveillance of the diaspora as part of its mission.

like these that proved that fear of widespread surveillance was "not paranoia," as Hussam Ayloush, a Syrian American activist, emphasized. When his parents were told by officials in Syria that Hussam should stop going to his local mosque in Texas because anti-regime persons were in attendance there, he knew that "one of their informants was either at the mosque or at the college." Moreover, Syrians who had been summoned to the London embassy recalled that they had been questioned over matters that could have only become known to officials through local informants.

The regime also repressed the diaspora through their gatekeeping functions, as when respondents were forced into permanent exile *after* emigrating to the United States and Britain for speaking out, or even for being perceived simply as too pro-democracy. Some interviewees found themselves blacklisted after protesting or participating in covert anti-regime meetings abroad, meaning that returning home would likely result in being seized at the airport and imprisoned. Assia attested that after her father and his friend attended an NFSL meeting in the United States, her father's friend "returned to Libya and was jailed immediately" as a result of having been informed upon; her father was forced into exile thereafter. The regimes also held sway over students on state-sponsored scholarships, as when Libyan officials coerced students to demonstrate in support of Gaddafi during his speech at the United Nations in 2009 by threatening to withdraw their scholarships (Hill 2011).

3.1.1 Fear and Fragmentation

The threat of transnational repression spread fear, mistrust, and division because fraternizing with the "wrong" Libyan or Syrian could pose a serious danger. Fear was particularly pervasive among Libyan dissidents since exiles had been targeted directly in the past. Assia, the daughter of an NFSL activist, recalled ruefully, "We were very distrustful of Libyans we didn't know. We didn't *mingle* with Libyans we didn't know, and my mom would tell us, don't *talk* to a Libyan you don't know because you don't know their alliance." She continued, "If we heard Libyans speaking in the US and we don't know you, we don't talk to you. Can't risk that. It was a real danger." Respondents also concealed their Libyan identities from others out of fear. M., another NFSL descendant, described the situation:

We couldn't really say that we were Libyan a lot of the time, for safety precautions. So my parents were always on their toes, always looking over their shoulders, *who could that be? Is that somebody that we trust?* So when you meet another Arab, they never said that they were from Libya. They said that they were from Egypt or Tunisia, you know, so that way it doesn't put us in any kind of unsafe situation.

Adam from Virginia also recalled that when he was very young, "My dad would pull us aside and be like, look, if anyone asks you where you're from, say you're from Jordan."

The threats posed by the regime meant that few Libyans felt safe enough to be open in their opposition, particularly in the 1980s and 1990s when murders in Britain were more common. Those who did so were few in number, and they expected retribution for their troubles. Khaled, a second-generation exile whose father was a wanted man, recalled that the fear of being kidnapped or harmed by Gaddafi's men was "really at the forefront of our lives." His father used an alias abroad, and he and his siblings were instructed never to use their dad's real name in public. "There was no way around it for us," Khaled explained, describing how the children of the opposition had to live day to day with the assumption that Gaddafi's men could be waiting around the corner. Libyan American Ahmed echoed this experience, recalling that "If a Libyan just showed up out of the blue without an introduction from some trusted person, it was always viewed with suspicion." Out of fear of proxy punishment, dissidents like Nagi, who lived for many years in Britain, "kept everything incognito. When we did these demonstrations, we had these masks on. We didn't show our faces. The problem we had is not for ourselves, but for our families who were [in Libya] – because those are the tactics."

NFSL activists and their descendants additionally attested that the possibility of lethal retribution also affected where they settled. Heba, who was raised by exiles, reiterated just how fearful their family was of strange Libyans:

We lived in Michigan for a short time, and I remember my parents packing up one time in the middle of the night because an "antenna" had moved in next door. *Antennas –* that's what we called a Libyan spy. *Literally* in the middle of the night, we got picked up and stayed with some friends for a few days until we found a different place to live.

Problems like these motivated some NFSL dissidents to move together to the same neighborhood in Lexington, Kentucky; besides an affordable cost of living, there was safety in numbers. By residing together "in the middle of nowhere, [with] just white people," according to Khaled, the community could more easily identify threats and warn each other about the presence of strangers, should they come knocking. Activist Dr. Mohamed Abdul Malek, founder of Libya Watch, likewise reported that every morning he would ask his children to wait inside while he checked the underside of his car for bombs. He said, "I think that was being overcautious, but it is something that anyone, *any* Libyan, would *expect* from Gaddafi."[2]

Libyans and Syrians who were not part of dissident families reported experiencing the same anxieties. Nebal, a Syrian studying in London, explained that "the regime made us fear each other because you don't know *who* works for

---

[2] Mohamed was not alone in being concerned about car bombings. Writer Hisham Matar (2016: 6–7) describes that his father would do the same: "Before getting into the car, he would ask us to stand well away. He would go down on his knees and look under the chassis, cup in his hands and peek through the windows for any sign of wiring. Men like him had been shot in train stations and cafes, their cars blown up."

the regime. Just saying hi to the old opposition is a crime." Malik, a member of a London-based exiled Syrian family, remarked,

Those who used to visit Syria regularly didn't want to associate themselves too closely with those who didn't in case the authorities found out and they get arrested in the airport or they get hassled.

Niz, a Libyan doctor from Cardiff, Wales, recalled that although his childhood memories of being around other Libyans were good ones, he developed a sense of unease and caution around community members as he grew older.

I had in me a paranoia of Libyans for fear of the regime's long tentacles, reaching out to the UK. You hear of informants, you hear of the foreign services and security services of Gaddafi being in different parts of the world. I certainly don't think it was a point *over*emphasized to us by our parents, but along the way I fell in line with the notion that Gaddafi was a bad person, and Gaddafi had bad people working for him, and that these bad people were keeping an eye on us abroad, and that I needed to be careful. I assimilated a lot of information along the way with news of assassinations abroad, news of Libyan family friends who had been killed, the realization that there were families out of Libya who weren't in the same situation as us – who were out of Libya for reasons of their personal safety.

Sarah, a British Libyan whose parents were deeply concerned about regime informants, developed a similar sense of fear even though, as she recalled, "In the early '80s, my dad just came here for work and it wasn't for political reasons. We lived outside of central London in order to remain independent, not get involved in politics because we'd always go back to Libya and my dad had family there." Because of their travels back and forth, it was imperative for Sarah and her family to distance themselves from anyone affiliated with Libyan politics, dissidents and potential regime agents alike. Sarah continued,

If you saw a Libyan on the street, you would cross over. You would never just talk to somebody you didn't know [or] make independent Libyan friends. It was always keep your head down, because you want to protect your family in Libya and you want to go back to Libya. You don't want to be on a watchlist, you don't want to be in anyone's peripheral vision on their radar. It was always understood that we're here for work or education and then we'll go back to Libya. So you'd just hang out with Libyans that you know – family friends, people that my parents knew from back in Libya and their children. You wouldn't make *independent* Libyan friends.

Just as longtime diaspora members were fearful of consorting with strangers, respondents reported that temporary migrants and students on scholarships were likewise terrified to be affiliated with residents. Because permanent residency abroad was often equated with being in political exile, some exiles attested to avoiding migrants out of concern that they would incriminate the newcomers. Dr. Abdul Malek of Libya Watch explained,

I tried to keep away from the Libyan officials and the students – unless they were somebody you really know from back home already. Otherwise, we don't mix.

Because if you have somebody coming to study in the UK and mixes with any of us who are the people who are really against Gaddafi, when they go back, they will be in trouble.

Likewise, Firas, a Syrian student in California, echoed this claim: "You stay away from the classic opposition because you know somebody is observing them!" The only way to overcome this estrangement, according to Sarah, the British Libyan mentioned above, was to do what she called a "background check." She recalled one incident that took place during her time at university:

People were like "I know this Libyan guy, I want to introduce him to you." [But] we were both very wary of each other. Our friends didn't understand; they were so keen to introduce us. But then it turned out that our moms knew each other. I told my mom what his surname was and she said "oh yes, I know his uncle," and he did the same thing, and then we both found out that the other was okay. You always did a background check.

This vetting system was imperfect, but it was often the only option for determining who to trust. As a result, as scholar Alice Alunni writes,

The mistrust and suspiciousness among Libyans abroad resulted in relatively isolated and small networks of people tied by political ideology and/or kinship. This prevented the establishment of a diasporic public space where all Libyans could come together in the host countries to openly and freely 'imagine' their nation and discuss its characters collectively, something that should be facilitated by ... the ability to communicate more easily and freely. (2019: 254)

This was also true for the Syrians, since – even if they did not fear for their personal safety – anti-regime diaspora members remained deeply concerned that one wrong move could put their relatives in danger.

3.1.2 Muted Voice

As suggested in the testimonials above, the threats posed by transnational repression constrained voice, literally and figuratively, in a number of ways. As a Syrian American speaking at a fundraising event I attended in late 2011 explained to the audience, "You would think that America's this free society, with freedom of speech, and we're comfortable speaking on things, but it has real ramifications back home." A young immigrant named Assad, who came to London from Libya to seek employment, affirmed this problem. Despite his opposition to the regime, when being around "other Arabs or other Libyans – the rare time I would come across them – I just wouldn't discuss it. Because you didn't know who you were dealing with." Hamid, a second-generation Libyan exile from Missouri, reported that broaching the subject of Gaddafi with non-exiled youth would be quickly shut down. "When we met Libyans, a lot of them were scared," he told me. "If I say hey, 'Gaddafi-this,' everybody was like, 'shut the hell up. I can't even hang around with you!' They're here in the US and they didn't even have free speech."

The limits imposed on diaspora members' speech reinforced the need to keep community events apolitical. Rafif, a Syrian American living in the Washington, DC, area, affirmed that the presence of informant networks in the community rendered gatherings into "shallow social events." Gaddor, co-founder of the Libyan Association of Southern California, remarked that rumors about who was informing for the regime made others "uncomfortable. Some people actually used to come to the Association and then decided not to because of these individuals." Ayman, a doctor who had settled in Manchester prior to the revolution, also affirmed that

[Pro-regime Syrians] would take part in our community affairs and gala dinners, but we would never have the confidence or relaxation to speak in front of them *openly* about anything to do with the regime. For fear for ourselves, because we were going regularly back home, or for our family back home.

Furthermore, unlike the Gaddafi regime, the Assad government sponsored Syrian organizations and social clubs that were understood as part of the regime's infrastructure of control. Sarab, an activist based in New York, attested that "most of the Syrian-associated organizations or entities had some sort of close connection with the embassy." Even purportedly apolitical humanitarian associations, such as the Syrian American and Syrian British medical societies, were not perceived by respondents as neutral or independent. Hasan, a second-generation exile in London, attested that these organizations "were based around what the *regime* wanted. You couldn't have an independent community of the regime." Kenan, a Syrian American activist, likewise reported that no organization "could operate independently of the Syrian government," and as a result, "we had no civil society."

Transnational repression continued to hinder mobilization during the so-called Damascus Spring in the early 2000s. Although the Syrian American Council (SAC) was founded in 2005 to support Syrian civil society and was not an anti-regime group by any means, Hussam recalled that recruitment into the organization was extremely difficult due to the threats posed by transnational repression. He explained,

In 2005, I was approached by a few Syrian Americans who I knew, mentioning to me that there's a new organization that was started called Syrian American Council. I can tell you it [was] a secretive process – not something they announced in the media or on Facebook, because there's so much fear that no one wanted to be associated with that publicly. [Only] through trusted sources, word of mouth, will they tell you about this meeting. On the day when [the first SAC meeting was held] somewhere in Orange County, that day I was traveling, but I told them you have my support. And I tried contacting a few people to encourage them to be part of it. *Not a single person that I know* who I contacted agreed to. The gathering was so small, maybe ten to twenty. And it didn't go anywhere, because everyone was afraid to even be part of something. But that's the irony of things. It was almost impossible to get a group of people to form a chapter in 2005 and '06 and '07 and '08. Every time they talked to people, people didn't want to do it because they understood the consequence would've been very severe if you were visiting Syria or they might visit your family members in Syria.

The regime also punished Dr. Radwan Ziadeh, who had traveled from Syria to Chicago to give a speech at SAC's opening conference in 2005. Dr. Ziadeh reported that after returning to Syria, "I was interrogated by the security forces and been banned from traveling because of my traveling into Chicago to participate." (As referenced in Chapter 2, Dr. Ziadeh was forced to escape soon after to the United States.) SAC was the only organization in either the United States or Britain that attempted to mobilize the Syrian diaspora for both immigrant empowerment and political liberalization in the home-country, but it remained largely memberless and dormant before the 2011 revolution.

For some Libyans, the era of Saif al-Islam's purported reforms in Libya and a decline in known murders of dissidents abroad in the 2000s lessened the sense of threat. Other respondents, however, felt *less* safe, or just as unsafe, as they had before. During this thaw in Western relations with Libya, the United States and Britain both partnered with Gaddafi to render former members of the Libyan Islamic Fighting Group to Libya for interrogation and torture, just as Egyptian secret services had done with Hisham Matar's father in the previous decade. The regime also leveled accusations of terrorism against its opponents to pressure Western governments to give up wanted refugees, including against Ashur Shamis, a peaceful activist and refugee residing in London.

The organizers of regular demonstrations, whether in Manchester or New York, also recalled that participation in such events remained sparse during the era of Saif's so-called reforms. Ahmed and Khaled reported that when they went to New York in 2009 to protest Gaddafi's UN appearance, many of them – including Ahmed himself – covered their faces with masks, scarves, and sunglasses for fear of being identified and incriminating their families back home. Acting with the same caution as London protesters had done in 1984, past incidents of regime violence remained at the forefront of activists' minds. As Monem attested, "*everything* is possible. You can't trust a regime like that."

The public meeting of Libyan opposition members in London from across the diaspora in 2005 also reinforced, rather than assuaged, concerns about regime surveillance. Sarah recalled that after making friends with a "normal" Libyan named Ahmed, she invited him and his family to a family celebration at their home. But after telling her parents about the invitation,

a few days later, my mom said, "Is there any way politely to un-invite them?" It turns out that [Ahmed's parents] were in town because there was a big opposition conference going on, and my parents were paranoid that everyone's being followed. So you'd think that everything is more open at this time, but no. For sure, people *were* being followed during the opposition conference. Even though the situation wasn't as bad as the '90s, there were always reminders [that little had changed].

Characteristic of the regime's paranoia, the social groups formed by community members also came under suspicion. Zakia, who founded the Libyan

Women's Association in Manchester in 2003, attested that becoming a public face of this nonpolitical "society" put her family at risk back home in Benghazi. She said,

I thought, because it's a *social* organization, you know, it's not about politics, I wrote my name and gave a [local] talk. So everyone knows me in Manchester. But at that time, my brother-in-law phoned me from Libya and said *Zakia, what you did do?* He said the *Mukhabarat* [Intelligence] come to me and said "your sister-in-law made a group which appears like a social group, but inside we *believe* it's a political group against Gaddafi."

Accordingly, Zakia refused an invitation to participate in the 2005 conference over fears that the regime "will go after my parents."

The regimes also continued to hold sway over Libyan and Syrian students through their state-sponsored scholarships. Zakia from Manchester attested, "Those who come to study from Libya, they're scared to contact us if they are a relative. Because they sign a paper there that says if you want to come to study, you agree that 'I will not contact my sister or my brother-in-law when I go' – like a contract." By threatening to withdraw their scholarships, Libyan officials paid for and coerced students to demonstrate in support of Gaddafi during his appearance at the United Nations in 2009 (Hill 2011). So just as the regime forced the masses in Tripoli to perform their loyalty, migrants were forced to do the same.

For all of these reasons, being "publicly anti-regime was fringe," as Syrian American Sarab from New York recalled. Abdullah, a Syrian who became active after moving to Boston in 2008, explained that only "a few people, using aliases [online], were comfortable talking about things that no one dared to otherwise." While small groups of Kurdish Syrian and Arab Syrian exiles in London periodically held protests, these events were considered to be high-risk because Syrian officials filmed the demonstrators and blacklisted those who were not already in exile, preventing participants from returning home. These fears were realized in some cases. When one first-generation Kurdish Syrian youth named Tha'er found out through his contacts at home that he was wanted by the regime for participating in a protest outside the London embassy, he was forced to remain in Britain thereafter.

These threats plagued Libyan commemorative demonstrations as well. Dr. Abdul Malek's daughter Sondes mused, "We'd done demonstrations for Libya in the past, but they always had limited numbers because of fear of what the regime would do. A lot of the time, people who went to these demos would wear masks for fear of what would happen to their family members if they were recognized." Hamid reported that his father and some other members of the US-based Libyan Human Rights Commission, a small group active in the mid-1990s, used aliases in the media "because they were scared for their family back home." Accordingly, anti-regime movements remained small and estranged from the broader community. Mohamed S. of London lamented that because "everyone was [so] scared, they got no support."

The reproduction of repression abroad meant that diaspora activists were unable to fully deploy their resources and exploit their political opportunities to wield voice after exit. Until the unthinkable (Kurzman 2004) occurred in 2011, the majority of anti-regime members in the diaspora remained silent in their views. Dissent networks remained isolated, and no member-driven organizations existed in the United States or Britain.

3.1.3 Weak Threats from the Yemeni Regime Abroad

For the Yemenis, a relatively weak authoritarian regime at home meant that the anti-regime diaspora felt a comparatively weak sense of threat abroad, although concerns about transnational repression and the hazards of surveillance were not entirely absent. According to Halliday (2010[1992]: 142), Yemeni authorities engaged in the "monitoring of exiles' political loyalties," and several pro-secessionist southerners reported the fear of being exiled because of their activism. Many of those interviewed also attested that embassy officials effectively meddled in the affairs of the diaspora and attempted to undermine or co-opt organizing efforts. Ragih, a community leader in Sandwell, mentioned that the Yemeni government had paid people to demonstrate on behalf of Saleh in London, providing for their travel and giving them sandwiches and *qat*, a tobacco-like leaf that is chewed recreationally in Yemen (and was legal in Britain at the time). Additionally, another respondent in northern California accused their local consulate of undermining the work of the American Association of Yemeni Scientists and Professionals by meddling in its affairs. While I could not independently verify these accusations, it appeared to be a common belief that the Saleh regime officials acted as a saboteur in the community from behind the scenes.

Unlike their Libyan and Syrian counterparts, however, none of the southern anti-regime Yemeni activists in Britain reported hiding their faces or their identities during protests or in petitions. This suggests that while Yemen's weak authoritarian regime attempted to surveil and intimidate the diaspora, it lacked the necessary capacity to enforce compliance and deter mobilization. Others believed or knew that they had been surveilled but believed that this was more of a distraction than an actual threat. For example, Hanna Omar of the US-based South Yemeni American Association recalled,

Constantly, *constantly* in our rallies, we would have one, three, four pro-Ali Abdullah Saleh [guys] coming in and seeing what we're doing, coming to our meetings. It was just something we had to live with. The only thing I didn't like about that is that it would take away the focus on what we were doing. Our own activists [would] concentrate on, well, this guy is pro-Saleh and what are we going to do about him? And then finally we were just like, it doesn't matter. *There's nothing to hide.* Everybody's out here, everybody's face is out in the open, everybody's names are out in the open. It's not like we're going to hide this from the government there. So it doesn't matter who's pro, who's not. Let's just focus on our main goal and that's it. That, of course, was easier said than done.

Additionally, most respondents did not take the threat of exile seriously, arguing that their families at home lived in rural, tribal areas largely outside of the regime's jurisdiction, or that they could bribe their way back into Yemen were there to be a problem at the airport.

3.2 CONFLICT TRANSMISSION

While transnational repression deterred voice in the Libyan and Syrian communities, *conflict transmission*, which was caused by the reproduction of divisive homeland conflicts in the diaspora, plagued community organizing in all three national communities across the United States and Britain. As conflicts and mistrust of politics traveled abroad through emigration and were inherited by 1.5- and second-generation youth, home-country fights divided conationals and undermined their mobilization potential. These divisions constrained the formation of movements for regime change and depressed initiatives for charity and development, even when organizers intended for these events to be apolitical affairs.

3.2.1 Factionalism during Libya's Era of "Reform"

After years of crippling economic sanctions and the fall of the Soviet Union, Gaddafi's anti-Western façade crumbled. As the Clinton administration initiated secret talks with the regime, Gaddafi began to settle his international debts by agreeing to pay settlements to the victims of its terrorist attacks, including the 1988 Lockerbie bombing. The subsequent attacks of September 11, 2001, also worked in the regime's favor. After the invasion of Iraq by the US-led coalition in 2003, Gaddafi declared himself an ally in George W. Bush's so-called War on Terror and agreed to give up Libya's weapons of mass destruction. Libya was able to reopen its embassies and consulates, and by 2004, Prime Minister Tony Blair was flashing a toothy grin for the media while shaking Gaddafi's hand.

As Saif al-Islam made gestures of goodwill, some regime opponents in the diaspora decided to take the opportunity to reconnect with their homeland. For Mohamed Shaban in London, "The first trip I and the family made to Libya was around 2004. That was partly because Saif was trying to be open, trying to attract Libyan talent back to Libya, so we started visiting, dipping our feet back in." Adam of Virginia also recalled that Saif sent some of "his people" to Los Angeles to coax the second generation to meet with regime representatives in 2010. Adam attested that Saif's reforms appeared to be the only plausible inroad to help the homeland at the time.

I looked at it like, let's see what they have to offer. I'm willing to sit at the table and talk. At the end of the day, it's a free trip to LA. So, I came out and I sat with [Saif's right-hand man] and I told him, look, I know you're part of the Gaddafi family. I don't care.

My dad is anti-Gaddafi, I have best friends that are anti-Gaddafi. That's not what I'm looking at. You said you want to open up a window, a door for us to help the Libyan youth, I'm there. And I told him about a [Libyan] scholarship fund that I started [here in the US]. He loved that idea.

A Washington, DC-based exile named Fadel explained, "That was a big debate – because is my problem the regime's policies, or the regime itself? Can I work to change the regime's behavior, or I just have to work until I get rid of the head?" For Fadel, dialogue seemed like a logical pathway to liberalization.

Isolation is better for dictators. They love it because they just can live and control their own people, and you don't have any leverage over them. Look at North Korea! So I was against the isolation. I was more for constructive engagement, to make a change. So that was part of the divergence in thinking about can I make real change – if the regime has five thousand political prisoners, if I can get five hundred out, is that good? Or is it five thousand or nobody? Ask for [Gaddafi's] head, or nothing else?

Likewise, the Libyan Muslim Brotherhood-in-exile represented by Dr. Abdul Malek in Manchester joined the reformist camp out of what he characterized as "pragmatism." He explained that during this time, "Gaddafi was a fact of life" and "if we can get something for the people and at the same time Gaddafi is still there, then we will work on that. That is why we had dialogues with Saif and others in the government hoping that we could carry out some serious reforms in Libya. But the opposition did not see that."

Saif's efforts to woo Libyans back home and incorporate them into the reform process divided the dissident community. Some came to believe that the campaign was a complete shill, and a dangerous one at that. Amr Ben Halim, the son of a prominent political figure from the time of King Idris, recalled,

A lot of us thought that there was some hope in [Saif's reforms] because we never hoped it was possible to remove Gaddafi from power. He was so entrenched, he was so pervasive, that the idea of him being removed from power in a peaceful way or normal way was just not possible. Clearly, his son is preparing himself, so let's see what can be done with the son. He speaks the right language, he says the right things. But then after the fact, over time, we found out that it was not legitimate. It was really more a manipulation that allowed him to the point where he was set to take over. He had some very bad dictatorial instincts that he would hide when he would meet the foreign press, the foreign politicians. But when he came back here [to Libya], he was a very brutal kind of person, very much in his father's mold.

Others condemned the normalization of relations with Gaddafi without preconditions for human rights reforms. Hamid, a young activist who had grown up in exile in the United States and whose relatives had been executed by the regime, explained that he and his friends remained strongly opposed to Saif's half-hearted measures. "We always tried to educate the other Libyans [about] what was really happening," he remembered. "We were like, no, you *can't* side with the devil. Our parents and our great grandparents are expecting us to carry this torch." Adam attested that his trip to LA estranged him from others in the exile community. "When I came back to Virginia and called up a few friends and told them what had happened, I got a lot of negative feedback," he said. "Some people cut me off completely. Someone went as far as to say that's blood money that's on your hands. Hold on, blood money from who? Who did I kill? Who died because I went to LA? They were like, no, because you sat down at the same table."

Owing to conflict transmission, anti-regime diaspora members from Libya were deeply divided. Split over whether to negotiate directly with the regime for reform or remain steadfast in demanding that the regime pay for its crimes, the eve of the 2011 revolution was a time of strong disagreement among those few who were working for change in Libya.

3.2.2 Syrian Divisions

Conflict transmission was likewise a problem for Syrian activists in exile. Though Syrian Kurds and Muslim Brotherhood-affiliated activists shared deep histories of repression, these groups remained split internally and with one another over the solution to their common foe.[3] As a persecuted ethno-religious minority facing region-wide threats of ethnic cleansing, Kurdish activists viewed secession and the establishment of an independent Kurdish state as the solution to regime repression. Arabs with Muslim Brotherhood affiliations, on the other hand, looked toward a political transition that would give their representatives and the Sunni majority a dominant role in government. Regime opponents were therefore divided in significant ways over their goals such that they not only opposed the regime, but each another as well.

Furthermore, second-generation-exile activists were also highly discontented with the opposition politics of their elders.[4] The Syrian Justice and Development Party, for example, sought to distance itself from what co-founder Malik al-Abdeh described as an outmoded opposition. "The Muslim Brotherhood," Malik explained, "are not really effective, like old fogies. They're not doing anything. We need[ed] to do something to re-galvanize the opposition scene. And we need to have young people involved. It's a new generation." However, this stance isolated them in the opposition community due to a sense of competition and threat from other groups.

We came under a lot of pressure from the Brotherhood because they saw us as a threat, [and] that we're going to draw away their youth to us. And the whole point of the

---

[3] Raphaël Lefèvre's important book *Ashes of Hama* (2013) describes in detail how the Syrian Muslim Brotherhood was and continues today to be factionalized by city of origin, anti-regime strategy, and leadership. See also Dara Conduit's work (2019) for more details on intra-Brotherhood fissures.

[4] I was told that the "elder"-led movements also included "classic" communist opposition groups based primarily in France.

Movement for Justice and Development was to have some sort of classic-liberal party, which is pro-business, free market, that isn't Islamist. We also came under fire from a lot of these old communists who thought, who are these new kids on the block? A lot of them thought we were like a Trojan horse for the Muslim Brotherhood, which wasn't true. And funny enough, the Muslim Brotherhood thought we were a Trojan horse for *another* Muslim Brotherhood breakaway faction. We couldn't please anybody!

Thus, organizing done independently of established factions was met with suspicion and criticism by many older exiles and elites.

As a result of conflict transmission, various members of the community were constantly accused of trying to dominate the opposition on behalf of the Brotherhood regardless of whether they were personally affiliated with the movement or not.[5] As such, the anti-regime movement as a whole suffered from a significant degree of mistrust about who-was-who and working-for-whom, as well as splits with Syrian Kurds who had lost faith that they could ever attain freedom in the Syrian Arab Republic.

3.2.3 Yemeni Divisions

Conflict transmission hindered the transnational mobilization of the Yemeni diaspora before the Arab Spring in several ways. As referenced in the previous chapter, "Yemenis have divided along fractures imported from their home country" (Halliday 2010[1992]: xiv) in the diaspora since their first major wave of emigration to the United States and Britain in the 1880s. Because anti-regime activism was dominated by calls for southern autonomy following the surge in secessionist activism and regime repression in 2007, opposition to the Saleh regime became a partisan issue that divided Yemenis along pro- and anti-unity lines.

Interviewees also reported being generally mistrustful of community elites with political ties to the homeland due to cronyism, corruption, and a general state of institutional dysfunction in Yemen. Yemenis from North Yemen were divided by political party and the issue of meddling by Saudi Arabia. Halliday (2010[1992]: 56) likewise observed that "division between the mainstream of the community and a newer grouping derived from *Al-Islah* (Reform), a party in Yemen itself which received support from Saudi Arabia and was propagating an Islamist politics," was prominent in British Yemeni communities by the early 1990s. As a result, many of the youth interested in mobilizing their communities before the Arab Spring perceived community elites as part of a corrupt

---

[5] Lefèvre (2013: 189) argues that such accusations are also due partly to the mischaracterizations made by outsiders in their discussions of exiled Islamist groups; he writes, "The landscape of political Islam has become highly heterogeneous and complex since the Brotherhood was forced out of Syria in the early 1980s. Many opposition figures classified as 'Islamists' ... actually do not belong to the *Ikhwan* and are even personally and politically hostile to them, if not ideologically so."

system who were highly suspect and incapable of promoting genuine social change. This suspicion extended to *any* person associated with home-country politics writ large. Because being associated with politics in the Yemeni diaspora was inherently problematic, the mobilization efforts of non-secessionists were focused on immigrant empowerment, such as literacy, in a "nonpolitical" way.

The Yemeni Community Associations (YCAs) in Britain, for example, had been impacted by authoritarianism in Yemen since their founding. In the Liverpool and Birmingham YCAs, respondents claimed that pro-Saleh individuals had corrupted the organizations and rendered them impotent to help their local communities. Respondents viewed the YCA in Liverpool, for example, as an insular crony organization that provided no benefits to its constituents because of its regime-like functioning. Omar Mashjari, a Liverpudlian youth, explained,

They'd been a corrupt and incompetent body for a long time. They never actually *did* anything. They never hosted any organizations, any dialogues, any parties whatsoever. They host elections once every ten years. A ten-year term! Most of them supported Ali [Abdullah Saleh].[6]

Respondents had similar complaints about the YCA in Birmingham. Several interviewees involved in the leadership confirmed that there had been no elections held there before 2007, and that the former president had run the organization like an autocrat. Nageeb, the subsequent head of the YCA, recalled of this period that "They'd pretend to have elections and cancel them at the last minute." He argued that the former heads had personal relationships with Saleh and that the Yemeni government helped to fund a legal case for the old leadership to retain the property after they ran the organization into the ground (which they eventually lost in court). Nageeb assumed leadership of the Birmingham YCA in 2007 to reform the organization and immediately set about instituting elections every two years. However, he lamented that they were still far from being the fully functional organization that their community members were calling for.

Furthermore, constant fighting between North and South Yemen, especially during the civil war of 1994, led to antagonisms between these communities and a separation of their organizations. As Halliday (2010[1992]: xi) writes, "On a visit to Birmingham in October 2007, I was particularly struck by the chasm between the two, each with their own buildings and social centres – the Northerners in one part of town, the Southerners in another." I observed the ramifications of this division myself in 2012. According to interviewees on

---

[6] At Omar's encouragement, I interviewed the chairman of the YCA in Liverpool named Abdul Alkanshali. He did not deny being affiliated with Saleh, and he concurred that the organization had significant solvency problems.

all sides of this dispute, the YCA in Birmingham was plagued by a feud with southern members over the use of the building. Nageeb explained,

A lot of the friction, the problems, that have happened between the Yemeni Community Association and the separatists were around that building, around that resource. No Yemeni woman in the last ten, fifteen years [had seen the inside of that building]. We were trying to change all of that but we came across so much opposition from those people.

"Those people" he was referring to were southerners who had become vehement supporters of separation in 2007. On the other hand, Ali, one of the outspoken leaders of the southern secessionists in Birmingham during this period, argued that northern and corrupt Al-Islah Party–affiliated elites[7] controlled the YCA and the local Amaneh Center, a community institution that served the wider Muslim community. Ali described a crisis in 2010 when "they," referring to the northern YCA leadership, "caged up" the South Yemeni building. Southern Yemenis had to break down the bars with the help of the police. "That's the only thing that we had left [and] they stole it," he decried, adding, "The same ideology they use in Yemen, they implement it *here*, in the UK." While Nageeb felt that the YCA should be used for everyone and that he had been wrongly slandered as a northern "Islahi," Ali felt that the pro-unity Yemenis were attempting to appropriate what little resources the southerners had left.

Haashim, Nageeb's successor and head of the YCA in Birmingham at the time of my fieldwork in 2012, attested that these forms of conflict transmission had made it very difficult to provide services for the community. He believed that southerners were "blaming the unity of Yemen for all of the problems" that had been plaguing Yemen for decades. But Haashim also sympathized with the southern people "who feel let down." If the community was not so divided over political problems in Yemen, he explained, "we would have been able to build a strong institution." Instead, he lamented, "We at the YCA haven't done nothing, even though we [Yemenis] are the oldest immigrant community in Britain."

Because community organizers perceived that home-country politics had polluted diaspora organizations, and community cohesion more generally, leaders credited successful civic efforts with the firm dissociation of their initiatives from politics. The YCA in Sandwell was widely cited by respondents across England as a counterexample to the dysfunctional associations in Liverpool and Birmingham because their leaders had successfully *insulated* their organization from politics. Saleh, an organizer who grew up in the Sandwell Yemeni community, reported getting together with his friends in the 1980s to try to "do something about the situation about the Yemeni diaspora."

---

[7] Al-Islah is Yemen's ("reform") opposition party and includes the Yemeni branch of the Muslim Brotherhood. For more detailed analysis of the Islah party, see Schwedler (2006).

They felt that because their parents came from rural areas with little education, the Yemeni children were at a huge disadvantage in terms of their socioeconomic status, education, and potential for social mobility. He said, "We knew as a community that we weren't doing well." Saleh further explained,

The politics of Yemen, north and south – that got in the way. After unification, we managed to unify our efforts in the UK. And the younger generation was saying, you know what, leave the politics aside, the UK is our home. Yemen is our beloved and cherished heritage, but we need to get things right here, our home, and help set up something that will establish ourselves as a successful community. We set up the YCA to support Yemenis here with *the principle of no politics*, and that's been a very successful ingredient in moving us forward. The benefit has meant that we have now been able to deal with the challenges that the community has faced – social, education, religious, health, recreational. All of the things you expect a community [association] to address.

These sentiments were echoed by Afraf and Ragih, a wife-and-husband team who ran the YCA in Sandwell in 2012. While Ragih was from the South, he attested that they maintained the association as a strictly nonpolitical organization because of the turmoil surrounding the issue of southern secession. Even celebrations of national Yemeni holidays, such as Unity Day, were banned within the Sandwell YCA because commemorations of the 1990 unification process were controversial to many southerners. Like Saleh, Afraf and Ragih credited their association's success in implementing social welfare programs to their strict dissociation from home-country politics. They acknowledged that politics were discussed in the Center, particularly during the once-weekly permitted qat chews. However, members were banned from distributing political materials or hosting political gatherings on-site. In order to combat accusations of cronyism, they published annual reports on their finances and held regular elections.

In a parallel example, Saleh A., former head of the YCA in Sheffield, also credited the organization's functionality with its insulation from politics. Saleh explained that he maintained neutrality in running the organization, but that the 2007 uprising in the South produced a notable degree of conflict. As a result, his role as head of the YCA eventually clashed with his sympathies for the separatist movement. He explained,

Whilst I was clearly in support of the southern movement, and I made it clear that was my *personal* view, I was also conscious of the fact that I was the chairman of the Yemeni Community Association. I didn't want the politics to get involved with the work that we were doing at the time. I remembered the day that the National Board of South Yemen was established that year, and standing in the meeting saying, please, we can express our politics and views, but let's not allow it to divide the community – and automatically we should separate personal views or political activities from the Community [Association].

After four years as chairman, Saleh came to feel that "it was wrong of me not to be, not to offer my abilities as simple as drafting letters and petitions to governments" on behalf of the southern cause. He then resigned from the

YCA and joined the National Board. But because separation was maintained between home-country politics and the YCA, Saleh stated that they managed community "coherence [with] less conflict, fewer problems" than in the Liverpool and Birmingham YCAs.

The reproduction of home-country conflicts influenced the anti-political character of diaspora mobilization in the Yemeni American community as well. My request for an interview with representatives of the Yemeni Association of Scientists and Professionals – the only functioning organization I could locate at the time – was politely declined because representatives viewed my research as political, and therefore outside the purview of their organization.

The British Yemeni youth who had formed new groups on the eve of the Arab Spring also reported that their initiatives were plagued by divisions from home-country politics. For example, Awssan, co-founder of the Yemen Forum Foundation, aimed to mobilize the broader Yemeni-British diaspora for the purposes of domestic empowerment, and specifically "to bring the youth together first because they don't have the politics or the [boundaries] or the sectarian ideologies some of the elders had. So we traveled to most of the cities in the UK and tried to bring them together." To that end, they had planned to partner with the Birmingham, Brighton, Liverpool, and Sheffield communities. At the same time, Awssan and his colleagues' status as "independent youth" also paradoxically hindered their mobilization efforts because they lacked legitimacy among the "elders" with ties to the Yemeni political establishment. He explained,

We weren't in touch with Yemen, which made our lives a lot harder. The community organizations were in touch with the ambassador or the embassy at the time. For us, it's difficult [because we're] not known. It was like, who are these three young guys with this radical ideology of bringing Yemenis together?

Though a southerner, Awssan was not a secessionist, and he had a difficult time convincing southerners in Birmingham to get on board with their plan while they were involved in a conflict over the YCA. The Yemen Forum Foundation, he explained, was just getting off the ground as an incorporated organization when the revolution began in 2011.

In sum, Yemeni diaspora mobilization before the 2011 uprisings was hindered by conflict transmission stemming from regionalism and corruption in the homeland. Community leaders correspondingly viewed the infiltration of home-country politics as toxic to their efforts to empower local communities. As a result, leaders involved in YCAs and development had to avoid appearing political in any way, including eschewing any mention of the very events and practices that *made* the diaspora a national community, such as Yemen's Unity Day. Other associations remained dysfunctional or sites of contention. So even though Yemeni Community Associations might have served as vehicles for collective action, these organizations were either undermined by crony politics or kept strictly apolitical. Furthermore, youth organizers who were motivated to overcome the divisions that plagued the diaspora were paradoxically hindered by their status as independent youngsters. Lacking social and political clout with older elites, their initiatives were sparse and largely informal. In all, like their counterparts in the Libyan and Syrian diasporas, Yemeni activism in the United States and Britain was rife with fissures before the Arab Spring.

3.3 CONCLUSION

As Chapter 2 elaborated, exiles and émigrés from Libya, Syria, and Yemen capitalized on political opportunities to mobilize on behalf of home-country affairs from their places of settlement and refuge. However, this chapter has demonstrated that diaspora members' transnational ties also acted back on them to constrain and contain voice. As elaborated above, diaspora members' ties to the home-country subjected them to transnational repression and conflict transmission, both of which mitigated opportunities to protest, lobby, and organize from abroad. In line with Alunni's research on the Libyan diaspora (2019: 258; 2020), "divisions in the diaspora together with the regime's policies at home and persecutions abroad were overall detrimental to the establishment of an all-Libyan diasporic public space." Syrians experienced the same problems. While the Yemeni regime was not strong enough to enforce the same degree of threat abroad, all three communities were subjected to conflict transmission. As a result, the use of voice immediately preceding the Arab Spring was considered a highly partisan, if not downright risky, political endeavor.

At the same time, it is precisely because of members' simultaneous embeddedness in home-country conditions (Levitt and Glick Schiller 2004) that the disruptions wrought by the Arab Spring had such powerful mobilizing effects on diaspora activism. As the revolutions disrupted the normative, everyday effects of transnational repression and conflict transmission, diaspora members became motivated to come out and come together for home-country change as never before. The next chapter elaborates how disruptions to social control and conflict at home had far-reaching effects on the diaspora, leading to a new wave of mass, public transnational contention against authoritarian regimes.

4

Coming Out and Coming Together

By 2010, the dictatorships ruling the MENA region seemed more self-assured than ever. President Assad retained an iron grip on Syria, President Saleh of Yemen was preparing to alter the constitution to stay in power for life, and Colonel Gaddafi in Libya was now a partner, rather than an enemy, in the global war on terror. But just when the power of these regimes seemed so secure, the despair of a single person ignited a volcano that had been boiling under the surface for decades. In the Tunisian city of Sidi Bouzid, a young man named Mohammed Bouazizi set himself on fire following humiliating abuse by municipal officials in December. His fellow Tunisians came out within hours to protest on his behalf. After the state-sanctioned murder of protesters produced a predictable backlash (Hess and Martin 2006), mounting demonstrations and the demurring of the military successfully pressured President Ben Ali and his family to flee the country on January 14, 2011.

Egyptians then took up the mantle, confronting President Hosni Mubarak's police state head-on. Given Egypt's regional and symbolic importance, activists across the region knew that whatever happened next would signify whether the Arab Spring was going to become a game changer or get passed off as a fluke. After protesters from Cairo's Tahrir Square to Alexandria and Port Said endured a series of state-sanctioned attacks and patronizing speeches, the Egyptian people pushed back, paralyzing the country with sit-ins, strikes, and riots. After the military decided to take control on February 11, 2011, Mubarak stepped aside, at least for the time being (Holmes 2019; Ketchley 2017; Said 2020). The impossible was really happening, and populations around the world cheered in celebration.

As discussed in the book's Introduction, the Arab Spring inspired protests across the region and the world over. Among the six countries[1] hosting

---

[1] According to popular demands for the fall of regimes, these countries were Tunisia, Egypt, Yemen, Libya, Bahrain, and Syria.

uprisings demanding the fall of ruling regimes, protesters in Libya, Yemen, and Syria became embroiled in prolonged battles against dictatorships over the course of 2011 and beyond. The regimes' violent responses to peaceful protesters calling for bread and dignity sent shockwaves into diaspora communities. These uprisings were what many exiles had been waiting for their whole lives, and the rebellions at home reinvigorated their activism. The Arab Spring also transformed many diaspora members' suppressed anti-regime sentiments into public calls for liberation and voice.

The emotions that these groups felt while watching the uprisings unfold from afar – rage, horror, hope, and excitement – might have been sufficient to inspire mobilization (Goodwin et al. 2001; Jasper 1998, 2018; Nepstad and Smith 2001). For the diaspora members in this study, however, two hurdles posed significant obstacles to voice, that is, public, collective claims-making against authoritarianism. As I explained previously, the operation and effects of *transnational repression* made non-exiles too fearful and mistrustful to wage either horizontal or vertical voice against the regimes. *Conflict transmission* also divided anti-regime members, sapped their efficacy by directing grievances toward one another, and undermined their willingness to act collectively for a common goal. Emotions played an important role in what happened next, but diaspora members needed other conditions to fall into place in order to overcome these obstacles to transnational activism.

In order to explain the Arab Spring's significant effects on diaspora mobilization, this chapter builds on the theory of "quotidian disruption" proposed by sociologist David Snow and his collaborators (1998). Snow et al. argue that major disruptions to the quotidian – that is, the normative routines and attitudes that guide everyday life – stoke mobilization by motivating previously disempowered actors to engage in activism. Extending this theory to diasporas and their transnational practices, I propose that the disruptions caused by the Arab Spring stoked public, collective claims-making in the diaspora by undermining the normative operation and effects of *transnational* deterrents to activism – albeit in different ways and at varying times for each national group. Once these deterrents fell, diaspora members could at last capitalize on their civil rights and liberties abroad to express voice and consort with "stranger" conationals, thereby forging new protest movements, organizations, and coalitions for change at home.

As this chapter explains, the Arab Spring first undermined the normative operation and effects of transnational repression for Libyans and Syrians by changing the circumstances of their loved ones at home. First, when diaspora members' relatives and friends were harmed, forced to flee, or became embroiled in the fighting, individuals abroad were *released from the obligation* to keep their anti-regime views a secret in order to protect their loved ones in the homeland. Second, acute regime brutality against peaceful, vanguard activists – such as Hamza al-Khateeb, a young Syrian teenager who was mutilated and tortured to death in unspeakable ways by regime agents early in the uprising – led diaspora members to take a principled stand *in spite of* the potential risks of coming out. As many in the United States and Britain came to believe that it would be shameful to hide their views to protect themselves or their families when protesters and innocent civilians were being slaughtered, their objects of obligation (Moss 2016b: 493) expanded from kin to the national community writ large. Third, activists decided to go public after deducing that the risks and costs of activism had been reduced. They did so after observing that the regimes seemed incapable of making good on their threats against the diaspora while waging a full-scale war for survival at home.

The Arab Spring also broke down the normative operation and effects of conflict transmission, albeit for different durations across national groups in the United States and Britain. After regime violence unified political groups and factions in the home-country, I find that previously fractured conationals followed suit and came together to support their compatriots. While activists did not always join the same group or organization, they came to engage in a common tactical repertoire to facilitate rebellion and relief (which I discuss at length in Chapter 5) and rallied around the anti-regime revolutionary struggle. Thus, the formation of revolutionary coalitions at home against a common enemy, which Beissinger (2013) calls "negative coalitions," was transmitted abroad through members' ties. This led regime opponents to forge new diaspora movements and coalitions.

At the same time, the emergence of diaspora movements against authoritarianism was not a linear, uniform process. While Libyans came out rapidly in public *and* reported a strong degree of solidarity for the duration of the revolution in both host-countries, Syrians and Yemenis residing across the United States and Britain faced challenges due to *persistent* fears of transnational repression and *resurgent* conflict transmission. Because the Syrian regime remained relatively intact during the revolution's escalation, transnational repression continued to pose a threat to the diaspora during the first years of the revolution. As a result, anti-regime diaspora members only gradually joined the public pro-Arab Spring movement, with many guarding their identities and voices throughout the revolution's early stages. As the Syrian revolution became plagued by infighting, mistrust, and competition, diaspora activists too became subjected to conflict transmission and began to splinter apart once again.

Meanwhile, Yemenis did not have to overcome the hurdles posed by transnational repression because the regime was too weak to effectively repress voice after exit. Accordingly, regime violence and the outrage it caused were sufficient to motivate anti-regime individuals to come out against the regime. However, it was only after revolutionary coalitions formed at home that they overcame conflict transmission and formed new protest movements abroad. Obstacles to *maintaining* a unified voice for regime change reemerged, however, after regime violence prompted northern elites in Yemen to defect to the revolution. This move irked southern separatist supporters at home and abroad – the diaspora's key anti-regime force before the Arab Spring – since the revolution coalition now included the perpetuators of southern oppression. Mirroring their compatriots at home, some Yemeni groups and activists withdrew their support as a result. In other words, conflict transmission reemerged as Yemen's revolutionary coalition between north and south became redivided. Yemen's Arab Spring therefore created its own hurdles to solidarity and divided the diaspora shortly after movements emerged to contest Ali Abdullah Saleh.

Taken together, the findings of this chapter demonstrate how home-country conditions and changes therein travel through cross-border ties to influence the use of voice (Hirschman 1970). The transnational effects of the Arab Spring had a significant, positive impact on diaspora mobilization not simply by stoking emotional distress or excitement but also by upsetting the transnational deterrents that had suppressed voice and divided their loyalties for so long. At the same time, the quotidian disruptions that brought people out and together to engage in public activism were also fleeting in some cases. As I show here, changes at home continuously shaped diaspora mobilization dynamics over time, leading to durable long-distance nationalism in some cases, and fissures or withdrawal in others.

4.1 THE BREAKDOWN (AND PERSISTENCE) OF TRANSNATIONAL REPRESSION

4.1.1 The Libyan Case: The Implosion of Regime Control and the Diaspora's Coming Out

Libya's Day of Rage was announced on Facebook as planned for Thursday, February 17, 2011, a day that commemorated regime violence against protesters in Benghazi in 2006. However, protests exploded two days early on February 15 after the regime cracked down on activists and arrested Fathi Terbil, the lawyer representing the families of the Abu Salim Massacre victims. This gave already-aggrieved activists and the relatives of slain prisoners a reason to riot. As regime forces mowed down protesters with lethal force, civilians and army defectors overran the military's barracks, forcing the brigade stationed in Benghazi to retreat. In this stunning turn of events, protesters claimed Benghazi as liberated territory. Protests then spread rapidly across the country to cities such as Misrata, Derna, Bayda, Ras Lanuf, Zawiya, and to the western capital of Tripoli. Within a week, Benghazi's uprising had become a national revolutionary movement.[2]

The regime attempted to reassert control by offering meager concessions while simultaneously killing protesters, conducting mass arrests, and shutting down the Internet. On February 21, two Libyan air force pilots flew to Malta

---

[2] For a detailed breakdown of these events, see Bassiouni (2013).

and defected, claiming that they had been ordered to bomb Benghazi. Saif al-Islam responded by threatening to crush the uprisings in a televised address, which signaled the "final chapter in the comedy that was reform," according to one of his advisors (Pargeter 2012: 229). On February 22, Gaddafi also gave a long-winded speech; blaming foreign powers and drug-addicted protesters for the disruptions, he promised to "cleanse" Libya of "rats" and "cockroaches." This proved to be a huge mistake, as it justified a multilateral and militarized intervention against him (see Chapter 7). Regime violence also induced widespread defections in the military, which all but imploded under the force of the exodus. Defectors formed what became known as the Free Libya Army, a loose conglomeration of underequipped fighting forces. In response, Gaddafi supplemented his loyalist forces with foreign mercenaries. Some protesters had secured small arms from abandoned military depots, but they were badly outgunned and largely untrained.

These developments were followed by a series of high-ranking defections by figures such as Mustafa Abdul Jalil, Gaddafi's former justice minister, on February 21. He warned the international community that Gaddafi would not hesitate to annihilate entire populations, claiming, "When he's really pressured, he can do anything. I think Gaddafi will burn everything left behind him" (Al Jazeera English 2011a; Black 2011). International institutions and heads of state condemned the "callous disregard for the rights and freedoms of Libyans that has marked the almost four-decade long grip on power by the current ruler," as Navi Pillay, the UN High Commissioner for Human Rights, announced (Al Jazeera English 2011b). Within a week of the initial protests in Benghazi, the protester-regime standoff had escalated into a nationwide war that left approximately one thousand Libyans dead. On February 27, elite defectors and commanders announced the formation of the National Transitional Council (NTC) in Benghazi, giving the Free Libya Army official representation and what was to become an internationally recognized government-in-waiting.

As described in Chapter 3, Libyans in the diaspora had been largely silent on matters of home-country politics and regime change due to the threats posed by transnational repression. For this reason, the emergence of the rebellion was insufficient to automatically induce *public* mobilization in the diaspora. Libyans who were not previously "out" against the regime had to carefully consider whether or not to lend their faces and names to the cause out of concern for their family members at home. And yet, the majority of these respondents came out publicly against the regime in protests, community gatherings, and online forums during the onset of the revolution for three reasons.

The primary reason cited by respondents for using voice was because the conflict rapidly engulfed their relatives. When their family members joined the revolution, fled the country, or were harmed by the regime, this released persons in the diaspora from the obligation to hide their anti-regime sentiments. For example, Sarah – introduced in the Introduction – decided to attend protests at the London embassy because her family in Benghazi had joined the revolution. When Sarah called her aunt, her aunt declared,

"The whole family's outside" – where people were being shot! And I said, "Go back inside!" and she was like "No!" You could hear shooting on the line, and she's like, "It's either Gaddafi or us. For us, Sarah, the fear is gone."

For this reason, Sarah decided to do the unthinkable and go to the London embassy to protest against Gaddafi. From the Washington, DC, region, Dr. Esam Omeish, who went on to co-found a new anti-regime lobby called the Libyan Emergency Task Force (see also Chapter 5), had a similar experience. He also felt empowered to speak out in the media because his parents' escape from Tripoli "helped us to increase our activities without fear for any reprisals against them there." Violent repression therefore upset the relational mechanisms that had previously forced those abroad to keep their anti-regime sentiments private.

The second factor prompting activists to come out occurred after they observed vanguard revolutionaries taking brazen risks and sacrificing themselves for the cause of dignity (*karamah*) and freedom (*hurriyah*). This led respondents to embrace the potential costs of coming out for moral reasons. Even though some continued to receive threats, as when Mohammad of Sheffield received a threatening anonymous email and had his computer-based communications hacked, he said,

[With] women being raped, children being killed, innocent people being killed, I didn't care, you know. I mean, compared to what the Libyans are going through while I'm sitting in an office in the UK, trying to help, and compared to what they do in [Libya], it is nothing.

Ahmed, a British Libyan doctor, also decided to reveal his identity during the second day of demonstrations because "there was a fire in me. People are dying! I'm talking to my friends who are protesting in central Tripoli and I'm wearing a mask? That's ridiculous! It just didn't seem right." Even after agents inside of the London embassy were observed photographing the participants, Sarah recalled that "it was too late. We were out already." Likewise, Ahmed H., a Libyan American who had been active anonymously before 2011, stated that despite the fact that his sibling was trapped in Tripoli, identifying publicly with the revolution was important for the collective effort.

I wouldn't cover my face at that point. I made it a point to do everything – [in] all of my online communications, all my appearances, my name was being spoken. To make sure that people understood that if people are going to be out there on the front lines, sacrificing or risking their lives, then the very least I could do from the US was to make my name known and to say I'm with you, no matter what.

Adam of Virginia felt the same way, scoffing, "Everyone was just like, you know what? Screw it. If people in Libya are willing to die for it, I mean, what are you going to do? Take my picture? All right, *here*, I'll take it for you – I'll pose."

FIGURE 4.1. An anti-Gaddafi protester demonstrates voice by holding a sign reading "We're not afraid of you anymore" from London in support of the Libyan revolution against Muammar al-Gaddafi.
(Photo credit: Mike Kemp, In Pictures Ltd., 2011/Corbis via Getty Images)

Abdullah also recalled that Libyan students abroad came to side with the revolution rapidly in the United States, even though these students risked having their scholarships withdrawn and their families harmed. When Abdullah and his colleagues in Enough Gaddafi! talked to them in Washington, DC, "We said, 'Aren't you afraid? You have family in Libya!'" He recalled with admiration,

They're telling me, "Those guys are facing bullets! The least I can do is come to a protest, you know?" [They] had this confidence and this loyalty to the lives that are being lost, the people who were dying, and the idea that, hey, we're really on the cusp of a real change. And those were a lot of the *same students* who were *forced* to come out for Gaddafi at the UN [in 2009], protesting on the other side of the line from us.

As journalist Evan Hill (2011) reported for the Doha-based news agency Al Jazeera English, this shift in moral obligation also led students to explicitly refute regime threats.

For some of the students in the United States, the sight of citizens publicly calling for Gaddafi's ouster was enough to inspire them to defy the embassy's demands to come to Washington, DC. "I was up late all last night watching the videos of masked youths pleading to the Libyan people to rise against the oppression," one of the students wrote in an email. "These videos have been circulating on Facebook, and after watching them I broke into tears. I will no longer accept this oppression."

This sea change in respondents' orientations toward risk and a new obligation to fellow nationals was both a strategy of resistance and an expression of newfound empowerment. As Mahmoud, a lifelong activist who had been shot by regime agents in London in 1984, stated, "The mask came off. It became [about] facing them *eye to eye*."

As the regime was put on the defensive in Libya, the third factor prompting participants to come out was the regime's relatively weak response to dissent in the diaspora and the rapid collapse of its outposts and informant base. Initially, activists expected a significant counter-mobilization effort because of the heavy-handed tactics used in the past. As Dina of California explained, some people refrained from joining the diaspora's first anti-regime protests because "they thought that others were going to report back to the regime, take pictures, and take down names and send them back to Libya. So people were still afraid at first." Osama, an organizer of the first demonstration held on February 19 in Washington, DC, recalled that they made plans for "security because [we] had an expectation that Gaddafi would send his people" to confront them and instigate a fight to discredit pro-revolution demonstrators. But while the presence of pro-Gaddafi demonstrators "shook up" those who traveled periodically to Libya, as a participant named Manal recalled, these efforts came to be perceived as an empty "scare tactic." Mohamed of London also attested that the students who were initially coerced into attending pro-regime protests rapidly defected to the revolution side, and the throngs of pro-Gaddafi supporters that many expected to materialize never did.

The regime's inability to deter dissent through threats and counter-demonstrations further empowered activists to confront the institutions and agents that had long terrorized them. Tamim, co-founder of the Libyan Emergency Task Force, attested that the Washington, DC-area community spoke out to harass and shame the Libyan ambassador, Ali Aujali, after he refused to side with the revolution in an interview on CNN. After Aujali officially resigned from his post on February 22, protesters entered the DC mission, which was still under the regime's jurisdiction, and ripped down pictures of Gaddafi, shouting, "Is this a free country or is this Libya?" (Fisher 2011). Exhilarated by this previously unthinkable showing of dissent, participant Rihab recalled that it was about "*finally* being able to do something and [making] a statement on behalf of the martyrs." A similar incursion occurred in London on March 16 when demonstrators stormed the embassy and raised the revolutionary flag.

Ten of my respondents reported guarding their identities beyond the first days of the revolution because their family members were trapped in Tripoli or because they were corresponding directly with rebels on the ground.[3] As Dina from California attested,

---

[3] Six Libyan respondents joined the insurgency in Libya during the first week of the revolution. I treat anonymous mobilization in war as distinct from the guarded advocacy approach adopted by Syrians in the diaspora because of the obvious differences in risk.

During Tunisia, I was tweeting in my own name. When Libya started, the first thing my mom said was change your name on everything, take down any pictures, because my entire extended family is in Tripoli.

Yet, respondents attested that anonymity was relatively rare, and did not hinder their efforts to form new movement groups under the banner of the revolutionary flag. Because the regime proved incapable of making good on its threats at the onset of the revolution, members of the diaspora largely experienced a rapid liberation of their own. The murders of protesters in the early days of Libya's uprising not only backfired at home, therefore, but also abroad, as the barrier caused by fear of consorting with the "wrong" Libyan largely dissipated.

4.1.2 The Syrian Case: Persistent Fears of Transnational Repression and Guarded Advocacy

In contrast to the swift eruption of a regime-rebel standoff in Libya, Syria's uprising resembled a "slow motion revolution" (International Crisis Group [ICG] 2011a). Calls on Facebook for a "Day of Rage" on February 4 failed to materialize on the ground, and the regime attempted to stave off protests by implementing a series of concessions, including lifting the bans on YouTube and Facebook.[4] Yet, many Syrians were aggrieved by years of growing inequality, corruption, and everyday abuse. In light of the new mood induced by Egypt's Arab Spring, individuals and crowds in Syria began to spontaneously challenge regime officials in ways that were previously unimaginable (ICG 2011a). For example, about a dozen children were arrested by security forces on March 6 for chanting slogans against the regime in the city of Dara'a. After their families rallied to demand the children's release, security forces used live ammunition to disperse them. This incident motivated this group to escalate their demands from releasing their children to demanding the end of the regime itself. Other collective displays of dissent emerged in Damascus as well, as when small groups held vigils to support neighboring revolutions. Cell phone videos of protests being harshly dispersed, including one that showed security forces dragging activist Suheir al-Atassi by her hair and throwing her in jail for demonstrating peacefully, affirmed to many observers that Bashar al-Assad was not interested in change.

On March 15, the moment that many regime opponents-in-exile had been waiting for arrived. A small demonstration in the central market of Damascus' Hamidiya neighborhood was recorded and disseminated to international news channels for the first time, and the territorial scope of the protests expanded shortly thereafter. Assad's March 30 speech denounced dissenters as traitors and foreign conspirators (ICG 2011b). Attempts by demonstrators to form a Tahrir

---

[4] According to the International Crisis Group (2011a), much of the internet-connected population were already using these sites before 2011 through proxy servers.

Square–esque sit-in movement in Homs were brutally crushed by a military siege in late April. During a subsequent siege in Dara'a, a young teenager named Hamza al-Khateeb was detained by regime forces. On May 25, his corpse was returned to his family displaying evidence of burns, broken bones, and dismemberment. Images of his body circulated on the Internet and were broadcast on Al Jazeera, stoking outrage inside and outside of the country.[5]

As the Syrian army moved to quell protests in Baniyas, Homs, Latakia, Hama, the Damascus suburbs, and other cities in May with lethal force, their brutality provoked defections and increased anti-regime sympathies. As reports circulated about mass detainment, torture, rape, and massacres of entire families by *al-Shabiha* loyalist militias, the death toll hit approximately one thousand five hundred in July. But even as protests and riots continued through the fall of 2011, the regime retained control over broad swaths of the population and its territory through a range of coercive tactics, including stoking fears of an Islamist-extremist takeover among minorities. The pitting of an Alawite-dominated security force against a Sunni majority and the Kurdish minority stoked further ethno-religious divides on the ground. As the International Crisis Group reported (2011c: 2),

Denied both mobility and control of any symbolically decisive space (notably in the capital, Damascus, and the biggest city, Aleppo), the protest movement failed to reach the critical mass necessary to establish, once and for all, that Assad has lost his legitimacy. Instead, demonstrators doggedly resisted escalating violence on the part of the security services and their civilian proxies in an ever-growing number of hotspots segregated from one another by numerous checkpoints.

As a result of these dynamics, the Syrian revolution unfolded in phases that were distributed unevenly across the country. The uprising was first characterized by pockets of protest and riots that gradually spread to many cities and towns, but it did not constitute a national rebellion until many months later. International condemnation did little to temper the regime's brutal approach. In December, the UN High Commissioner for Human Rights reported the death toll as having reached approximately five thousand; by the end of 2012, that figure would increase at least tenfold.

Syrians in the diaspora went public in their opposition to the Assad regime over the course of 2011 and beyond. This was because the three factors enabling Libyans to wield voice also became operative in the Syrian case: (1) the engulfment of their significant others into the conflict; (2) the embrace of risk-taking and cost-sharing for moral and ethical reasons; and (3) the perceived decline in the regime's capacity to target individuals abroad. However, the *pace* at which Syrians went public was staggered because regime control in Syria was largely held in the initial months of the uprising. Correspondingly,

---

[5] See Munif (2020: ch. 1) for a detailed discussion of regime violence and "necropolitics" in Syria during the uprising.

regime agents and loyalists continued to threaten activists in the United States, Britain, and other host-countries during the revolution's first year and beyond.

The threats posed by agents of transnational repression were realized in some cases. For example, after protesters met with the ambassador to Syria in Washington, DC, in mid-April to discuss their grievances, some of their relatives in Syria were detained or disappeared, and others received death threats (Public Broadcasting Service 2012). Additionally, when Syrian artist Malik Jandali performed at a July rally in Washington, DC, in support of the 2011 revolution, regime agents kidnapped his father and beat his mother in Homs, telling her, "We're going to teach you how to raise your son" (Amnesty International 2011). The brutalization of Jandali's parents was cited by activists across the United States and Britain as a deterrent to using voice. Media reports also detailed additional instances of Syrians' relatives being harmed after they spoke out against the regime over the course of the uprisings' first year (Devi 2012; Hastings 2012; Hollersen 2012; Parvaz 2011). Batul, a student who later became active in a youth chapter of SAC, explained that these reprisals made her family too fearful to go public in 2011. Her mother told her,

"I understand we all want to voice our opinions. I understand we live in America, it's a free country. But you've got to think of the others. Don't be selfish. You're not the one that's going to face the harm – *they* are." That's why [we were] quiet for a year.

Fears were also heightened by the presence of counter-demonstrators at protest events. Pro-Assad protesters took photographs and video recordings of revolutionary gatherings and verbally threatened individuals in Arabic, as I observed firsthand in Los Angeles in 2012. This marked a notable difference from the Libyan situation. Libyan American activist Dr. Saidi, whose wife is Syrian, attended protests for both causes; he attested that

When I was marching with Syrians in the beginning, we always had people intimidating, taking photos. Sometimes they are on the streets, sometimes they are in a car. [This happened] much less with the Libyans. *Much* less. Because [although] there were a few pro-Gaddafi, because they saw everyone is against Gaddafi, none of them were willing to stand up or do this intimidation.

These acts of intimidation by pro-Assad Syrians were not always empty gestures. One man named Mohamad Soueid was in fact arrested and convicted of documenting the DC-area opposition with the intent to "undermine, silence, intimidate, and potentially harm persons in the United States and Syria who protested," according to the indictment (United States of America v. Mohamad Anas Haitham Soueid 2011: 3).

Pervasive regime threats also made my presence at protests suspicious to some participants. In January 2012, a woman observed me jotting down the names of protesters I recognized during a sidewalk rally in Anaheim. She asked in a flat tone, "Why are you writing names?" As I hurried to introduce myself, she remained standoffish and seemed unconvinced. Another woman who was listening to the conversation turned to me and explained in a Syrian accent, "We're not afraid for ourselves, but for our families." British Syrians also reported that the presence of outsiders at their events raised serious concerns. Ayman, a doctor who had been living in Manchester since the 1980s, recalled that public events did not start in his city until "late 2011" and that he was "very afraid" to participate because "I have elderly parents in Syria and I don't want them to be harassed, and we know that people have been." The counter-mobilization of pro-regime groups meant that just because revolution sympathizers were out demonstrating in public did not mean that they necessarily felt free to be *identified* as revolution supporters.

These fears led some activists to engage in what I call "guarded advocacy" by covering their faces during protests, posting anonymously online or not at all, and refusing invitations to speak to the media in order to avoid being identified as pro-revolution. Sarab, for example, first helped activists in New York organize from behind the scenes "because I hadn't gotten approval from my family to be public." The guarded character of activism also meant that public events took on a semi-private character. For example, despite declarations by a speaker that "the wall of fear has come down!" at a SAC-LA community meeting in December 2011, I was explicitly instructed not to photograph the audience. Persistent concerns about infiltration also led activists who went public early on to be suspected as agents provocateurs. Susan of Southern California, who had gotten permission from her father in Syria to come out, recalled that "people were like, why is she doing this if her family is home? Why is she not scared for them? Reality was, I was scared to death." In this way, respondents reported that their mobilization efforts suffered from enduring suspicion between conationals. As Rafif from the DC area recalled,

Many people used pseudonyms for a very long time. Other people would sort of mask their faces or something so they wouldn't be recognized on camera. So people took their pace, whatever they were comfortable with, in terms of coming out publicly in support of the revolution. That also created some mistrust, right? [Because it raised questions as to] why is one guy completely out there and not afraid, and then somebody else is still protecting his identity?

Mistrust in the community also created a challenge for Syrian organizers, because early supporters of the revolution could not get significant numbers of sympathizers in their communities to sign their names on petitions, join organizations like SAC, or affiliate with public calls for regime change. This was a problem because organizers wanted to combat regime propaganda that slandered the revolution as a conspiracy of foreign powers and a terrorist plot. As Said Mujatahid, one of the early SAC organizers, recalled, because of the "phobia in the Syrian community to say anything against the Syrian regime,

I would say the first four months was difficult. Even some of your closest people will stay away from you because they are afraid of being associated." In another example, Belal formed the National Syrian American Expatriate group in Anaheim, which he hoped would bring individuals with varied political views together to support gradual liberalization in Syria. This group of a dozen or so individuals put together a list of requests for Assad, including presidential term limits, in March 2011. However, Belal's expatriate group was formed in secret out of fears of transnational repression, and Belal was the only member willing to sign his name to the group's demands.

4.1.3 Syrians' Gradual Coming Out and Risk-Taking Strategies

Despite the challenges of going public, Syrians reported doing so after regime violence converted their families to the cause or forced their loved ones to flee. Sharif observed this shift among his conationals in Bradford, who began to tell him, "Look, if my family in Syria are going on the street, why do I need to be frightened here in England?" Similarly, Batul was able to "open up" in 2012 after her relatives in Syria decided to make their anti-regime position known and gave "their okay" for their relatives to come out. Washington, DC-based Mohammad al-Abdallah, a political exile whose father was imprisoned by the regime at the onset of the uprising, likewise reported being able to escalate his public criticisms of the regime after his father reached out to condone his son's activism. He said,

When the uprising started, I was on TV commenting and basically criticizing the government. But I had that concern about my family's safety because members of my family were in prison. In April, I get a phone call from my father inside the prison. He managed to basically bribe a police officer and use his cell phone. And he called me, [saying] they're arresting lots of people from the street and bring[ing] them to the prison here, but they tell me they see you on TV and they're very proud of you. So please continue doing that regardless of what's happening here.

The victimization of loved ones also compelled respondents to transition from guarded to public advocacy. Nebal, a student in London, emphasized that although an embassy official had contacted him to demand that he attend pro-Assad demonstrations, he felt that he had "no choice" but to go public after his brother was imprisoned. Others did so after experiencing a personal loss. As Abdulaziz Almashi, a founder of the Global Solidarity Movement for Syria, attested,

When I start joining the anti-Assad demonstrations in late April, we used to hide our faces with scarves because we're not sure about the consequences, we're worried about loved ones in Syria. In late May, my friend was killed in Hama and I saw the video on Al Jazeera. One week after that, the Syrian embassy again contacted me to ask me to join *their* protests, and I made my decision. I said "look, I'm not joining you, you are killing our people." The person said to me, "if you don't join us, that means you are against us." I said "I *am* against you, go to hell!" I was using the megaphone, shouting. They were [taking pictures of] me. And I didn't care at that time. It was the spark of my activism in the *open* way.

Respondents also came out after the scope and brutality of regime violence transformed their sense of obligation to encompass the broader national community, rendering nonfamilial Syrians as significant others. Omar, an activist from Houston, recalled, "My brother and family are in Syria, but people were losing their lives. And I don't think *our* lives are more precious than those people who lost *their* lives." Similarly, Firas of Southern California came out after the regime sent tanks to put down protests in Dara'a in April 2011. Before this incident, he had covered his face in protests, and

[I tried] to avoid mentioning my name in any petition. But after using the tanks, it was like, no, screw it! Why should I worry about my family when *all* of the people are getting killed? I know that this regime uses collective punishment. But I was like, I'm not going to care. I'm going to go public.

FIGURE 4.2. Syrians and SAC organizers call for outside powers to "Stop the Bloodshed in Syria" at the Federal Building in Los Angeles, California, on June 9, 2012. (Photo credit: Dana M. Moss)

Fadel, a doctor in London, refuted peer pressure not to go public by referencing Syria's most famous child martyr: "You can't only be concerned about yourself and your family. If you think Hamza al-Khateeb is not part of your family, I think you are very selfish." Ahmed of London also attested that he came out after Hamza's mutilated body was posted on YouTube. "The thing that affected me most was the murder of Hamza al-Khateeb. Before that, I was reluctant to do protests. When that happened, the next day I was protesting outside the embassy."

The perception that costs should be collectively shared sometimes forced activists to choose between their families and the cause. Muhammad N., exiled to London at the time, described the agonizing decision of whether or not to give a televised interview because his family in Aleppo might be subjected to reprisals. His brother advised him, "This is a duty on every one of us. If all of us are cowards because we have family in Syria, then it's treason." Muhammad decided to speak to the media, but the decision pitted his family's safety against his principles. For other Syrians, the decision to embrace the potential costs of coming out led to familial discord. Fadel in London reported,

I was in a big dispute with my mother. She said, "aren't you risking yourself?" I said "I'm not, I am safe here." Then she said, "you have a brother and sister back home." I said, "Mom, I have to get out of my silence and talk and protest. Those people on the ground, they are brave enough to sacrifice their lives. And I'm sitting here, knowing that nobody is going to shoot at me, and I'm still hesitating? *No way*. This is the least I can do."

Some experienced significant social costs for choosing the cause over their familial obligations. When Nour, an independent activist from a Christian family, set up a Facebook page in February 2011 calling for liberty for Syrians, some of his family members in the United States called him very "angry" to say that "if you don't care about *yourself*, fine, but *we* want to go to Syria." Friends and family abroad and in Syria then began to sever their connections with Nour for fear of "getting in trouble," and he "started to unfriend a lot of people just to spare them the headache." Because two of his uncles in Syria were interrogated by security forces about Nour's social media posts, he published an announcement on Facebook that his family had rejected him. That way, he reasoned, if the regime questioned any of his relatives about him again, they could see that he did not represent their views. "But it wasn't an easy call," Nour explained. "I experienced extreme isolation and social stigma. I lost everything, all my social connections." In a parallel case, Hussam stated that coming out early on as a member of SAC was a strategy "to help others break the fear, the wall of fear. Because it was unusual for people to go public criticizing the regime." At the same time, "We got a lot of heat. I had family members calling me from Syria like what the heck are you doing? Relatives from all over. All of us went through that, although our [initial] letter [to the regime] was very respectful." Many participants reported that they had to cut all forms of communication with their families at home so as not to incriminate them by association, which was emotionally trying.

Lastly, activists came out because they perceived that the Assad regime's increased use of collective and arbitrary violence in Syria meant that going public no longer posed additional risks to their significant others. As L. A. from California explained, such escalations signaled that her family's fate was no longer in her hands.

Even if I didn't do anything, if they want my family, they will take them for no reason. When my mom tells me you are [putting a] target on us, I say mama, when they want you, they won't wait for me to protest or not to protest.

Sabreen also stated that although her mother initially asked her to remain anonymous, she later told Sabreen, "It doesn't matter if you speak or not, because they are targeting everybody." As such, members of the diaspora went public because they came to perceive that the regime was no longer willing or able to sanction them in a *targeted* fashion. As Y. explained,

In the beginning, because everything was so slow in Syria, the regime was able to crack down on everyone who talked. Then it got to a point where they're not going to keep up. When the conflict escalated militarily, we're like, okay, their focus is not on Facebook anymore.

This rendered formerly high-risk activism abroad as low-risk, enabling activists to transition from guarded to overt advocacy.

In summary, Syrian anti-regime mobilization in the United States and Britain emerged as never before over the revolution's first year. As Qayyum (2011: 4) writes, this coming-out process cultivated a new consciousness in public space, as Syrians came to "link their names to their stories and opinions as an act of defiance . . . [and] to rebuff intimidation tactics facilitated by the Syrian government." However, transnational repression also obstructed diaspora solidarity and mobilization by perpetuating mistrust and fear, and by imposing costs. As Sarab explained, the decision to "cross that line of fear" was belabored.

After I put my first post on Facebook condemning the regime, my finger was trembling and my heart was racing. So it gives you a sense of how repressed and how conditioned we were to be quiet and never express ourselves as long as I've been alive.

Furthermore, because many of their family members still resided in Syria, some Syrians chose to only use their first names or to remain partially hidden online or in public.

As numerous members of the anti-regime diaspora began to come out on behalf of the revolution, Syrians attested that the cause lumped and split the community into pro- and anti-regime camps. The fear of being informed upon by fellow conationals also increased polarization within the diaspora. Respondents reported cutting off communications with those who came out on behalf of the regime and avoiding or boycotting businesses known (or believed) to be pro-regime. Though the respondents interviewed in this study affirmed that they would continue to be public regardless of the eventual outcome of the revolution, many knew of others who remain silent or guarded.[6] Hassan of SAC-LA cited this as a pervasive dilemma for Syrians because "we enjoy freedom and democracy. We came to this country for those things. That fear should not be there. And still, people are afraid."

4.1.4 The Yemeni Case: Regime Repression's Effect on Public Mobilization

Protests broke out in Yemen's capital city of Sana'a on January 15, 2011, in support of Tunisia's revolution, and street-level demonstrations grew steadily each week across the country. Calls by demonstrators known as the "independent youth" for Saleh to step down were intertwined with calls by the legal opposition, including Yemen's Al-Islah Party and the Yemeni Socialist Party, for reform. After Yemen's first Day of Rage on February 3, protesters pitched tents at the newly christened Change Square at Sana'a University and in Freedom Square in Ta'iz. Regime forces killed several participants in response and spurred a steady growth in protests and sit-ins.

The resignation of Egypt's president on February 11 escalated Yemen's uprising. Thousands took to the streets to demonstrate in at least eight cities across different regions of Yemen, including in the restive South and its largest city of Aden. In the North, the regime deployed *al-baltajiyya* – plainclothes security forces and thug groups – to disperse protests by force. Repression in the South included a series of coordinated attacks, firing on fleeing civilians, preventing doctors and ambulances from reaching injured demonstrators, and disappearing victims (Human Rights Watch 2011a). In the capital and elsewhere, erratic shootings by Saleh's forces killed about a dozen protesters each week. By the end of February, regime violence prompted Hussein al-Ahmar, a paramount leader of the prominent Hashid tribal confederation, to rally thousands of tribesmen to the cause. He also urged northern Houthi insurgents and southern secessionists to "drop their slogans, adopt a unified motto calling for the fall of the corrupt regime" (ICG 2011d: 5). In February and March, some southern protest factions acquiesced to requests by northerners not to raise the secessionist flag.

In early March, Saleh announced that he would implement reforms while also deporting as many foreign journalists as his enforcers could get their hands on. Soon after, the regime attempted to clear Sana'a's Change Square for good. During a day of protest dubbed the "Friday of Dignity," or *Jumaat al-Karamah*, Saleh loyalists shot and killed more than fifty unarmed protesters

---

[6] Several participants in LA-area protests declined to be interviewed in 2014. A mutual friend explained that because the territories in which their families reside were constantly changing hands, they no longer wanted to be publicly identified as supporting any one side in the conflict.

in the square and injured hundreds (Ishaq 2012). The massacre backfired, however, by drawing international condemnation and stoking key defections. Saleh's former ally and commander of the First Armored Division, General Ali Mohsen al-Ahmar, announced that his unit would defect to protect the protesters. Sadeq al-Ahmar, another prominent figure in the Hashid confederation (and of no relation to Ali Mohsen), also came to side with the revolution. This gave the sit-in movement in Sana'a armed protection by Mohsen and his division. At the same time, other protests and sit-in movements across Yemen remained exposed. The regime continued to target them with regularity, leading to dozens of deaths each week.

The Yemeni diaspora did not experience the same degree of threats or fear as their Libyan and Syrian counterparts, as Chapter 3 describes, owing to the regime's relative weakness and inability to effectively intimidate Saleh's opponents abroad. Several activists, particularly those from the South, were concerned that they might have trouble returning to Yemen for going public. That said, many of these individuals took that risk out of a sense of moral obligation. Arsalan of Sheffield said that his family worried about potential retribution from the regime, but "I couldn't stand to stay home and watch TV while my brothers and sisters were being killed back home and not do anything." Furthermore, unlike their Syrian counterparts, no Yemeni diaspora respondents reported covering their faces at protests or witnessing others doing so, and only one interviewee guarded his identity online.

Respondents reported that regime violence also undermined the sway of the regime over students on state-sponsored scholarships. Hanna, who had been active before 2011 organizing with southern Yemenis in New York, recalled,

In the beginning, a lot of Yemenis, mainly from the North, were pro-Ali Abdullah Saleh. So that was one of our main challenges. [At] the first rally that we had, we had a group come rally against us. And it was mainly people from the embassy, mainly students that the regime was paying for, they said well, we're paying for your schooling, you have to come out to this rally and support the regime against the other activists. [But] a lot of them, after the killings and after just the tortures and a lot of things that were going on, [those] Yemenis came to our side. So the pro-government rallies started dissipating.

Furthermore, while a core group of activists had already begun mobilizing on behalf of the revolution in February and March, the Friday of Dignity Massacre on March 18 spurred a dramatic spike in protest participation in the diaspora. Adel of Michigan described it as a "turning point" because the killings motivated many who were not previously active or were pro-regime to join their calls for Saleh to step down. Idriss of Washington, DC, recalled, "At that point, there was no going back. Whatever happens, we weren't going to stick with Saleh anymore." Respondents attested that they found the footage of the protests appalling. As Ali from the DC-area community described,

Personally, what motivated me most was all those videos I watched on Facebook and on the news. All those young people getting killed by Saleh's army. I felt like I have to do something. If those people over there are facing the army with guns and everything, the least I can do is support them with my voice.

For Haidar of Birmingham, the massacre also affected him personally. He said,

Initially, Yemenis in the UK were not involved in the revolution heavily, until what happened in March 2011 in [Change] Square, *Jumaat al-Karamah*. I remember that day, it was – a black day – when we saw the blood of our friends, our colleagues. Some of my best friends were injured in this massacre. Since this day, we started to move.

FIGURE 4.3. Yemeni community members shout slogans against Yemen's embattled president Ali Abdullah Saleh during a demonstration in front of the White House in Washington, DC, on March 26, 2011. The large banner reads "Ruling Yemen is not a family business."
(Photo credit: Jewel Samad/AFP via Getty Images)

Mahmoud of Sheffield described the effect of the massacre as "shocking" in its scale. Referring to another well-known community figure and longtime regime opponent named Abdallah al-Hakimi, he said,

It [became] not only about me or Abdallah calling people and saying, let's go out. It was amazing how people were calling *us* to say, look guys, you have to do something, we need to mobilize. I think we had one or two demonstrations beforehand, but they were not as big as after *Jumaat al-Karamah*. The response of people was very enormous to that.

Morooj also attested that the massacre inspired activists across different US cities to begin working together to launch national days of protest in

Washington, DC. She recalled, "After that day, we really began to start working with other cities and start connecting our actions together and [planned] a national day of action in solidarity with Yemenis. So that day definitely was a big turning point. [I]t brought the movement home [to us]." Nadia reported that this event motivated her to galvanize other women in Birmingham to participate in the London-based protests.

> The women weren't involved as much in the organizing for the revolution. They weren't normally invited. When they killed that many people in one day, that was *it* for me, I had *had it.* I felt that it was *my* children who were getting killed and hurt, [so] I went and booked a coach [to London]. [My husband] said "why did you do that? you haven't even spoken to the men about it." I said that "we're going to fill the coach, even if we fill it with women." That was the turning point where I was prepared, if anyone was to say to me, "You don't have the right," I would say, "*Yes I do.*" There's a point where you go past thinking, am I supposed to do, am I not *supposed* to do. It's something you *have* to do, it's obligatory. So for me, [*Jumaat al-Karamah*] was the turning point.

As the experiences of activists like Nadia and others illustrate, Yemen's revolution not only brought diaspora members out in public to protest, but also increased the political participation of Yemeni women as well.

From one of Yemen's largest concentrated communities in the United States, a community organizer named Adel also observed that the massacre had a counteractive effect on the pro-regime protests in Dearborn, Michigan.

> At the beginning, just a few people showed up to a small demonstration. But especially after the Friday of Dignity, lots of people showed up. There were also two demonstrations that were big in numbers that were pro-government. And those were the people who were members of [Saleh's] *Al-Mu'tamar* [General People's Congress] party. They showed up with the president's pictures. But after that Friday, I don't think they did anything after that. Some of them kind of joined the revolution and some of them just stayed on their own. And the last [pro-Saleh] one was kind of an embarrassment because only like ten or eleven people showed up to the city hall.

In all, regime repression at home undermined the weak effects of transnational repression in the Yemeni diaspora and, as I explain below, stoked the outrage needed for community members to condemn Ali Abdullah Saleh. As a result, anti-regime activists, both new and old, came together to wield voice as never before.

4.2 THE BREAKDOWN (AND RESURGENCE) OF CONFLICT TRANSMISSION

4.2.1 The Libyan Revolution and Diaspora Solidarity

In addition to upending transnational repression, the rapid escalation of a zero-sum standoff in Libya also undermined conflict transmission and induced solidarity between conationals for the Arab Spring. As Noueihed and Warren (2012: 180) write,

[Gaddafi's] now-infamous pledge to go "zanga zanga, dar dar" or from "alley to alley, house to house" to "cleanse" the "rats" and "cockroaches" carried echoes of the 1994 genocide in Rwanda, when Hutus described the Tutsis in similarly insect-like terms. Saif al-Islam's calls for dialogue and a "general assembly" were ignored by both the opposition and the outside world, while his rambling speech threatening "rivers of blood" prompted Western politicians to fall over each other in their rush to distance themselves from Libya's heir apparent ... Even though Gaddafi promised an amnesty to those who gave up their weapons, threats of "no mercy" to those who resisted suggested that a terrible vengeance would be visited upon Libya's second city [of Benghazi].

Thus, the revolution created shared anti-regime grievances between revolutionaries in exile, reformists who had treated the regime as a bargaining partner in recent years, bystanders who had eschewed home-country politics in the past, and students abroad on state-sponsored scholarships. As a result, regime repression and revolutionary backlash in Libya produced a newfound alignment that paired a "diagnostic frame" attributing the Gaddafi regime as the problem with a "prognostic frame" naming the armed revolutionary movement under the National Transitional Council (NTC) as the only legitimate solution (Benford and Snow 2000; Snow and Benford 1988). These conditions motivated mobilization among a wide cross-section of Libyans in the United States and Britain and produced a newfound sense of nationalistic solidarity among conationals. As M., a second-generation exile and member of the Enough Gaddafi! network, explained,

It was incredibly unfortunate, the severity of the crisis, but it left a very clear line for us. There wasn't any doubt if Gaddafi was doing this or he was not doing this – like in Syria, where there's a lot of doubt floating around regarding who did what, and what was going on, who's the good guy or the bad guy. We were lucky enough to have all of that very black and white. The severity of his actions made it very clear. Whether or not [others] had been supportive of Gaddafi before, it changed a lot of people afterwards, not to mention those who had already been affected.

Dina from California also attested to how important Saif al-Islam's threatening reaction to the uprising was in discrediting the regime. A young professional from Southern California, Dina had spent time working in Libya during Saif's "liberalization" period before being imprisoned for a brief but terrifying time over government suspicions that she was a spy. She said,

Many people actually, at the beginning of the revolution, did not expect Saif to react in the way that he did. People forget that, but that's still really an important part of the whole puzzle – the way that he came out so strongly in those first days. His hatred was just so shocking.

Saif's speech also prompted individuals like Adam, who had engaged with regime representatives through Saif's diaspora outreach initiative in 2010, to change his mind. He explained his decision in the following way:

If I'm having a debate with somebody and the person decides to slap my sister, the debate is _over_. I understand we want to limit as much bloodshed as possible. But when you're fighting a rabid dog, you can't speak with it, you can't calm it down with words anymore. That's it. You've got to put it to sleep, end it then and there. The point of return is long gone. And [the regime] passed it.

Abdullah of Enough Gaddafi! also recalled the transformative effect of the revolution in unifying members' grievances. He reported that during the initial planning meetings for the first protest in Washington, DC, on February 19, he and his fellow organizers debated,

What if people bring [the] green flags [of the regime]? What if people don't want to see posters that are cursing Gaddafi? There were all these things that we were trying to accommodate so that we'd get as many people to come out as possible. But when the nineteenth came, all of that went out the window. When people were getting killed, people could see the bravery of the youth in the street, and it was all the independence flags, _down with Gaddafi_! It was just unified all of a sudden.

Niz, a Libyan doctor-turned-revolutionary who was living in Cardiff at the time, also noted that the regime's use of overwhelming force was critical in legitimizing armed revolution as a necessary method of resistance. He explained,

Very quickly, the realization was that Gaddafi is not Ben Ali or Mubarak. They are all brutal and corrupt dictators, but Gaddafi is a different breed, and public protests at squares – these things were not going to bring the regime down. And that the Gaddafi regime would easily kill 90 percent of the population if it meant him staying in power. They would continue to gun down protesters. And very quickly, the idea came about that this _cannot_ be a mass peaceful protest movement. It needed to become an armed uprising.

For this reason, respondents came to validate the armed struggle by the Free Libya Army (also known as the National Liberation Army) and to back the NTC.

Respondents overwhelmingly reported experiencing a newfound sense of community that brought exiles, refugees, non-activist immigrants, migrants, and even some formerly pro-regime individuals together for the same cause. As Abdo G. of Manchester recalled, "It unified the Libyan community. Because before February 17, the Libyan community in Manchester was in silence. There _wasn't_ a community." But after the onset of the revolution, he exclaimed, "People [were meeting] new people. My own brother met his future wife at one of these events!" This sentiment was echoed by activists based in the United States as well. As Khaled recalled, the first Washington, DC, protest on February 19 was the biggest thing I've ever been a part of. Usually when we protest[ed], I would have spent my last dime driving to New York or DC for a protest that had maybe thirteen people. The DC protest was the most Libyans I have seen in one place in America ever. It was [hundreds of] people who had never been politically active, who had never met before.

Osama, who at the time of the revolution was living in Chicago but had grown up among other Libyan families in Tucson, Arizona, echoed that at informal community events, such as "the picnics that happened during the revolution, suddenly everyone [is] singing freedom songs, singing the national anthem – any picnic it would be like that." The contrast in community relations before and during the Arab Spring could not have been starker.

Of course, neither the revolution itself nor the diaspora's response was a purely harmonious effort. There were underlying conflicts and mistrust between groups, including violence between anti-regime forces in Libya itself, as well as lingering resentments by long-standing regime opponents of those who had jumped on the anti-regime "bandwagon," as Ahmed H. recalled. Several members of Enough Gaddafi! who helped to organize the February 19 protest also recalled competition between opposition figures to dominate the event. Ahmed explained that he spoke with the leaders of other groups in order to tell them,

Listen, we just need people to show up. If you want to demonstrate solidarity with the people who are on the front lines going through it right now, [then participate]. That's the objective more than anything else. We want to present a common front, a unified front, to the world.

Mohamed of Manchester also referenced an underlying "competition" over who would appear in the media. However, despite these wobbles in community cohesion, respondents reported experiencing a sense of solidarity as never before. Mohamed said his experience protesting in Manchester around February 19 "was in and of itself amazing" because

We were rubbing shoulders with everyone. The thing that brought us together was being Libyan and being anti-Gaddafi. I was talking and standing together with socialists, communists, liberals, Islamists, we all had one goal and one pain and we were happy to be together.

Furthermore, despite some tensions, collective action in the diaspora was fundamentally unified around a set of anti-regime grievances and demands. As M. stated, "There was one goal to be achieved. Yes, we all have our differences, but the main goals were to get Gaddafi out, and to stop the killing of people." Mohamed of Manchester also recalled that Libyans were joined together by the fact that the revolution had escalated immediately into "a fight to the death" – and that despite the disparate groups involved, the revolution-supporting opposition was "united in one fight" against Gaddafi, as Adam from Virginia recounted. As a result, their various strategies to intervene in the revolution itself, described in the next chapter, remained complementary and largely unified for the duration of the fight.

For Libyans, the Arab Spring not only prompted individuals to ally themselves under the banner of the revolutionary flag, but also enabled them *convert all known preexisting diaspora groups and organizations in the United States and Britain to the cause* (see Table 4.1). This not only empowered individuals to unite in new ways, but also allowed diaspora members to use previously "neutral" or apolitical "indigenous organizations" (McAdam 1999[1982]), that is, community associations and groups formed prior to the revolutions, as spaces for conationals to congregate. In this way, the Arab Spring transformed Libyan organizations into "mobilizing structures" for activism (McAdam et al. 1996), providing leaders with a base of support and collective resources for intervention at home. Although the NFSL and other groups formed in the 1970s and 1980s were no longer in operation just before the revolution, many of their participants immediately came to support the struggle. So too did Dr. Abdul Malek, founder of Libya Watch and representative of the Muslim Brotherhood from Manchester. He recalled that he and the Brotherhood came to ally with the revolution because of the regime's severe response.

When we went to the general meeting, which is the highest authority in the *Ikhwan* [Brotherhood], we expected something to happen on the seventeenth of February. The argument was over what to expect. Would we expect an outright revolution? Would we expect just some people to come out and then go home, or what? Our position at the end of the day was this: if something happens on the seventeenth, then we will have to wait for the response of the regime. If the regime uses brutal force and kills demonstrators, then we will go out right [away] with the revolution and there will be no going back. But if the regime backs away and allows these young people to vent their energy and their steam without an incident and without killing anyone, then the reform prospects that we are very keen on will continue. But obviously, the regime decided to act brutally against the uprising and started killing right away, and immediately we moved into the revolution mode.

TABLE 4.1. *Libyan groups and organizations converted to the revolution and/or relief during the 2011 Arab Spring, as reported by respondents*

Diaspora Group/Organization	Converted?
USA	
Enough Gaddafi!	Yes
Libyan Association of Southern California	Yes
National Conference for the Libyan Opposition[a]	Yes
Britain	
Libyan Muslim Brotherhood[a]	Yes
Libya Watch	Yes
Libyan Women's Union	Yes
National Conference for the Libyan Opposition[a]	Yes

[a] Denotes multinational membership.

The revolution also transformed previously apolitical organizations for empowerment and socialization into politicized groups for the Arab Spring. Dr. Saidi of the Libyan Association of Southern California remarked that "when the revolution started, *every* Libyan gathering became political." While attending one of these events in Fountain Valley, California (which convened just a few days after the October 2011 killing of Gaddafi), I observed that the event was entirely revolution-themed: children gleefully swatted at piñatas draped with pictures of the Gaddafi family, and different men gave a series of speeches while wearing the revolution flag like a cape, heralding the triumphs of their compatriots. Participants wore clothing adorned with the revolution flag, ate revolution-flag-colored food, and sang revolution songs, both old and new. British Libyans witnessed this transformation as well. Zakia, founder of the Libyan Women's Union in Manchester, explained that her organization transformed from a social empowerment group into an activist organization dedicated to intervening in three areas: "one for charity, one for media, one for protests." As these examples show, diaspora organizations and community events came to be pro-revolution in orientation and mission, giving activists the structural foundation and legitimacy to launch collective actions for rebellion and relief.

4.2.2 The Syrian Revolution and the Diaspora's Gradual Coming Together

As in the Libyan revolution, the onset of protests in Syria re-energized existing activist networks that had previously opposed the regime. For groups like the Syrian Justice and Development Party in London, the onset of the protests in their home-country presented a welcome opportunity to support and incite resistance. Co-founder Malik al-Abdeh recalled that his group began to play amateur footage of protests in Syria repeatedly on Barada TV to prod Syrians into doing "more of this kind of stuff." Exiles such as Dr. Radwan Ziadeh and Marah Bukai in Washington, DC, also came out immediately to support the uprising. They used their political connections to meet with US officials on Capitol Hill and speak out in the media. After Suheir al-Atassi was released from prison in Damascus, Marah recalled contacting her friend to affirm that "we'll do what we can do here to support your aims and targets."

However, not all activists in exile were comfortable with the prospect of a Libya-style revolutionary war. Ammar Abdulhamid, an activist in exile and co-founder of the Tharwa Foundation, expressed grave concerns about the poor state of rebels' preparedness. Recalling his thinking at the time, Ammar said, "If people are in the street, I'll be with them, [and our] Tharwa network is part of it anyway." Still, he recalled warning other exiles and regime opponents that "we're not ready," expressing concerns about the lack of vision and planning on how to overcome the challenges inherent in launching a successful revolution.

The uprising also breathed new life into the Syrian American Council (SAC), but the gradual emergence of the revolution meant that SAC's reform-oriented stance did not automatically convert into a pro-revolutionary one. Hussam, who helped establish the Los Angeles chapter of SAC and would later became its national chairman, recalled that the council's first statement on the uprisings was laughably humble in hindsight. He said,

It wasn't asking for changing of the regime. It was still addressing Bashar al-Assad as the legitimate president – *Dear President Assad*, basically. We stated support for the demands of the protesters, which at that time were very, very simple. It was very peaceful. It was about political reforms, freedoms, release of political detainees. And the argument behind it was that's what they're asking for in Syria. And we can only support what they're asking for on the street. There's no need to push the envelope higher than they're doing. As long as the regime is willing to compromise and come to somewhere in the middle, that's my insistence. We made it a condition [that] anyone joining SAC or speaking for SAC [had] to abide and be committed to a peaceful revolution, a nonviolent one demanding freedom and democracy and a slow process of change.

This initially put SAC at odds with longtime activists calling for regime change. When Marah Bukai was invited to SAC's first national meeting in May, she recalled asking them, "'What is going to be your major statement?' They said, 'We want to see some changes in Syria.' I told them, 'I'm sorry, you should go and knock on the door of someone else. For me, I want this regime to go.' So their ceiling was different than my ceiling."

Just as many Libyans had believed that Gaddafi's son Saif al-Islam would be the harbinger of reason in the early days of the uprising, many Syrians also held out hope that Bashar al-Assad would do the same. Belal, a Syrian American from Orange County, California, had represented the Syrian expatriate community in dialogues with Syrian regime officials in the past. He explained,

When I met [Assad] face to face and we were talking, you know, he really showed humility and he showed passion. He was very passionate about making change and I believed him. So that's why I became part of the expatriate [group] that wanted to build a bridge between here and Syria.

However, after sending a letter to the regime and receiving a favorable response, Belal was left waiting in vain as violence on the ground escalated into the summer of 2011 and produced over one thousand casualties.

Once the regime escalated its retaliatory response to protests by laying siege to entire cities and towns, reformist groups mirrored calls for the fall of the regime that were spreading across Syria. Hussam of SAC recalled, "After the regime showed that they had absolutely no interest in reforming or changing their ways, that's when I said dialogue cannot work." In an evolution of SAC's position, he explained why the organization transitioned from supporting a peaceful revolution to armed resistance:

Initially, most people truly believed the nonviolent path was the only path. It started changing, [but] the change didn't happen overnight. That transition first included: what do you do with soldiers who defect? These people are being tracked down by the government and killed, and their wives were being raped and their parents were being shot. So there was a debate, can they defend themselves and their own families and villages? The first transition was yes, they have the right, actually they have the *responsibility* to refuse these orders. And when they go in hiding, if the government is pursuing them, they have the right to defend themselves and their families. And the next phase became, what about these soldiers defending their whole village, their whole town, or their neighborhood? Because the regime is coming to practice collective punishment on the cities. Can they defend their own villages and neighborhoods? The answer was yes. And then the next question becomes, what if a young man joins them because there weren't enough defecting soldiers to defend the village? What if a young man says, I will join you? Yes. And that transition eventually became, what if we [the revolutionaries] raid [government forces] before they raid us? What if we go and raid a Syrian army base and take the weapons so that they don't use them against us? Yeah, that sounds good, too.

He added, wryly, "I know from here, it sounds great to be Gandhi." Yet, because regime forces and militia known as *al-Shabiha* were hunting down pacifists and defectors, this left the opposition with no choice but to fight back. Belal, despite having initiated dialogue with the regime in the past, also came to side with the revolution by the end of the summer. He said,

When people rise up for a change, you should accept that. I learned that here [in the United States]. People were going out in their bare chest, they're resisting, they're asking for change. And they were met with weapons, machine guns, and attacked. Basically they were paying the price with their life. Even *we* supported that they carry arms because they were getting killed and slaughtered.

As violence worsened significantly over the course of 2012, activists reported that many members in their respective communities came to sympathize with the uprising within a year of its onset. Sabreen, a youth activist from Southern California, reported that different events, including a slew of massacres occurring in people's hometowns and cities, "hit different people at different points. So there wasn't one specific event. [But] you can't really go back on all those massacres, you can't go back on all those deaths. And you can't just accept the regime after all that." The escalation of the conflict over the course of 2011 *gradually* brought different politicized factions into alignment with the view that the regime must fall.

As a result, Syrians converted many preexisting organizations to the Arab Spring (see Table 4.2). Groups such as the Syrian American Council, which lay relatively dormant since its founding in 2005 due to the threat of transnational repression (see Chapter 3), and elite-led organizations like Ammar Abdulhamid's Tharwa Foundation and Dr. Radwan Ziadeh's Center for Political and Strategic Studies, immediately converted their groups to the Arab Spring. Activists also converted professional service organizations,

TABLE 4.2. *Syrian groups and organizations converted to the revolution and relief during the Arab Spring (2011–14), as reported by respondents*

Diaspora Group/Organization	Converted to the Rebellion and/or Relief?
USA	
All4Syria	Yes
Syrian American Association (Southern CA)	*No*
Syrian American Club of Houston	*No*
Syrian American Council	Yes
Syrian American Medical Society[a]	Yes
Syrian Center for Political & Strategic Studies	Yes
Tharwa Foundation	Yes
Britain	
Syrian British Medical Society[a]	Yes
Syrian Justice & Development Party	Yes
British Syrian Society (London)	*No*
Syrian Observatory for Human Rights	Yes

[a] Denotes an exclusively charitable/service nonprofit organization.

previously perceived by respondents as co-opted by regime elites, to the cause of relief. The two medical associations that operated in the US and British diasporas before the revolution – the Syrian British Medical Society and the Syrian American Medical Society, both founded in 2007 – came to channel their resources to the conflict after pro-revolution humanitarians and activists mobilized to liberate these organizations from regime loyalist control.

Dr. Fadel Moghrabi of London, who came out early for the revolution, attested that he joined the Syrian British Medical Society during the revolution in 2012 "for one reason: because corruption was everywhere [in Syria], and it was reaching here as well. When the people were killed in the street, the Syrian British Medical Society was silent because half of the leaders were connected to the government." Fadel responded by mobilizing his colleagues to threaten a mass resignation unless regime loyalists were removed from the society's leadership. After these doctors succeeded in pressuring the organization to hold new elections, Fadel and his colleagues joined the board so that "now we can open up, we can talk freely, we can talk as a medical society looking at the scale of atrocity going on against doctors, against medical facilities, hospitals, paramedics, all those things." The Syrian American Medical Society did the same, enabling the organization to "fulfill its potential," according to one respondent, as a bona fide relief agency working inside and outside of Syria to save civilian lives.

That said, conflict transmission over the revolution and the presence of loyalists in Syrian communities meant that not all groups followed in lockstep, as in the Libyan case. Three social clubs mentioned by interviewees – the Syrian American Club of Houston, the Syrian American Association of Southern California, and the British Syrian Society of London – did *not* convert to the revolution. Omar Shishakly, a board member of Houston's Syrian American Club who had come out on the side of the revolution early on, maintained that the Houston club *had* to remain neutral. As an organization dedicated to providing scholarships and hosting community gatherings, he argued that it was required to adhere to its nonpolitical bylaws and continue serving the broader community regardless of their political views.

However, another activist from Houston attested that the club's neutrality made it pro-regime by default because they would not allow community members to use the space or the listserv to advertise events, such as fundraisers for humanitarian relief or documentary films on the uprising. This respondent told me with more than a hint of disdain, "I see the club as kind of an extension of Damascus – Little Damascus thinking they can stay neutral and everything will be okay." Associations in California and London were likewise perceived by outsiders as taking Assad's side once the conflict began because they were run by loyalists and remained silent on the crisis at home.

Nevertheless, as Table 4.2 shows, most Syrian diaspora organizations – including those with long-standing political claims and capacities to deliver much-needed aid – were converted by their leaders to the revolution, granting the anti-regime diaspora an institutionalized means of raising attention and aid for the cause.

4.2.3 The Resurgence of Conflict Transmission in the Syrian Diaspora

The escalating conflict in Syria produced an unprecedented surge in anti-regime activism, as I detail further in Chapter 5. However, the revolution was also represented by and divided into a multitude of groups without a unified leadership. Over the course of 2011, numerous revolution-supporting organizations emerged across Syria. These included the Local Coordination Committees, which promoted nonviolent civil resistance and broadcast the Syrians' plight to the outside world. On July 29, defector Colonel Riad al-Asa'ad announced the formation of the Free Syrian Army (FSA) and later merged his loyalists with another group called the Free Officers Movement. The Syrian National Council was established in Turkey in August 2011, initially recognized by foreign governments as an umbrella body to coordinate and lead the internal opposition (Carnegie Endowment for International Peace 2013).

Yet, many opposition groups operating inside of Syria contested the Syrian National Council's authority. In addition, while defectors and volunteers formed FSA units to protect their towns and neighborhoods from regime violence, the disjointed character of these armed units made the rebel army "more a wild card than a known entity" in the conflict (ICG 2011c: 6).

The FSA's lack of coordination with the Syrian National Council also posed significant challenges in unifying the opposition. As Yassin-Kassab and Al-Shami (2018: 57) argue, "The Syrian revolution wasn't led by a vanguard party and wasn't subject to centralised control. It didn't splinter, because it was never a monolith." Many other groups were coordinating resistance at the local and national levels, including the militarized Syrian Revolution General Commission, the Syrian Revolution Coordinators Union (Yassin-Kassab and Al-Shami 2018), and the Supreme Council of the Syrian Revolution (O'Bagy 2012).

Many defectors and civilians later allied themselves with the Free Syrian Army, but this force was comprised of multiple factions that lacked a central command structure. Various coordinating groups emerged inside and outside of Syria to represent the opposition, but these groups lacked a common vision and often contested each other's tactics and legitimacy. As a result, Syrians came to share the demand that "the regime must go!" but lacked consensus over a prognostic frame of who should lead and represent this effort (Snow and Benford 1988). This lack of coordination and consensus in the home-country was reproduced in the opposition abroad. So just as the Syrian community was beginning to join together and publicly support the revolution, emergent pro-revolution groups in the diaspora became redivided by conflict transmission.

A major hurdle in sustaining cohesion among the anti-regime diaspora was the fact that leaders of pro-revolution groups and organizations were perceived as trying to co-opt the movement for their own gains. As Malik of the Syrian Justice and Development Party recalled, the London pro-revolution scene quickly succumbed to infighting and competition that was easily observable during street protests.

The demonstrations caused a lot of problems within the community itself. The same problems, the same divisions that were happening in the Syrian opposition were reflected in this microcosm of the Syrian community in the UK. Because you had the professionals who were like – there was a guy and he wants to be basically the head of whatever revolutionary body that represents the Syrian community in the UK, even though he was very close with the ambassador until very recently, before the revolution. On account of the fact that he thinks he's clever and he's got a high position and he's highly regarded in the community, he has to be the boss. And then the Muslim Brotherhood came along thinking oh, hold on a second. We've been doing this for years, this is *our* gig! So then they started muscling in. We tried to set up a protest coordination committee, but it kept falling apart because whenever there was a Muslim Brotherhood guy involved, they would say, oh, Muslim Brotherhood is hijacking this thing. It just became extremely messy. And basically, it got to a point where there isn't really any organization in the UK that represents Syrians who are against the regime. And this is the challenge when it comes to organizing anything Syrian in the UK, because you have certain political forces that believe that they have an automatic right to assume leadership regardless of who created the body or whatever. One of those forces that was probably the most influential was Muslim Brotherhood.

Making the situation more difficult was the fact that active members of the Syrian Muslim Brotherhood were (and are) a part of the opposition, but have not been card-carrying members of an official organization with a brick-and-mortar headquarters. This made it all the more confusing as to who was truly a Brotherhood member and who was not, which created mistrust and suspicion over activists' underlying agendas. In addition, many interviewees who denied having a Muslim Brotherhood affiliation were nevertheless accused by others of being secret members working as a fifth column for a Brotherhood takeover. For instance, when the name of a widely known anti-regime figure in London was raised in an interview I was conducting with an independent activist, this respondent interjected, "He is *Brotherhood*, by the way." When I replied that this person explicitly denied being affiliated in any way with the group, he said with a raised eyebrow, "Do you think he would actually *tell* you that he is?" suggesting that I had been easily deceived.

In this way, I came to learn that the Brotherhood was used as a label to refer to actual members of the opposition-in-exile forced to leave Syria in the early 1980s, as well as current factions within Syria's revolutionary movement perceived as working in the service of the transnational Brotherhood movement and on behalf of Islamist principles more generally. Activists also branded other dissidents as "Brotherhood" when they perceived them as co-opting the revolution on behalf of a conservative Sunni Muslim agenda, regardless of their actual intentions and identities. According to Conduit (2019: 167), Walid Saffour, the longtime Syrian activist in exile in London who represented the Syrian Human Rights Committee on the Syrian National Council, was later appointed as the Opposition Coalition's ambassador to London. This gave "the Brotherhood an important formal diplomatic link to the UK through an undeclared member" (Conduit 2019). However, Conduit also reports that "a Brotherhood associate was highly critical of the decision, arguing that Saffour was unqualified for such an important diplomatic role and that the Brotherhood's push to have one of their own represented amounted to 'gross incompetence' on the group's part" (Conduit 2019). This criticism followed in line with the Brotherhood's compromised reputation in Syria as being linked clandestinely to "front" groups that had not been open or honest about their ties to the *Ikhwan* (Conduit 2019: ch. 6). It also followed concerns among Syrians at home and in the diaspora that the Brotherhood was attempting to dominate the opposition.

This mistrust exacerbated long-standing conflict transmission and factionalism in the community; as Ahmed of London lamented, "you always had this accusation against people, that they're Muslim Brotherhood." After joining a pro-revolution activist group in London, he found himself shunned as a result of this accusation.

They identified me as being Muslim Brotherhood. I tell them I'm not and I haven't got anything to do with them. I mean, my father was part of them but he left them when I was very young. He is very religious. I'm not as religious as he is, by the way. And well, they made it very clear that they didn't like my presence with them.

Diaspora organizations were also accused of being Brotherhood-run. As Hussam reported, the decision of a SAC founding member to exit the organization and start his own group raised accusations in the broader community.

I hear from community members telling me that [this] person told people that [he] decided to quit the organization because it's a Muslim Brotherhood organization. It's easy to throw these accusations – completely baseless, by the way. I heard that even when I wanted to join. But I checked and I talked to people who are members and I talked to people who know them, [and] they said no. Some of them do have sympathies. Some of them are Christians, some of them are Alawites, some of them socialists. They were everybody. And in this case here, I was laughing. I said, "you know, did that person tell you [that he] was the president of the local [SAC] chapter? That person must be Brotherhood then, if that organization is Brotherhood!" But it's easier to throw these things in the community because they resonate.

Other groups were perceived to be Brotherhood-affiliated because they were comprised of the older generation of opposition activists, or because activists felt that their leadership style was too domineering or religiously oriented. Abdulaziz of London, for example, said that despite the fact that protests in London brought Brotherhood and non-Brotherhood members together, he stopped participating in them because

[Their] style was mainly [supporting] the Muslim Brotherhood objectives. And we are not really happy with the ideology of Muslim Brotherhood, because [they] are in exile since the 1980s. And the people who started the Syrian revolution were the Syrian people *inside* [of the country]. So basically, we believed it is good to listen to the people from *within* Syria. We can work accordingly with what they want us to do. The Muslim Brotherhood didn't really want that. They thought they are the only opposition party. They are organized, but they are this kind of dictatorship to some extent. Unfortunately, they are still living in the 1980s.

Belal of California also emphasized that the assortment of various groups affiliated with the revolution inside and outside of the country raised a series of unanswerable questions that ultimately hindered solidarity among opposition sympathizers. "Unfortunately," he stated,

some groups are working under the radar. They're attracting others and they're organizing things, but we really don't know who those groups are. Who do they represent? What are their intentions? There are religious groups, but then who are they? After the revolution, can I get along with these people? Are they really pro-democracy, or are they planning for their own agenda? Are they Muslim Brotherhood, are they Salafis, are they extremists? I don't know. People are just jumping and joining groups, and [they] don't know who they are.

As Syrian activist and author Yassin al-Haj Saleh (2017: 122–23) argues, this "persistent infighting, which is most likely driven by attempts at self-promotion; and the deeply mediocre standing of most opposition spokespersons, manifest in their lack of discipline and a clear, shared vision" contributed to the collapse of trust in the opposition by Syrians and outside powers alike (I take up the issue of outside powers in Chapter 7).

In addition to religious and generational divides, Kurdish separatists who had mobilized against the Syrian regime from Britain before the Arab Spring also quit the protest movement early on because they felt disrespected and marginalized by the Arab-dominated opposition. Dr. Jawad Mella, founder of the pro-secessionist Western Kurdistan Association, remarked that he had initially encouraged his colleagues to participate in anti-Assad protests with the Syrians in London. However, Syrian Arabs at the protests "did not allow them to raise the Kurdish flag." For this reason,

I then told them: you don't go and I don't go if the exiled Syrian people will be just like the Syrian government! They are *as bad* as the regime when they will come to the power, or be worse. So since the revolution, I didn't participate in *any* demonstrations, when before that we had many demonstrations in all locations. We are against the regime, and *we are against this opposition as well.*

These strains were further exacerbated by the fact that many Arab Syrians raised the Turkish flag at pro-revolution protests because of the Turkish government's support of the revolution. This was an insult to many Kurdish Syrians, since Turkey has long repressed Kurds and their separatist aspirations. On the other side, Ahmed attested that the Kurds made "trouble" at the revolution protests in London. He felt that they attempted to dominate the Syrian nationalist cause with their ethnic and separatist grievances. Ahmed recalled,

We used to have a lot of problems with the Kurds at the first protests. They would attend and they would bring the Kurdish flag, so *it would look like a Kurdish protest*. And then Syrian Arabs would protest, and then sometimes fights happen. Especially once when some people wore Turkish flags. The Kurds didn't like that.

As a result, many Kurds like Dr. Mella broke away from the Syrian opposition, choosing to withhold their support of the revolution altogether, or forming new organizations dedicated to pursuing distinctly Kurdish claims, such as youth activist Tha'er's decision to form a group called the Syria Future Current Party.

While some respondents perceived the proliferation of pro-revolution groups as a healthy expression of Syrians' newfound freedom to use voice, others argued that the fragmentation of the opposition, both at home and abroad, was counterproductive. Hussam of SAC stated, "The unhealthy part was when people insist on remaining part of a one-man organization because they don't want to dilute their power or authority." This led to an atmosphere of competition and slander within the opposition community that shocked many activists. As Razan from Britain said while shaking her head, "I felt like we're protesting for freedom, campaigning for freedom. And despite that, we've got this disease within us – this competition. I couldn't understand it." Her brother Hassan echoed in a separate interview, "Why have twenty groups? It's better to have one or two. People are still learning that we need to have unity." Unfortunately, the resurgence of conflict transmission compromised activists' abilities to unite the anti-regime diaspora and led to infighting and withdrawals as time wore on.

In summary, the anti-regime uprising in Syria released a sufficient number of Syrians in the diaspora from the deterrent effects of transnational repression. After experiencing the liberating effects of the revolution, activists mobilized to use voice by launching protests and social movement organizations for rebellion and relief. At the same time, the revolution lacked a unified and inclusive representation and a corresponding prognostic frame around who should lead the anti-Assad movement. This conflict was reproduced in the diaspora, as exemplified by fights over suspected Muslim Brotherhood agendas and by Kurdish Syrian representation in the nationalist cause. So although the Syrian revolution stoked a heightened degree of mobilization abroad, it did so slowly and without the sense of solidarity experienced by activists' Libyan counterparts.

4.2.4 The Yemeni Revolution and the Resurgence of Conflict Transmission

In February 2011, Yemenis in the diaspora began to meet to discuss how to support their compatriots back home. Organizers held community meetings and formed committees, applied for permits to demonstrate, and reached out to activists in other cities to launch cross-community protests in Washington, DC, and London. In addition to organizing these events through their preexisting networks, several started Facebook groups, such as the Yemen Revolution UK page, to disseminate news reports from Yemen and coordinate local actions. These efforts marked the first time that Yemenis in the diaspora launched anti-regime protests that were not about the South. Dr. Ibtisam al-Farah, a women's rights activist from Sheffield, recalled, "Positively, it was the first time that the community was brought together. It got new faces involved in the Yemen issues. [This] never would have happened without the revolution."

The defection of former regime allies after the Friday of Dignity Massacre in March presented a dilemma for Yemenis at home and abroad, however. The newfound allegiance of General Ali Mohsen and tribal elites to the revolution was especially problematic for southern separatists (*al-Hiraak*) because Mohsen had spearheaded violent attacks against them in recent years. Protesters in Aden also condemned the infiltration of their movement by pre-existing political parties, decrying the fact that "Islah began to dominate the protest venues and antagonised independents and protesters who sympathized with the Hiraak" (ICG 2011e: 11). Reports also circulated that Al-Islah supporters were attacking independent youth protesters in Aden. Southerners told the International Crisis Group (2011e: 12) that their counterparts in Sana'a were ignoring their grievances.

Ultimately, the chief obstacle to cooperation lay in the fact that, by April, Southerners feared the revolution would fail and that it had been compromised by opposition parties and regime insiders such as Ali Mohsen. . . . As it were, after his encounter with Northern protest leaders, a Southern representative remarked: "Youth in the North have the same mentality as the rulers." . . . Distrust and differences grew over time, and by late April the initial euphoria over coordination with the North had faded. Protesters throughout the South once again vocally called for separation.

When the revolution emerged, activists abroad who supported southern secession were split on how to respond. Some perceived the uprising as a natural extension of their anti-regime grievances, while others viewed it as a threat to their demands for autonomy. As a result, the Arab Spring produced heated debates within southern activist circles. Fathi, a journalist from London with origins in the South, described that some of his friends and colleagues felt they should wait and see what would happen, while others came out immediately for or against the revolution. Fathi himself decided to join the protests immediately, and urged other southerners to do the same.

Just as elites in Yemen had asked southern protesters to lay down the flag of secession and mute their calls for independence, so too did organizers in the diaspora try to convince southern Yemenis to join northerners in support of regime change. Nadia in Birmingham recalled negotiating with southern leaders over the phone to convince them to participate in the protests without carrying their flags because revolution was for *all* Yemenis. She urged them, "It's totally humanitarian. We will go to London just to show that our aim is to get [Saleh] down. It's not about north and south. If you want to split later, you can. It's not the time to talk about it [now]." Mazen O. of Washington, DC, reported doing the same and stated that early negotiations with southerners not to raise the South Yemen flag were successful.

There [was] a group from the southern *Hiraak* movement. They came and they were raising the southerners' flag. And then we had to, you know, communicate with them. We came to a common ground that this regime is killing everyone, whether they were northern or southern. So they have to come and raise the current Yemeni flag and join us with our effort. So we unified against the regime.

Some pro-unity organizers also promised not to raise the national Yemeni flag or chant slogans about unity in exchange for the southerners' support. These negotiations initially forged pro-revolution protest coalitions that converged in DC, New York, and London during the initial weeks of the uprising.

However, many southerners reported changing their views shortly thereafter, echoing claims by southerners in Yemen that northern military elites, Islahis, religious figures, and tribal elements in Yemen were working to subvert the southern people. Saleh of Sheffield recalled that the revolution lost its potential for meaningful change as soon as these elites sided with the uprising after the Friday of Dignity Massacre. He explained,

Momentum was gradual, and it was meaningful, and it was making progress. And then as soon as you got these [people like] Hamid al-Ahmar all of a sudden becoming revolutionaries, I thought, *it's the end*. What can we do? We need them, because they're powerful, in order to get rid of the regime. [But] it just distorted the whole momentum that was going on.

Understandably, Saleh and his colleagues in Sheffield found the slogans of "unity or death" proclaimed by Sana'a-based elites such as Hamid al-Ahmar and General Ali Mohsen to be both threatening and insulting. Fathi in London also recalled that rather than benefitting his homeland, "We realized that the fall of Saleh [would be] to the benefit of Hamid al-Ahmar and Ali Mohsen. They are as bad, if not worse, than Ali Abdullah Saleh in terms of [stolen] land acquisition" in the South. In the eyes of many southerners at home and abroad, northern defections had hopelessly compromised the uprising.

In addition to losing their faith in the revolution itself, many southern respondents also withdrew their support because they came to feel marginalized in pro-revolution protests abroad. Ali from Birmingham stated unequivocally that the revolution period presented another example of how northerners were speaking over southern voices and muting their demands in Britain. This claim was further substantiated, according to Ali, by the displaying of the Yemeni national flag at these protests, which for him and many others was a symbol of occupation. He recalled,

In 2011, we went to London to support the anti-Saleh demonstrations with our brothers and sisters from the North. We thought that this is going to bring change. When we went as one, we forgot [about] all the [different] parties. The main objective was one: to get rid of Ali Abdullah. Everyone forgot their own objective – the Houthi, the South. We had an agreement before we left that the banners should have only "get rid of Ali Abdullah," nothing about the South. But when we went there, we were shocked to see them lifting different banners. Even some of them were speaking [against] the idea that we agreed [upon]. I saw that people were trying to show themselves as a leader, they're trying for their own benefit. They had their own agendas. [So] the wool [was pulled] off our eyes. They were trying to fool us. Islah party jumped on the bandwagon of the revolution, the Islamic ideology, and took it over. They were taking advantage of this opportunity and not being fair.

Other southerners also found newcomers to the anti-regime movement to be untrustworthy partners. Fakhary, a southern youth activist in Sheffield, felt that because the pro-revolution protests were organized by many people who had "switched sides" from pro- to anti-regime over time, "how would you trust people like that?" he exclaimed. When meeting with a pro-revolution organizer who was trying to convince all Yemenis to come out and support them, Fakhary recalled,

I stood up and said, "hold on a minute. [Before], you were protesting *for* Saleh in London. Today, you're asking us to protest *against* Saleh! Why didn't you come with us in the previous protest? We'll come and protest with you, but on one condition: that you come and protest with *us* on the southern issue." And then after that, they faded.

Abdo Naqeeb of Sheffield, who had been an organizer on behalf of the South for many years, stated that both he and his colleague Dr. Mohammed al-Nomani initially supported the revolution and even connected with activists in Ta'iz to give a speech through Skype. He said, "We ask them to recognize our revolution in the South, to recognize our specific goals and aims. I am not against the public in the North, but against the mafia, the corrupt people." However, after the Islah party and Ali Mohsen sided with the uprising, he viewed the revolution as antithetical to the southern cause. When organizers in Sheffield approached him and fellow Southern Democratic Assembly (TAJ) members to join them, he refused.

I had a discussion with people who came to convince us to join them. I said, why didn't you recognize *our* marches [from before] February 2011? You didn't recognize our movement and our rights, our people's aims, what they experience and how they suffer! If you don't recognize that, how will we be together? They said you are calling to divide the country. We said that our differences are not only with Saleh *but also with you.*

In addition to being upset that purported opportunists were trying to "jump on the bandwagon" during the revolution, as Ali put it, southerners expressed how northerners were being callous by pushing aside their grievances. Ali lamented that after he tried to raise southern grievances on the Yemen Revolution UK Facebook page, he was lambasted for being partisan. "They said it's nothing to do with the South, that the main objective is the Yemeni revolution," he explained. "'Don't bring North and South into it.' *What do you mean, don't bring North and South into it?* They're neglecting the southern issue. It really *hurts.*" His Birmingham-based colleague Abdul Hamid agreed, adding, "They don't understand us. They don't feel our pain. I thought the revolution would change them a little bit, but it's the same." The dismissiveness with which some treated the southern issue at this time also led to renewed disagreements on- and offline. Adel of Sheffield described his disgust at the fact that pro-revolution Yemenis at home and abroad did not demonstrate goodwill by drawing up concrete plans to address the problems in the South. He argued,

They said this is a chance to get rid of Saleh and build a new Yemen when I'm still discriminated against, with no house, no job, a lot of people have been killed since the unity and since 2007. You want us to *forget* about that? Do you have a *solution* for these problems?

As Abdul Hamid told me, "Everyone is opposing us, even here, since 2007. When the revolution come, people join us. They say oh, there will be change. And then they hijacked the whole thing." Accordingly, as southern separatists in Yemen became disillusioned with the revolution, so too did secessionists in the United States and Britain.

On the other side, the demands of pro-secessionists to prioritize the southern issue offended activists who came to feel that the southerners were the ones trying to hijack the revolution for themselves. Yazan, a youth protester from Sheffield, was outraged that some southerners at the London protests "tried to push their agenda." He recalled,

We stopped them instantly. They were never going to be allowed to push their *agenda* in a protest about the revolution. No – don't be cheeky, put your flag down. [If] you want to protest that, protest it later. Right now, the South isn't suffering on its own. "The South's suffering, the South's suffering." We're *all* suffering right now, mate! We're all here for a common cause that involves the whole of Yemen, not just one bit. I was so upset, I was so angry. Because it was like some of them tried to hijack the entire thing. I was like, Yemen right now is at its most delicate. It's just so opportunistic and I really didn't appreciate that. But when you're in such a sensitive state and then you go and create more division, it ruins it for everybody.

Activists in the United States experienced the same tensions. Hanna, who had taken part in the pro-southern protests in New York before the revolution, said that when southern Yemenis came out for the revolution early on,

One of the great things we were able to do was also bring the South Yemen Association into the movement for Yemen as a whole. Bringing everyone together, fighting for one cause, fighting for democracy and human rights, was one of our major achievements early on. [But] a couple months afterward, when a lot of southern Yemenis just got really tired of the promises and a lot of that base started remobilizing [for the South] again, the huge solidarity that we had in the beginning was starting to break.

In addition, some protesters in the United States sported T-shirts with the slogans "New Yemen, United Forever" and the unity flag. Morooj from Washington, DC, reported that this made southerners feel "very marginalized." She continued,

And they *were* [marginalized], honestly. Because [organizers] were like, oh, that's not our messaging now. We're one. And so they stopped coming. They didn't feel like it was their space, and it was unfortunate. Because we all need to be united for the Yemeni people. That doesn't mean that we can't have our different opinions about what Yemen should look like or whatnot. So it was difficult to have the activists from the South participate. They did in the beginning, but they weren't respected.

While Morooj recalled that some southerners rejoined them for specific events later on, they did so while holding the southern independence flag and came to speak specifically about the southern issue. "I don't blame them," as Fouad from New York grimaced, since all that southern Yemenis have received in general "is a lot of talk – about nothing."

Overall, as in the case of pro-secession Kurds in the Syrian diaspora, Yemen's ethnic and regional divisions were exacerbated by the revolution at home. Southern grievances were perceived by pro-unity Yemenis as subversive to the broader cause, while pro-unity messaging came to be perceived by secessionists as corrupting and co-opting. As a result, the only public anti-regime movements in operation before the Arab Spring did not remain part of the broader nationalist cause for long.

4.2.5 Contestation over Preexisting Yemeni Groups and Organizations

As a result of fears of co-optation and the problem of regional Yemeni politics, no preexisting Yemeni organizations were converted to the revolutionary cause by their leaders (see Table 4.3). Instead, the organizers of functioning diaspora empowerment and social organizations discussed in Chapter 2, including the Yemeni Community Associations in Britain and the American Association of Yemeni Scientists and Professionals, worked to *insulate* their organizations from the effects of the revolution. Because YCA leaders considered home-country politics as toxic to the work of diaspora empowerment organizations, they reported making the strategic decision to enforce a no-politics rule during the revolution. Respondents argued that they were required to adhere to bylaws stipulating a nonpolitical mission and as necessary to maintain their organizations' legitimacy and service provision. As Saleh of the Sandwell YCA recalled,

Our response as a management committee, of which I'm a part, is that, look, this is a free country here, and we want a free country in Yemen. You go and do what you want as an individual, but not under the banner of the Yemeni Community Association. Because

TABLE 4.3. *Yemeni groups and organizations converted to the revolution and/or relief during the 2011 Arab Spring, as reported by respondents*

Diaspora Group/Organization	Converted to the Rebellion and/or Relief?
USA	
South Yemeni American Association	No
American Association of Yemeni Scientists and Professionals	No
Yemeni American Association of Bay Ridge	No
Britain	
TAJ – Southern Democratic Assembly	No
National Board of South Yemen	No
Yemen Forum Foundation	No
Yemeni Youth Association	No
Yemeni Community Association, Birmingham	No
Yemeni Community Association, Sandwell	No
Yemeni Community Association, Liverpool	No
Yemeni Community Association, Sheffield	No
Yemeni Migrant Workers Organisation	No
Yemen Refuge Organisation	No
Yemeni Education and Relief Organisation	No

[our] principles are no politics. When the revolution came about, politics reared its head within the community. And there were elements within the community that felt, for example, that, yes, we should be very pro-revolution and go out there and demonstrate. It was hard because it started fragmentation in the community. But *alhamdulillah* [thank God], [we were able to] enforce our decision. And of course, we should not be putting in barriers to stop them to do that. But we won't open up the center to facilitate that kind of activity because it puts the objectives of the organization at risk.

The YCAs of Birmingham and Sheffield reported adopting the same strategy in order to prevent their facilities from being used as a "political tool, either pro- or anti-revolution," as Nageeb of Birmingham stated. Mohammad al-Sahimi of Sheffield echoed this view, stating, "If [the association is] going to say that we support the revolution, we're also going to have to say that we support the *Hiraak* (the southern secessionist movement). Let's leave the Yemen Community Association as a voluntary organization, not involved in politics." Awssan's nascent organization, the Yemen Forum Foundation, was also left unconverted to the revolution because of the rules stipulated in its bylaws. This foundation became dormant as he and his colleagues went on to form a new group to support Yemen's uprising.

That said, the Yemeni Community Association in Liverpool, which was perceived by revolution supporters as dysfunctional, corrupt, and an arm of the regime (see Chapter 3), became itself the target of anti-regime diaspora mobilization. As members of the community held meetings to debate how to respond to the uprising in early 2011, some of the independent youth decided to take action to force a change to the YCA's leadership. As Kamal recalled, their youth movement "all wanted to do something *locally*. The idea was, let's oust the old regime from the community association – they're all supporters of Ali Abdullah Saleh anyway." His brother Omar attested, "The YCA is important to us because it has a distinct status in the sense that it's approved by the Ministry of Foreign Affairs in Yemen; it's approved by the embassy." Omar explained that their aim was to "change the direction of the organization democratically." To do so, organizers set out to register new members of the YCA in the hopes of voting out the incumbent leadership in an upcoming election. Another participant in this campaign named Bashir recalled that they recruited between seventy and eighty people in the community by having them fill out a YCA membership application and pay a three-pound fee. Their expectation was that with a surge of new members, the community would vote out longtime incumbents who had left the organization in "tatters," according to Abdul Basit, who had served as the YCA's secretary in 1997.

Despite their enthusiasm, however, their campaign was ultimately unsuccessful. Neshwan recalled that the YCA was only open one or two afternoons a week – an accusation that Abdul Alkanshali, head of the YCA in Liverpool, denied to me in a separate interview – which made it difficult to deliver the applications. Once election-drive volunteers found the YCA to be open and rushed to deliver the applications, Omar reported that trying to convince the association chair to accept the applications posed another obstacle. According to Neshwan, Alkanshali refused the applications by claiming that the YCA required each new applicant to present their paperwork in person. Alkanshali affirmed this response in an interview with me, accusing the group of violating the association's rules.

[They submitted] forged documents. First, they didn't use the proper documents from the YCA. They printed their own stuff. And then they went round getting signatures. The rules said that the person himself must come into the YCA, fill the application form, and none of that happened.

Neshwan recalled retorting that they would bring each new applicant to the YCA to do so, but that Alkanshali said, "'No, we can't accept you.' Why? '*Because you are coming here to overtake.*' That was explicit. *Overtake*. 'And we can't let you do this.'" Bashir said that in response to the YCA's refusal to accept the new applications, they launched a spontaneous protest. In the end, however, the campaign to reform the YCA failed, "And now it's still a problem," he said.

Since this campaign, Bashir explained that they decided to ignore the YCA because it was a failing organization that was "collapsing within itself." But despite the fact they failed to reclaim the YCA, respondents described this campaign with relish in light of the community's past ennui and passivity. Abdul Basit reported,

[The revolution] activated the *challenging nature* within us. Before, we were just like, accepting we [have a] dysfunctional community association. We [had] a dysfunctional *country* [i.e., Yemen] – and we just accepted it. What the revolution did is make that initial jumpstart for us all.

Kamal also explained how this campaign signaled to local elites and elders that the youth were not going to be so accepting of the status quo in the future.

We've reached that here [in] the diaspora itself *and* in Yemen – we've reached that point now where there is no going back to the old ways where you get elders who come and do nothing and talk rubbish, and then wreck the community like they've done.

The YCA in Liverpool represented a microcosm of Yemen's electoral authoritarianism to pro-revolution activists in the community. While their campaign failed to reform the organization by democratic means – in contrast to Fadel's experience reorganizing the Syrian British Medical Society in London – these efforts nevertheless demonstrate how Yemen's uprising created an impetus for change within the diaspora community itself by promoting new forms of civic engagement. That said, the YCAs and other organizations remained unconverted to the cause. In the United States and Britain, activists who worked to mobilize protests, community meetings, and other initiatives were therefore forced to do so without the backing or the resources of existing organizations and their members.

At the same time that many southerners came to boycott revolution events and protests, pro-unity activists also reported being threatened by the efforts of elites and elders to dominate their coalitions. Activists in Liverpool, for example, commented that this dynamic was pervasive from their very first community meeting about the revolution. Former regime allies dominated the discussion, which made the youth angry. "While they've got a voice in the community and a valid voice," Kamal of Liverpool explained, "they're not representative of all of the voices, and they were trying to be dictatorial in how they did it." As a result, the youth broke off to form their own independent group. But as Awssan of London recounted, "Even when protests were initiated successfully, the problem was people were put off because the actual youth leadership were pushed aside." He found it highly questionable that community leaders who used to be friendly with the Yemeni ambassador were now drowning out independent youth voices during demonstrations and in the media. These dynamics created a significant "division within only five hundred or three hundred or two hundred people who would come out." Awssan's colleague Anter agreed, stating that it was difficult for the participants to keep working together because they all had their "own agendas."

Rabyaah, a New York–based organizer, likewise lamented that certain figures within the pro-revolution movement tried to co-opt the protests.

We had some within our group who were more conservative, working for their own agenda – essentially for the Islah party. I had a big argument with one of the organizers. We wanted to keep it non-partisan. We're not going to say Islah – we're just an [independent] group, no Islah, no socialists. We're not going to associate ourselves with any party. [But] they wanted to bring their Islah banners. We were at a rally and I said, you had better bring that down right now. It doesn't represent us, it's not what we're here for. Here we are, already glorifying *Bayt al-Ahmar* [the Ahmar family] and this *hizb* [party]! Have we not learned *anything* from this revolution?

Dr. Ibtisam al-Farah of Sheffield also noted that the main reason that solidarity for the revolution started to break down was because certain figures were taking advantage of the situation. She found pro-Saleh individuals who were throwing their support behind the revolution in demonstrations to be highly suspicious. That said, other respondents mentioned Dr. Ibtisam as an example of a pro-regime infiltrator, signifying prevalent mistrust between supporters of regime change.

The lack of trust between participants in the protest movement was also apparent through respondents' personal stories of being slandered as pro-regime spoilers. Speaking of her activist colleague Ibrahim, Safa in London recalled, "You'd get idiots in Sheffield accusing Ibrahim, who are you to lead the movement? Who are you, the London people? And you think, bloody hell, who are *you*?" Mazen O. of Washington, DC, attributed this infighting to elders and elites wanting to do things the "Yemeni" way, rather than the

"Yemeni American" way. He lamented that "They want to control things. They want to be on top, in power. They want to have their names published in articles. And [lead in] the protest. For example, we did protests here. A lot of people, especially from Michigan – everyone wants to deliver a speech."

Because trust and solidarity were tenuous within the movement, many organizers paradoxically sought to support the revolution while distancing themselves from "politics." For this reason, respondents used broad rhetorical strategies to avoid accusations of being proxies for any particular political party or elite "agenda." When Safa joined the first youth meeting of activists in London, she found that the group was being extremely careful of who they included and were intentionally vague in their anti-regime claims and slogans. She recalled,

Not all of them wanted to have a political framework, which seemed odd to me. They just wanted to basically say that they're not happy with tyranny in Yemen anymore and they wanted to see radical change. The odd thing was that they wanted to see regime change, but I didn't feel that there was anything else [to their demands]. As an older person, who comes with experience, I needed to feel that I was with people who had a common vision. I think they misunderstood me by thinking, "Oh, she wants us to get *political*. She wants to direct us into this political minefield."

Eventually, Safa warmed up to this way of thinking because Ibrahim convinced her that having more specific political claims would "open a can of worms." Summer from New York also attested that she had to keep her discussions general in order to avoid appearing political and rousing North-versus-South sentiments. "I just talk[ed] about just the general," she said. "We want to kick Saleh out because we want a better life, we want education. So it was just a *general* type of talk."

In sum, the Yemeni movements that emerged in the United States and Britain in 2011 were primarily led by youth activists who had previously been involved in diaspora empowerment initiatives. After the Friday of Dignity Massacre, organizers attested that revolution sympathizers and some Saleh supporters came to side with the revolution and join their protests. Many who had mobilized on behalf of abuses in Yemen's southern region also joined in and acquiesced to the requests of organizers not to raise the South Yemen independence flag or secessionist slogans. However, after many southerners in Yemen came to feel betrayed and withdrew their support from the national revolution, so too did secession-supporting activists in the diaspora. Independent youth activists also observed attempts by elites to co-opt the diaspora movement, just as had happened in Sanaʻa. In response, organizers attempted to keep their calls for change "general" and their movements informal so as to be inclusive. Even so, as the Yemeni Spring turned into summer, pro-revolution movements in the diaspora experienced a heightened degree of conflict transmission that proved taxing to their efforts over time.

4.3 CONCLUSION

As the Arab Spring took the world by surprise and the region by storm in early 2011, the moment that many political exiles had been waiting for arrived. In the Libyan case, the sudden eruption of a nationwide revolt at home produced the quotidian disruptions necessary for activists abroad to back the revolution and justify armed resistance against the Gaddafi regime. These disruptions enabled fearful regime opponents and revolution sympathizers to overcome the deterrent effects of transnational repression and use their voices publicly on behalf of the uprising. As regime opponents were relatively united under the banner of revolution led by a singular cadre, this correspondingly unified the revolution-supporting diaspora around a common cause.

The emergence of the Syrian uprising, on the other hand, was far more piecemeal than in the Libyan case. As a result, the quotidian disruptions necessary for Syrians to overcome the deterrent effects of transnational repression occurred gradually over time. The revolution in Syria also succumbed to power struggles and infighting between groups. This dynamic was transmitted to the diaspora through a resurgence of conflict transmission. As a result, just as Syrians began to come out against the Assad regime as never before, so too did revolutionary movements fall victim to infighting over who should lead and represent the opposition. Suspicions over Muslim Brotherhood "agendas" at home and abroad were widespread, and Kurdish separatists withdrew their support after becoming marginalized within the Arab-dominant opposition. These dynamics exacerbated long-standing fault lines between ethnic and religious groups, as well as between older and younger generations, and factionalized the anti-regime diaspora.

Yemenis in the diaspora did not report the same degree of fear of the regime as their Libyan and Syrian counterparts. They came out against Saleh en masse after the Friday of Dignity Massacre because regime violence stoked a sense of outrage and urgency to use voice against the regime. Just as in the Syrian case, however, the opposition at home and abroad splintered along preexisting fault lines. Many southerners came to feel betrayed by what they perceived as northern co-optation of the movement, and independent activists also perceived that elite elements were working to co-opt the revolution on behalf of existing political parties and Islamist factions. As a result, the Yemeni revolution produced a heightened degree of both mobilization and factionalism in the diaspora, and as in the Syrian case, activists' efforts were plagued by mistrust, in-fighting, and frustration.

Nevertheless, while diaspora mobilization was far from a seamless process, the activist groups that emerged did far more than hold demonstrations in their free time or post headlines from their laptops. Beyond coming out and coming together to hold lawful demonstrations on the streets of London or

Washington, DC, respondents – whether divided or unified with their conationals – worked in a variety of ways to support the rebellions and facilitate relief efforts for the humanitarian crises that followed. The next section of this book explains these dynamics, comparing how and to what extent voice transcended their local communities and became a transnational force against authoritarianism at home.

5

Voice for Rebellion and Relief

As the Arab Spring revolutions escalated over the spring and summer of 2011, the Libyan regime battled NATO-backed insurgents in a fight to the death; the Syrian regime waged a scorched-earth campaign against rebelling cities as foreign extremists declared war on all sides; and regime loyalists attacked peaceful protesters and fought with defectors in Yemen. As each revolution became prolonged and increasingly bloody, these conflicts and ensuing humanitarian crises presented a unique opportunity for anti-regime diaspora activists to intervene in their home-countries. For newly invigorated anti-regime activists in the American and British diasporas, mobilizing for the Arab Spring did not simply involve protesting on the weekends or issuing Tweets during passing moments of distraction. Instead, they wielded voice against authoritarianism in order to fuel rebellion and relief using a common tactical repertoire, summarized in Table 5.1.

Activists' first type of intervention was to *broadcast* revolutionaries' grievances and demands through protests, online, and other awareness-raising efforts. Second, they *represented* the cause abroad by acting as formal delegates and informal proxies of revolutionary organizations to outside audiences, especially through lobbying. Third, they *brokered* between insiders at home and outsiders abroad to channel attention and resources to their allies. Fourth, they *remitted* tangible and intangible resources homeward to rebels and civilians under siege. Fifth, activists *volunteered* on the front lines as humanitarian relief workers, interpreters, citizen journalists, fighters, and leaders. Many of them combined overtly political activism with relief work, since the regimes blocked aid delivery to liberated areas. Others focused primarily on relief efforts due to their unique skills, as in the case of doctors who volunteered in field hospitals.

The first part of this chapter elaborates on this repertoire, demonstrating how activists worked creatively across a variety of venues to help their comrades. Because not all diaspora groups gained the capacity to fulfill their goals

TABLE 5.1. *Typology of diaspora interventions in the Arab Spring*

Broadcasting	Disseminating facts and claims for a shared cause through protest, online activism, and by holding awareness-raising events.
Representing	Serving as formal delegates or informal proxies for home-country causes and organizations to outside audiences and decision-makers, including through lobbying and in the policymaking process.
Brokering	The linking of previously unconnected actors and entities inside and outside of the home-country for the purposes of facilitating anti-regime mobilization and relief on the ground.
Remitting	The channeling of tangible and intangible resources to the home-country for the purposes of rebellion and relief.
Volunteering on the front lines	Traveling to the home-country and its border areas to participate directly in rebellion and relief efforts.

consistently over time, the second part explains how diaspora movements' collective repertoires varied (see Table 1.3). As I illustrate here, only Libyan movements in the United States and Britain were able to meet the needs of their compatriots and enact what I call a *full-spectrum repertoire* of interventions over the course of the revolution. Syrians and Yemenis, on the other hand, faced a number of challenges and obstacles in doing so. Chapters 6 and 7 then explain how this variation was determined primarily by two causal factors: the different capacities of diaspora movements to *convert resources* to the revolutions and relief efforts, and the varying degree of *geopolitical support* they received from states and other third parties. When resource conversion and geopolitical support were absent or died off over time, activists became disempowered to do much more than voice their solidarity and support from afar.

5.1 BROADCASTING

In the wake of the Egyptian revolution's ousting of President Hosni Mubarak on February 11, 2011, respondents across the three diasporas were both buzzing with anticipation and gravely concerned. While the protests in Cairo's Tahrir Square were broadcast live on Al Jazeera day and night, the only media allowed to operate in Libya and Syria in 2011 were state-controlled. Yemenis had more press freedoms, but their people had a long history of being neglected in the international media. Movements outside of the capital Sana'a were also prone to being ignored. Furthermore, internet penetration, particularly in Yemen, was spotty at best. As a result, observers in the diaspora worried that movements following in Egypt's footsteps would be crushed in the dark.

5.1.1 Disseminating Facts and Movement Claims

In light of these concerns, longtime regime opponents prepared themselves to remedy their compatriots' isolation and neglect on the world's stage. Brainstorming privately with family and friends, many reported setting up social media accounts dedicated to publicizing events underway at home. Libyans in Enough Gaddafi! (the US-based youth activist network founded in 2009) worked to relaunch their anti-Gaddafi information campaign days before the planned Day of Rage on February 17. Raucous protests erupted in Benghazi on February 15, however, and within days, rioters had liberated the city from regime control, prompting soldiers to defect or flee. As protests spread like wildfire from the east to the western capital of Tripoli, Gaddafi's stronghold, and confronted a media blackout, diaspora activists took up the task of broadcasting events on the ground via the Internet. Ahmed of Enough Gaddafi! explained, "We knew that in Libya there was no such thing as an independent media that could effectively report on what was taking place." He continued,

We understood our role in the beginning to be the media team. We needed to do whatever we can to make sure that the world knows about what's going on. We [planned] to essentially flood all media outlets with as much information as we possibly could to bridge the gap between [them and] the credible on-the-ground presence. So we thought of our role as being the bridge. We could report [through] our networks on the ground what was happening [until] the time when somebody from those Western or other media outlets could actually be on the ground reporting in the first person.

His colleague M. echoed, "Information is key. And whenever it's able to be disseminated, the situation becomes a global issue – no longer just something that happened in Libya that was wiped off the face of the planet." Abdullah attested that this "bridging" work was vital if "people on the inside were going to stand a chance." Libyans outside of the United States had the same idea. Ayat, a Libyan Canadian from Winnipeg, launched *Shabab Libya*, the Libya Youth Movement, with activists across the United States and Britain to broadcast on behalf of the revolution. "Obviously, we *had* to," she recounted,

because there was nobody [inside the country] who's going to put Libya on Al Jazeera for twenty-four hours and show us what's happening. We worked primarily in English. What we wanted to do was tell the world to help those people making decisions to make decisions in our favor.

To undertake broadcasting, Enough Gaddafi! activists established a "central place on the Internet to get news" about Libya, according to Hamid, by launching the website Feb17.info. Assia, one of their longtime friends who was living in Dubai at the time, recalled, "We were all around the world. We would run it in four-hour blocks to keep it twenty-four hours. Our houses were newsrooms." M., who was working with the Enough Gaddafi! team from her home in Pennsylvania at the time, recalled, "I remember the first week, there was no sleep. We literally overnight just became like a source of information for the outside world." Hamid also contacted activists in Cairo over social media who had done similar work during the Egyptian revolution for help in getting around Libya's internet blackout. His colleague, Abdulla Darrat, Abdulla's spouse and media professional Sarah Abdurrahman, and a Senior Researcher at the University of Toronto's Citizen Lab, John Scott Railton, build @feb17-voices (Railton 2012). This platform allowed Libyans to call a phone number and record their eyewitness accounts in English and Arabic, with translation provided by Abdulla and Sarah; Hamid also linked this information to Enough Gaddafi's website. According to Railton, after the media "showed up in Benghazi," they switched to broadcast from more isolated places such as Misrata and the Nafusa Mountains.

A youth named Haret worked simultaneously and independently from Birmingham, England, to set up a Twitter account and website called LibyaFeb17 to "translate and transcribe" all news coming out of Libya in Arabic to English. Haret said,

I wanted to make that media window for the international world to look at what's happening without any bias. I say the word bias loosely, because I was really focusing on the pro-revolution events. But without any additions from myself.

A handful of Libyan American women activists in the Washington, DC, area also formed a group called Libya Outreach that issued regular "situation reports" about the uprising and emailed them to government bureaus and think tanks.

Assia recalled that a key part of their work in the early days of the revolution "wasn't just spreading information but capturing misinformation and labeling it as misinformation." In doing so, activists worked to monitor and triangulate reports and counter rumors. Ayman in Oklahoma took it upon himself to post near-hourly updates about the situation on the ground on the website of the National Conference for the Libyan Opposition, "in Arabic – so targeting the Libyan people." By broadcasting information abroad and into the home-country, activists combatted regime propaganda. Tasbeeh of Los Angeles recalled, "It did feel like we were *transistor radios* because there was no one else to take up this mantle. We felt a responsibility to transmit those voices."

Like their Libyan counterparts, Syrians who dared to resist the Assad regime inside the country faced extreme risks for participating in pro-Arab Spring candlelight vigils and filming protests on their cell phones. In response, Syrians abroad broadcast information coming from the ground to global audiences in the hopes of gaining outside sympathy and support for the cause. Razan, daughter of an exiled Syrian dissident in London, worked directly with a network of activists on the ground on Twitter to do just that. Her responsibilities included

live-tweeting their protests, for example. I had a lot of contact with people on the ground. We had online meetings. Several would tell me, "I'm going out on protest now, please tweet it." That was probably the best work I ever did, being in contact with people on the ground, translating for them. [They produced] a magazine and I was also part of the translating team. The Arabic one was distributed inside Syria – a very dangerous business – and the English one was online.

In addition to criticizing the Assad regime by publicizing videos showing acts of defiance and state violence, activists also worked to name and shame entities who supported the dictatorship. Kenan, a Syrian American law student from Chicago, helped to launch an awareness project on Twitter called "The Syria Campaign."

It was a core group of seven or eight or so Twitter users who were Syrian, and we would come up with a hashtag and try to do whatever we could to get that hashtag to trend. We had a few really memorable ones. I remember we did a campaign in summer of 2011 against Shell Gas because they were still operating in Syria. So we got an audience in the media because the media was following [our] weekly Twitter campaigns, and we were able to deliver messages.

Respondents who participated in the Syrian uprising on the ground testified to the importance of this broadcasting work. Ibrahim al-Assil, a student in Britain at the time that the revolution broke out, returned to Damascus in the summer of 2011 to join protests and organize what became known as the Syrian Nonviolence Movement. He attested how Syrians abroad played a pivotal role in helping publicize their amateur videos of protests.

They were in the US, the UK, Qatar and the UAE and other countries as well. I used to ask for a lot of help from them, especially because they have faster [internet] connections. In Syria, we used a kind of VPN to be secure, which made the connection even slower. So for anything that needs to be done online, anyone outside Syria was very helpful – and also to get in touch with the media. So for example, when civil disobedience took place in Syria in December 2011, the majority of the work [publishing] documentation of it and getting in touch with the media was done *outside* Syria.

When Ibrahim was forced to return to Britain, he then took up this work himself, hoping that diaspora campaigns to name and shame the regime would prompt their host-country governments to intervene.

Syrians also held "teach-ins" and other awareness-raising events at universities and places of worship. Haytham, leader of the Rethink Rebuild Society in Manchester, held a tribute to a British doctor named Abbas Khan who worked as a medical volunteer in Syria before he was tortured to death in a regime prison in 2013 (Siddique and Borger 2013).

His two brothers came here, and [one] gave a very emotional speech. Three members of Parliament, the Greater Manchester Commissioner, and the mayor of Manchester were there also. It was a memorial for Dr. Abbas, but we also told the audience, look, he is just one example of tens of thousands killed in Syria and tortured. We called on the UK government to act on [behalf of those inside] Syrian prisons.

Meanwhile, as Yemen's revolution evolved into a series of prolonged and predominantly peaceful urban sit-ins across the country, Yemenis in the United States and Britain also worked to broadcast the claims of independent protesters to the public and the press. This was important because although freelance journalists and some Al Jazeera reporters managed to evade the regime's deportations of journalists in March, these brave individuals faced numerous obstacles to reporting on events outside of the main protest encampment in Sana'a. Yemenis initiated broadcasting work on social media, posting updates on forums such as the London-based Yemen Revolution UK's Facebook page. Ahlam, an activist in New York, worked with her colleague and friend Atiaf, a Yemeni American then working in Sanaʻa, to publish photographs of the protests on a website called Yemenis for Justice. Atiaf recalled that while she was in Change Square,

We would send Ahlam the photos, the information, and the idea was to have an interactive map of where the protests are, reports related to the revolution, things like that. A bunch of them [abroad] were also very active on Twitter, sending information. Specifically, I had given Ahlam my number, [telling her] "in case something happens, I will message you immediately so that you can tweet it." Once or twice she tweeted for me while I was at a protest; I texted her, international texts.

From her home in New York, Summer also received information from her relatives in Aden about events on the ground and published them on her blog. In light of the near absence of independent media outside of Sanaʻa, she recalled,

[Information was] hard to verify. If I'm hearing about shellings or things like that, I would call back home [to family in Aden] at the time and be like, did you hear this, did you hear that? Are there people in the hospital dying of sniper wounds? And then I'd confirm [through them].

Yemenis also broadcast information about the revolution by putting on photography-based events in Washington, DC, and San Francisco. Some also gave talks about their experiences, as when journalist-intern Abubakr talked about his experiences participating in Change Square at universities and think tanks in London. With these strategies, diaspora members enacted voice against the regime in new ways.

5.1.2 Holding Demonstrations and Protests

As discussed in Chapter 4, the breakdown of transnational deterrents to mobilization enabled Libyans and Syrians abroad to express their voices openly for the first time en masse and hold protests against the regimes. This form of broadcasting attempted to signal to the public, the media, and policymakers that regime atrocities warranted outside attention and support.

Libyan activists held several notable gatherings at the White House and outside the Libyan consulate in Washington, DC. Residents of Manchester and London also demonstrated outside the BBC building and the Libyan embassy regularly. Syrians held demonstrations outside the Syrian embassy (before its closure by the Obama administration), on the Washington, DC, National Mall, and in other city centers. As a participant-observer of these protests in Southern California, I spent Saturday afternoons driving from my home to places such as the shopping district of Costa Mesa, the Little Arabia section of Anaheim, and the Chinese Embassy, the Federal Building, and City Hall in Los Angeles to attend demonstrations for the Syrian revolution. Whereas we usually chanted slogans and sang songs in Arabic, I was sometimes asked by participants to write placards in English. Others had pre-printed posters that were carted by organizers from one event to the next bearing slogans such as "Save Syrian Children" and "Shame on CNN" for its perceived neglect of the crisis. Organizers aimed to broadcast these events into Syria in order to lend moral support to their allies. As Firas recalled, "We chanted in Arabic. We feel we have to do the same as Syria. We know everything is getting recorded, so it will reach over there." A. A. in Michigan also recalled,

The most important thing that really moved us to do some demonstrations here is for us to take videos of us demonstrating and to send it to our people in Syria to encourage them that you have people supporting you from outside of Syria – to say that we are all in this together, [to provide] emotional support. When I echoed the same chants that I used to hear from videos on YouTube of people back home in Syria, it gave me the feeling that I'm there, I'm actually part of this whole thing. This was, we would say, the happiest days of the revolution.

FIGURE 5.1. Syrians and their allies gather in Costa Mesa, California, during a "Global Walk for Syria" on November 17, 2012. This event, co-sponsored by the Syrian American Council and the Karam Foundation, raised proceeds for internally displaced children in Atmeh, Syria.
(Photo credit: Dana M. Moss)

Syrians in the United States also counter-demonstrated against pro-regime events hosted by home-country elites, loyalists, and pro-regime spokespersons. Firas, who was then a member of the Southern California Coordinating Committee for protests and fundraising, recalled that events held by pro-regime groups, often referred to as *al-Shabiha*, bring us all together. In front of the Federal Building, it was like hundreds of people against the *Shabiha*. And in front of the hotel where Bashar Jaafari[1] came, all organizations decided that we're going to go over there. The enemy was bringing us together, unifying us.

Hussam of SAC attested that it was easier to bring people to protest against a specific pro-regime target "because you're channeling anger at the regime," rather than in an "open-ended" way to the public at large.

FIGURE 5.2. Anti-Assad posters adorned poles around the Federal Building in Los Angeles in 2012. This was a common site of protest for pro- and anti-Assad diaspora members to face off against one another from different sides of the intersection at Wilshire and Veteran avenues. The small print of the poster reads, "He killed 15,000+ in 15 months!" (Photo credit: Dana M. Moss)

---

[1] Bashar Jaafari was the permanent representative of the Syrian Arab Republic under the Assad regime to the United Nations in New York from 2006 until 2020.

Activists also lobbied locally against individuals affiliated with the regime to pressure them to resign and to shame their affiliated sponsors and organizations. For example, Syrian American students and local activists launched a campaign against Dr. Hazem Chehabi, the Syrian Consul General in Newport Beach, California, and president of the University of California Irvine Foundation. They organized these events in conjunction with other student groups at UCI to pressure Chehabi to resign from his post. As I observed firsthand, our silent demonstration during a UCI Foundation fundraiser caused a significant disturbance in the proceedings as guests in their black-tie attire gawked and pointed at us from the red carpet.[2]

Other Syrians got creative in their broadcasting work after weekly and monthly protests died down in 2014. Lina Sergie of Chicago launched the One Hundred Thousand Names Project to communicate the extreme costs of regime repression during the third anniversary of the revolution. Partnering with activists in SAC, she recounted,

I saw this video online that had a graphic visualization of different facts about the Syrian revolution. One of the facts in that video says, if you were to read one hundred thousand names of the people who have died in Syria so far, it would take you seventy-two hours. So I emailed [my colleagues] and I told them, let's read the names of the dead for March 15 [2014 anniversary] in front of the White House for seventy-two hours. We got tons of media. We repeated this again in June in front of the UN. It was a global reading. And in several cities, including inside Syria, the hundred thousand names were read in twenty-four hours during the "election" of Bashar al-Assad, the reelection. We did it again in August 2014 in front of the White House where we read fourteen hundred names [of the chemical weapons' attack victims from August 2013]. There are two components of the memorial: the Oral Memorial for Syria, the actual reading of the names. Also, the book of names. We printed out fifteen copies. We hand delivered them to the fifteen ambassadors of the UN Security Council in coordination with the Syrian National Coalition. Not everybody accepted the book, but we tried to take it to everybody. [US Ambassador to the UN] Samantha Power still has the book, according to Qusai Zakarya,[3] on her desk.

Yemenis also staged regular demonstrations. Activists in the United States gathered regularly in front of the Yemeni embassy and White House, the United Nations in New York, and in their local communities in Dearborn and San Francisco. As a New York–based organizer named Rabyaah recalled, "We were like, as long as there are people on the streets every day in Yemen, for

---

[2] Chehabi later resigned from his post as Consular General after the United States and other governments, including the Cameron administration in Britain, expelled diplomats in response to the Houla Massacre of May 2012. During this terrible event, more than one hundred civilians, including families with their children, were slaughtered at close range by regime forces.

[3] Qusai Zakarya is the nom de guerre of Kassim Eid, a Palestinian Syrian activist from the Damascus suburbs of Mouadamiya, Syria. He gained international attention with the help of diaspora activists during his hunger strike against regime violence from his home. He was gassed during the August 21, 2013 chemical weapons attack by the regime; he eventually escaped Syria as a refugee. See Eid (2017) and Eid and di Giovanni (2018) for his personal account of these trials.

us, the only practical way to support is at least once a week we have to hold some sort of rally or town hall meeting." Participants traveled on charter buses from cities such as Dearborn and New York to converge on Washington, DC, for mass rallies on several occasions, including the weekend following the Friday of Dignity Massacre in March. Likewise, respondents in Britain organized weekly protests in London, busing in hundreds of participants from cities such as Liverpool and Birmingham. They also demonstrated outside the Yemeni embassy and in front of 10 Downing Street and the US embassy to protest US and Britain's financial support of the Saleh regime. Occasionally, Yemeni diaspora events were coordinated across countries. Mazen O. from the DC area recalled that their group held demonstrations with Yemenis in Germany on one occasion. Activists from Britain also used Skype to share their experiences with their US counterparts during a town hall event in Dearborn, Michigan.

Yemeni activists worked proactively to draw media in advance of these events. Mahmoud of Sheffield attested, "We knew journalists, we had a good list of journalists from all channels, from the BBC to Al Jazeera to Al-Hiwar. And we informed them in advance that we are moving and we make our point clear and publicize it." After sending press releases to different channels, respondents such as Safa in London reported garnering BBC, Al Jazeera, Press TV (an Iranian international satellite channel), and Al-Hiwar coverage (a London-based satellite channel). Abubakr in London stated that they worked to gain the sympathy of bystanders as well, recalling that the conversations they initiated with passersby "felt good" because "it wasn't just about shouting Arabic chants. It felt like we were actually doing something" to educate the public about the cause. Morooj of the DC-based movement also made short films of their protests and posted the videos on YouTube "to try and get the word out there." Ahmed of San Francisco emphasized the importance of this broadcasting work for their compatriots and in the political arena.

It's a small thing, but we used to contact people from there, from Change Square in Sana'a. And those small things for them were big. First of all, they see that their families outside Yemen, they're supportive of whatever they're doing there. They know that they're not alone in this struggle. Second, the regime used to say that those people who are protesting there in Yemen, they're just odd voices there, trying to make the international community think there is nothing there in Yemen. We wanted to show that, no, it's *not* just people who are there. Even Yemenis who are *outside* Yemen are protesting. Yemeni people deserve to live freely just as the American citizens do. There was a lot of aid going to the Yemeni government which was used to kill the Yemeni people. We wanted that to be stopped, too.

Arwa in London also described the importance of demonstrating their support to Yemenis back home by sending them videos of their protest events: "The most way we were connected to the Yemenis there, after we made the videos of the demos, we made sure that the Yemenis know that we are with them and that we are making *their voices heard*." In these ways, the literal voicing of revolutionary chants, slogans, and demands in the diaspora diffused the revolution abroad.

5.2 REPRESENTING

While the broadcasting of facts and claims online, in the streets, and in public forums was a key component of diaspora mobilization for the Arab Spring, activists sought to do much more than act as "transistor radios" for the revolution. They also worked to *represent* the revolution directly by lobbying for outsiders to take action, joining revolutionary groups and leadership cadres, and acting as spokespersons for the cause in the media.

5.2.1 Lobbying outside Powers

Libyans served as representatives first by lobbying their host-country governments for limited military intervention. They did so because even though Libya's military members began defecting en masse immediately during the uprising, loyalist brigades buttressed by mercenaries from neighboring countries began to retake towns one by one and moved to launch a major offensive against Benghazi in February using airpower and tanks (Bassiouni 2013). In the view of revolution supporters abroad, these threats warranted militarized counter-measures to save lives. Second, Libyans in the diaspora echoed calls from Libyans on the ground for protection and support in the fight against Gaddafi. Third, diaspora members viewed limited military intervention in the form of no-fly zones as distinct from Western interventions undertaken in Afghanistan and Iraq; no one wanted a ground occupation, they emphasized to me repeatedly. At the same time, stopping Gaddafi from obliterating entire liberated zones (as Assad has done since) was mandated, in their view, by the UN's Responsibility to Protect doctrine and international law.[4]

To that end, Libyan representatives on both sides of the Atlantic advocated for a no-fly zone using congruent framing strategies, arguing that intervention was in their governments' economic and security interests. They also contended that democratic Western powers had a moral responsibility to intervene and prevent a massacre in Benghazi. Mazen R. from Seattle, who lobbied his US congressional representatives before joining the National Transitional Council (NTC) himself, explained that in order to get anti-war Democrats on board, "You had to shape it or frame it in an American way. Explain Gaddafi, how horrible he is and that he's *killing* people. This is the humane thing to do. And explain that it's not going to cost the US lives as well." To that end, the Libyan Emergency Task Force in Washington, DC, worked with the report-issuing group Libya Outreach and other activists to lobby officials. Parallel efforts were established in Britain by longtime dissidents like Mahmud, who had been shot in the leg protesting against Gaddafi

---

[4] See my earlier work (Moss 2016a, 2017) for a more detailed analysis of Libyan and Syrian demands for limited military intervention from the West. These works explain why activists viewed outside military intervention pragmatically as the best bad option available and necessary to save lives in the short term according to the Responsibility to Protect doctrine (see also Nahlawi 2019). According to testimonials, missives, communiqués, and their personal relations with activists on the ground, such as Raed Fares of Kafranbel, Syria, respondents also argued that it was what Syrians and Libyans themselves were calling for from the front lines.

in 1984, a group of young professionals who organized themselves at the onset of the uprising to form the Libyan British Relations Council. Dr. Abdul Malek of Libya Watch in Manchester also met with various European governments to convince them to recognize the NTC, Libya's government-in-waiting, as the legitimate representative of the home-country.

Even after winning support, which I discuss at length in Chapter 7, A. R. of the Libyan British Relations Council recalled the strategic importance of wielding voice through lobbying over time:

Before [the intervention], people had no idea what was going on. After, Parliament wanted to make sure that they were fighting a good fight, and we knew that NATO's involvement was vital. So the main purpose was to keep them *committed* to the fight at the same level of operations and not to feel under political pressure to withdraw. The other purpose was that we wanted to be an alternative face of Libya. Because you had the diaspora here, educated people, speaking the language of the country they live in. The only thing that was known about Libya was created in Gaddafi's image, and we wanted to show people that, no, Libyans are a well-educated people who can *speak*.

Lobbying efforts were also initiated by exiled Syrians who were already public in their anti-regime sentiments prior to the Arab Spring, such as Marah Bukai and Dr. Radwan Ziadeh in the United States. After newcomers to activism began to organize and come out publicly for regime change for the first time, these efforts expanded and grew to be represented by such organizations as the Syrian American Council, the DC-based Syrian Emergency Task Force, and the group British Solidarity for Syria by the end of 2011. Dr. Ziadeh and Marah reported that their earliest meetings with US Secretary of State Hillary Clinton were productive. They presented several requests, according to Ziadeh.

The first meeting we had was with Secretary Clinton at the State Department. This was in June 2011, before any of the opposition organizations had been established. At that time, actually, the meeting was very good. We requested from Secretary Clinton four things: for President Obama to ask Bashar al-Assad to step aside, which he did not do until August; to increase the sanctions on oil companies; then to work with the UN Security Council to [pass a] resolution condemning the violence in Syria; and to work on the sanctions against people in the Syrian government, ban them from traveling, stop giving them visas. Secretary Clinton, at that time, took things very seriously. My focus at that time was to get any kind of international support. Because we know what's happened before in Syria in the '80s when there was no reaction from the international community. My focus at the time was to get a special session on Syria with the UN Human Rights Council in Geneva. We had many meetings at the State Department to convince them to request special meetings. That was in April 2011.[5]

After the regime escalated its violent response over the course of 2011, many activists also came to advocate for the implementation of a no-fly zone to stop the regime from bombing liberated and civilian areas. Activists argued that this was both necessary and obligatory under the principles of the Responsibility to

[5] The UN Human Rights Council held a special session on the "Situation of Human Rights in the Syrian Arab Republic" on April 29, 2011.

Protect doctrine, a global agreement reached by UN member states in 2005. As Y. of Manchester, an activist and scholar of international law, argued,

The idea behind this principle is that where there's a mass atrocity situation as in Syria, the international community has a responsibility to step in if the government is failing to protect its people. You can find a lot of differences between Syria and Libya that would make intervention less favorable in Syria. Okay, fine. That doesn't mean that the international community no longer has a responsibility.

By the end of 2013, however, it became clear to activists in the United States and Britain that their governments were not going to intervene decisively against Assad by enforcing a no-fly zone or by launching punitive strikes against his use of chemical weapons. Nevertheless, they continued to lobby for more effective assistance to vetted units in the Free Syrian Army, to request funding for civil-society-building initiatives in Syria, and for expanded humanitarian aid. Syrians attested that their lobbying work also included arguments about how regime violence enabled the spread of extremists like Ahrar al-Sham and the Islamic State (ISIS, referred to by President Obama as ISIL). As Hussam, national chairman of the Syrian American Council, recalled,

Early on, I will say until [2013], we focused on pressuring and convincing the Obama administration to arm and train the Free Syrian Army. The argument is that unless we do so, Assad will continue to engage in murder, shootings, sending barrel bombs, missiles on people. And as the regime weakens, that vacuum would be filled by extremist groups such as ISIS. So there's a threat in allowing for the FSA to be weak. As of 2014, we're focusing on reminding the Obama administration that as they're engaged in defeating ISIS, there is no solution to the threat of ISIS *without* the elimination of the Assad regime and the establishment of a strong, democratic Syria. Otherwise, the conflict with ISIS will go on indefinitely – and Assad is actually benefitting from this targeting of ISIS. Our argument is that ISIS is a result of Assad's oppression and a result of the vacuum created through repression by Assad's regime. So that is our main focus. Other areas include pressuring the administration to increase their foreign humanitarian aid to Syrian refugees around the world.

Abdulaziz likewise attested that members of Britain's Syria Parliamentary Affairs Group, which was formed in late 2013, did the same.

We are trying to do our best to show, look, what's going on in Syria is mainly caused by Assad, and that the extremism is because of the lack of action from the international community. I mean, if you look at ISIS, they just appeared about fourteen months ago. And the Syrian revolution has been going on more than three years and a half. If the international community, the UN Security Council, [upheld] their responsibility, we wouldn't have reached the point where we have this extremism.

Around the time that some politicos in Washington, DC, and Britain were suggesting that their governments partner with the Assad regime against ISIS, the DC-based Syrian Emergency Task Force helped to launch a major campaign to pressure foreign governments into rejecting this option. This effort, referred to by Mouaz as the "Caesar file," publicized the testimonials and evidence of a regime defector who had photographed thousands of deceased detainees murdered by torture and starvation in regime prisons. The task force brought Caesar to testify at hearings in Congress (much to the consternation, he added, of certain US officials who did not want these atrocities to be exposed) in order to pressure the US government not to ally with the regime.[6]

The Caesar file is unprecedented in that it's something that can start tying the noose around Assad's head – not for the legal process, which is important for accountability and justice. But more important for me is how we can use that politically to prevent any thought of [the US government] working with the regime. It would just be embarrassing for President [Obama] – impossible – if he knew everything [in the Caesar file] and still worked with Assad.

FIGURE 5.3. Mouaz Mustafa, head of the Syrian Emergency Task Force (left), speaks with unnamed Syrian regime defector "Caesar" (right) while waiting to brief the House Committee on Foreign Affairs in Washington, DC on July 31, 2014. Caesar smuggled fifty-five thousand photographs out of Syria that document the torture and killing of more than ten thousand detainees by the Assad regime. Some photographs depicting the corpses of starved prisoners have been enlarged and are displayed behind Chairman Ed Royce. Mouaz has worked as Caesar's partner and broker across a range of venues to publicize these atrocities, including in Congress and the Holocaust Museum in Washington, DC.
(Photo by Erkan Avci/Anadolu Agency/Getty Images)

---

[6] As articles by Simon and Bolduan (2019) and Kossaify (2020) explain, Caesar's defection and testimonies in front of Congress, which displayed photographic evidence from more than fifty thousand images of Syrians who had been starved and tortured to death in regime prisons, was shepherded by Mouaz Moustafa of the Syrian Emergency Task Force. This broadcasting work

The task force also established a partnership with the Holocaust Museum in DC, which publicized the Caesar photographs and hosted events featuring prominent members of Congress, Syrian prisoners-turned-refugees, and Holocaust survivors.[7] Activists like Ayman Abdel Nour of Syrian Christians for Democracy (later changed to Syrian Christians for Peace) also worked to combat regime propaganda that Assad protected minorities by informing "the West and the leaders that the Christians are not as the regime is trying to portray." This was especially notable due to the regime's long-standing and utterly false declarations that Assad is the protector of Christians and minorities in Syria.[8]

Yemeni respondents served as representatives of the revolution by meeting on several occasions with a range of officials in the US and British governments to express their grievances and lobby on behalf of their demands. These included asking their host-country governments to voice stronger support for the revolution, to pressure Saleh into halting attacks on protesters and to resign, and to cut financial backing of the regime. As Faris, spokesman for the DC-based Yemeni Youth Abroad for Change, recalled,

> The only thing we really wanted to do for [the revolution] was to vocalize, or at least show support, or put some type of pressure on the Yemeni government to try to stop the killing and the oppression that was occurring at that time. So we wanted to put pressure [on the US government] to put boundaries on the violence that was taking place.

To this end, organizers from a cross-community delegation met with officials in the White House, the State Department, the National Security Council, and various congressional representatives to put forward these demands. London-based activists calling themselves the Yemen Revolution Support Group also delivered written demands to the Prime Minister's office and to the Home Secretary, members of Parliament (MPs), Foreign Secretary William Hague, the Department for International Development, and the Saudi embassy "to say that you need to be more serious about what's happening in Yemen," according to Haidar in Birmingham. Safa, who was responsible for writing for this group, attested that she worked up draft template letters for community members to send their MPs and petitioned the Department for International Development (DFID) for emergency humanitarian aid.

---

was eventually used as the basis of bipartisan legislation sanctioning the Syrian regime and individuals and entities for working with Assad. The Caesar Syria Civilian Protection Act, which Moustafa helped to draft, was in the works when I spoke with him in 2014, but it only gained bipartisan support after Obama's second term in office. President Donald Trump signed it into law in late 2019 and it became effective in June 2020.

[7] The Washington, DC-based Holocaust Museum has featured a number of exhibits on mass killings in Syria, the first of which featured photographs from regime-defector Caesar and was coordinated in conjunction with the Syrian Emergency Task Force (O'Grady 2014).

[8] Members of Syrian Christians for Peace and SAC penned a compelling opinion-editorial for *The Hill* refuting this myth. See Yamin et al. (2017).

5.2.2 Joining Revolutionary Groups and Cadres

Activists also represented the revolution by serving as delegates for the various arms of the Libyan and Syrian opposition in an official capacity. For Libyans from the diaspora, much of this work took place while volunteering in the Gulf region or within Libya itself. After the regime severed communications between Benghazi and Tripoli, a number of respondents were recruited by newly appointed NTC information minister Mahmoud Shamman to launch a pro-revolution satellite station. Broadcasting in Arabic out of Doha, the station was dubbed Libya AlAhrar. Shamman designed this station as an alternative to Libya's state-run channel and to promote the revolution in coordination with the NTC. Shahrazad, who had traveled to Washington, DC, during the first week of the revolution to participate in protests and lobbying, was one of the many diaspora members who helped to run the station in Qatar. She explained,

Our TV station became the focal place for people to look for information. We were trying to connect with the east and the west because Gaddafi controlled the west side of Libya at that time. I had a program called *Libya al-Naas*, Libya The People, targeted to Libyans. My show was in the Libyan dialect [because] I was trying to get in touch with the common Libyan person and bring people together. Gaddafi at that time was trying to divide the people and say that the west is doing this and the east is trying to confuse you, the east is this and the east did that. So every night, I showed a map of Libya with the green flag on it and the new flag closing in on the green to show people visually how things are liberating and progressing in the different parts. Because they would not get the news [otherwise].

Syrians too came to represent their revolution as long-distance members of Local Coordination Committees (LCC), an anti-violence activist network based in Syria. Others joined the Syrian National Council, formed in August 2011 in Istanbul to represent the revolution to the international community, before it was subsumed by the Syrian National Coalition the following year. Playing a role as representatives was critical, recalled Marah in Virginia, because, "We have the opportunity to go on TV, to communicate with the international community and to deliver their message." Mohammad al-Abdallah, a civil society activist who came to the United States in 2009 as a political refugee and headed the Syria Justice and Accountability Centre as of 2014, recalled,

I started working with a group of activists trying to organize activities on the ground. After the Local Coordination Committees emerged, I became one of their spokespersons for six months, from almost April to October in 2011, to communicate some of the demands of Syrians to the [US] government. I *had* to do it, because there was a vacuum. After that, I joined the Syrian National Council when it started.

Rafif Jouejati, founder of FREE-Syria, a humanitarian organization and think tank in Washington, DC, also came to translate and speak for the Local Coordination Committees.

I responded to a Facebook post that was asking for someone to translate some news of what was happening on the ground, and I responded; they invited me to join the translation team. This was back before every news bureau had a correspondent either on the ground or near Syria. When the LCC spokesperson left to do other things, they asked me to take on that job, so I did. [In addition] to posting on YouTube and Facebook, we developed an impressive media list. There was an email service that went out, and the daily summary of the death toll, the destruction. We posted everything to the LCC's Facebook page where we uploaded videos. Anybody who wanted to receive the news had access. Our goal was to make sure that the average reader or listener had access to information about what was happening on the ground. It was very important to us – and it still is – that events in Syria don't go unnoticed.

Activists likewise served as informal representatives in the media by holding press conferences, giving interviews, and helping the revolution with its public relations. Malik, co-founder of the Syrian Justice and Development Party, recalled being catapulted into the position of unofficial spokesperson for the revolution from London.

After the protests [first] happened, [a journalist] called me straight away and got me an interview on Sky News, and that was the start of probably hundreds of interviews. I'm not exaggerating. Everyone from BBC World, BBC News, ITN, Channel 4 News, CNN, you name it, all wanted someone who speaks English and who can put some context. So I was kind of like a de facto spokesman for the opposition even though I never had any kind of official role.

Similarly, Haytham represented the anti-regime cause from Manchester by giving the media information and testifying about his experiences as a former political prisoner.

We addressed the media [by] responding to their requests. When they needed somebody to talk about refugees, to talk about the peace conference in Geneva, they call us. We are one of the resources to talk about the Syrian cause. Second, we advocate the Syrian cause doing work with ordinary people. We go to places like mosques, churches, universities. About twenty times we have given a talk called "Voices from Syria." The first [part] is about the situation in Syria, the political situation before the revolution, why the revolution happened, what was the response of the regime. I [also] give my personal story – why they imprisoned me, what happened to me in prison.

A. A., a youth from Michigan, worked as a volunteer for the Shaam News Network, which was founded by Bilal Attar (Conduit 2019) to act as a global network of citizen journalists and volunteers dedicated to promoting international publicity.

We were contacting [American] news channels urging them to cover demonstrations back home in Syria. All of this was done under the Syrian American Council. A couple of months later, through some connections of Syrian friends here [in Michigan], I started working with Shaam News Network, which is a news channel run [from Syria] using social media websites. It's one of the sources that the media here in the US and international media used to start covering what's happening in Syria. The media used a lot of the materials that

Shaam News Network would provide on their Facebook page and YouTube channels. My involvement was to moderate their English channel on Facebook and translate the Arabic news into English news, and post all of this on Facebook.

Yemeni respondents also served as representatives of the revolution in the media when invited to do so. Mazen O. of Washington, DC, recalled that "because we're basically the voice of the peaceful protesters here in the US [in] the local media, to the American public," the Yemeni Youth Abroad for Change group appointed a spokesperson, an activist named Faris, to speak on networks such as Al Jazeera and MSNBC. He explained that their roles were to transmit the general grievances and claims of anti-regime youth, who were consciously leaderless and anti-hierarchical. As Ahlam of New York attested, "What we were doing – or what we thought we were doing – was amplifying the voices of the people in Yemen. Simply amplifying." However, unlike the Libyan and Syrian cases, no Yemeni activists in the United States or Britain reported acting as deputized representatives of any revolutionary groups in Yemen.

5.3 BROKERING

Activists worked as brokers – intermediaries who linked together previously unconnected entities – for the purposes of channeling attention and resources to the Arab Spring. They did so in two main ways: (1) by connecting revolutionaries and aid workers on the ground with geopolitical actors such as host-country policymakers, journalists, NGOs, and international agencies, and (2) by connecting rebels at home with one another. Libyans and Syrians reported engaging in both sets of actions; for Yemenis, rare instances of brokering involved connecting outside journalists with Yemenis in the sit-in movement in Sana'a.

5.3.1 Brokering between Revolutionaries and Geopolitical Actors

Activists worked as *brokers* for their compatriots – what Tasbeeh, a Libyan American, called "remote fixers" – to connect them with journalists for major networks, governments, and donors. Heba, for instance, put a cousin and a friend living in Benghazi in touch with CNN and Al Jazeera for interviews since they were "not afraid to talk" and could communicate in English. Likewise, Ahmed of Enough Gaddafi! contacted a Libyan American named Rahma, then living in regime-controlled Tripoli with her family, over Facebook, and (with her permission) introduced her to a news organization. This single connection, they attested, snowballed into regular calls from NPR, the BBC, Al Jazeera English, and the *Los Angeles Times*.[9] This kind of brokerage enabled Libyans

---

[9] Eventually Rahma and Ahmed were married. This echoed many stories I heard during my fieldwork of how the Libyan revolution had forged new ties between conationals who were previously estranged from one another because of Gaddafi's repression.

to "speak for themselves," Abdullah of Enough Gaddafi! affirmed. Farah from London similarly emphasized that while diaspora voices were important, they were not the most important voices. "*I* did *not* want to be the voice of the revolution in Libya," she exclaimed. "That was really important to me." To that end, brokerage enabled revolutionaries and relief workers on the ground to speak to the outside world directly.

Ayat additionally attested that an important part of brokerage included vetting her contacts to cultivate trust with journalists and prevent the spread of misinformation. "People I was talking to [in Libya] just kind of assumed that I was a journalist," she mused. "And I said, no, I'm the middleman here, I just basically have to vet you." Amna from Manchester reflected that some of her relatives in Libya "were surprised at how much we actually knew. I don't think they realized that a lot of the information that was in the media was actually [from] the Libyans who were abroad, getting the information from Libya, and sending it across." The preexistence and expansion of activists' transnational network ties, as I detail further in Chapter 6, proved vital for brokering work.

Syrians reported that connecting insiders with outsiders was important for overcoming a deficit in outside awareness about how bad the situation had become in besieged areas. Writer-activist and Karam Foundation founder Lina Sergie reported that in the early days of the uprising,

We really were in the mindset that "the media doesn't know what's going on, nobody knows the truth. If only they knew more, then there would be a change." We felt it was our duty to tell people what was going on, circulate the videos, and connect the media to different people like doctors and activists and fighters on the ground. I got connected with people in Homs, during the Baba Amr siege [in February 2012]. That was the moment when journalists were looking for people on the ground constantly; I would connect journalists and the media to the activists all the time.

Haytham in Manchester likewise attested that this work was vital in empowering Syrians to speak for themselves whenever possible. "When the media called me," he explained, "I said, okay, you want somebody from Homs? I will bring somebody from Homs. It's not *me* who gives the information [about Homs]. It's about *linking*."

Maher Nana, a Miami-based doctor and co-founder of the Syrian Support Group, further reported that brokerage was predicated on facilitating trust and understanding between insider and outsider political forces.

We were actually bringing and introducing people, officers from the Free Syrian Army, to the US government and helped with vetting them. I mean, the most important thing that we did really was making the connection. So our role mainly was two things. Number one, to present the US side to the Free Syrian Army and let them know the United States stands for freedom, liberty, democracy, equality. We were raised [in Syria] on conspiracy theories – on the belief that the United States and Israel are evil, the sources of all the problems in the world. So when the Free Syrian Army was formed, we really wanted to let those guys know that this is not true. They were hopeful that the United States was going to provide support. We wanted to assure them that we live here, we are American citizens, we know how the system works, we know what the United States stands for, and all of those myths are incorrect. So we were trying to present the US side of the equation. At the same time, we wanted to connect those FSA members to the United States administration and tell them that those guys are really freedom fighters, they really have a cause, and they are fighting for that cause. They are not warlords, they are not gangsters. We helped in making that connection, basically.

FIGURE 5.4. Syrian peace activist Kassem Eid presents a talk about the Assad regime's siege on his hometown of Moadamiya, Syria, with organizers from the Syrian American Council (April 25, 2014, the University of Southern California). He had met with US Ambassador to the UN Samantha Power on April 14 to testify about the regime's sarin gas attack on August 21, 2013. This attack, which nearly took his life, killed more than one thousand seven hundred civilians.
(Photo credit: Dana M. Moss)

Complementing these efforts, the Syrian American Council brought nonviolent figureheads of the anti-regime movement, such as civil society champions Raed Fares and Razan Ghazzali, to the United States to give a speaking tour to the media and meet with members of Congress.[10] They also brought victims of

---

[10] Syrian activists Raed Fares and Razan Ghazzali went on a speaking tour co-sponsored by SAC in 2013, which I had the privilege of attending in Los Angeles. During Fares' radio interview with National Public Radio, his dear friend Kenan Rahmani, a Syrian American activist, provided

regime violence and chemical weapons to the United States, such as Kassem Eid, a peaceful activist known by his nom de guerre, Qusai Zakarya.[11] The talk of his that I attended at the University of Southern California with SAC members and student activists on April 25, 2014, moved me to tears. Eid almost died from the sarin gas attack in the Damascus suburbs in August 2013. In addition to describing his experience of being gassed, which stopped his heart, Eid's talk detailed the relentless siege underway in Moadamiya at the time. He also spoke about his experiences at the United Nations and his meetings with US Ambassador Samantha Power, which gained national media attention. These efforts, supported by diaspora activists, provided important counter-evidence to Syrian and Russian regime propaganda that the rebels had been the ones to perpetuate chemical warfare.[12]

Diaspora activists like Ibrahim al-Assil of the Syrian Nonviolence Movement reported that brokerage put Syrians in touch with potential international donors as well.

When some groups became more mature, they were asking more to get in touch with international NGOs. Not only those who work in humanitarian aid but also those small groups in Syria who were trying to spread awareness inside Syria and to help some development of projects. At that time, they realized they needed to get in touch with international NGOs, to know how to register their NGOs, to get funds for their organizations, for their managerial expenses, to get trained so they can grow more in a professional way. So mostly these were the tasks of all members in the US and the UK, to expand our network with the media and to get in touch with international NGOs to help (them) grow and develop strategic planning for the future.

In contrast, Yemenis reported a few, albeit rare, instances of brokering with the media. Fathi, a London-based journalist with the BBC, served as a broker by sharing a database of activist contacts in Yemen with other journalists. Atiaf, who was in Yemen at the time, said that her New York–based colleague

---

"voice" on the program through interpretation (Gaylon 2013; National Public Radio 2013). Fares was gunned down in his hometown of Kafranbel in 2018, a most tragic end to his courageous commitment to civic activism.

[11] I had the privilege of attending Eid's speaking tour, which was also facilitated by SAC, at the University of Southern California in April 2014.

[12] Kassem gave testimony at the United Nations about being the victim of the Assad regime's sarin gas attack on August 21, 2013. During this visit on April 14, 2014 he met US ambassador Samantha Power. His testimony was vital in refuting Syrian, Iranian, and Russian regime propaganda that the rebels had perpetrated the attack. He later lambasted Power for "lying to my face" about wanting to help Syrians, given her later defense of President Obama's reticence to intervene. He writes,

Caesar also gave Ms. Power a handwritten note to deliver to President Obama, but he never received any response. I also requested a meeting with President Obama as a survivor of the war crimes in Syria on multiple occasions, through the White House, the State Department, and Ambassador Power, but all of my requests were also denied. Neither Ambassador Power nor President Obama wanted to acknowledge the truth. (Badran 2018)

Ahlam contacted her to facilitate the entry of journalists into Yemen. However, this activity was rare when compared to broadcasting for Yemenis in the two host-countries.

5.3.2 Brokering between Allies on the Ground

Libyans and Syrians additionally worked to connect various parties of the conflict inside their respective home-countries to one another. This coordination was crucial, as Abdo G., a British Libyan, told me, because ad hoc revolutionary forces were often disorganized and isolated from one another. For example, Monem, who was living in San Jose, California, at the start of the revolution, heard from contacts in his parents' hometown of Khoms, Libya, that "all political activists and people that were doing activities in Khoms were being killed." In response, he sought to help the resistance movement by asking his brother to deliver satellite phones to trusted contacts in Tunisia for delivery to Khoms. Using his smartphone, Monem "connected them with the central command in Misrata and Benghazi. One of the guys in Misrata was the point of contact with NATO," he explained, "and I said, please, I have information for you because the cells in Khoms could not communicate with Misrata directly." In this way, Monem helped to link these fighting forces to one another.

Syrians in the United States and Britain also brokered between dissidents inside of Syria to help them coordinate civil disobedience. Ala'a Basatneh, a Syrian American college student who became the subject of a documentary called #*ChicagoGirl: The Social Network Takes on a Dictator* (Piscatella 2013), performed this work from the Illinois suburbs. She assisted activists in Syria by serving as an intermediary between clandestine organizers, helping to plan protests and plot escape routes using Google Maps. This brokerage enabled activists inside of Syria to keep their identities hidden from one another for protection. Nebal in London, co-founder of the group British Solidarity for Syria, explained how he also came to be a middleman for the Syrian Revolution General Commission in Aleppo. After going on British television to discuss the revolution at a time when "not a lot of Syrians were speaking out in the media," he recalled,

I was contacted by people from Aleppo saying that we need a contact from outside Syria and we've seen you on TV, and we think that we can trust you. We'll provide you with photos, we'll provide you with videos. It was me and another girl in Saudi Arabia, working with these guys inside Aleppo, a core of five people from different areas who don't know each other. And they should *not* know each other so that if one is caught, he can't tell about the others. This happened in another [case] – one was caught, and all the nine working with him were caught because he had no choice but to tell about it. So that's why it was our duty to connect them, to agree about the timing and the place of the demonstrations and then spread it to all other activists inside, so that if one of them was caught, he doesn't know any other ones. They were providing me with information about how many people had been killed, what's going on inside Syria. We pass [that information] to the media, because at that point, the media didn't have those contacts.

Brokerage between insiders thus helped rebels to continue resisting in the face of extreme threats and brutality.

5.4 REMITTING

Diasporas are well-known for remitting resources homeward to crises and conflicts in their homelands, and many diaspora groups for the Arab Spring mobilized to do just that. Libyan activists channeled resources that included satellite phones, bulletproof vests, medical aid, and cash homeward from the first week of the revolution to its conclusion. Ayman, founder of the US-based organization Libyan Humanitarian Action, attested that they worked to send the rebels communications equipment before NATO stepped in to fill this role.

The Libyan freedom fighters didn't have material support or weapons before the March intervention of NATO and other countries, so I did fundraising to buy some equipment and logistical stuff, like military-grade Iridium satellite phones. We had a hard time convincing the Iridium company to [let us] buy them, because they have restrictions on what you're going to use them for. But finally I was successful in buying a good amount of them, and we sent them to the Libyan Transitional Council. These phones were sent to the freedom-fighter leaders in Misrata, Benghazi, and the Nafusa Mountains. After that, in March, they got a lot of support. At the beginning, it was a small amount – it's not like a country is supporting them, it's just *people* supporting them – but we tried our best.

The need for tangible remittances also increased as the war left thousands of casualties and displaced people in its wake. Women's participation in remitting was vital, since the humanitarian aid assembled for the revolution included supplies that "the men weren't thinking of," Rihab from Washington, DC, noted. Heba of the Libyan American Association of Ohio echoed,

One of the number-one things needed was feminine products, and because of the psychological trauma, a lot of the adults were needing adult underwear. We went out to get the products, and also bought bottled water and non-perishable foods that we could send without a problem. Our forty-foot shipping container was filled to the end.

Ayman from Oklahoma also channeled funds to Libya and Tunisia using global wire transfer services. These methods enabled activists to get money into areas beyond their reach. "When the Gaddafi brigades were sanctioning the Nafusa Mountain area, people suffered from hunger and misery there," he grimaced. "They needed money to buy food, so I sent money through a MoneyGram. It was quicker." Salam, a Libyan American who spent most of the revolution mobilizing from within Tunisia and Libya as part of a diaspora-founded charity called Libya AlHurra, also set up a system whereby donors in the diaspora could purchase mobile service for the rebels' satellite communications. He said,

"We posted a list of satellite phones, I think a hundred and fifty of them, that we as a charity had donated. I posted it in a Facebook group. I was like, if you have ten bucks, go online and [purchase] credit for it. And that's what Libyan Americans did." By purchasing essential items, diaspora donors helped to pay for the supplies and fuel that kept the revolution running.

Other forms of aid that activists sent to Libya included basic necessities such as maps. Mohamed of Manchester explained, "I attended a meeting and there was a request for a satellite up-to-date picture of Misrata because missiles were being fired from certain locations, but they could not pinpoint where they were coming from." As Gaddafi's forces pummeled Misrata and the Nafusa Mountains, activists also mobilized to assist the harder-hit areas that lay outside of the NATO-protected zone. Assad of London's World Medical Camp for Libya recalled,

We started initially on the eastern side. That was liberated very quickly, so we only sent one shipment of food and medicine to that side, because after that, the big organizations got involved – the big charities and United Nations. So we moved to the west. We sent two people at the charity's expense to Tunisia and to Malta. These guys were in charge of receiving the goods that we sent and finding a way to send them into Libya. From the Tunisian border, we used to smuggle from there into Libya. In Malta, we hired some fishing boats and some of the Libyans who came in fishing boats as refugees to Malta. We filled them with as much as we can. After that, there was a boat we used to charter to take the stuff out into Libya. We sent food, medicine, and either satellite phones or satellite-based internet systems to some of the hospitals, and we carried on doing that the whole time.

For Syrians, the revolution and subsequent humanitarian disaster, which escalated into the largest refugee crisis since World War II, led diaspora activists to remit a range of resources to the revolution and humanitarian relief. Initially, as in the Libyan case, these remittances included communications equipment, such as satellite phones and covert recording devices, for the purposes of exposing events on the ground. Mohammad al-Abdallah, director of the DC-based Syria Justice and Accountability Centre, affirmed,

One of the earlier strategies the government did inside Syria was when they surrounded and besieged a city, they basically stopped the communications. The response from the community here was let's equip the activists there with satellite phones and satellite internet so they can reach out to TV stations and to media and to human rights groups and tell them about how Syria was. So that was one of the main activities that happened in the beginning, mid-2011 to early 2012.

Dr. Nana of the Syrian Support Group went to Aleppo in June 2011 to observe what was going on for himself (Ward 2012). After joining the protest movement there, he recalled,

I came back to the States and at that time all our activities were how to send hidden cameras in pens or in glasses or in the shape of a lighter or a watch, banners, computers, laptops, satellite phones, satellite internet, and so on.

As more and more Syrians were forced to flee their homes, activists also fundraised for aid. A member of Syria Relief in Manchester recalled,

Initially it was informal. We recognized there were a large number of people who tried to flee from Syria into Turkey and were stuck at the borders. They were sleeping on the ground and when it rained, they had to sleep in the trees. It was just awful to hear about that. We didn't even see it at that time because there wasn't footage or reports, but we heard about it from contacts and friends and families and what have you. So at that time we decided amongst us to raise as much as we could. It was all done on trust. We'd ring people and say we need money for this purpose. We can't really provide a receipt or confirmation where the money went for but if you trust me, please do send the money. [Some] guys who went over bought tents and blankets and clothing, and got it across the border to these people that were displaced.

Nebal in London echoed that remitting was often learned on the fly. "I was a PhD researcher," he said. "I had no idea about how to do charity work. It wasn't organized work in the beginning. We were just sending the money straight away to the activists inside Syria." As the number of refugees swelled into the millions and they grew increasingly fragmented, apolitical humanitarian aid became the major focus of the diaspora. Though the exact figure has been impossible to track, the US and British diasporas have donated anywhere from tens of millions of dollars to over half a billion US dollars to the humanitarian effort alone since 2011 (Alloush 2018; Svoboda and Pantuliano 2015).

Activists also founded professional organizations during the revolutions to assist with humanitarian aid delivery and reconstruction. Syrian American engineer Khaled, for example, founded the Syrian American Engineers Association to work on near- and long-term rebuilding projects. Khaled said that by searching for like-minded organizations on the Internet in Arabic, he located engineering groups dedicated to rebuilding and supporting liberated areas around Damascus and Dara'a. To begin helping them, he said, "You contact them, you send them your name. Usually they are skeptical, but once you have their trust, then you'll start working with them." In so doing, Khaled assisted by "planning out what areas they need help in so you can alleviate those needs and help them work through those issues." As a result, Khaled transferred his expertise to help with rebuilding infrastructure, including the installation of water purification systems and the building of flour mills in areas facing aerial bombardment and widespread hunger.

Others worked to advise the Free Syrian Army and various military and political leaders at the forefront of the anti-regime insurgency. Dr. Nana of the US-based Syrian Support Group worked in an advisory capacity to help bolster the practices and legitimacy of the armed resistance.

When the Free Syrian Army was formed, which was defected soldiers who refused to fire on civilians basically, me and a bunch of guys thought that the Free Syrian Army is made of people who are not really organized. They don't have a long-term plan, they don't have experience in organizing or leadership or how to run a country. We helped them develop what is called the *Proclamation of Principles for the Free Syrian Army*. I put it online. It's twelve points talking about liberty, democracy, freedom, equality of treatment to all citizens, condemning revenge killing, condemning use of chemical weapons or weapons of mass destruction, [having] peaceful relationships with neighboring countries, restoring order and peace in Syria. The people there, the officers there, they were very receptive. They were very enthusiastic that they are doing this because they really believe that this is what they stand for, and they signed on it. They formed what is called the Military Councils for each province that were supposed to lead the effort and the organization among the fighters and prevent them from those battalions turning into gangs or warlords.

Syrians also traveled to opposition hubs in Turkey or Qatar to deliver workshops on political leadership, human rights, international law, and citizen journalism, as well as on how to "document all of the crimes and human rights abuses," according to Ahmed from London. Ammar Abdulhamid of the US-based Tharwa Foundation established an initiative to work on transitional planning for a post-Assad Syria in partnership with the Public International Law and Policy Group. Dr. Radwan Ziadeh, head of the Syrian Center for Political and Strategic Studies in Washington, DC, reported undertaking a similar initiative. In these ways, Syrians in the diaspora worked to channel their professional experience and expertise to the revolution, the humanitarian crisis, and into short- and long-term development and political capacity-building.

In contrast to the aforementioned interventions, I did not find any evidence that Yemeni movements worked *collectively* to channel resources to the rebellion or its medical volunteers during the main Arab Spring period, which lasted from January to November 2011. No diaspora movement leaders report fundraising for Sana'a's field hospital, for instance, or sending donations to any of the other protest sites. Instead, interviewees like Adel in Michigan attested that some individuals and families channeled funds to victims of regime violence in Change Square by wiring money to people they knew on the ground.[13] One Yemeni American reported sending several cameras to Change Square, but he never received confirmation of whether these cameras ever reached their intended recipients. From London Safa, Awssan, and several others shipped a container of food, clothes, medicine, and medical equipment to Aden, Yemen's southern port city. They did so by partnering with an Aden-based charity, *al-Firdos*, whose head arranged to receive the shipment. Awssan said that the community's response to this project was "excellent." This charitable initiative occurred after the Arab Spring had waned, however, and the aid was intended for Yemen's needy writ large, rather than for anti-regime protesters.

---

[13] When I visited Sana'a's field hospital in June 2012, the head doctor attested that his team had received donations from abroad. However, it is unknown how much money was channeled to the field hospital from various sources overseas.

5.5 VOLUNTEERING ON THE GROUND

Libyans widely reported volunteering on the ground in order to contribute to the rebellion and relief directly. Volunteers initially flocked to Cairo to amass supplies and drive them into Benghazi as it was being liberated and faced regime shelling. Amr Ben Halim recalled, "We would travel fifteen hours by car to drive all the way into Libya [to make] deliveries [from Egypt], but also we wanted to see what's going on and see what help we could offer." Assia from Kentucky echoed that many volunteers, including her brother, went to Benghazi to "fill the gaps" of what needed to be done. Ahmed of Enough Gaddafi! attested that he and other volunteers filled these roles on the fly in order to help the effort.

From Cairo, there just happened to be this team of journalists who were looking to get into Libya. We were like, well, let's go! We started as their translators and their fixers. We got to Benghazi on the twenty-fifth or the twenty-sixth of February to see what we could do to better coordinate a couple different things. Number one, when medical supplies came into the country, we made sure that they actually got to where they were supposed to go to different hospitals in Benghazi. The other things were to try to make sure that different journalists who came in actually had an appropriate understanding of the context that they were reporting on. We did our best to set up the right interviews for different folks, and tried to translate as much as possible.

Libyans also worked within regime-controlled territories. Dr. Niz Ben-Essa, a young Libyan doctor from Cardiff, managed to catch what he attested was the last flight into Tripoli to join the protest movement. After demonstrators were mowed down by live ammunition and arrested en masse, Niz joined an underground resistance unit called the Free Generation Movement.[14] Their clandestine group undertook a number of activities that included stealing Internet and satellite-based communications equipment from regime installations for the resistance. Niz explained that they did so because they knew that "If we don't have a means of communicating with the outside world, much of what we do here is going to be fruitless." The Free Generation Movement also facilitated independent media reporting from inside Gaddafi's stronghold by helping foreign journalists escape their government-enforced lockdown. He recalled,

We were smuggling out the international media, who were effectively under arrest in the Rixos Hotel, to demonstrate that there was resistance and opposition to Gaddafi in Tripoli. Because Gaddafi was spinning the idea that everyone in Libya loved him and that there were no protests in Libya, no problems in Libya, it was just Al Qaeda elements causing trouble. We were taking journalists to speak to people and see sporadic small protests happening in Tripoli.[15]

---

[14] Niz communicated with journalists via Skype during his time as a leading dissident in the Free Generation Movement, which worked underground in Tripoli during the Libyan revolution to sabotage regime censorship and infrastructure; see Kofman (2011) and McKenzie (2011).

[15] Having visited the Rixos Hotel during my fieldwork in Libya, I asked Niz how it was possible that he and his colleagues smuggled journalists out past the hotel's fortifications, which included

In addition to facilitating relief, diaspora activists also helped to monitor the work of international aid organizations. After visiting one UN Refugee Agency campus, Abdo G. of Libya Link attested that the conditions were appalling. Libyans lacked food, toilets, and supplies for basic hygiene. His group responded, pressuring officials by threatening to report the conditions to the press unless the situation improved. Likewise, Salam, a Libyan American, addressed this problem by supplementing services and negotiating with the managing officials.

I thank the UNHCR for everything they did, but the amount of care that I thought was humane was very different from what they thought was humane. I understand, as an agency their resources are limited. So as a charity, we did what we could. We provided a mobile hospital and a refrigerated pharmacy. My role fit in with trying to coordinate with the internationals because I speak English.

He also rented apartments for Libyan refugees in Tunisia, negotiated with Tunisian authorities to allow Libyan fighters to receive medical treatment, bought fuel to send into Libya, and purchased walkie-talkies and "all types of communication devices." Salam stressed the fact that "it was a free for all. Whichever way we can help, we were going to help."

As the Free Libya Army and NATO liberated additional territory over the summer, other members of the diaspora went home to help their compatriots directly, and even to join the fight itself. Adam of Virginia recalled that in addition to his combat training in Benghazi,

We were helping with the journalists, doing translations. There were also a few startup newspapers and they were all [run by] young guys. We were helping with the English side. This is all going on while we were training. Finally, once we were done training, my brigade leader was like, all right, you're going over to the western mountains. And it was literally like taxi drivers, students, doctors, regular bakers-turned-soldier. It was college students like me who are now holding an AK and we're in charge of five other guys.

a long driveway and a gate. He said that by communicating with journalists via email and using moles who worked within the hotel, they would make arrangements for the journalists to venture outside the gate, ostensibly for a cigarette, and then jump into a waiting car (Many journalists got deported after their escapes were discovered). Niz explained that the poor training of the security services provided opportunities for them to exploit as a guerilla movement:

You have to understand something, I'm not trying to belittle what we did or what anyone did, and I'm not trying to belittle what the risks were, but Libya has been very neglected for forty-two years. Not only from an education or healthcare or infrastructure point of view, from every aspect you can think of, but also the quality and the standard of training and expertise of the intelligence service. And the security services. Put bluntly, I think there were a lot of them, they were brutal, they were aggressive, but they weren't intelligent and they weren't well-equipped and they weren't well-trained.

This situation made such high-risk resistance possible. See Bassiouni (2013) for more information on the lack of preparedness and investment in the Libyan Army by the Gaddafi regime.

FIGURE 5.5. Two men walk past a mural in Tripoli, Libya, paying homage to Libyans from Manchester, England, who joined the revolutionary brigades in 2011.
(Photo credit: Joseph Eid/AFP via Getty Images)

FIGURE 5.6. The Martyrs' Museum in Zawiya, Libya, photographed here in 2013 by the author, displayed photographs of Libyan Americans, including a father-and-son pair, who had died fighting in the 2011 revolution. The upper floors of the building were destroyed by the fighting in 2011.
(Photo credit: Dana M. Moss)

Some volunteers arrived to help the Free Libya Army break the summer stalemate. Abdulssalam, then in his fifties and living in California, arrived in Benghazi from Cairo using his American passport, to join the *thuwar* (revolutionary forces) to "pay my share for the revolution." His brother, who had been living in Libya, connected him with the Libyan Martyrs Militia.

They took my name and said they would call me when they were ready. One day early in the morning, [my brother] called me and said go to the airport, there was a flight that was going to take me to Nalut. With no training, nothing – zero. It took us about five hours to get permission to fly, because of NATO. Then we went to Misrata. At that time there was heavy fighting. We landed on the road, on the highway. You're scared, you don't know what's going to happen.

Members of the diaspora also became members of the "supporting cast" for the National Transitional Council, as Fadel from Washington, DC put it. Dina from California volunteered as the press coordinator for the interim prime minister. Mazen R. from Seattle joined the NTC to help with logistics, as he explained with a wave of his hand, because "wars *are* logistics." He ran the NTC's Oil and Finance Department and coordinated the Temporary Finance Mechanism, which enabled the NTC to receive outside funding by borrowing money against frozen assets to keep the country functioning during the war. As the finance mechanism coordinator under NTC minister Ali Tarhouni, Mazen R. worked to keep oil and electricity flowing to Benghazi and distributed cash in the Nafusa Mountains. He said, "I was a volunteer the whole time, so there was no salary or anything. I had three phones that wouldn't stop ringing, each for one area: One for the Temporary Finance Mechanism, one for the fighters, and one for the administrators."

Like Mazen R., Syrians from the United States and Britain ventured across state lines to volunteer in Syria and its border zones. Dr. Nana from Miami, for instance, escorted journalists into Syria, as when he brought reporters from CBS's *60 Minutes* team into Syria in the fall of 2012 (Ward 2012). "We went inside Aleppo," he said. "I hosted them in my family's house with all my family members and we showed them the city, we show them the destruction. We also introduced them to those leaders of the Free Syrian Army." In addition to working on the front lines as brokers and interpreters for journalists, others participated directly in protests. Ibrahim al-Assil of the Syrian Nonviolence Movement traveled from Britain back home to Syria in 2011 in order to participate in civil resistance before being forced to escape through Lebanon that same year. He said, "In mid-2013, I started to visit Syria again from the north. Going to Aleppo and at that time even to Raqqah before it was occupied by the Islamic State." He and his colleagues from the Syrian Nonviolence Movement did so because,

We had different goals. One of them to coordinate and to meet people we work with inside Syria. For me personally, I felt that after being outside Syria for a year and a half, it became more difficult for me to understand what is going on. If you are Syrian and

even if you are in the US or UK, you *are* part of what's going on, but being geographic-
ally far away is not helpful for understanding what's going on. From another side,
activists and people on the ground aren't always willing to listen to people who have
been outside Syria for a long time because they feel that [those outside] are emotionally
disconnected. Many of them started to say, you don't feel us – especially when you are
asking them to stay peaceful. They say you don't know the brutality we face, you don't
know the horror of the Syrian army, the Syrian *Shabiha* [loyalist militias and thugs]. So
I felt that I need to start to go back to Syria to understand what's going on. That will help
us to plan for our movement in a better way and to get more in touch with other
activists, to rebuild the trust with people on the ground and to be more effective.

For physicians like Dr. Ayman Jundi in Manchester, going home also
enabled volunteers to lend their labor and expertise in medicine.

We went down [to Syria] and did a few courses. We've been organizing trips for people
to go and operate in field hospitals. That kind of activity started very early on. Very
quickly, the [Syrian British Medical] Society became *seen* as an arm of the revolution,
but it's *not* a political organization. It's just, as it happened, the medical need is in the
areas that are being bombed by the regime. The regime's hospitals are still functioning,
they're still working, they're getting their supplies – not so the hospitals on the other
side! So the emphasis of the Society has been where the need is.

Others transported medical aid and equipment to liberated zones. Ousama of
the Syrian Bristol community, for example, drove ambulances as part of a
volunteer convoy into Syria several times, which he arranged in coordination
with medical councils.

We used to take the powder called Celox, very famous in Canada, used by loggers who
cut trees using chainsaws. It stops bleeding straight away. In the city of Aleppo, they
formed the medical council and they started coordinating all the activities, overseeing
about eighteen hospitals in the north. So we found that the best way is to take everything
to them. They sort it out and they see where everything is needed and they divert it.
Because there are a lot of amputees as well, one of the things we concentrate on taking is
wheelchairs and crutches.

Mohamed Taher Khairullah, an activist and the mayor of Prospect Park in New
Jersey, also began to travel into Syria in December of 2012 to deliver humanitarian relief. He said,

It started as an individual effort and it developed into joining an organization. Right now
I work with Watan USA, which is a 501(c)(3) organization. We're approved by the IRS and
we're tax deductible. I've been to Aleppo and many villages in the governorate of Aleppo,
Idlib, Hama, mostly to deliver aid and to make contacts on the ground for future projects.
Because the needs are rapidly changing, I stay in touch with people who do work on the
ground, and through them we assess what we need to do. Obviously, as an organization, we
also have projects that are consistently running such as school and two bakeries.

Only one Syrian I interviewed attested that he had fought with the Free
Syrian Army before 2013. He did not come from a political family or have any
experience in political activism before the revolution. This interviewee first

traveled into Damascus in 2011 in order to understand what was happening in Syria for himself. Going against his parents' wishes, he then joined the protest movement and worked with the anti-regime Damascus Media Center. As the revolution escalated, this respondent reported undertaking aid delivery and weapons smuggling, as well as fighting on the front lines with an FSA brigade in Aleppo. Unlike my Libyan interviewees, however, he did not report fighting alongside other members of the Syrian diaspora during this period.

Several respondents also reported volunteering in Yemen during the revolution, although this was not a part of activists' collective strategies of intervention. Some simply decided to put their lives on hold to venture home and see what they could do. Raja, a student in New York, for example, was motivated by the Friday of Dignity Massacre to take a leave from her university and become a citizen photojournalist in Sana'a. Because the regime deported many foreign journalists the week before the massacre, these circumstances gave her a unique opportunity to document the violence. Armed with her Yemeni residency card and her camera, she recalled,

I don't need a visa to get into Yemen, and at that point they weren't issuing visas to anyone, especially from the US. So I went, it was pretty easy to get in. I can blend in and integrate and report. I speak English, I have media contacts, so my added value was sky rocketing at that point.

Raja went as an independent observer and published her photographs and writings on her blog and on social media. She remained in Yemen from March through August. Lacking a journalist's background, she learned how to document the conflict on the fly.

Summer from New York also returned to her family's residence in Aden several times during the revolution. She avoided joining the protests, however, because she did not want to become embroiled in the controversy surrounding southern separatism. Instead, Summer worked to document stories and events on her blog. In one other case, I found that a London-based journalist named Abubakr joined his family in Sana'a during the revolution for about a month in April, working as an intern for the *Yemen Times* during the day and participating in the sit-ins at night. That said, Yemeni diaspora movements did not incorporate volunteering on the ground into their tactics or goals. Instead, activists made the decision to participate directly in Yemen's Arab Spring on a selective, individualized basis.

5.6 VARIATION IN DIASPORA INTERVENTIONS

As illustrated above, diaspora movements from the United States and Britain performed a range of critically important roles in Arab Spring. When compared by national group and host-country, these roles varied widely, as summarized in Table 1.3 in the Introduction. The riots that kick-started Libya's revolution escalated into a national revolutionary war that "needed *everything*," as one respondent recalled, and Libyans abroad took up the call, becoming a *full-spectrum auxiliary force* for rebellion and relief as broadcasters, representatives, brokers, remitters, and volunteers on the front lines for the duration of the revolution, as Table 5.2 illustrates. Activists also frequently reported swapping indirect, lower-risk forms of support (like broadcasting) for direct, higher-risk ones (like volunteering on the front lines) over time. All respondents were keen to point out that the true sacrifices were those of their allies at home. Nevertheless, by undertaking a full-spectrum intervention consistently over time, Libyan diaspora activists from both the United States and Britain became an important transnational source of support from the first hours of the riots in Benghazi through the liberation of Tripoli in August 2011. As one Libyan American activist attested, "Not a single thing was left undone by Libyans abroad."

In contrast, Syrian interventions were far more variable by host-country and changed significantly for both diaspora groups over the course of the revolution and internationalized civil war. Although Syrian activists initially undertook the same repertoire as their Libyan counterparts to bolster a badly outgunned insurgency and escalating humanitarian emergency, their roles differed in two main ways. First, their collective interventions differed by host-country in that Syrian activists in the United States played an elevated role as *representatives* who lobbied consistently over time, while their British counterparts rarely reported doing so. Second, Syrian activists in both the United States and Britain faced significant challenges in sustaining their respective repertoires as revolution wore on. Both sets of respondents overwhelmingly reported a steep decline in their broadcasting, representing, brokering, remitting, and volunteer work by 2014. Although some efforts continued – and still do today at the time of this writing – Syrians' voice for regime change was largely *muted* by the time I conducted interviews in 2014.

As in the Libyan and Syrian cases, Yemeni activism in the United States and Britain also marked an unprecedented shift in the voice and visibility of their members for liberal change at home. However, efforts to broker, remit, and volunteer on the front lines were not a part of the diaspora activists' *collective* tactics. Instead, Yemeni activism focused primarily on broadcasting and representing the independent youth movement from their places of residence. Thus, in contrast to the full-scale interventions of Libyans, the repertoires of Yemeni movements in both host-countries remained *selective* over time.

Of course, it is important to note that the Yemeni revolution had different needs than the Libyan and Syrian insurgency. Yemenis, having successfully launched a durable, peaceful, popular uprising, did not rely on activists abroad to augment a war effort or a government-in-waiting. Yet, it was also the case that the Yemeni revolution was hugely under-resourced. For example, the Sana'a field hospital, which I visited during a trip to Yemen in 2012, was little more than a shed – the size of a walk-in closet with the sparest of equipment. The protest encampment in Ta'iz also faced violence by regime forces and arson

TABLE 5.2. *Collective tactics to support rebellion and relief during the Arab Spring (→ refers to change over time)*

National Group	Host-Country	Broadcasting	Representing	Brokering	Remitting	Volunteering on the Ground	Voice in the Arab Spring
Libyan	USA	X	X	X	X	X	Full-spectrum
	Britain	X → Declined					
Syrian	USA	X → Declined	X → Declined	X → Declined	X → Declined		Full-spectrum → Muted
	Britain		–	X → Declined	Declined	X → Declined	Constrained → Muted
Yemeni	USA	X	X	–	–	–	Selective
	Britain						

a number of times, but had essentially no outside support. So too were southerners in places such as Aden coming under constant attack. In light of these disparities, organizers in the diaspora often expressed frustration that they and their fellow Yemenis lacked a concrete way to help their compatriots beyond holding protests and lobbying from afar. As Shaima from Birmingham lamented,

Even though I want to help Yemen, I just don't know how I would. Here, we're educated, we have resources, we have activist resources. So what I want to know is how we can use these resources and *get them over to them*. I don't know how! . . . Even if you're not educated to a certain level, there's opportunities here. It's about just being able to pick it up and move it. But *how do you do that*?

This dilemma was echoed by respondents across the diaspora. Omar from Liverpool too reflected on their movement's inability to tangibly help the revolution after the Friday of Dignity Massacre.

We were more saddened on an individual level. But we thought, they died, what can we do? We can't do anything particularly for them. All we can do is give them our emotional support. It brought their reality of the revolution home to *us* more than anything. The diaspora was very much on the back foot. We didn't quite know what to do, to be honest with you.

Other participants expressed skepticism about the utility of protests. For example, Afrah of Liverpool mentioned,

I think even sometimes it's not even about getting [a] reaction. I think *we* felt a bit better. We felt that at least *we've* done something, *we* worked on something. Because sometimes we're looking at the news and thinking, *what can we do?* We live so far away from it. We want to show and let them know that we are there, we are listening and we are proud, so I think it's as much to make us feel better as well as [showing] our support.

This gap in their response left many respondents feeling that the diaspora had failed to meet its mobilization potential. As Ahlam of New York lamented, "At a point you realize, what is there that you can do, you know?" Hany of Sheffield surmised,

It was good in the sense that it's woken a lot of people up. It's good in the sense that it brings out this new talk, how we can improve Yemen, as opposed to just complaining. It gave us a platform to talk about and deal with issues now. But I don't think it's manifested as much as we have wanted. There's a lot more that we can do – and that we need to do.

In all, by the end of the Arab Spring period in Yemen, activists from the United States and Britain were both proud of the work they had undertaken and deeply perplexed about why they could not do more.

5.7 CONCLUSION

This chapter explained how and to what extent Libyan, Syrian, and Yemeni groups across the United States and Britain contributed to the Arab Spring revolutions in their home-countries. However, it leaves unanswered why diaspora movement interventions varied significantly when compared by national group and host-country. The following two chapters provide the answers by demonstrating how the additive processes of *resource conversion* and *geopolitical support* shaped diaspora mobilization for rebellion and relief. In so doing, I show that the emergence of voice, as explained in Chapter 4, does not in-and-of-itself transform diaspora activists into interventionists. Instead, their interventions vary according to whether members have the respective network ties, wealth, and skills to convert to a shared cause and whether activists gain the backing of geopolitical powerholders, such as government leaders, the media, and international bodies. The remaining chapters demonstrate how these processes transform anti-regime movements from long-distance supporters into a transnational auxiliary force for change.

6

Converting Resources to the Cause

Social movement scholars have long held that resources increase a movement's readiness to engage in collective action and the likelihood that movements will survive and achieve at least some of their goals (Edwards and McCarthy 2004; McAdam et al. 1996, 2001). These resources often come from organizations that sponsor social movement activity, such as NGOs and professional organizations (McCarthy and Zald 1977). The catch, however, is that elite sponsorship puts limits on what movements can do (Jenkins and Eckert 1986; Staggenborg 1988) because revolutionary change inherently threatens sponsors' social standing and power. As a result, patronage can make mobilization possible, but it also compromises activists' abilities to achieve radical social change. Constraints imposed on the grassroots by elites can therefore become a major dilemma for movements that require external resources to fulfill their missions.

While the top-down sponsorship of movements is an important subject that I address here and in Chapter 7, relatively little scholarly attention has been paid to how activists serve as *peer patrons* of allied movements for the express purpose of revolutionary, radical change. Yet, this is precisely what makes diaspora mobilization so important in world affairs (Adamson 2002, 2004, 2016; Smith and Stares 2007; Vertovec 2005). As the previous chapter illustrates, diaspora movements can ameliorate resource shortages in highly repressive, underprivileged locales by remitting a range of tangible and intangible resources homeward. Based on my analysis of the Arab Spring abroad, this chapter argues that doing so hinges on a process I call *resource conversion* – that is, the capacities of diaspora activists and their movements to convert personal and collective resources to shared political projects rooted across borders.

Here, I argue that two major types of resource conversion mattered during the Arab Spring abroad. The first type consisted of activists' *transnational network ties* to family and friends in the home-country. Once converted to the revolutions, these ties became cross-border conduits for information and material exchange (Kitts 2000). They also enabled activists to expand their contacts from kin to previously unknown partners through introductions, vetting processes, and referrals. Both preexisting and emergent cross-border ties deputized activists abroad as broadcasters, representatives, brokers, remitters, and volunteers for resistance efforts and made the channeling of remittances possible.

The second type of resource conversion that made the Arab Spring abroad possible was the conversion of diaspora activists' *capital* to rebellion and relief efforts. Capital took *fungible and material* forms, such as when activists moved cash and medical equipment to home-country locales under siege. They also converted their expertise and skills – what social scientists call *social capital* – to the Arab Spring (Portes 2000). Social capital ranged from doctors' medical knowledge to activists' language interpretation and translation skills, previous experiences in public relations, and technological savviness. Capital conversion lent invaluable resources to the revolutionary struggles and gave activists a way to participate in the action, whether directly or indirectly. Taken together, these different forms of capital facilitated each tactic in the transnational repertoire.

To evidence this process, this chapter illustrates how Libyans in the United States and Britain had few problems overcoming the hurdles posed by physical distance to help their compatriots due to *sufficient* resource conversion. Syrians and Yemenis, however, faced a number of different challenges owing to waning or absent network ties and insufficient capital. As Table 1.3 (column 5) summarizes, Syrians' resources decreased from being largely sufficient to insufficient over time, and Yemenis' resources remained insufficient for the revolution's duration.

The comparison illustrates how resource conversion to political causes transforms distant sympathizers into transnational forces for radical change. While diasporas channel considerable resources homeward to their families amounting to billions of dollars each year (World Bank 2018), this chapter demonstrates that whether or not those resources get channeled to *politicized* causes is another matter. Owing to differences in community-level wealth, education, and activists' emigration circumstances, diaspora movement capital may be or become insufficient to address needs on the ground, even when demand for their support is high.

6.1 THE CONVERSION OF CROSS-BORDER NETWORKS

6.1.1 The Conversion and Expansion of Libyans' and Syrians' Cross-Border Ties

The conversion of Libyans' and Syrians' ties to family and friends in the home-country was the first type of resource that made diaspora intervention possible during the Arab Spring. By serving as the diaspora members' eyes and ears, sources on the ground provided them with testimonials and information for use in their roles as broadcasters and representatives of the revolution. At the onset of the Libyan uprising, for example, activists began "calling up friends, calling up family, getting all of these [pieces of] information," as M. of Enough Gaddafi! explained.[1] Their allies also sought out sympathizers in the diaspora to help them smuggle out information. As Muhannad, an independent Syrian American activist from Southern California who had lived for part of his youth in Hama, affirmed,

People were sending me videos of anything they can document, any kind of crime or shooting at a protest so they can clear it off their phone and I can upload it to social media. It would all go to YouTube. We'd also get phone calls: "can so-and-so send you this and that?"

Because being caught with video recordings could be a matter of life and death, connections to persons like Muhannad provided the means for dissidents to smuggle out information as quickly and safely as possible using the Internet. In this way, transnational networks provided the infrastructure needed to engage in information wars (Keck and Sikkink 1998), refute regime propaganda, and attract favorable attention from outside media.

Activists' preexisting contacts also snowballed into a widened network of pro-revolution activists on the ground seeking to broadcast their plight. Referring to her colleague Omar in the Libya Youth Movement, Ayat recalled, "When things began, I called my cousins, Omar called his, we started asking people on Facebook for their contacts – whoever was willing to talk." Having direct contacts with protesters and fighters on the ground was also important in establishing activists' credibility and legitimacy. As referenced in Chapter 5, activists were keen to voice demands on behalf of the Arab Spring, but not to speak *for* the revolution or revolutionaries who were facing the greatest risks and costs of dissent. Abdulaziz Almashi, a doctoral student in London who became a full-time activist after the Assad regime cut off his scholarship, attested that they amplified revolutionaries' demands by broadcasting their allies' exact claims.

On the outside, we must reflect what our people need on the inside of Syria. We have a connection with media activists in every single city in Syria via Skype or Facebook, and we are always in touch with them. We ask them, what do you *exactly* want? What message do *you* want us to deliver on the outside? So we take our instructions from *them* and deliver it to the public, the media.

---

[1] Respondents perceived that Skype was a safer method of communication than speaking over the phone, because those using the phone from regime-controlled areas such as Tripoli had to speak in a kind of impromptu code. The platforms that became popularized and normalized in 2020 as a result of the global COVID-19 pandemic, such as Zoom, were not yet available.

In turn, dissidents at home were often eager to team up with members of the anti-regime diaspora to amplify their long-repressed voices and play a role in resistance. Rahma, who worked with Enough Gaddafi! to speak with foreign media from Tripoli, attested, "I kept changing my SIM card. I was kind of scared. But I wanted to try and do *something*."

Network ties to persons at home also made the sending of remittances possible. Based in London, Assad, of the organization World Medical Camp for Libya, recalled,

Using our own connections in the country, we started to make contact with people – the hospitals and doctors in the hospitals that we know in areas that were either liberated or where they were fighting for it to be liberated. We distributed through smuggling some satellite phones to each of these hospitals so they can call us with their needs. They also confirmed deliveries. We carried on doing that the whole time.

For some, these contacts solidified into direct, sustained communications with persons on the front lines. Dr. Shalabi of London attested,

Through Skype, a friend got me the details of a doctor in Canada. This doctor got me the details of a friend of his who ran the Misrata port and had satellite internet. I was able to speak to him, but it was very hard to gain people's trust. When I called him, he was like, "who are you?" I was like, "I got your contact details from this chap in Canada. I'm Ahmed Shalabi, a Libyan doctor working from the UK. I want to help, but I need to know what you guys need. Get me a doctor." He said, "Okay, give me one hour, I'll get you a doctor from the hospital where all the injured are being taken and he'll tell you what they need." So I got him, an hour later, and this doctor now is a friend for life. It was an honor working with him. He told me, "I need *this, this, this*."

Diaspora members also relied on their contacts at home to smuggle and deliver the aid they had acquired to hard-to-reach areas. Salam recalled that getting supplies to these areas was dependent on the extraordinary resourcefulness and bravery of smugglers and fighters.

At one point, the World Food Program wanted to go deliver food, but they couldn't because of protocols. Because we'd been going and coming from Zintan back and forth and we had a great relationship with the fighters there, we decided we would create a post in Zintan and deliver all the food there. Once we got there, we were still worried about how are we going to get this [aid from Zintan] to Yefren. We decided to seek out the Boy Scouts – not the children, the Boy Scouts organization [in Libya].[2] We purchased, I think it was like seventeen, mules. They carried it to Yefren on mules, because there was no other way to get it in there, the roads were occupied by Gaddafi's troops.

Taregh of Oxford also reported that his contacts made the movement of volunteers possible, both Libyan and foreign, from Cairo into Benghazi.

---

[2] Colonel Gaddafi was a Boy Scout in his youth and allowed the organization to operate in Libya.

He said, "We were connecting people together so people who wanted to go over there to help out would have [other] people that would wait for them and look after them." Ayat recalled,

There were a lot of journalists who we gave instructions to go to the Egyptian border, and we had our relatives go meet them and bring them in early on. Technically, anybody could've driven in, but it was very early and nobody really knew how to assess the situation. So we said, okay, if it makes you feel better, they'll drive you in.

Taken together, activists' preexisting cross-border connections and the new-found alliances forged over the course of the revolution enabled them to get information out and resources in. According to Assad of London, this was all made possible through

Contacts. You know that theory, six degrees of separation? In Libya, it's probably three. If you think about the logistics, they're almost impossible to do in these circumstances. But because people knew each other, and we could talk to each other, and this person vouch for this person and this person vouch for that person, we managed to create the network that actually functioned.

As Sarah of London recalled, "Everyone tried to use their own contacts and expertise" in some way, often at the request of revolutionary forces themselves, to address needs on the ground.

6.1.2 The Decimation of Syrians' Network Ties over Time

While Syrians initially had sufficient network ties to undertake the same kinds of interventions as their Libyan counterparts, these critically important relationships were decimated over time by the regime's systematic targeting of activists in Syria and its depopulation of the country. Lina of Chicago, for instance, recalled that as of 2013, "I stopped doing any of the Skype work anymore [because] a lot of the people I knew are dead or they disappeared. Most of the people I knew in Homs, they all died, one after the other." Razan from Britain similarly attested that the hemorrhaging of activists from Syria left her without a clear way to contribute to the revolution.

I had a lot of contacts with people on the ground, [working] with them secretly, translating articles for them. They'd be inside Syria or they'd tell me we're going offline; if anyone asks about us, don't worry, we're going to go to such-and-such base. All of this happened the first year of the revolution. Those are probably the best kind of moments of my life, where I actually felt like I was part of the revolution, because I was helping facilitate protests inside wherever it was by being in contact with these people. But then I lost contact with [almost] all of them. They either left Syria or died.

Ibrahim al-Assil in the United States, who continued to work with activists on the ground as of 2014, confirmed that the overall number of available volunteers had been slashed drastically by regime repression.

In Damascus now, it's also very, very difficult to find activists because most of them got killed or detained or they had to flee the country, or they are now very afraid to become involved. Because now if someone is detained in Damascus, most probably they will never be released again and they will die in a detention center. So whether inside or outside Syria, it's now more difficult to find volunteers.

As activists' cross-border contacts were depleted by violence, so too were their abilities to broadcast, broker, and remit aid. In this way, no-holds-barred repression by the Syrian regime has largely succeeded in severing the links forged between insiders and outsiders, and the transnational advocacy networks that made auxiliary activism possible.

The fragmentation of the Syrian opposition on the ground, discussed at length in Chapter 3, also damaged activists' network ties over time. Nidal Bitari, a Palestinian Syrian activist with the Syrian Expatriates Organization, stated that the problem with mobilizing to support the revolution was that "you don't know for whom you are promoting now or advocating." For this reason, Dr. Radwan Ziadeh and Marah Bukai, who had joined the Syrian National Council at its founding in August 2011,[3] withdrew from this body in 2012. Explaining her decision, Marah said,

---

[3] The Syrian National Council was formed in August 2011 to represent the revolution from Istanbul. This included those who had been a part of the 2005 Damascus Declaration (see Chapter 2), the Kurdish Future Movement, Muslim Brotherhood members (who held over a quarter of the seats), and members of the Local Coordination Committees. However, the council lacked authority and a grounded presence in Syria and was subject to internal disagreements (Yassin-Kassab and Al-Shami 2018). Several leaders resigned in March 2012 citing corruption, Muslim Brotherhood domination, and a failure to gain international support for the Free Syria Army (FSA). A Kurdish coalition known as the Kurdish National Council (KNC) also departed over differences regarding the Kurds' regional sovereignty. In November 2012, a more sweeping National Coalition for Syrian Revolutionary and Opposition Forces was formed in Doha as a result of international pressure; this body absorbed the original SNC and included more FSA representatives and liberals. Coalition offices, referred to as the *Etilaf* (https://en.etilaf.org/, accessed November 27, 2020), were granted as foreign missions under the leadership of Ahmad Jarba. Optimism was short-lived, however, as the coalition suffered from the same problems. Muaz Khatib, the coalition's first president, resigned after only six months in response to a lack of support and meddling by outside states. By May 2013, major groups condemned the coalition and demanded more representation. As described by Yassin-Kassab and Al-Shami (2018: 188),

The Coalition, like the SNC before, produced the ugly spectacle of factions and personalities squabbling over the throne of a country which was going up in flames. . . . The ability to put aside personal and factional interests for the sake of a common goal, to adapt, to accommodate the other's point of view, requires a background level of trust in the national community and its institutions, and long experience in democratic collaboration. Syria had been a cast-iron dictatorship for four decades, so these conditions did not apply. Beyond that, the Syrians had no Benghazi in which to base themselves, no field on which to enact transitional authority.

Accordingly, "despite its hard work and diplomatic progress, all the Coalition won on the ground from its participation was the heightened disgust of activists" (Yassin-Kassab and Al-Shami 2018: 190).

There is no transparency. From where are [the SNC members] getting the money to hold their huge meetings? We've never seen any of their sources. And was this money used to buy arms? And then sent *to whom*? We don't know. *From* whom? We don't know. And I don't want to be part of that. I told the head of Muslim Brotherhood frankly, if we don't know from where you are getting the money . . . I have no interest. You cannot *use* me. Use someone else. [With this] mistrust, corruption, lack of transparency, no accountability, no responsibility – who will trust you? How could United States of America trust you? How could the Syrian *people* trust you?

Dr. Ziadeh also withdrew in November 2012 after being with the council for almost a year because there was "too much in-fighting, too much losing focus." Sabreen, an activist from Southern California, left her position working for the Syrian Interim Government's Assistance Coordination Unit in Turkey for similar reasons. She explained,

In the unit, there was a lot of corruption going on. People were directing humanitarian aid to some of their hometowns so they would gain credibility in it. And the people who founded this unit – who are some of the most legitimate people I've ever met in my life – a lot of them left because they couldn't handle the corruption. People that stayed are the ones who went on strike basically. So then we went on strike and they decided to bring us a new CEO who turned out to be just as corrupt.

The opaque dealings of various groups representing the anti-regime movement also undermined ties between veteran activists abroad and their allies on the ground. Malik al-Abdeh, co-founder of the Syrian Justice and Development Party and Barada TV in London, withdrew from publicly supporting opposition forces after he uncovered a scandal implicating a member of the Syrian National Council.[4] Malik said,

---

[4] According to Malik,

Around February 2012, one Syrian opposition figure who was big within the Syrian National Council, his brother was murdered in Aleppo in mysterious circumstances. So he went on *Al Jazeera* and said my brother is a martyr, the regime killed him because they couldn't get to me so they killed my brother instead. On the same day, an armed group from Aleppo called the Abu Amara Brigades claimed on their Facebook page that they had killed him because he was a regime spy. Then later that day, they took down this post from their Facebook. So I thought, this is interesting. It's one or the other, it can't be both. So I got one of the journalists at Barada TV to look into the story. Eventually we spoke to the members of the Abu Amara Brigades and they said, yeah, we killed him because we warned him several times, he was with the pro-regime militia, was using his restaurant as a meeting place and he was supporting them . . . I asked them, why did you take it down on the Facebook? Well, he said that what happened was the brother of the guy who was killed was so embarrassed by the fact that his brother was supporting the regime and he's supposedly this opposition guy. There were bribes going down. So I said, are you prepared to go on the record and say this? They're like, yeah, fuck it. We're going to go on the record and expose this. Okay, fine. So I said that this is investigative journalism at its best, right? So to be fair, we need to phone the guy [in the Syrian National Council] to get his story. We called him and spoke to his right-hand man, his personal secretary. The personal secretary went crazy. He said, we're gonna fuck you up. Tell Malik that 'this is like a personal challenge. You mustn't

In my very naïve British kind of upbringing, this is a citable offence! You can't have a politician lying in that way. So I spoke to the head of the whole channel [of Barada TV] and said, look, here's the story. And he's like, *what are we going to gain from exposing this? We've got everything to lose and nothing to gain. The regime is going to love the fact that an opposition leader is lying. We're just going to be seen as causing a shitstorm within the opposition, and we're going to get hassled from that guy. So just drop the story.* I said, alright. But that evening, I went home and I thought, how am I any different than the editor of those government-run state-owned newspapers in Syria? This is self-censorship. This is not what the revolution is about, and if I can't hold those people to account now when they're in opposition, imagine when they're in a position of power! They'll probably send people to kill me in the TV station. I'm living in London and I'm subject to censorship. Where is this revolution going? So that made me say, this is completely messed up, and there's a lot of corruption and incompetence on the part of the opposition. [After that], I decided to take a step back. People called me [for interviews] and I said, I'm not available. I turned down all these requests to go on TV.

As Malik's case illustrates, the questionable – if not outright authoritarian – practices of some opposition leaders and rebel groups led many activists to rescind their support for the official bodies and organizations representing the Syrian revolution in 2012 and beyond.

6.1.3 Yemenis' Shortage of Cross-Border Ties to Arab Spring Participants

In contrast to their Libyan and Syrian counterparts, Yemeni activists in both host-countries reported being plagued from the start by network ties shortages with Yemenis on the ground. Some southern activists did have direct ties to various wings of the southern secessionist movement, as mentioned in Chapter 2. These activists withdrew their support shortly after the onset of the revolution due to concerns about northern co-optation, as explained in Chapter 4. Accordingly, their direct ties were diverted from the revolution effort back to the secessionist cause. Furthermore, while some non-secessionist activists had relatives in the protest encampments, activist leaders with no direct kin living in major urban centers reported feeling separated from revolutionaries on the ground. Besides those Yemeni Americans who were in contact with individuals such as Atiaf and Raja (see Chapter 4), few respondents reported connecting with activists outside of their kinship networks in Yemen. Shaima, one of the most active organizers in Birmingham, recalled that having relatives in rural areas left her disconnected from revolutionary centers.

say this.' He also said that's not his brother, it's just a guy who has the same surname or something. Anyway, just complete bullshit. So I said okay, fine, but those guys are prepared to go on the record and say he was a regime stooge and they killed him. So what's the response? He went crazy. At that point, I realized, this is the big story, this is the big political scandal. Because that means that guy's a liar. He went on *Al Jazeera* and said my brother's a martyr knowing that he wasn't a martyr.

When we were getting reports from Yemen ourselves, from my cousins in the village, you didn't *feel* it. Even though they held an opinion, they didn't feel part of the revolution. They didn't live it because they weren't in the city.

Awssan, an organizer in London, emphasized that without family in Sana'a, he too felt detached and uninformed about the movement in Change Square. While his colleague Ibrahim could "contact his cousin in Sana'a" to get information,

Trying to find out what's happening in Yemen was the most difficult thing. Getting in contact with the right people in Yemen, independents who would give me an idea of what's happening on the streets, it was [difficult].

Disconnection between insiders and outsiders therefore limited activists' abilities to serve as broadcasters and representatives or to channel resources to field hospitals and media centers in the encampments. Ahmed Alramadi, who participated in the Change Square movement and was detained and tortured by regime agents before gaining a visa to come to the United States in May 2011, explained to me that this was due to "a lack of connections. The Yemenis abroad had [few] informants or local links inside," he recalled. Instead, he affirmed that the focus of Yemenis on the outside was on broadcasting, "like protesting in front of the United Nations to get us attention." Because many of the most active organizers in the diaspora did not possess direct ties to activists on the ground, their roles as Arab Spring supporters were more indirect, and even ambiguous.

In light of this chasm, some activists were fearful of *mis*representing the revolution. Ahlam in New York, for example, was extremely concerned about people in Yemen "telling us to back off. I just had thoughts about, like, what is my role as somebody who hasn't really lived there? I'm privileged, and [do] I have the right to speak on behalf of these people? It was really bothering me." This self-reflexivity was echoed by activists across the three communities, but Libyans and Syrians were able to assuage this concern by communicating revolutionary demands strictly as instructed by their partners on the ground.[5] Furthermore, the only method to get aid into the revolutionary encampments was either for Yemenis to wire funds to individuals on the ground, such as their family members or activists like Atiaf, for in-person delivery to the squares. Yet, useful connections in this regard were sparse at best.

---

[5] Yemeni regime corruption and sabotage also stood in between diaspora members and the contacts they did have on the ground, which remained a significant obstacle to remitting resources. To illustrate, when Safa and her colleagues in London worked to ship a container of aid to Aden in partnership with a local NGO in 2011 (after the revolution's end), Safa reported that doing so created "a fucking nightmare. In Yemen, they tried every trick to block it, saying that the papers are all wrong. To the last second, this shipment was not going to happen. We had so many people trying to sabotage it." While getting about thirty thousand pounds' worth of aid to Yemen was a "beautiful" thing, Safa described the process as perilous because the diaspora remained dependent on corrupt or incompetent Yemeni bureaucrats to allow the aid in.

6.2 THE CONVERSION OF CAPITAL: FUNGIBLE RESOURCES, MATERIAL AID, AND SOCIAL CAPITAL

6.2.1 Libyans' Capital Conversion: Sufficient over Time

Libyans and Syrians alike intervened by tapping the wealth of the anti-regime diaspora, thereby converting cash into funds for rebellion and relief. Given Gaddafi's long-standing expulsion and isolation of the business classes, civil society leaders, and other elites, his repression came home to roost as wealthy individuals funded insurgent action against him. But so too did ordinary Libyans, including students and non-wealthy families forced to leave Libya with very little, make tremendous sacrifices to channel resources to the cause. Among Libyans in the United States and Britain, no respondent reported difficulties in converting fungible resources and acquiring material goods for the Arab Spring from their conationals. Dr. Mahmoud Traina recalled that after getting to Cairo, for instance, he found that Libyans there "had amassed a crazy amount of money – about one million dollars – from different expats," which they used to purchase aid and drive caravan of medicine and food into Benghazi. Another US-based activist recalled,

We had a registered bank account and an EIN number so we could collect money. We collected about twenty thousand dollars' worth of funding and about three hundred thousand dollars' worth of medical equipment. I took these boxes with me over to Malta, and this cash. There was a group of Libyan businessmen. They had these ships and were sending supplies, arms, and stuff like that, over to Misrata. They also had a shortage of milk and medical supplies and diapers, [so] that's what we spent a vast majority of our cash on. It was just kind of, how do you get these needs covered?

Activists also poured their own individual capital into the cause. As a medical doctor working in Cardiff, Niz used his personal finances and social capital to recruit five co-workers to treat injured fighters in Libya.[6] He explained, "We paid and planned everything down to the last little detail for them to fly from Cardiff to London to Egypt, to be driven into Benghazi, to be driven to Ajdabiya and back to Benghazi where they were staying in a safe house." In another case, an activist from Manchester attended a psychiatry conference in Norway in order to beseech doctors to come to Tunisia and volunteer their services with refugees. Using private donations from fellow Libyans, this individual helped to arrange for nine doctors from Norway to come to Tunisia in June to address the needs of traumatized Libyan women.

---

[6] According to Benamer (2012), 707 doctors registered in Britain had obtained a primary medical degree in Libya as of 2012. He cites the number of Libyan doctors in the United Kingdom, United States, Australia, and Canada as about 1,120 without disaggregating these numbers. These figures do not count those who completed their primary medical degree in USA and Britain or those working toward an MA or PhD in the medical sciences.

TABLE 6.1. *Libyan groups and organizations created for revolution and relief during the 2011 Arab Spring, as reported by respondents*

Diaspora Group/Organization Name	Exclusively an Apolitical Charity?
USA	
Lawyers for Justice in Libya[a]	No
Libya Coordinating Group	No
Libya Outreach	No
Libya Youth Movement[a]	No
Libyan American Association of Ohio	No
Libyan Council of North America	No
Libyan Emergency Task Force	No
Libyan Humanitarian Action	No
New Libya Foundation	No
Britain	
Lawyers for Justice in Libya[a]	No
Libya Link[a]	No
Libya Youth Movement[a]	No
Libyan British Relations Council	No
World Medical Camp for Libya	No
Other	
Libya AlAhrar[a] (Qatar-based)	No
Libya AlHurra[a] (Tunisia-based)	No

[a] Denotes multinational membership.

In addition to remitting directly, diaspora activists also channeled resources into the formation of new organizations staffed to support lobbying and relief efforts. These groups are listed in Table 6.1.

Because the revolution was relatively short-lived – lasting from February 2011 until Gaddafi's capture and execution in October – respondents reported that they were able to donate their time and resources to sustain a new set of pro-revolution diaspora organizations. Furthermore, those who traveled to Doha to work on the revolution satellite station had their hotel expenses paid either by funds supporting the National Transitional Council (NTC) or by wealthy Libyan donors. To that end, the creation of new organizations with low-to-no operating costs by the rank and file enabled activists to channel additional donations directly to the rebellion itself.

Libyans' full-spectrum role in the revolution was further bolstered by their social capital, including skills and experience in the areas of media, law, business, medicine, technology, politics, and civil society. Because knowledge and skills in these areas were needed to buttress a revolution that "needed everything," activists reported that their expertise came to be converted to the revolution in different ways. For instance, Fadel, a Libyan American who had worked for the US State Department in the past, was contacted by NTC

Chairman Mustafa Abdul Jalil to help them in lobbying the Obama administration for assistance. Fadel recalled that as an ad hoc advisor to the NTC, he helped them to formulate an argument for intervention based on the Responsibility to Protect doctrine. Having worked previously in the NGO world of Washington, DC, he recounted,

I have a lot of American friends who were involved in the Responsibility to Protect. I said we have to use this, and I sent it to them [the NTC] in English in an email – I still have this email – and they said, can you send this to us in Arabic? They couldn't read it because in the '80s, Gaddafi banned English. So I sent it to them [in Arabic] and said this is what we're going to do. It has never been used before, but we know Gaddafi is going to [retaliate] at that level. So that was the first advice, in terms of how we can go about getting the support of the international community and the framework we can use.

Fadel, among other respondents, continued to advise the NTC informally as a member of "their supporting cast" throughout the revolution.

In another example, Dina converted her skills in communications to assist in brokerage with dissidents and CNN. She recalled,

I ended up getting contacted by a producer from Anderson Cooper. I'm sitting here aspiring to get a job in the media; my master's is in communications. So I'm getting firsthand experience in something I really wanted to do and hopefully really contributing to a cause at the same time! I had all these media contacts that just converged. People that I hadn't heard from in years were like, "Hi Dina, so I'm working on getting some contacts for Libya and was hoping [you could help]." It's just because, you know, there's not very many Libyans. From that day, I was literally the on-call consultant for *Anderson Cooper 360°*, really working closely with the entire editorial production team to figure out what we're doing for the show for the night, five days a week.

Activists also used their social capital to address the traumas of sexual violence among Libyan refugee women. They did so by mobilizing to change the norms surrounding the social stigmatization and shaming of assault victims. Salam, for example, said,

We tried very hard to raise awareness in Libya about rape. We produced these [recordings], one in the Amazigh language, one in a Tripoli accent, one in a Benghazi accent, where boys, young men, would speak, explaining to people that, listen, these are victims. They didn't do anything wrong. You shouldn't be ashamed of them. We wanted to get the message out that, one, these people need help, and for a long time. It's not like, oh, your physical wounds are healed, you're fine. I don't think that Libyans understand culturally that the psychological effects of rape are sometimes lifelong. And we kind of wanted to stress that. I know that Libyan expats, especially the female Libyans in America, were just adamant on this.

Diaspora members also came to represent the revolution itself by joining the NTC to fill in gaps in leaders' professional expertise. After working with CNN, Dina of Southern California came to be recruited by the NTC as an advisor and assistant due to her professional expertise in communications. After working for Mahmoud Shamman at the AlAhrar satellite station, he introduced her to the Interim Prime Minister of Libya, Mahmoud Jibril. "I ended up managing all of his press," she recalled, and she traveled during the revolution back and forth from Doha to Libya to assist the prime minister directly.

Others remitted their much-needed expertise in medicine to the conflict. Dr. Ahmed Shalabi in London, for example, was relied upon by donors and his colleagues in the newly formed World Medical Camp for Libya to determine exactly what types of aid should be purchased and sent to the front lines.

They needed a doctor's touch, and that's when I really came in. People were already flying to Egypt to get stuff into Libya. They were asking me for a list of things, saying I have this amount of money, tell me what I need to buy. I told them what I thought we should buy, one, two, three, four, five. I [also] started trying to get meetings with other doctors, Skyping my doctor friends here in the UK with a variety of specialties and asking them, okay, bone injuries, what do I need? Anesthetics, what do I need? That's the first-ever list I formed.

Dr. Traina of Southern California also emphasized that activists relied on doctors to determine what supplies to purchase because "some requests were for things that they had been living without for twenty years and other things were more medically urgent. You'd have to sort through these lists and see what was most urgently needed. That was mostly my role."

Activists additionally lent legal expertise to the revolution. M. in the United States and Mohammad in London, for example, joined a transnational network of Libyan lawyers to assist in the documentation of the revolution and to help build a case in the International Criminal Court against the regime. She said,

I got on this call [with] these Libyan lawyers, all fairly young, I would say forty years old and under, all living abroad. They were trying to handle all of the different requests that they were getting in, because the foreign governments in whatever country they lived in were looking for some consultations. At the same time, there were things going on in the ground that needed to be addressed as far as collecting evidence, fact-finding, investigating, so I started working on that as well. I was a law student, but it was really interesting because we basically were helping set up investigative committees in Libya to collect evidence.

As the war progressed, activists also lent their strategic and logistical know-how to the revolutionary forces who were largely comprised of inexperienced or civilian volunteers. Abdo G. from Manchester attested,

We set up something called Libya Link. We founded this as a way to provide expertise in international law, humanitarian law, as well as our own strategic tactical type skills. So if you had the skill, the strategy, you could pool your opinions or even get involved in logistics to save a life, and maybe win a battle. Objective number two was to help empower the youth, and there were two types. One was the youth who were playing their parts in the operation centers on the front lines. We were providing support to train them up, give them strategies and tactics, logistical type stuff, as well as [for] the youth who were working on the humanitarian side.

When I asked Abdo how he was able to advise a nascent army using a professional background in business strategy, he replied,

Our background was not primarily military, but we all had to do what we had to do. So if we had to develop military expertise, we developed military expertise! A lot of it was actually the experience from the business world. Strategy is strategy at the end of the day. If you're from the business world or commercial space, you're being competitive and we took some of those ideas and strategies to the opposition space. Scenarios were done using various game theories. For training, we looked at the needs and developed on that. We had access to skills in those respects, and we had ideas about what can be done.

In addition to applying their social capital to the revolution directly, activists also expanded upon their existing skill sets to convert their professional expertise into activism. For example, Dr. Shalabi described that his role was not only that of a medical consultant for the London-based charity World Medical Camp for Libya, but that he also became a buyer and supplier of aid. He described how, after receiving a list of needed medical supplies to send to Libya, he was left with the question:

How do I get them? So I started Googling pharmaceutical companies in the UK, equipment companies, I went to my local pharmacist in the hospital asking him about costs. I needed to know everything! I started getting lists of companies and calling them about antibiotics, external fixators, [asking] which ones are the cheapest? I managed to find a company that sold used medical equipment, contacted them, and I got great prices from them, it was like a godsend. The next problem was, how do I get them to Malta? We have to find air shipping! One of the other guys in the charity managed to get a Libyan friend who coordinated with this freight company, they stored everything we got for free, and they managed to get all of the stuff air-freighted all the way to Malta. We had to make sure that everything was in place, that all the boxes were ready. It was nonstop. At the time, I was a foundation year-one doctor, someone who just recently graduated, [and] I was given the full responsibility of getting the lists, making the purchases, talking to the companies.

Like Dina and Dr. Shalabi, many other respondents found themselves promoted beyond their years in their roles as revolution supporters.

Many diaspora members traveled to the front lines to convert their capital to the effort. Abdallah Omeish, a Libyan American filmmaker from Los Angeles, snuck into Benghazi during the first week of the revolution to film a documentary on the resistance. He focused on telling the story of Mohammed Nabbous, a revolutionary activist in Benghazi who became a hero for broadcasting a livestreamed video of the city on the web before he was killed.[7] Others lent their medical expertise to the injured. Dr. Traina, for example, volunteered to transport aid and lend his skills in Benghazi.

We were getting reports of people getting killed and the hospitals being short-staffed, [and about] a lack of medicine and supplies, and I started talking with some of my

---

[7] See *Libya 2011: Through the Fire* (Omeish 2011).

childhood friends [about this]. [One of them] called me and said we need to help, we're trying to get some medical supplies in. [Around] the twenty-second, I went to Cairo. While in contact with hospitals in Libya, we immediately went about arranging a caravan of medicine and food. We went to Benghazi so we drove through the border. People from all over were coming [to Cairo], it was a diverse group. By the twenty-seventh, we had a shipment put together of four trucks of medicine and another three or four trucks of food items and drove them into Libya. Then I went to help in one of the hospitals in Benghazi and they were pretty overwhelmed. The hospitals were not equipped to handle the amount of major trauma that they had to deal with.

M., who was in her second year of law school when the revolution began, also recalled an opportunity to serve on the revolution's transnational, diaspora-driven legal team even though she had not yet obtained her law degree.

I attended a training there at the ICC, which was really interesting because it was only for lawyers with ten years' experience. Ten years ago, I was in fifth grade, you know! So after I completed that training, I then went to London to meet up with some of the lawyers I was working with, but only really on the internet. There was one in London, one in Paris, one in Spain, one in Dubai, some in Libya. In London, we had a series of consultations with [Parliamentary Under-Secretary of State at the Foreign and Commonwealth Office] Alistair Burt [to] discuss with him the issues that were going on, and we'd phone in someone on the ground in Libya to explain more, or what the UK could do to support them. So we did a lot of that that summer – ICC cases, investigating, but also advocating in general. My colleague who was with me went to the UN to advocate there, we had a lot of things going on at that time. We created guidelines for pro-revolution fighters once the armed conflict began on how they could comply with international rules of engagement without violating any sort of human rights. We did so at the request of the National Transitional Council. Basically we boiled them down to little flip cards that they could carry with them, laminated little cards, which was a flow chart of if you're in this situation, what do you do, what don't you do. So we were engaging at all different levels on the legal front.

In all, by pushing many of Libya's most well-to-do and highly educated out of the country in search of freedom and opportunities, the regime produced a highly skilled and well-resourced diaspora primed to mobilize against the regime under the right conditions. As M. remarked,

Those abroad ended up becoming very educated, very well-connected in their societies, and they were able to influence from the outside. That was something that Gaddafi did to himself, because he did forcefully exile those people. Everyone used their kind of expertise and their skills to contribute in any way they could. A lot of influential Libyans were consulting other governments, and were well-connected enough to raise a lot of funds for aid. Not a single thing was left undone, I think, by Libyans abroad.

6.2.2 Syrians' Capital Conversion: From Sufficient to Insufficient

The exact figures remain unknown, but there is no doubt that Syrians abroad have remitted tens of millions of dollars to Arab Spring organizations and charities over the course of the rebellion and war (Svoboda and Pantuliano 2015).

The fundraisers I attended during my ethnographic observations of the well-to-do Southern California community, for instance, raised tens of thousands of dollars for SAC and humanitarian aid from a single event. Leaders also used their resources to establish a number of new organizations dedicated to rebellion and relief, listed in Table 6.2.

TABLE 6.2. *Syrian groups and organizations created for the revolution and relief during the Arab Spring (2011–14), as reported by respondents*

Diaspora Group/Organization Name	Exclusively a Charity/Service Org?
USA	
American Relief Coalition for Syria	Yes
American Rescue Fund	Yes
Coalition for a Democratic Syria	No
FREE-Syria	No
Karam Foundation	Yes
Maram Foundation	Yes
Southern California Coordinating Committee	No
Syria Relief and Development	Yes
Syrian Support Group	No
Syrian American Engineers Association	Yes
Syrian American Humanitarian Network	Yes
Syrian Christians for Democracy/Peace[a]	No
Syrian Emergency Task Force	No
Syrian Expatriates Organization	Yes
Syria Justice and Accountability Centre[a]	No
Syrian Institute for Progress	No
Syrian Sunrise Foundation	Yes
Texans for Free Syria	No
United for a Free Syria	No
Britain	
Bristol Justice for Syria	No
British Solidarity for Syria	No
Global Solidarity Movement for Syria	No
Hand in Hand for Syria	Yes
Help for Syria	Yes
Human Care Syria	Yes
Rethink Rebuild Society	No
Syria Relief	Yes
Syrian Christians for Democracy/Peace[a]	No
Syrian Legal Development Programme	No
Syrian Parliamentary Affairs Group	No

[a] Denotes multinational membership.

The sufficiency of Syrians' resources is not surprising given their relatively high degree of wealth and educational attainment in comparison to other immigrant groups. Syrians' socioeconomic and educational mobility have been high in the United States due in part to the fact that their origins were middle-class to begin with, as well as the fact that many came abroad specifically to obtain advanced degrees and white-collar work. Of course, not all Syrian activists were wealthy. However, their community-level wealth was initially sufficient to fund the pro-Arab Spring effort in different ways. In the United States, for instance, the median annual wage for Syrian immigrants was reported as $52,000 in 2014, compared to the $36,000 median wage for all immigrants and $45,000 for US-born workers (Dyssegaard Kallick et al. 2016). In the same year, 27 percent of Syrian immigrant men held an advanced degree of some sort; 11 percent were business owners compared to 4 percent of immigrants and 3 percent of US-born persons; Syrian business owners additionally earned an average of $72,000 per year (Dyssegaard Kallick et al. 2016). Researchers also report that Syrian immigrants have relatively elevated levels of English-language abilities, home ownership, and naturalization compared to all immigrants and the US-born (Dyssegaard Kallick et al. 2016).

Correspondingly, Syrian activists reported converting their social capital to the anti-regime effort. As mentioned in Chapter 5, engineers like Khaled worked to lend their expertise and skills by partnering with Syrians at home to rebuild infrastructure destroyed by the regime and its backers. Lobbyists like Mouaz Moustafa, with years of experience working as a congressional aide in Washington, DC, and then as a member of the Libyan Emergency Task Force, went on to form the formidable Syrian Emergency Task Force to lobby for sanctions against the regime. Law students like Y. lent her legal expertise to the cause, arguing that the Responsibility to Protect doctrine should be applied in the Syrian case, and not just the Libyan one. Youth activists like Razan and Alaa, mentioned in Chapter 4, used their tech savviness to communicate with activists on the ground to coordinate and publicize protests. Doctors like Fadel and Ayman lent their labor by working with groups like the Syrian American and Syrian British medical societies to perform life-saving surgeries inside liberated zones and refugee camps. Syrian Americans like Hussam, with years of experience as a civil rights activist for Arab and Muslim minorities, transferred his organizing and fundraising expertise to the Syrian American Council. I watched in awe firsthand as he helped to raise tens of thousands of dollars for the Syrian American Council in community meetings held in hotel ballrooms in Anaheim, California. In all, a well-educated and highly professionalized activist community offered an immense degree of intangible support to the revolution and relief efforts.

However, as the need for aid increased over time with Syria's growing humanitarian emergency, these organizers' main donor base in the anti-regime diaspora came to be tapped dry. Dr. Ziadeh in DC attested that the millions of Syrians who had been displaced and rendered unemployed over the course of the war came to be wholly reliant on the support of their family members in the diaspora, which diverted aid from the political to the personal.

When we talk about four million refugees in neighboring countries and nine million displaced, everyone has his family affected. My mother crossed the border into Turkey[8] along with my sister. I have another brother in Jordan and a sister in Lebanon. I'm responsible for [them]. No one can afford that for two or three years, no matter the income you have. This is why the Syrian communities here [now] focus much more on their immediate families.

This is not to say that members of the diaspora ceased to donate to charitable organizations or to volunteer altogether. But at the same time, the anti-regime community could no longer be relied upon by organizers to write enough checks to supply the donations needed to meet the ever-expanding needs of millions of Syrians. As Nebal of London explained, "What's the point of asking someone, some Syrian, to donate money when you know he himself has to provide food for three, four, five families already?"

Organizers also reported that protest participation had waned significantly by 2014 for all events except commemorative activities in large part because of financial difficulties. Haytham in Manchester explained that they amassed funds to pay for protesters to travel to London for "six, seven months until we were exhausted financially, because every coach costs one thousand pounds." Nebal, an organizer with the group British Solidarity for Syria, attested that participants came to feel that their time and resources would be of better use elsewhere.

At the very beginning, it was easy to go every Saturday to demonstrate. Nowadays, many in the community would say, what's the point of spending two hours every Saturday protesting? – it would be better for me to work and make some money to send to Syria instead. And I totally agree with that. But as a symbol, it's [important to have] big marches to mark the anniversary of the revolution, to mark the big massacres.

Overall, fungible resource conversion declined as the revolution became prolonged and created an extreme humanitarian crisis.

The conversion of Syrians' social capital to the revolution was also compromised due to their dependence on insiders willing to receive and use this resource in local contexts. Many activists found that they had no one, and nowhere, to channel their skills *to* once their allies were killed, captured, or displaced, as discussed above. As their abilities to convert social capital

---

[8] For detailed information about Syrian refugees in Turkey and across Europe, see Carlson and Williams (2020).

consistently declined over time, this deprived Syrians of the "brain gain" (Kapur 2010) needed to supplement the underequipped resistance.

6.2.3 From Resource Shortages to Professionalization

A decline in fungible resource conversion among anti-regime Syrians in the United States and Britain caused many informal groups to die off after volunteers and donors became exhausted. I found that organizations without the financial backing of a board or wealthy donors to pay for one or two full-time staff by 2014 had since closed or become comatose. At the same time, organizers responded strategically to these hurdles by channeling remaining resources into the formation of formal, professionalized organizations that specialized in addressing a specific dimension of the rebellion or relief effort. This professionalization enabled some activists to withstand unfavorable conditions by switching from a self- or community-sustained emergency response to long-term advocacy focused on a particular area of need. The legal accreditation that came with formalization also enabled activists to solicit funding from sources outside of the Syrian diaspora, such as by NGOs, which counteracted resource depletion and fears that informal remittances would become associated with support for terrorism (see Chapter 7).

At the same time, formalization imposed regulations and constraints on activists' work, which limited their abilities to adapt creatively and spontaneously[9] to needs on the ground. Respondents attested that the formalization process required donors to divert some portion of their contributions to the maintenance of diaspora organizations themselves. Haytham, director of Manchester's Rethink Rebuild Society, described how his organization's survival depended on the commitment of wealthy private donors to pay for staff salaries.

From January 2012, we had an office for our British Syrian Community of Manchester. At that time, I was doing my PhD. I opened this office daily for three hours in the evening time and it stayed like that for one year. At that time, the money came job by job. Let's say that, okay, we need the coach to London [to hold a protest], we need one thousand pounds. After I finished my PhD, I told them, look, I have to find a job or continue with you for any amount of money just to live on. [The donors] said we need you, so stay with us. Two years ago, we started to make it more systematic. So now people are paying, let's say, a regular payment of twenty pounds a month, and we have some businessman paying more to cover the cost of the office, employees, some activities. Now we are five people after a long journey. We moved here to this proper office one year ago.

---

[9] On creativity in the Arab Spring, see Bamyeh (2014); on the importance of spontaneity in social movements, see Snow and Moss (2014).

FIGURE 6.1. The Rethink Rebuild Society advertises its mission to the diaspora community during a Syria Day celebration in Manchester, England, in 2013. The last line states, "We believe that our work with the Syrian diaspora will strengthen the determination to rebuild Syria, in spite of its destruction through war and conflict." (Photo credit: Dana M. Moss)

Mouaz Moustafa, the full-time executive director of the Syrian Emergency Task Force in Washington, DC, also explained that his political advocacy work is funded by his organization's board.

The boards of my organizations are all Syrian and they donate for the salaries and the office space and so on for the team that we've got. That's why we've lasted a really long time, four years of doing this regularly and it's a lot of money, even though compared to other organizations and lobbies it's little money. But for them to sustain that for a very long time is admirable.

In contrast to the formation of these DC-based lobbying organizations, I did not find any interest group organizations in London dedicated full-time to lobbying or political advocacy as of 2014. While official statistics on their community wealth is lacking, this suggests that the smaller community in Britain, which is also made up of more recent immigrants, lacks the wealth of their counterparts in the United States. Though respondents reported some ad hoc volunteer-based lobbying efforts, including by a handful of volunteers comprising the Syrian Parliamentary Affairs Group and Syrian Christians for Democracy, most interviewees lamented the weakness of the British Syrian community's lobbying efforts. The Parliamentary Affairs Group, for example, was only formed *after* the failure of the British government to launch strikes in retaliation to the regime's chemical weapons attacks of August 2013. This group was also comprised largely of Syrian doctors who volunteered on a part-time basis.

Other informal organizations that had previously engaged in advocacy, such as the British Solidarity for Syria, were inactive by 2014. Nebal, a former coordinator of this group, explained, "To be honest, we've got no resources." Mazen E. of London agreed, describing in a separate interview, "We have some small groups, lobbying groups or parliamentary groups. They're not professional by any means. These things need a lot of financial support and professional support. Unfortunately, we haven't got it." Syrian American professional groups, on the other hand, continued to represent and broker with a range of officials across governmental institutions and think tanks. While these groups were unable to change the Obama administration's policy on Syria outright, as the next chapter explains, they continued to work with allies in the US government to provide information to and consult with policymakers. Some, like Mouaz, continue their work years later, including at the time of this writing.

Another benefit of movement formalization was that the specialization of the pro-revolution diaspora's work enabled them to address needs in a way that used limited resources efficiently. M. of the nonprofit organization Help for Syria in London recalled,

To start with, we were not professional. Everybody – one a doctor, one a teacher, one a businessman – all wanted to help, and in the beginning, *everybody* was doing *everything*. We were going out demonstrating in front of the embassy, we were trying to go to the parliament in here, we were communicating with the newspapers, with the news, with the TV, networking, doing humanitarian work. Then we started realizing you have to specialize in something. It's wrong to do everything. Leave the doctors to do the medical field. Leave the psychiatrists to do [mental health] support. Even if you're going to do humanitarian, specialize either in nutrition or homes or clothes or children or women. That's why I withdrew from where I used to work in Turkey and Lebanon and Jordan. I am from the city of Suwayda. It's inside Syria and is very difficult to get to, it's in a city still under government control. There are a lot of displaced families in there, really in need. They cannot go to the Red Cross under their names because of their relations, their husbands and kids who are fighting. So that's where I concentrate my work, in an area where I can be more effective.

Lina of the Karam Foundation, based in Chicago, also realized after a time that doing both political and humanitarian work was unsustainable. Referring to her experience and that of her fellow activists in SAC, she remarked, "We were so tired [because] we were so focused on the next emergency. We [decided that we] have to change our lifestyles because this thing is going to go on for a very long time." For this reason, Lina came to prioritize the humanitarian work of the Karam Foundation and to focus on food deliveries and education, leaving medical aid to fellow organizations like the Syrian American Medical Society. Ibrahim al-Assil additionally recalled, "There is a huge need inside Syria. But at the same time, if we decide to do too many things, we will end up doing nothing." Accordingly, once carried out solely through informal networks, aid work came to be conducted through formal Syrian-led organizations.

Relief-oriented activism was critical in reaching populations within Syria who were blocked by the regime from receiving aid from international organizations. Omar, an activist from Houston, described how his brother Yakzan, founder of the Maram Foundation, was compelled to formalize his efforts.

[My brother] was going inside Syria to the liberated areas along the border and then saw that there were a few hundred people in need. So we raised some funds [for] tents and things like that. The problem about this camp is that it's not a regular refugee camp .... The United Nations can't give aid to those people. Red Cross cannot give aid to those people. At the beginning, we were tapping the local community here in Houston and a few people that we know to raise funds and to help those people. And then the numbers [of internally displaced persons] increased dramatically. We went everywhere trying to get funds for them. If you're not an organization, then you can't, [you don't qualify for aid]. So then we established Maram Foundation to be able to raise funds to aid those people.[10]

Likewise, M. from Suwayda argued that the best use of his limited resources was to fill in the gaps of the relief efforts among the internally displaced and most needy inside Syria.

I decided that I'm going to do some things mainly [for] the children with special needs. Children being traumatized and badly affected by witnessing torture, rape, killing, things like that, together with the women and their families who have special needs as well. I set up a center in the city [where] we've done psychodrama, psychotherapy. We managed to enroll about seven or eight thousand children from the families who came to the city in the normal school in Suwayda. Any funds I get, I get whoever donated to transfer it directly to the people, and we don't have any expenses because we are all volunteers. If they can't get it to Syria, I'll send it to Lebanon, and from Lebanon, they send it to Syria.

While funding from larger organizations enabled Syrian diaspora movements to survive and conduct life-saving work, this adaptation also brought its own sets of challenges. Reflecting upon his experience trying to fund the Syrian Nonviolence Movement, Ibrahim explained that one problem with relying on international NGO funding is that these organizations often dictated the work of the diaspora from on high.

---

[10] See also Malek (2013) for media reporting on Yakzan's activism.

To become full-time, [Syrian organizations] need a source of money and to be employed. Some of them, they got funds for that from NGOs, or they were employed [directly by] other NGOs. That has pros and cons. That means they're more professional, they have access to more money. But at the same time, they have less freedom to choose what they want to do. Because when you are part of an international NGO, they plan for you already what you can do. There are actually some NGOs who are ready to fund Syrian groups and give them kind of freedom and space where they can decide what they want to do. But also some of them, they have a clear or certain agenda and they say this is our goal and this is the kind of project we want you to do, [or] we don't support you.

Ibrahim also recalled that these organizations tended to sponsor projects with delimited start and end dates, rather than promoting long-term projects or empowering the growth of Syrian organizations themselves.

That said, some diaspora organizations have been able to harness funding from larger NGOs and major private donors to supplement their broader goals. Dr. Jundi of Syria Relief in Manchester explained,

[These organizations] have been raising lots of money in the name of Syria, but in reality, they haven't been able to use it because they either cannot take it into Syria or they opted to use it in the [easier] environment of refugee camps. Yes, there is a need there, but nowhere near as much as the need inside. So we have developed a very good working relationship with a number of major NGOs. We've managed to put proposals together that they would fund and cover part of our administrative cost. They couldn't deliver it, so *we* can deliver it, acting as their agent, and they'd get all the documentation that they need [from us]. That's been an important part of our success, because although a lot of our fundraising relies on the five, ten, twenty pounds that people give, the big bucks come from either big NGOs or charitable organizations that want to do something for Syria but cannot, or want to do something but are reluctant to be seen openly doing it. There are also a number of industrialists or businessmen of Syrian origin working in the UK, made their fortunes in the UK, and they want to give something back. Some of them actually cooperate with us in support of our programs. So that means we don't have to worry about these programs – we can focus on stuff they're not interested in, like food supplies and that kind of mundane thing that isn't visible.

At the same time, Syria Relief was not in any way allowed to be "political," to discuss or affiliate with the revolution, or even use the opposition's flag or logo. This created a delicate situation for the organization. Dr. Jundi said that in one case,

We had somebody who, on his website, was openly selling items [with the revolution flag on them] and donating 20 percent of the money he raised to Syria Relief. We got reprimanded by the Charity Commission for it, even though we had nothing to do with it. We didn't ask for it, we didn't know that he was doing it – just because we were mentioned in the same sentence as revolutionary items, that was a no-no. So we have to be absolutely squeaky clean when it comes to abiding by the regulations.

Lina of the Karam Foundation lamented that despite the importance of fundraising, their efforts were woefully inadequate in addressing the needs of millions.

The problem is the work that we have to do is not the work of organizations – it's really the work of *nations*. Because no matter what we do, it's never enough. We can't give out enough food, we can't set up enough schools. The Syrian American Medical Society can't help every single person that's injured.

L., who had worked within Syria to deliver aid and fight with the Free Syrian Army for a time, noted that the formalization of aid transfers from the diaspora was problematic for both practical and moral reasons. He lamented,

When I gave out cash to families in need in Syria, to widows and orphans, [Syrians in the United States] told me it's illegal for me to give out cash to civilians. That I need *receipts*. I'm like, are you *kidding* me? You *have* to break rules. That's how you get results. You can never even *have* a revolution if you follow the rules! *The whole revolution is illegal!* It makes no sense.

As the poor response of states and international institutions to the Syrian crisis increased the need for diaspora intervention, activists shifted into full-time professionalized advocacy, thereby establishing a sustainable transnational advocacy field. While formalization had its limitations, this was the only option for movements facing an expanding humanitarian emergency and a losing war at home. That said, even as diaspora activists in the United States and Britain performed a number of critical roles in the cause through capital conversion, they nevertheless perceived their efforts as insufficient to meet needs on the ground.

6.2.4 Yemeni Challenges to Converting Material and Fungible Aid to the Revolution

Yemenis faced a different situation. In order to keep the pro-revolution protest movement legitimate in a diaspora plagued by conflict transmission (see Chapter 4), organizers deliberately did not establish formal organizations out of concern that participants would accuse them of co-opting, or speaking over, revolutionaries in Yemen. Mahmoud of Sheffield said that Yemenis had not "moved" to that extent in their history and that mobilizing the community became a big job. However, they "tried to make it less formal in order to keep everybody involved and not to create political fractures or fights for representation." They were also "cautious about finances, because we were independent. We asked people to pay for themselves and we collected donations from people to pay [for others]" to go to London for demonstrations. Financial sponsorship of the pro-revolution movement came to be associated with co-optation, and for this reason, organizers relied on individuals to fund their participation and kept their initiatives informal. The activist groups they formed are listed in Table 6.3.

Keeping their claims vague and their movements informal was tricky for organizers, however, for several reasons. Ahlam, a Yemeni activist youth with

TABLE 6.3. *Yemeni groups and organizations created for revolution and relief during the 2011 Arab Spring, as reported by respondents*

Diaspora Group/Organization Name	Exclusively a Charity/Service Org?
USA	
Popular Support Committee to the Youth Revolution in Yemen	No
Yemeni American Coalition for Change	No
Yemeni Youth Abroad for Change	No
Yemeni Youth for Change in California	No
Britain	
Change Point Liverpool	No
Independent Yemen Group	No
Liverpool Yemeni Youth Movement	No
Yemen Revolution Support Group	No
Yemeni British Coalition to Support the Yemeni Revolution	No

prior experience organizing for other minority rights campaigns in the United States, exclaimed,

It was a whole new ballgame because I realized I wasn't working within an *organization*. I haven't had any experience working with loosely affiliated groups, so I wasn't quite sure how the democratic process was working. People were like, don't tell so-and-so about this meeting! It's like, what is going on here? [laughs] But *it mirrored what was going on in Yemen*, all of the fractured things that were happening and how people were losing sight of the larger picture. How do you keep their morale up, and keep things really organized and clear, and not leave people out? Because people were coming from different places, and get really offended by little things. It's hard to deal with it when this isn't people's full-time job and coming to the table with a variety of skills. Really, *we should have just had one person manage that full-time*, but it was just different people.

Many respondents additionally attested that strategies to maintain the integrity of the diaspora movement by keeping it informal exacerbated the literal costs of movement participation. This was due to the fact that a significant proportion of the Yemeni diaspora community in the United States and Britain was working class to begin with. New York–based organizers also reported difficulties in sustaining protests because many of their supporters worked day and night running small businesses like bodegas and were preoccupied with child care. Morooj likewise attested that their Washington, DC-based movement lacked the resources to continue bringing attention to the Yemeni crisis in an effective way.

There was this sense of urgency, and that always is problematic because how do you build something that's long-term while still addressing the urgency of the situation? Does [protest] really create change? It creates awareness, yes, to some degree. But ongoing protests, not really. You have to shift your energy towards something else. I was like, visibility is important. What else can we do instead? We tried to get more creative. [Tactics such as] flash mobs or messaging around the city, like wheat-pasting posters about Yemen. I could have taken it upon myself, but *it also takes resources and bodies to do that.*

Mahmoud, a Sheffield-based organizer, described that relying on self-funded volunteers and private donations to keep their movement independent and credible made it difficult to keep protest events going.

Honestly speaking, it was a high cost because the mobilization of people across cities exhausted us financially as well. With all of this, we do our normal jobs [at the same time]. The level of pressure that was on me was just crazy. Safa [in London], she was going mad because she is doing her full-time job and she put a lot of commitment into these activities.

Though some organizers sustained protests into the fall, others – such as in the Liverpool community – reported that their local movements were "well and truly dead" by the summer. Morooj of Washington, DC, echoed this, explaining,

[Protesting] was a weekly thing for a very long time. And then it just started trickling down. Not so many folks were coming down anymore, [feeling like it] doesn't make a difference. I would say [that the movement died] maybe towards the end of September. And it was just kind of like, what should we do? Should we gather? That's when it kind of died out. People were working, have families. They can't just dedicate six hours a day.

As a result of these resource shortages, organizers overwhelmingly reported feeling frustrated over their limited role and weak sense of efficacy. Adel of Dearborn cited that their Popular Support Committee to the Youth Revolution in Yemen was formed as "a reaction to what's going on back home. So if there is something major, then somebody will do something about it. And if there is not, it would just stay quiet." Amel of New York also lamented that their ad hoc mobilization efforts had "no long-term strategizing, there's no long-term planning. You do last-minute protests. I feel that that works for the short term, but I don't feel that's effective in the long term." Hanna echoed this sentiment, lamenting that for both the pro-secession and pro-revolution protests, "I've always felt our efforts were reactionary and we lose momentum after a rally or protest was over." Without a sustainable organizational field, as in the Syrian case, Yemeni activists often felt left on the "backfoot," as Omar in Liverpool attested.

As explained in Chapter 4, Yemenis' collective tactics focused on broadcasting and representing the revolution. To this end, many were able to convert their social capital to the mobilization effort. Safa, who had previously worked in public relations, issued press releases to the media about protest events in London. Awssan, with experience networking with Yemenis across Britain for the Yemen Forum Foundation, converted these skills during the Arab Spring into organizing protests. Ibrahim Al Qataby, with years of experience under his belt mobilizing for human rights in the nonprofit sector in New York, transferred his skills in framing, internal organization, and communicating with the media to bring attention to protest events. That said, organizers attested that they carried a disproportionate burden when rallying inexperienced compatriots to the movement. Ibrahim, for instance, explained the problem with relying on volunteer labor and amateur activists during the revolution. At that time, he said,

We had lots of challenges. Our community was not very much involved in any political or human rights advocacy in the US. They were political in the sense where they understand what's going on, but they never took it to the streets in a form of organized advocacy. They read news, and specifically Yemeni news, but they never organized themselves into lobbyist groups . . . . Especially when a lot of them work twelve hours a day, seven days a week, when is the appropriate time for them to come out? And a lot of community [members] hardly understand how to use the media and the political system, how to navigate it. That was another challenge. When I first started doing this with my colleagues, almost everyone did not know how to get a police permit. Basics [like] how to phrase slogans, signs, how to frame [their messages]. And the few who know how to do it were completely swamped with a lot of extra burden. A number of us were overwhelmed. You're starting from scratch trying to guide people how to do advocacy, show them A to Z.

Accordingly, diaspora movements in the United States and Britain only possessed some of the social capital needed to organize and sustain community-wide mobilization. This dynamic was later echoed in a 2019 report from the Brookings Doha Center, which argues that although Yemenis abroad serve as a valuable resource for their war-torn homeland, "the poor mobilization and coordination among these Yemeni professionals is a major challenge" (Aboueldahab 2019: 1).

Another difference between Yemenis' group-level experiences and those of the Libyans and Syrians was the fact that little of their social capital seemed to reach the protest encampments in Yemen itself. According to respondents, this was due not only to their sparse network ties but also because the advice from the diaspora was not always needed or welcome. As Atiaf, a Yemeni American who participated in the uprisings in Sanaʿa, lamented, "Yemeni Americans would get into details about where people should march. I would say, leave it up to the people *in Yemen* to decide where to march!" The relational disconnection between insiders and outsiders plagued efforts among activists abroad to help their allies in concrete ways over the course of the revolution.

6.3 CONCLUSION

Diaspora movements that converted network ties and capital to rebellion and relief became transnational players in the Arab Spring in different ways.

Cross-border network ties with allies became crucial for broadcasting, representing, brokering, remitting, and volunteering on the ground. Fungible and material resources gave activists the means to augment anti-regime efforts directly and the capacity to build a new transnational organizational infrastructure. Social capital elevated activists' voice as advisors, interpreters, and participants in the revolutions. At the same time, not all diaspora movements were equally well-resourced and able to convert resources to the Arab Spring. When movements lacked or lost these varied forms of resources, as the Syrian and Yemeni cases across the United States and Britain illustrate, their voices in the revolutions become less effective and muted.

While resource conversion is a critical process for diaspora interventions, it is also insufficient to explain diaspora movements' roles in anti-authoritarian mobilizations at home. The following chapter demonstrates how the added factor of geopolitical support is also vital in facilitating diaspora movement interventions, including the movement of resources across state lines. Without this support, diaspora activists and their resources become caged inside host-country borders, and their voices in homeland struggles are rendered into merely symbolic displays of support.

7

Gaining Geopolitical Support

Social movements do not operate in a vacuum, and they do not fulfill their goals on their own. As a number of pioneers in the field of movement studies have demonstrated, activists operate in contexts populated by a range of political players, including government officials and the media, who have the potential to help or hinder the realization of their goals (Lipsky 1968; McAdam 1999 [1982]; McAdam et al. 2001; Meyer 2004; Tilly 1976[1964]). Accordingly, while the process of *resource conversion* discussed in Chapter 6 is necessary for diaspora intervention against authoritarianism, it will only get activists so far. This chapter demonstrates that just as local- and national-level social movements are bolstered by the backing of their proximate governments, the media, and civil society (Amenta 2006; Gamson and Wolfsfeld 1993; McAdam and Boudet 2012), so too is transnational diaspora activism facilitated by the *geopolitical support* of international actors such as states, media, international NGOs (Keck and Sikkink 1998), and multilateral bodies dedicated to regulating the behavior of states.

Geopolitical support is necessary for diaspora activists to fulfill their goals for several reasons. First, even if activists return home to instigate insurgency or channel weapons homeward (Anderson 1998; Hockenos 2003), they cannot take down powerful authoritarian regimes on their own. Instead, they need the backing of states and institutions with the capacity to counter authoritarian regime violence and support rebel groups directly (Betts and Jones 2016). Second, diaspora members are literal outsiders to the homeland, separated from their allies by borders and distance. Activists who seek to intervene in their home-countries by remitting and volunteering are therefore reliant on gatekeeping authorities who control the movement of people and resources in geographical space. Of course, activists can often find a way around these gatekeepers through smuggling and circuitous routes. Nevertheless, states can significantly hinder remittance-sending and cross-border travel by making it an illegal or otherwise impossible ordeal for ordinary people.

Geopolitical support is of particular importance for groups that have become stereotyped as threats to national security, as with Libyans, Syrians, and Yemenis in the United States and Britain (Godwin 2018; Shain 2007: 49). When activists seek to fundraise for insurgencies and regime change – as when Golda Meir raised $50 million from her supporters in the United States in 1948 to purchase arms in Europe for Haganah militants in Israel (Shain 2007: 50–51) – their actions will be greatly facilitated by a permissive political environment. Otherwise, movements seeking to amass resources for radical change overseas may pay a steep price. For Arabs, Muslims, and many South Asians, the transfer of funds to the region for political change, or even simply for charity, has been another story altogether. As sociologist Ali Chaudhary's (2021) research on Pakistani immigrant organizations across the United States, Britain, and Canada reveals, remittances for charity have been caught in the war-on-terror dragnet, which has imposed significant burdens and barriers on cross-border relief efforts.

For Middle Eastern emigrants, both clandestine and legal measures have prevented the channeling of funds to insurgents categorized as inimical to host-country interests since at least the 1960s (Pennock 2017). While persons of Arab heritage have not been the only activists targeted by state surveillance and harassment for their ties to foreign liberation struggles, historian Pamela Pennock (2017: 143) observes that "The government's persecution of Arab Americans [has been] unique in its aim to link their activism to foreign terrorism." Furthermore, after the terrorist attacks of September 11, 2001, security agencies in the United States and Britain paid even more scrutiny to funds moving from diasporas to Islamist actors and networks at home (Horst and van Hear 2002: 49). Today, as members' home-country ties render them as suspects in the war on terror, "the voice of Arab Americans is muffled or magnified" according to host-country geopolitics and its interplay with events in the region (Pulcini 1993: 59). Because Middle Easterners in the West are particularly vulnerable to scrutiny by security agencies for channeling resources homeward, they require a significant degree of geopolitical support to help level what is a deeply unequal playing field for transnational activists.

In light of the importance of geopolitical support for diaspora activism, this chapter demonstrates how two kinds of geopolitical support, in conjunction with resource conversion, facilitated diaspora movement interventions in the Arab Spring. The primary form of geopolitical support that facilitated activists' transnational interventions was the backing provided by *states*, and especially activists' host-countries, via their foreign policies and practices in activists' homelands. Diaspora movements that gained the assistance of powerful states during the Arab Spring acquired unique kinds of leverage, including policies aimed at protecting their allies and sanctioning their enemies, the provision of intelligence and logistical support, and favorable votes in the UN Security Council, as the Libyan case shows. As Betts and Jones (2016: 9) argue, host-country support "animates" diaspora movements by elevating their voices in the political arena. I also argue that friendly states other than the host-country – such as Libya's border-sharing neighbors of Egypt and Tunisia – also facilitate the literal movement of diaspora movements by leaving border crossings open, or by turning a blind eye to the movement of people and resources across borders. As transnationalism scholar Thomas Faist (2000: 218) argues, remittances may appear ubiquitous, but they do not flow over a "magic carpet" in deterritorialized space. Accordingly, state support is key in fostering activists' abilities to remit and volunteer on the ground.[1]

This chapter also demonstrates how assistance by influential third parties in geopolitical conflicts and crises – including the media, international NGOs, and multilateral bodies – further facilitates diaspora activism. For instance, when media organizations deploy reporters to cover activists' home-countries, journalists are more likely to grant diaspora members a voice as translators, interpreters, brokers, and experts. While much of this work may occur from behind the scenes, the adoption of activists into the process of media coverage elevates their abilities to channel favorable attention to their allies. Another important form of third-party support stems from international bodies and organizations that aid dissidents and civilians in need (Keck 1995; Keck and Sikkink 1998; J. Smith 2004; Tarrow 2005; Tsutsui 2018), such as Amnesty International, the United Nations Human Rights Council, and the International Criminal Court. Agencies such as these create political opportunities for movements by defining, recognizing, and adjudicating transnational rights (Kay 2011). Such organizations can also go a step further by making demands on states and other decision-makers to change their policies and practices. Moreover, when these agencies take steps to intervene in a diaspora's home-country, diaspora activists gain transnational political opportunities to work with agencies as remitters and volunteers, as well as to pressure relief providers to do more for activists' constituents.

The challenge for diaspora movements in gaining geopolitical support is significant, however. As political scientist Clifford Bob (2005) argues, movements do not automatically receive support from international actors merely because they mobilize on behalf of the right causes, such as humanitarianism, freedom, and democracy. Instead, they have to market themselves to fit with the goals, agendas, ideologies, and interests of competing actors in the international

---

[1] Of course, external state support causes its own problems. It can compromise the legitimacy of local movements and channel mobilization into serving the interests of great powers; see Keck and Sikkink's (1998) discussion at the end of chapter 5 and in the conclusion in *Activists Beyond Borders*. That said, during periods of crisis and contention, the more support movements receive from states, the more formidable they become in fulfilling their short-term goals. See also Hironaka (2005) for the effect of external support on civil wars.

community. Research shows that activists can influence this process by deploying discursive frames and messages that resonate with trending geopolitical interests and values (Bob 2005; Koinova 2010a; Shain 1999). Yet, even when activists do all the right things, positive attention is far from guaranteed. The reception of states, media, and international bodies to revolutionary situations and humanitarian crises in today's world is embroiled in long-standing geopolitics that lie outside of activists' immediate control. Furthermore, international organizations like Human Rights Watch, which goes to admirable lengths to address abuses underway, simply do not have the capacity to channel attention and resources to all causes equitably. Diaspora advocates can certainly coax and cajole their elected representatives to pay attention to them, particularly when presenting themselves as voting constituents. However, activists do not themselves generate major shifts in foreign policy, reporting, or aid simply by virtue of their strategic savviness. Instead, the extent to which they do depends in large part on the *long-standing geopolitical orientation* of outside actors to the home-country, the interests and arguments that win out *internally,* within institutions, and the *adaptive responses* of political actors to emergent conflicts over time. It is only after diaspora movements are invited "in" by powerholders that they gain a seat at the table to weigh in on coverage, policy, and aid delivery. Those who are left out will instead face steep challenges – if not outright blockages – in mobilizing for rebellion and relief at home.

This chapter demonstrates how Libyans in the United States and Britain gained strong and sustained geopolitical support in 2011 that facilitated their full-spectrum intervention at home. Syrians faced more obstacles in intervening because geopolitical support was far weaker in Britain than in the United States initially. These obstacles increased for Syrians across both host-countries, however, after geopolitical support for regime change declined across the board and shifted to priorities dictated by the war on terror. In contrast, Yemenis gained only weak geopolitical support for their cause from each host-country and other third parties for the revolution's duration. Low-level assistance significantly limited these activists' efforts to represent the cause to outside decision-makers and remit aid. This chapter explains these dynamics in detail below.

7.1 STRONG GEOPOLITICAL SUPPORT FOR THE LIBYAN REVOLUTION

The progress that the Libyan regime had made in rejoining the international community by 2010 – giving up weapons of mass destruction, paying a settlement to the Lockerbie victims, and participating in the US-led war on terror – was lost after Gaddafi and his son Saif refused to budge on protesters' demands during the early days of the Arab Spring. In light of Gaddafi's disproportionate response and threats against external powers (Bassiouni 2013; Noueihed and

Warren 2012; Pargeter 2012), the emergent revolution gained geopolitical support for intervention on the basis of the Responsibility to Protect doctrine, which legitimizes intervention in order to stop genocide and mass killings. World powers imposed sanctions on the regime almost immediately after Gaddafi's forces began killing protesters, and the UN Security Council unanimously passed Resolution 1970 on February 26, 2011 to condemn the killings. Leaders of the revolution's newly formed and underequipped National Transitional Council (NTC) called on the international community to impose a no-fly zone, and the European Parliament called for the NTC to be recognized as Libya's legitimate government. The Arab League followed suit, excluding Libya from its meeting to decide on their position and agreeing to back the Security Council's decision.

On March 17 the UN Security Council passed Resolution 1973, which demanded a ceasefire and authorized the international community to use any means short of a ground occupation to protect civilians. No country opposed the measure, though five members, including Russia and China, abstained from voting. The resolution also authorized NATO forces to launch the first-ever intervention explicitly based on the Responsibility to Protect doctrine to stop atrocities. As Gaddafi's forces shelled Benghazi, French fighter jets helped launch an international offensive to push regime loyalists back. NATO subsequently took command of multilateral naval and air operations. By the end of March, the NTC published a manifesto for liberal democracy in Libya, and France recognized this body as Libya's legitimate government-in-waiting. The rebels now had the support needed to defend themselves and win the ground war against Gaddafi's forces.

The role of diaspora movements in the revolution was bolstered by this geopolitical support because US and British government officials not only met with diaspora members to listen to their grievances, but invited them into the intervention and policymaking process and relied on them in an advisory capacity for the duration of the war. These working relationships brought outside activists in and deputized them as representatives and brokers almost immediately. Sarah, a member of the Libyan British Relations Council, recalled,

We did lobbying in Parliament, we'd see 10 Downing Street, MPs [members of Parliament]. *Every week* there were meetings. They were asking about [the revolution], they wanted to see what was going on, briefings. It was amazing. We had a lot of support from that side. The MPs, they were more interested in the information gathering, and things that we talked about were creating humanitarian corridors, getting aid in. They wanted information and we were happy to provide it or provide them with contacts. So we definitely had support in the political establishment.

Mohammed in London also attested how the sympathies of the British government enabled them to work with officials on related issues. This allowed activists to suggest favorable policies and actions in line with governmental agendas.

The Foreign Office took us seriously. They were quite helpful. The fear I had is that I would call them and say, look, we have someone who wants to defect within the embassy but he needs certain guarantees, and I thought [this one important official] would not reply to me. But actually he would say, okay, come over, let's discuss it. And that's why I say I think they made a decision early on that Gaddafi's time was up. What we did wasn't to make the decisions *for* them, but make it easier for them to connect all the dots.

Thanks to the British government's geopolitical support, Mahmud A. also worked closely with a high-level British official to track down regime assets and transfer them to the NTC.[2]

[One official] was sort of the go-between for us and the Foreign Office, and he came to be very close to the Libyan community. That's why we came to him, and we start offering him every help they wanted from us. We worked as a team with all of them because we were trying to monitor the movement of money and companies linked to certain [Libyan] assets. *We* Libyans were aware of all these things – they don't know everything. So I was contributing mainly by giving them information. We didn't want the assets getting in the wrong hands at the time of the confusion.

On the US side, Rihab of the Libyan Emergency Task Force (LETF) reported that, initially, the response of officials was that they had no interest in Libya. However, after the situation on the ground escalated, departments across the broader establishment became eager to meet, receive information, and hear activists' arguments for intervention. Rihab said, "We didn't strategize for these things to happen. These people emerged as being interested in this issue naturally. We didn't line it up that way." Tamim of the LETF echoed this point, expressing how the support they received was widespread across different government branches and institutions.

We started setting up a strategy and working on developing relations with the White House, with the State Department, with Congress, the House and Senate, and with other organizations that could support and help our effort. It must be said that the welcome and the open arms that we received from all of these entities – NGOs, think tanks – there was some great people who helped us out, organizations as well as individuals. First of all, they opened their doors to listen. Second, they opened their doors to ask how can we help, how can the US government help Libyans? What is needed on the ground? Tell us. And that was at all levels. *At all levels.* This was an amazing experience for me.

---

[2] Colin Warbrick's (2012) research on Britain's response to the NTC reveals that even though the Cameron administration did not officially recognize the NTC as Libya's government-in-waiting until July 28, 2011, this was a highly unusual gesture of support for a government that did not yet represent or have control over a state. He writes, "After 1980 until the Libyan case, there were no examples of the Government making a statement recognizing a government in even the most intractable civil war, though forms of words were often found to indicate clearly where the Government stood" (2012: 51). Legitimation of the NTC by the British government therefore represented an exceptional showing of support for the anti-Gaddafi cause.

Tamim also affirmed that the support of Samantha Power – a former journalist and advocate for humanitarian intervention, advisor to President Obama, UN Ambassador, and member of the UN Security Council – elevated their voices in policymaking. Tamim became the contact person for Power during the intervention, and the group continued to meet with White House staff and kept in regular contact with the Libya desk at the State Department over the course of the conflict. Through their working relationships with these foreign policy elites, Tamim recalled that "Eventually we found doors open with the State Department, doors of communication open with the command center with Germany with NATO. And everyone wanted to help, [asking] *how can we coordinate, how can we solidify our position?*" They were also given opportunities to weigh in on the administration's options, as when the White House considered an offer by the Gaddafi government to split the country into east and west during the Nafusa stalemate in the summer of 2011. The LETF was invited to the White House to discuss this proposal, which they vehemently opposed.

The interventions by NATO after March 19 further accentuated activists' voices by turning information on the ground into potential intelligence to be used in the war effort. Mohammad in Sheffield recalled that through satellite phones,

We were talking to the people on the ground in Misrata and Brega, and we had different eyes on the ground. We used people we trust and we know because Gaddafi was dying to pass the wrong information and NATO will act on it, and then NATO will hit the target when the target is civilian. So we were so careful. We tried to make sure twice, three times, ten times, it's the right location, the right source. Otherwise, we will not pass it [to NATO].

Another respondent in Leeds who was incorporated into the war effort showed me the emails that she sent back and forth to her NATO contact containing the coordinates of enemy movements,[3] which were reported through her contacts on the ground and obtained through Google Maps. Abdo G. of Libya Link likewise attested that Google Maps was vital to this work, as it allowed members of the diaspora to pinpoint the precise coordinates of reported enemy locations. As Cardiff-raised Niz of the Free Generation Movement, the underground resistance in Tripoli, explained,

[NATO] would never tell me if the information I was providing was useful or was used. My understanding, having spoken to lots of people after the revolution, is that they were just gathering information from many different areas and seeing how it corroborated with their own intelligence.

Geopolitical support from third-party states was also vital in enabling the diaspora to move themselves and their resources across state lines. No

---

[3] This interviewee showed me her email communications with her contact in NATO. See the Methodological Appendix on the exchange of personal archival materials during interviews.

respondents who traveled to Malta, Egypt, or Tunisia to get into Libya from the United States or Britain reported being hassled or prevented from traveling beyond the additional scrutiny that Arabs and Muslims have commonly received in airports since September 11, 2001. For these reasons, activists were able to participate directly in the resistance and move resources homeward (see Chapter 5) without the obstacles commonly posed by border agents and travel embargoes. Furthermore, the fact that authorities along the bordering countries of Egypt and Tunisia allowed Libyans to travel back and forth to move supplies and help refugees also facilitated direct action. As Salam recalled of his experience traveling back and forth between Tunisia and Libya, "The amount of times we crossed the border, I was a familiar face. Sometimes it was multiple times a day." Activists' access to liberated space protected by outside states and the tacit permission they received to cross borders was fundamental in enabling them to volunteer on the ground.

Other respondents traveled from the neighboring island-nation of Malta to Misrata after the worst of the fighting to assist in the recovery. Taregh, a mental health expert from Oxford, recounted,

A psychiatrist friend and myself decided to go into Libya in June 2011. Misrata was under siege at the time, so we were smuggled in via one of the fishing boats. Our primary object was a needs assessment [of] the distress and trauma, because the city was under siege for so long. So I went around all the different hospitals, spoke to different mental health workers who had absolutely no training or experience in working with trauma. After about a week or ten days, I came back to England to raise money for a training program.

The Tunisian border region became a hub for diaspora relief work as well. After international organizations began to step in to assist Misrata, Rihab and other expat volunteers turned their focus to "support Libyan women off of the border" with Tunisia. After assembling private donations, they opened a center for women and their children in a local grade school in the Tunisian city of Tataouine to hold classes and provide social support.

This is not to say that moving supplies into Libya was easy. Assad of the London-based World Medical Camp for Libya attested, "With certain big shipments and sensitive equipment like satellite phones or internet satellite systems," he said, "we had to personally go so we could deal with the paperwork. It was logistically a very difficult situation. Some equipment you have to go and present papers and beg, and in some cases bribe." Despite these difficulties, no respondents recalled being blocked at any border crossings by authorities in the United States, Britain, Tunisia, Egypt, or Malta over the course of the revolution.

Media attention also elevated the anti-regime diaspora's role in the revolution for the duration of the conflict. Because the independent foreign press lacked contacts of their own and a presence in Libya before 2011, they relied heavily on diaspora activists to help make insider contacts and facilitate access to Libya. M. of Enough Gaddafi! recalled that soon after initiating the website Feb17.info, "We started getting phone calls from CNN, from BBC, can you get me someone to do an interview?" After journalists such as CNN's Anderson Cooper took a special interest in the Libyan revolution, Dina, a Libyan American with media expertise, was recruited by the network as a consultant to provide contacts. And even after members of the media began to communicate with Libyans inside the country independently of brokers like Dina, journalists nevertheless relied on bilingual activists from abroad to translate on the front lines. Haret, who had been working from Doha with the Libya AlAhrar satellite station, decided that he did not want to spend the entire revolution behind a computer in a nice hotel in Qatar. "It was too comfortable," he said. "When you're reporting about people who are in hell, it just didn't seem right." He decided to quit Libya AlAhrar in July and travel to Zintan, where his British Libyan father was volunteering in a hospital. After meeting journalists from Agence France-Presse and the Associated Press, he volunteered to be their interpreter. "Every morning, we'd wake up, we'd jump on the first truck heading to the front line," Haret recalled.

When the fight for the Nafusa Mountains was won in July, the final push for Tripoli began. Rebel forces drove into the capital city during Ramadan in late August to cheering crowds. Despite intermittent battles with the last of the loyalists, Libyans converged in Tripoli's main square to welcome the *thuwar* forces, celebrate their victory, and grieve their losses. Gaddafi's forces fled to Sirte before he was killed in October, and the National Transitional Council assumed control. Victory had been achieved, but at a high cost (and only temporarily, as a civil war broke out in 2014). By the end of the eight-month-long war in August 2011, at least twenty-five thousand Libyans had died, with many more tens of thousands displaced, missing, and injured.

Libyans from abroad recalled their work for the rebellion and relief with tremendous pride, and often in tears. They had indeed shared in these struggles and in collective jubilance and grief, mourning the sacrifices of their compatriots, the years spent in exile, and the losses endured in their families. Some shook their heads in recounting these events, as if they still could not really believe that the uprising – the dream that so few believed would ever happen – had been real. Those I interviewed in Tripoli marveled over the simple fact of being home again, talking openly in outdoor cafes about a tyrant who had once spread dread and terror across thousands of miles. As more than one activist said, "All of the stars had aligned" for their cause in 2011. My Libyan respondents added that, sadly, their Syrian friends and colleagues had not been so fortunate.

7.2 FROM VARIED TO WEAK GEOPOLITICAL SUPPORT FOR THE SYRIAN ARAB SPRING

The emergence of protests and civil disobedience in Syria's 2011 uprising accomplished what was previously thought impossible. Not only did Syrians refute the assumption that they were too loyal or complacent to rebel, but revolutionary collective action created space for dissidents of all types – including ethnic and religious minorities, Islamists, feminists, anarchists, and leftists – to speak out against oppression (Al-Haj Saleh 2017; Yassin-Kassab and Al-Shami 2018). However, as discussed in Chapter 4, as protesters were gunned down and detained by the thousands, the Assad regime's disproportionate response produced a predictable backlash. As members of the military defected and civilians mobilized to defend themselves, the rebellion took up small weaponry made available by defections and shadowy patrons from the Gulf region. The militarization of the rebellion was the subject of intense debate among Syrian activists, but the decision to take up arms by many was barely a choice (Yassin-Kassab and Al-Shami 2018). Various units comprising a resistance force known as the Free Syrian Army (FSA) emerged across Syria in early 2012 to protect their kin and liberate towns and villages from regime control and brutal retaliation. Revolutionaries also formed local councils to coordinate security, provide services, and even hold local elections in the wake of security vacuums and encroaching extremist movements.

By August, the UN Human Rights Council issued a damning report on the Syrian government's crimes against humanity, and a joint statement presented on August 18 by US President Barak Obama, British Prime Minister David Cameron, French President Nicolas Sarkozy, and German Chancellor Angela Merkel called for Assad to step down (Myers 2011). In 2012, the United Nations and the Red Cross dubbed the Syrian revolution a civil war (Charbonneau and Evans 2012), which angered many Syrians by mischaracterizing what was a disproportionately one-sided bombardment. The regime was especially brutal in dismantling the civic sector by killing, imprisoning, and forcing into exile progressives with nonviolent, democratic ideals. Nevertheless, "nobody could deny that a cycle of mutual violence had taken root" (Yassin-Kassab and Al-Shami 2018: 78). The rebels' desperate need for weapons and cash led to heightened competition between groups, and only some FSA brigades received nonlethal aid from the United States. This was followed by "light" lethal aid (Cornwell 2013), but nothing that could help the rebels actually win against their enemies. Weapons and funds from Gulf allies were also inconsistent. FSA troops often went hungry and lacked bullets with which to load their guns. Calls for a Libya-esque no-fly zone were raised by Syrian activists and rebels, but went unheeded by the international community (Moss 2016a).

Differences in geopolitical support between activists' host-countries produced variation in their abilities to serve as auxiliary forces for the Arab Spring. In the US case, host-country support for the rebellion was moderate after the Obama administration imposed sanctions against the Assad regime in 2011 and security agencies supplied and trained selected rebel groups in 2012. During this period, diaspora lobbyists gained the geopolitical support needed to serve as representatives and brokers with various congressional committees, security and defense agencies, and political elites. Activists also gained an elevated role in representing the revolution in comparison to their British counterparts. This was evidenced by Syrian Americans' working relations with an amalgam of allies in Congress and other political elites, including members of the Senate Foreign Relations Committee and House Foreign Affairs Committee, the Department of Defense, the National Security Council, prominent senators such as Lindsey Graham and John McCain, and former State Department officials such as Frederic Hof and Robert Ford, according to interviewees. As brokers between rebels and establishment representatives, activists forged connections by introducing Syrian rebels to government representatives, as Maher Nana recalled, and facilitated visits by officials such as Senator John McCain to liberated Syria (Kalin and Lukacs 2014).

The British government, on the other hand, lent weak support to the rebellion. While the Cameron government was involved in covert operations with the CIA from behind the scenes, the reticence of officials to acknowledge government involvement restricted British activists' capacities to serve as representatives and brokers in the political arena. MPs and other officials appeared hesitant to push the government into a leading role in intervention. This was likely due to popular fatigue over the Libyan intervention and wariness about following the United States into yet another unpopular conflict in the Middle Eastern region. Thus, British Syrians were largely excluded from consulting with the government on matters related to Syria because, despite officials' rhetorical condemnations of Assad, neither the Cameron administration nor any political party mobilized openly to support the revolution in a substantive way. British Syrian activists thus reported lacking a voice in the foreign policymaking process and receiving weak political support for their claims.

At the same time, Syrians in the United States and Britain – like their Libyan counterparts – worked closely with other geopolitical actors, such as members of the media and international sponsors of relief work, for several years. These agencies facilitated activists' interventions as representatives, brokers, remitters, and volunteers on the ground. Diaspora activists also capitalized on the support lent by Turkey, for example, which gave them a second hub from which to mobilize and cross into liberated Syria. All of the significant opposition groups formally representing the Syrian revolution met in Istanbul and Gaziantep, including the SNC,[4] the Syrian Interim Government, and the Syrian Muslim Brotherhood's coordinating offices (Conduit 2019). This support enabled respondents to move supplies through Syria's northern border and distribute resources on the front lines. Ousama from Bristol, for example, drove ambulances into Syria this way as part of a volunteer convoy several times. Others, such as New Jersey mayor Mohamed Taher Khairullah, delivered aid through an accredited organization to the internally displaced. After hitting a wall in

---

[4] As mentioned above, the SNC was later refashioned as the National Coalition of Syrian Revolutionary and Opposition Forces.

lobbying for decisive forms of intervention, activists such as Dr. Radwan Ziadeh of the Syrian Center for Political and Strategic Studies and Mouaz Moustafa of the Syrian Emergency Task Force set up shop in Turkey to order to contribute to the revolution more directly. During our conversation in 2014, Mouaz explained,

Lobbying wasn't panning out, so I went down to the border and opened an office in Antakya [in 2012]. Because first of all, to see if I can do something that helps people where I can *see* it translated into something [for myself]. Now we have an office in Antakya, four offices, and expanding inside liberated areas in Syria.

Mouaz also described in *Red Lines*, a documentary film about these activities (Kalin and Lukacs 2014), that he and an activist named Razan Shalab al-Sham from Homs worked in the liberated areas to establish civilian police forces and judicial councils. These projects were designed to fill the security vacuum left in the wake of war, as well as to serve as a model for civil governance in a post-Assad Syria. This project required going back and forth into Syria across the less-regulated northern border with Turkey on a regular basis.

Turkey's geopolitical support of the revolution meant that the Syrian-Turkish border became a hub for Syrians from across the world interested in assisting the revolution. Sabreen, who worked in Turkey for many months, said, "In every hotel in Gaziantep, you can walk in any day and find a training happening. No joke." During this period, Sabreen worked for the Syrian Interim Government as part of their Assistance Coordination Unit. This team organized the flow of aid into Syria to fill the gap left by the insufficient response of the UN Office for the Coordination of Humanitarian Affairs (OCHA). Sabreen's work in Turkey involved working as a broker between outside donors and needy insiders:

[In 2012], there was basically no coordination in Turkey among NGOs. So the opposition created this unit to fill that role, and I started working with them as a project coordinator for eight months. I was working with international donors and developing projects for them. I would do is talk to local Syrian NGOs and develop projects. I did a lot of grant writing. I was handling all donor relations, all external stuff . . . because they had no one who knew English. That's the reason why I was there. Donors, they have no connection to the inside and they also have a language barrier. So it's like nobody knows how to talk with anybody. There's a lot of international people, but they're in one world. And then there's people who are in-between, [like] me.

In response to gains made by the rebellion in the Damascus suburbs, the regime launched the world's worst chemical weapons attack in recent history on August 21, 2013. The attack killed approximately 1,730 Syrian civilians, including hundreds of children. A survivor of this attack, an activist named Kassem Eid later testified to the United Nations about the horrors of witnessing mass death by sarin (Eid and di Giovanni 2018; see also Chapter 5). This put an earlier claim by President Obama – that the use of chemical weapons by the Assad regime constituted a "red line" – to the test. These words proved to be empty, however, which further discredited the United States in the eyes of the Syrian opposition. After the British parliament voted against retaliatory strikes on August 29, the United States agreed to a Russian proposal that would allow Assad to remove his chemical arsenal over the course of the next year. This not only reaffirmed the regime's legitimacy in international relations, but also enabled the Syrian army to continue launching gas attacks, most notably in the form of chlorine, and killing civilians by barrel bombs and other extraordinary means.

The influx of Islamist fundamentalists into the war also drained outside geopolitical support for the anti-regime effort over time. In 2011, Assad released fifteen hundred Salafis from the nation's prisons, which a regime defector testified was a deliberate strategy to justify a violent response and to scare the country's minorities into remaining loyal. Not coincidentally, Assad's early claims about the revolution being the work of foreign conspirators came to fruition. Syria became a draw for jihadists from places such as Chechnya looking to fight infidels in the Alawite-dominated regime. The Al Qaeda–affiliate *Jabhat al-Nusra* (Al-Nusra Front) also joined the fight in the summer of 2012, bringing with them discipline, fighting experience, and resources from private donors in the Gulf region. Some extremist groups also stepped in to provide services to the population suffering from shortages of basic resources. Many were more disciplined, organized, and motivated to die in martyrdom in accordance with their apocalyptic beliefs than their FSA counterparts (Yassin-Kassab and Al-Shami 2018).

Having split from Al Qaeda over differences in how to establish an Islamic Caliphate, foreign fighters under the black banner of the "Islamic State" (ISIS, or *Da'esh*) flooded into Syria from Iraq in 2013. After being initially beaten back by FSA factions, they resurged with a vengeance following a successful assault in June 2014. Armed with American-made weapons and cash pillaged from Iraq, ISIS fighters opposed everyone, killing Syrians, beheading foreign journalists, and destroying the country's cultural heritage. Yet, the Assad regime maintained a nonaggression pact with ISIS at this time, bombing the FSA instead and using ISISs' presence to bolster the regime's standing in the international community. In November 2013, another faction called the Islamic Front was formed as a coalition that included the *Jaysh al-Islam*. This front, which was later accused of being involved in the disappearance of civil society activists in the Damascus suburbs, engaged in a fierce, win-or-die competition with the likes of Ahrar al-Sham, Jabhat al-Nusra, and ISIS.

In light of these shifts, activists from both the United States and Britain reported that geopolitical support for their cause waned. As a result, their roles as auxiliary forces for the rebellions declined. The first reason for this change was that the Obama administration's failure to punish Assad for the chemical weapons attacks – the regime's crossing of the "red line" – diminished Syrians' trust in the US government. By proxy, this refusal also chilled Syrians' trust in diaspora representatives and brokers. Dr. Ziadeh explained how the United

States' refusal to strike in August 2013 significantly strained his relationship with Syrians on the ground.

This was very disappointing and difficult to explain to the Syrians. Now I still have the same difficulties – to convince the Syrian people how it's important to work with the administration to fight against the ISIS because this is the only way you can [eventually] get rid of the Assad government. But the people in Syria have been frustrated because they're hearing from the media, the officials, the only focus was the ISIS, the terrorists. And everyone knows that the Assad machine has killed far more than what the ISIS killed among the Syrians.

The lack of US government support for the rebellion also led to the demise of the Syrian Support Group, an organization dedicated to supporting the FSA. Dr. Maher Nana, one of its co-founders, explained,

The lack of support, lack of arms, lack of money, lack of everything – [because of this], none of our work reached any [of its goals]. All the aid that has been sent has been given to small groups, very randomly distributed. Even the people there inside, their moods start turning against the United States and they were actually *blaming us, that we were the ones who let them down*, basically. And at that point, we really didn't have any leverage. *There's no reason for them to talk to us.* Even though we are Syrians, they still look at us as Americans. So we lost that strong relationship. Even I remember, I would talk to my family there and they would tell me, why should we keep talking to you? You disappointed us for two years. I left the Syrian Support Group almost a year and a half ago [in 2013]; it lasted for almost another year and it closed [in 2014] because of lack of funds, lack of anything, lack of purpose, basically. *The trust was broken, number one. And number two, there was no meaningful assistance.* The only assistance that was presented was the meal ready to eat [MRE] and the medical emergency kits to the Free Syrian Army. Now you go there and meet with people and they tell you, we have missiles coming on top of our heads and you're giving me meals? It was pathetic to them.

So too did Syrian American activist Yisser Bittar report that her journey into a town north of Aleppo under Free Syria Army control in December 2012 was a heartbreaking experience. She attested that the violence the Syrian people face on a daily basis makes them "feel and know [that] they have been abandoned. Whether it is by the diaspora, the Arab states or the West" (Bittar 2013).

Weakened support by the US government also damaged diaspora activism by stoking disillusionment with advocacy itself. As Dr. Ziadeh stated,

The special session requested [in 2011 by the United States at the UN Human Rights Council] issued a resolution requesting a fact-finding mission on what's happening. I testified on that session to send a strong message at that time to the Syrian government that things are not like in Hama in the '80s. Now you have Human Rights Council and the international community built a different system to not allow what's happened in the past to repeat again. But now we discover all of that is useless. Now, the UN confirmed the number of the victims exceed one hundred ninety thousand, [not to mention] the number of the mass atrocities, war crimes and crimes against humanity. And that affects, of course, the mobility of the Syrian diaspora. In the beginning, it was very active, mobilized. They tried actually to do very much lobbying pressure on the US government. But right now, it's less and less.

Marah Bukai also attested that protests came to be perceived by many community members as pointless because "by the third or fourth year, nothing has happened." She added, "I don't believe there is any reason to go shout next to the White House or embassy."

After the proliferation of religious extremist groups designated as terrorist organizations by the US and British governments, diaspora activists reported that the growth of these groups in Syria significantly damaged their abilities to support the vetted Free Syrian Army and civilians alike. Activists in both countries reported that donors had raised significant concerns about their remittances being tied in any way to the support of activities or groups deemed illegal by their host-countries. Aware that the security apparatuses in the United States and Britain were monitoring donations to Syria, fears of being caught in the war-on-terror dragnet stoked widespread worry and deterred community members from sending fungible aid to their allies. Furthermore, proving that resource deliveries were *not* going into the wrong hands placed an additional burden on Syrian activists abroad (Chaudhary and Moss 2019).[5] A member of Syria Relief remarked that concerns by governments and donors increased dramatically after the emergence of ISIS in Syria in 2013. He recalled,

In the beginning, the charity commission was a little bit more lenient with us. [Before], I really couldn't tell you the name of the person who received the food parcel. They wanted details, but when we said we gave it to *this* group of workers we have and they distributed it in *that* village, that was fine, they were happy with that. And they would even allow cash transactions, which are even more difficult to trace. Now, the instructions are if you cannot give us the name of the very final destination of your donation, don't do it. You can't even go there because they're so worried about money going into the wrong hands, going into aiding terrorism, going into buying arms. We have to be absolutely clear to the nth-degree as to where the money had gone. Otherwise, we'll be closed down, and we can't afford to have that happen because lots of people rely on us. We have schools that need to be funded, salaries of teachers that need to be paid, books and school equipment that have to be bought, et cetera – and that's only schools. There are hospitals and there are the food parcels and all that kind of [aid]. It all relies on the fact that we are functioning, and we cannot let them down.

Omar, a board member of the Syrian American Medical Society, also described the post-ISIS climate as "scary" because activists and donors could potentially be "considered terrorists." He added, "If you look at the history of some organization who were doing good work, later on, the US government changed the way they treat it and they consider them a terrorist organization." Ousama of Bristol attested that he had been questioned by the British police over his

---

[5] For a related analysis of the burdens placed on Pakistani charitable transnational organizations caught in the war on terror, see Chaudhary (2021).

volunteer activities such as driving ambulances into Syria. Respondents also affirmed that doctors they knew who had gone into Syria to do volunteer medical work had been hassled at airports.

Respondents likewise reported facing discrimination when attempting to register their organizations and wire funds to Syria. In one example, an activist working for the Syrian Legal Development Programme in Manchester told me that their group had difficulties opening a bank account, despite being an incorporated organization, because of their Syria-specific designation. This was not paranoia, as the British bank HSBC had closed down Syrians' personal bank accounts in 2014 (Bachelor 2014). For this reason, Haytham of the Rethink Rebuild Society decided not to put the word "Syria" in his organization's name because he worried about facing institutional and legal discrimination. Dr. Jundi of Manchester attested that local Syrian families faced additional difficulties sending remittances directly to their family members "because of the restrictions on money transfers, the sanctions that banks are imposing on bank accounts and what have you, even that simple process of family helping family has been crippled to a large extent." Mohammad al-Abdallah of the Syria Justice and Accountability Centre said that Syrian Americans were generally fearful of "getting calls from the FBI or other agencies saying, hey, your money ended up in terrorism and elsewhere," for obvious reasons.

The precariousness of liberated space within Syria, left undefended by outside powers, and ever-increasing restrictions on movement across borders into the country, significantly constrained the diaspora's abilities to serve as a volunteer force on the ground by 2014. Unlike in Libya, where liberated territory was protected and expanded by NATO forces, liberated Syrian territories were subjected to bombardment by the Assad regime and its allies, as well as constant power struggles between rebel groups and extremists. Most respondents had therefore stopped going into Syria in or by 2013 due to the threat of kidnappings (by either the regime, corrupt members of the Free Syrian Army, or criminal gangs), the expansion of extremist groups such as ISIS, and the retaking of territory by the regime. Rafif of FREE-Syria explained,

At the beginning, we used to be far more able to deliver humanitarian relief. We have more constraints now with ISIS operating as well as the regime. We were a little bit more optimistic about some women's initiatives earlier on. Those are now impossible. We're finding a lot of constraints and challenges.

L., who had fought on the front lines, also recalled that increasing desperation and criminality among opposition groups had made this work doubly dangerous. After explaining how two of his European aid worker friends had been kidnapped and ransomed by a corrupt FSA member, he remarked,

Now you can't trust anyone. Once they find out you're American – bare minimum, [that can get a ransom of] ten thousand dollars to any group. Imagine how fucked up that is.

Even though you're a Syrian, because you're American born, you're a target now – and people are greedy and desperate, so why not!

Over time, activists found that Turkey was the only country allowing relatively safe passage in and out of Syria; Jordan and Lebanon were reported to be far less accommodating for those seeking to volunteer to assist refugees or smuggle supplies to the front lines. Even the Turkish regime's support for cross-border movement became temperamental, however, with the rise of ISIS and terrorist attacks in Turkish cities, as well as the government's escalating belligerence against Kurdish factions in northern Syria. Even though activists could smuggle themselves in, this process became increasingly precarious.

In conjunction with declining resource conversion (see Chapter 6), diminished geopolitical support – which shifted in the United States from strong to weak and in Britain from moderate to weak – had a significant negative effect on diaspora activism by 2014. Despite the admirable efforts by Syrian organizations with the resources to sustain full-time activist work, the situation looked increasingly bleak as time ticked by. Backed by Iranian manpower and Russian airstrikes, the Assad regime remained intent on destroying what was left of the country in order to save it for itself. International actors, from Russia to the UN to the United States and Britain, came to agree that Assad must be a part of Syria's future even though mass killings continued. By the end of 2014, four million refugees languished in camps or risked death to reach Europe, over seven million Syrians had been displaced internally (a combined total of half of Syria's population), and at least two hundred and twenty thousand Syrians had been killed.

At the time of this writing, the Assad regime has produced the worst refugee crises since World War II, and while international agencies have stopped counting, it is likely that well over a million Syrians have been killed. More than one hundred fifty thousand prisoners face unspeakable treatment in prisons, an estimated eight hundred thousand Syrians have faced starvation, and major outbreaks of disease have occurred in towns and cities from Yarmouk to Madaya. The Syrian regime and Russian forces continue to bomb the last revolutionary strongholds in Idlib to dust, including its hospitals and schools. The resistance at home and abroad continues to suffer irreparable losses, muting the voice that Syrians had gained after the emergence of the "impossible revolution" (Al-Haj Saleh 2017).

7.3 WEAK GEOPOLITICAL SUPPORT FOR THE YEMENI REVOLUTION OVER TIME

Yemen's revolution began with street protests in January 2011 and evolved to include tens of thousands of Yemenis in mass sit-ins, protests, and strikes across the country. As I described in Chapter 4, the Friday of Dignity Massacre on

March 18 marked a turning point after plainclothes regime loyalists, *al-balti-jiyyah*, opened fire on unarmed demonstrators in Sana'a's Change Square. The killing of approximately fifty demonstrators stoked the defections of regime elites such as General Ali Mohsen, who brought his First Armored Division to defend the square. The defections of these elites and members of the Islah Party caused significant friction within the revolution and undermined its previously nonpartisan character. Other protest encampments in cities such as Ta'iz and Aden were also subjected to intermittent attacks over the following months.

By April, domestic and international efforts were underway to convince Ali Abdullah Saleh to agree to a peaceful transfer of power. The Joint Meetings Parties, Yemen's coalition of legal opposition parties, convened to offer Saleh a deal to transfer power to his Vice President, Abdrabuh Mansour Hadi. The Gulf Cooperation Council (comprised of Bahrain, Kuwait, Oman, Qatar, Saudi Arabia, and the United Arab Emirates) backed this idea, proposing their own agreement – what would come to be known as the "GCC agreement" or GCC deal – offering Saleh and his family immunity from prosecution in exchange for a gradual transition of power.

As Saleh stalled, hoping to win the standoff in the end, his attacks continued. These incidents prompted officials in the United States, Britain, the UN, and the European Union to make statements condemning the violence and calling for a transition of power. Saleh agreed to the terms of the GCC deal in late April but was given thirty days to sign it. He used this time to try and force protesters from their tents. On April 28, the crisis escalated when loyalist forces again shot at demonstrators in Sana'a, killing at least a dozen demonstrators and injuring approximately two hundred. Yemenis across the country launched coordinated strikes in response. Saleh's forces continued to try and disband the protest movement, cutting electricity to Change Square.

After Saleh refused to sign the GCC deal by allowing the thirty-day signing period to expire, Sheikh Sadiq al-Ahmar of the influential Hashid tribal confederation moved his fighters into the capital city. A street battle against loyalist forces ensued with artillery and mortars, claiming the lives of approximately 120 soldiers, tribal militia, and civilians. Six days later, Saleh's forces launched an operation to crush the protest encampment in Ta'iz known as Freedom Square using live ammunition and water cannons, killing dozens of unarmed civilians. Tribal leader and Islah Party member Sheikh Hamoud al-Mikhlafi, a powerful elite with his own formidable militia, mobilized to defend the square and forced loyalists to retreat.

These attacks prompted US President Barack Obama to call on Saleh to fulfill his commitment and sign the GCC deal at a joint press conference with British Prime Minister David Cameron in London.[6] But back in Sana'a, the street battle continued. On June 3, a bombing (for which no party claimed

---

[6] See the statement published by the White House's Office of the Press Secretary (2011).

responsibility) hit the presidential palace, badly injuring President Saleh and killing several guards. Saleh was flown to Saudi Arabia for medical treatment, and Vice President Hadi assumed office. This attack temporarily ended the street battles in Sana'a, but the standoff continued as anti-regime protesters occupied the streets.

Having survived the attack, Saleh issued a decree on September 12 from Saudi Arabia for Hadi to take up some of his presidential duties and authorized him to negotiate a transfer of power based on the GCC deal. However, a renewed crisis broke out on September 18 after government and *baltijiyyah* forces opened fire on protesters across Yemen in a series of coordinated attacks, resulting in the deadliest day of the revolution in months. More than fifty people were killed over the next several days, and Saleh's military forces fired rockets at Change Square in the capital, prompting General Mohsen's First Armored Division to strike back. Saleh returned to Yemen in October to the continuation of intermittent clashes. On October 21, the UN Security Council voted unanimously for Resolution 2014 that condemned the violence and called for an immediate transfer of power under the GCC deal. After an envoy to the UN worked to restart negotiations, Saleh signed the deal on November 23 and was granted full immunity.

How did these developments impact diaspora activism? Despite the valiant efforts of Yemeni activists to broadcast the demands of the youth movement, their voices fell largely on deaf ears due to weak geopolitical support from both host-country governments. Both the United States and Britain used a soft strategy of political pressure to convince Saleh to sign the GCC agreement in a clumsily designed effort to put Vice President Hadi in place as the new president. This effort, which was designed to *stabilize* the country through political continuity rather than induce radical democratic change, backfired after Saleh joined with northern rebel forces known as the Houthis to launch a coup d'état and instigated a devastating civil war. So while activists in the US and British diasporas reported that host-country officials were willing to *listen* to their grievances, they were not treated as partners or advisors in decision-making processes. Thus, unlike Libyans and Syrians who were treated as brokers and representatives on matters of policy, Yemenis were not treated as such by any sectors of their host-country governments.

Furthermore, as with their Syrian counterparts, the US' and Britain's war-on-terror security environment hampered organizers' potential to remit home-ward on a collective scale. These countries had long partnered with the Saleh regime, supplying him with weapons and cash to fight Al Qaeda in the Arabian Peninsula, and viewed Yemen primarily through the lens of terrorism and national security (Brownlee et al. 2015; Day 2012). Saleh, in turn, often diverted these funds to contest his domestic enemies (Knickmeyer 2010). Because Yemeni communities in places like New York had come under increasing scrutiny after the attacks on September 11, 2001, community members were logically fearful about sending remittances to anti-regime causes at home. Ibraham, an organizer in New York, explained that without official guidelines on how to remit aid, their movement lacked a way to safely assist revolutionaries.

When a lot of people were being murdered in the squares, we wanted to provide medicine and food. But we can't do it because we have concerns about the US policies when it comes to sending that kind of aid. They can prosecute anyone, saying that the food fell in the wrong hands. And the government did not provide us with guidelines or ways to send medicine and food. There is no designated list of organizations that we can work with on the ground, and no US organization that is willing to do that. So we had great difficulties trying to do that throughout the whole year. And it would be great if the US somehow, maybe through USAID program or another program, [could facilitate that] because the Yemeni community can contribute a lot in supporting the needy. I would say that the Yemeni community, especially in New York, is so wealthy. But our hands are very tied. Yemen needs food and medicine, and as Yemeni Americans – and even as *Americans* – we are very cut off in trying to send support or do fundraising for Yemen.

Accordingly, diaspora movements in both the United States and Britain lacked the geopolitical support needed to collectively remit to their compatriots at home.

In line with weak state support, foreign media penetration in Yemen was moderate in comparison with the rush of reporters to the front lines in Libya and Syria. Prior to the revolution, journalists had easy access to Yemen relative to other countries undergoing the Arab Spring, but a near-total lack of demand for coverage on Yemen on the part of media organizations meant that few foreign reporters were there at the start of the protest movement in January 2011. Most who came to report of the protests thereafter were expelled by the regime by March. Nevertheless, journalists from Al Jazeera English remained, along with a small cadre of Western freelancers and stringers – brave individuals like Laura Kasinoff, Iona Craig, Adam Baron, Jeb Boone, and Tom Finn – who managed to stay on and undertake important coverage from inside the revolution. That said, coverage remained limited outside of Yemen's capital, and unlike in Libya, journalists could not as easily smuggle themselves into the country.

Weak geopolitical support for the uprising by international organizations also limited diaspora activism during the uprising. No humanitarian agencies that I could locate mobilized to assist victims of regime violence inside the encampments during the revolution. Despite the presence of some international NGOs in Yemen, such as Islamic Relief, many activists did not perceive these groups to be trustworthy or useful. Because these organizations had to operate with the regime's permission, respondents noted that the aid would not reach revolutionaries. As Faris of the Washington, DC-based diaspora movement explained,

As far as NGOs, we were trying to reach out. We tried to go through them, whether it was Islamic Relief or other aid organizations that were already in Yemen – but there was an issue of actually distributing the supplies out to the people there. You have global NGOs that have been established for decades and the branches that were present in Yemen were being run by pro-Saleh officials. So in a sense, even well-noted NGOs were not able to distribute the funds that were allocated and for the people on the field, because of the fact that those people were anti-Saleh.

As discussed in Chapter 6, this problem was combined with the shortage of insider contacts available to receive humanitarian remittances. Thus, if activists did not have familial contacts in these places, they lacked the means to send help to protesters and the field hospitals. It is very likely that the individual donations made through personal contacts, such as those wired to Yemeni-American Atiaf in Sana'a, represented only a tiny fraction of what the pro-revolution diaspora could have contributed had they had state-sanctioned channels to do so.

Saleh's resignation on November 23, 2011, was a cause for celebration for some, while others in the encampments remained in their tents. Nevertheless, calls for the fall of the regime – now headed by the former Vice President Hadi – ceased at this time, signifying the end of Yemen's 2011 revolution. Saleh traveled to the United States for medical treatment at the end of January and returned to Yemen for the February 21 election. Vice President Hadi was the only candidate on the ballot and won easily, marking the official start of Yemen's transitional government. Yemenis residing in the United States and Britain had come out in force to show their support and viewed this time as a profound showing of newfound community empowerment. However, weak support by geopolitical powerholders had left them with few ways to facilitate rebellion and relief on the ground.

7.4 CONCLUSION

This chapter has demonstrated how geopolitical support from states and other third parties fueled transnational auxiliary activism during the Arab Spring, and how unevenly diaspora movements against authoritarianism gained such backing. Even though all of the Libyan, Syrian, and Yemeni movements discussed here advocated for democracy, human rights, and humanitarian relief, favorable attention from key actors varied significantly. While Libyan activists in the United States and Britain gained overwhelming support for the revolution's duration and geopolitical backing for the Syrian cause started off strong in the United States, other groups struggled to make their voices heard. British officials were reluctant to publicly support anti-regime interference in the Syrian conflict; assistance for the Syrian anti-regime cause declined across the board over time; and Yemenis across both host-countries received low-level support for revolutionary democratic change. When geopolitical support was weak, activists faced significant hurdles in gaining voice, and their resources were more likely to remain caged in their host-country communities. Correspondingly, this chapter demonstrates that the potential of transnational movements to undermine authoritarian regimes is – in conjunction with resource conversion, discussed in Chapter 6 – largely dependent on the support of states and geopolitical powerholders.

Conclusion

On a sunny December afternoon in 2011, I arrived in downtown Los Angeles for an event billed as "International Human Rights Day, Occupy LA, Solidarity with a Free Syria." The park surrounding City Hall, recently the site of the Occupy LA movement, was enclosed with a mesh fence after the movement's eviction. However, the western steps were still open for demonstrations, and a huge banner stuck between two planters let me know I was in the right place. It read, in all caps, *SYRIANS ARE DYING, WHERE IS THE MEDIA?* A few men I recognized from past protests for Syria were standing together to one side. In future months, we would greet each other with enthusiastic hand-shakes. On this day, they simply murmured hello and turned back to their conversation.

I looked around and spotted a petite young woman with a glowing face wearing sunglasses and a Free Syria T-shirt. Spotting my own shirt, which displayed a photograph of Hamza al-Khateeb, Syria's most well-known victim of regime brutality at the time, she bounded over to me. In an Arabic accent, she asked, "Are you Syrian?" I had not seen her before; I learned later that this was because she was visiting from her hometown in Texas. This organizer, whom I will call "R.," gave me an enthusiastic hug and kissed me on the cheek. R. then excused herself, yelling "MIC CHECK!" to the group. Surrounding youth sporting ripped jeans and bandanas echoed back "MIC CHECK!" in the call-and-repeat style of the Occupy movement. R. then asked the crowd of about thirty people or so to gather in front of the banner for a short "teach-in" about Syria.

She began by asking, "What would you say to a father whose son was killed? What would you say to a mother whose children are being killed, mutilated, and tortured? What do you *say* to the *free world*?" After a pause, she answered her own question: "Why are you not standing in solidarity for Syria?" She described how in the Syrian city of Dara'a, forty protesters were being killed every day – protesters just like us. She then taught the crowd a chant from the front lines: *"Allah! Suriya! Hurriya-wa-bas!"* meaning "God! Syria! Freedom only!" as in, freedom is all we want. R. then pleaded, "Cry their pain. Be one of them. *Speak for them."*

I have thought of R. often since that day. During a time when many were still too afraid to come out against the regime, R. was speaking out, using her voice to condemn the regime through a megaphone. At the time, I did not fully appreciate how brave such an act really was, but that was only the half of it. I attempted to reach out to her a few years later through Facebook for an interview, but I did not see or talk to R. after that. It turned out that she had left the United States to venture home to Syria and volunteer in places like Idlib, a liberated province that the Assad and Putin regimes were bombing into oblivion. Through her social media posts, I gleaned that she was publicizing information, putting her contacts on the ground in touch with helpers abroad, and distributing aid with her own hands. R., like so many of her conationals, had become part of a transnational auxiliary force for the revolution as a broadcaster, a broker, and a volunteer on the front lines.

As R.'s story illustrates, diaspora mobilization during the Arab Spring was about far more than retweeting headlines or holding demonstrations on the weekends. Instead, scores of anti-regime activists took on the revolution as a calling, fighting tooth and nail to support their compatriots. By helping to facilitate revolutionary political change and supply humanitarian relief, these activists found their voices as home-country nationals demanding freedom, as members of the free world with civil liberties, and as global citizens vying for universal human rights. As the previous chapters show, by broadcasting their allies' plight to the outside world, representing the cause to the media and policymakers, brokering between allies, remitting all manner of resources homeward, and volunteering in person, these diaspora movements brandished voice *after* exit as a weapon against tyranny and authoritarianism. They did so for a range of reasons, including out of nationalistic pride, concern for their relatives and hometowns, a belief in human dignity, indignation and outrage over regime brutality, and a desire to realize long-standing interests. Whatever the reasons, their interventions in home-country conflicts and crises demonstrate that diaspora mobilization is not something that observers should take for granted. As the *Arab Spring Abroad* argues, the ability of activists to help their allies during periods of acute need is highly contingent. By pinpointing the conditions giving rise to voice after exit, this book sheds new light on the conditions under which diaspora activists become transnational forces for change.

By comparing diasporas' collective action before and during the Libyan, Syrian, and Yemeni revolutions from the United States and Britain, I find that fear and mistrust resulting from *transnational repression* and *conflict transmission* can divide and silence anti-regime populations, thereby suppressing members' voices in democratic states. I then show how *quotidian disruptions* in the home-country upend these transnational deterrents by lowering the costs and risks associated with voice, motivating diaspora members to go public in spite of the risks, and by bringing people together against a common threat. During the Arab Spring, quotidian disruptions enabled anti-regime members to engage in public, collective claims-making against regimes and their abusive practices, albeit to different degrees over time. Yet, I also argue that diaspora movements need to do more than just project their voices on the streets of their host-country in order to meet their goals. As the final chapters demonstrate, activists require *resource conversion* and *geopolitical support* in order to contribute in meaningful ways to rebellion and relief. Otherwise, diaspora movements will be left without a way to support their allies in times when their help is most desperately needed.

By providing a new explanation of when and how diaspora movements mobilize against authoritarian regimes, this book demonstrates that such anti-regime activists are neither irrelevant to the study of contentious politics nor the ready-made "long-distance nationalists" who meddle in international affairs (Anderson 1998; Huntington 2004). Instead, I show that although the trappings of globalization make transnational activism faster and easier than ever before, not all movements are equally advantaged to intervene in the homeland. Rather, members' simultaneous embeddedness in home-country conditions after exit, their varied capacities to convert resources to politicized causes, and the different degrees of geopolitical support they receive for home-country liberation impact their transnational practices in significant ways. By specifying the conditions under which diaspora members come together against tyranny and suffering, the arguments presented here have a number of implications for future research.

THE VALUE OF A TRANSNATIONAL PERSPECTIVE
OF CONTENTIOUS POLITICS

The first implication of this book is the tremendous value of taking a transnational perspective of contentious politics. Revolutionary episodes like the Arab Spring are not just country-specific or region-wide events, but globalized phenomena that diffuse and activate constituencies across national communities. By systematically accounting for the "transboundary" dynamics of contention (Lawson 2019), we see more clearly how anti-authoritarian insurgency is fundamentally dependent on how and to what extent activists are able to channel their claims outward, acquire resources, and build alliances on a global scale (Keck and Sikkink 1998). As persons who "keep a foot in two worlds," as Peggy Levitt (2003) posits, diaspora members play pivotal roles in these processes. They are often the first to respond to conflicts and crises, fill in gaps in the international response along the way, and the last to leave the scene (Svoboda and Pantuliano 2015). Yet, studies of transnational activism overwhelmingly focus on the work done by formal nongovernmental organizations (NGOs) at the expense of diaspora movements. This is a major oversight, given the fact that diaspora activists are often responsible for supplying NGOs with the connectivity and insider information these organizations require to do their jobs. Accordingly, scholars would do well to pay serious attention to the role of diasporas in the dynamics of cross-border contention.

Building on this point, I echo calls by transnationalism researchers to be more conscious of the "methodological nationalism" (Wimmer and Glick Schiller 2002) that delimits what topics and actors we view as important objects of study. Of course, state borders matter a great deal in distinguishing liberal territories from illiberal ones and shaping the character of social and political life. Yet, the tendency of movement scholars to treat the dynamics of contention as a contained phenomenon has led to the neglect of the transnational alliances and geopolitics that shape resistance movements.[1] All notable rebellions in the modern world, from the anti-fascist movement in Spain, to "Third-World" liberation struggles, to demands by organized labor and the US Civil Rights Movement, have gained the attention of foreign supporters and detractors.[2] The framework elaborated suggests the importance of investigating how groups divided by social, political, legal, and physical borders transcend the boundaries that are designed to keep allies apart (Adler 2019; Russo 2018; C. Smith 1996). As scholars continue to debate the causes and consequences of events ranging from the French Revolution to the insurgencies underway in Libya, Syria, and Yemen today, it will be useful to investigate how peer patronage and foreign sponsorship impact "local" social movements.

Applying a transnational perspective also brings needed attention to the ways in which states and other illiberal authorities adapt to the threats posed by diaspora activism and act back on their nationals to impede voice. As this book shows, just as transnational *advocacy* poses a threat to illiberal authorities (Keck and Sikkink 1998), so too does transnational *repression* pose a powerful counter-threat to anti-regime activists – and not only for Libyans and Syrians (Hilsum 2012; Pearlman 2016, 2017; Shain 2007). A growing literature on this topic shows that transnational repression continues to present pervasive dangers to activists from Belarus, China, Eritrea, Iran, North Korea, Turkey, Saudi Arabia, Russia, and the former Soviet states, among other places (Cooley and Heathershaw 2017; Farooq 2015; Lemon 2019; Michaelsen 2018; Glasius 2018; Williamson 2015; see also Brand 2006; Miller 1981; Shain 2005 [1989]). This is a pressing subject of investigation as regimes deploy internet-based technologies, Interpol, and accusations of terrorism to impede the voices of human rights advocates around the globe.

---

[1] For a good example of a work that accounts for transnational alliances in anti-authoritarian mobilization, see Chang (2015).

[2] For sources on the transnational dynamics of these rebellions, see Carroll (1994), Lindsley (1943), Orwell (2015[1952]), Richardson (2015), McAdam (1998), and Skrentny (1998). More research is needed on foreign state support of movements, for example, Muammar al-Gaddafi's sponsorship of the Irish Republican Army and Louis Farrakhan's Nation of Islam.

Of course, it is not only authoritarian states that engage in such practices. This study also points to how democracies participate in transnational systems of repression and social control (Blanton 1999; Gordon 1987). The ongoing war on terror's impact is not only detrimental to realization of Middle Easterners' civil liberties (Cainkar 2009, 2018; Maghbouleh 2017; Naber 2006, 2012; Pennock 2017); as this book shows, it also impedes their abilities to support democracy, human rights, and humanitarian relief in their home-lands (Chaudhary 2021; Chaudhary and Moss 2019; Nagel 2002). If the West continues to justify its foreign policies on the so-called promotion of global goods such as democracy and freedom, the least that these governments can do is facilitate diaspora mobilization for humanitarian aid and human rights. Sociologists and policymakers alike would do well to pay further attention to these dynamics.

A transnational perspective of social movement activism can provide a useful framework to study mobilization *within* the nation-state as well. With so many territories internally divided by invisible but highly policed boundaries (Simes 2021), the question of when movement actors cross borders in a transgressive fashion is a critical one. In the US civil rights movement, which continues to serve as a bedrock in the study of contentious politics, northern Black activists and their multiracial, interfaith allies played a significant role supporting high-risk activism in the south. They did so by remitting resources to their repressed counterparts for bonds and legal fees and by participating in direct action campaigns, such as the 1961 Freedom Rides (McAdam 1986, 1988, 1999 [1982]). Crossing state lines for civil rights was extremely risky during this period due to the major differences in laws, policing, and white vigilante racism by state. Thus, while the border-crossing characteristics of movements are sometimes taken for granted, we would do well to remember that the literal movement of movements was absolutely essential in defeating Jim Crow. A transnational perspective reminds us of the importance of free movement in combatting apartheid and dehumanization, both within and beyond the nation-state.

QUOTIDIAN DISRUPTIONS BEYOND REVOLUTION

This book further contributes to studies of contention and social change by showing how quotidian disruptions (Snow et al. 1998) mobilize previously silenced and divided diaspora members by reducing the costs of activism, making members willing to take risks, and creating new solidarities against common threats. However, regime repression and revolutionary uprisings are not the only types of disruption that can mobilize people across borders. Environmental disasters, which are increasingly common owing to climate change, can have congruent effects. For instance, Grady Vaughan's (2020) research on Turkmenistan and diaspora politics finds that as of 2020, members of diaspora communities in Turkey, Cyprus, and the United States "have initiated a rare wave of demonstrations in response to Ashgabat's inadequate response to a raft of man-made and natural disasters." In light of President Berdimuhamedov's poor response to floods and economic crises, diaspora members' grievances have been further exacerbated by the 2020 coronavirus pandemic. In an effort to assert their power, Turkmen authorities have actually confiscated and withheld medical aid donated by the diaspora. Because Turkmenistan's regime is infamous for enacting transnational repression, voice after exit in the diaspora has been relatively rare, just as it was for Syrians and Libyans before the Arab Spring. Yet, as of 2020, Turkmen abroad have begun to protest against Berdimuhamedov and have vowed to overcome their internal divisions (Vaughan 2020). Accordingly, the overlaying of urgent crises and fresh grievances may push diaspora members to engage in high-risk activism (Hechter et al. 2016) even when the chances of regime change are low. Additional comparative work within and across regions will help us to understand how the dynamics described here transcend regions and revolutionary waves.

It is also the case that diaspora members may come to exercise voice after exit when home-countries experience quotidian disruptions in the form of liberalization and democratic reforms.[3] As respondents reported in the Libyan and Syrian cases, perceived openings in their home-countries in 2004 and 2005 motivated some anti-regime members to embrace voice in new ways. However, the question of whether voice endures and grows in a community will depend on whether liberalization becomes sustained and meaningful in practice. If regimes do make meaningful progress toward reform, then we can expect these changes to impact voice in positive ways abroad. Otherwise, diaspora members are likely to remain skeptical of using voice as an independent means of expression – or else they may learn the hard way that doing so will put them in danger.

In democratic and semi-democratic sending-states, a key factor shaping the emergence of diaspora voice is whether home-country governments actively encourage transnational practices such as voting, bond buying, and migrant investment in public goods, as in the case of Mexico and Israel (Bada 2014; Goldring 2004; Lainer-Vos 2013; Shain 2007). In cases such as these, the initiation of meaningful political rights at home may extend into transnational citizenship and sustained political engagement in the diaspora (Gamlen 2014; Délano and Gamlen 2014). However, home-country attempts to foster diaspora engagement do not necessarily promote free-wheeling voice. Lauren Duquette-Rury (2020) finds, for instance, that migrants' efforts to support their hometowns with public good provision fail when local governments are disengaged and exclusive to ordinary citizens. Furthermore, out-of-country voting may not be the obvious indicator of transnational citizenship that it seems (Pearlman 2014). Research by Elizabeth Wellman (2021) demonstrates that

---

[3] I thank Dr. Erin McDonnell, Kellogg Associate Professor of Sociology at the University of Notre Dame, for encouraging me to address this point.

while one hundred countries across the world have extended out-of-country voting rights over the past thirty years, not all of these citizens abroad are franchised in a meaningful way. She finds instead that access to out-of-country voting for members of African nations is often selective and precarious. Governments have also *reversed* these rights when diaspora voters have shown insufficient support for incumbent parties.[4] In light of these nuances, scholars should avoid being overly focused on home-country voting as the true signifier of transnational citizenship. Instead, we need to look at the broader range of practices that signify diaspora political engagement in the homeland, including both institutionalized and contentious forms of political action.

This book also serves as a cautionary tale against labeling diaspora remitters as harbingers of peace *or* war (Smith and Stares 2007). When combatting totalitarian regimes and mass killings, armed resistance is often the only possible means to pursue liberal change. Accordingly, diaspora activists' support for Western military intervention needs to be evaluated with care by pundits and peace activists. UN-mandated interventions in Libya, for instance, were regarded by Libyans on the ground and in the diaspora as the only way to defend civilians against slaughter and uphold the Responsibility to Protect (Moss 2016a). Because humanitarian intervention and imperialistic interests collide in the geopolitical arena (Bob 2019), more attention to the ways in which diaspora activists manage these tensions is needed.

Relatedly, the blame that diasporas often receive for manipulating foreign affairs is deeply misplaced. While exile-lobbyist Ahmad Chalabi, who helped to justify the United States' invasion of Iraq in 2003, has been vilified as an example of a manipulative, scheming long-distance nationalist run amok, such characterizations obscure the true source of Chalabi's power. He was, in fact, placed on the CIA and State Department payrolls in the US government's years-long effort to overthrow Saddam Hussein (Roston 2008; Shain 2007; Vanderbush 2014). Without geopolitical support from the United States, Chalabi would have been like many of his counterparts longing for regime change in other countries – a lone figure left to voice his demands to a deaf public. We should be sure to attribute diaspora activists' influence not to their savviness or scheming, but to their resources and the geopolitics that undergird foreign policymaking.

The case of the Arab Spring abroad also points to the need for scholars to look beyond violent conflicts to understand the roles of diasporas in the aftermath of acute crises, as when their members flood back home to fill

---

[4] Diaspora engagement in democratic home-country politics can also contribute to outcomes that are unintended by home-country governments. Pérez-Armendáriz and Duquette-Rury (2021) find, for instance, that the more often Mexican hometown associations contribute to public goods in their places of origin, the more likely these hometowns are to produce militias that provide local security in the absence of state protection. For a comparative and historical perspective on immigrant associations, see Moya (2005).

political offices, establish political parties, man businesses and hospitals, and promote civil society initiatives (Baser 2015; Baser and Swain 2011; Koinova 2010b). Even when the resources and expertise of diasporas are needed for rebuilding purposes, significant tensions may arise between those who maintained a foot in both worlds (Glick Schiller and Fouron 2001; Levitt 2003) and those who never left – especially since diaspora members may exit again after conflicts reignite. The Libyans I met with in Tripoli in 2013, for example, attested how resentment over their repatriation was creating friction with those who had never left. Returnees were often referred to by their conationals as "double *shafras*," a pejorative term for those who carried both a Libyan and an international SIM card in their mobile phones. Indeed, many of the respondents who moved home after Gaddafi's fall were forced to leave again after renewed fighting and the influx of ISIS in 2014. The question of whether and how returnees achieve social reintegration into their home-countries remains an open one. Future studies would do well to investigate how different quotidian disruptions impact the process of return and reintegration, and how diasporas shape economic, social, and political life after exit and return.

BROADENING OUR VIEW OF DIASPORA AND IMMIGRANT VOICE

This study also has implications for understanding the effects of diaspora activism on the political practices of immigrant communities. As we have seen in the previous chapters, whether conationals come together or splinter apart shapes "horizontal voice" in fundamentally important ways (O'Donnell 1986). As studies of Balkan diasporas (Koinova 2011, 2013), Somali refugees (Besteman 2016), and Latin American immigrants (Guarnizo et al. 1999, 2003) demonstrate, acute conflicts at home can divide conationals as easily as unify them. This suggests the importance of disaggregating groups by the ways that they identify *themselves*. The Libyans, Syrians, and Yemenis featured in this study are too often lumped together in sociology as Arabs and Muslims, despite the fact that many of them are neither and do not identify as such (Brubaker 2013). If sociologists rely primarily on the pan-ethnic and racialized categories used by host-countries to identify minority groups, we miss how these groups are socially constructed (Brubaker 2004, 2015) and how internally fractious their intra-group politics can be. We will also neglect to understand the roles that national and ethnic groups play in politics, especially when they are treated as too statistically small to be counted in census data. Without attention to this heterogeneity, we will miss some of the most important and interesting mobilization dynamics underway in minority and immigrant communities (Pupcenoks 2012). Observers will also erroneously take instances of nationalistic solidarity for granted. As Rogers Brubaker (2004, 2015) argues, "groupness" is a dependent variable rather than a constant, and should be treated as such by investigators.[5]

The effects of immigrant identities on coalition building remains another important but neglected topic in the study of diaspora mobilization. Many of the activists in this study had previously mobilized as part of pan-Arab and Muslim coalitions in defense of Palestinian rights along with white-majority anti-war and pro-peace Jewish American and British groups. The Arab Spring undermined this solidarity in a variety of ways, however, as many pro-Palestinian, pro-Arab, and so-called peace groups came out on the side of Bashar al-Assad in Syria due to his long-standing anti-Western, pro-Palestinian rhetoric.[6] These pro-regime alignments have ignored the terrible crimes that Assad has inflicted on Palestinian refugees in Syria (Chatty 2018) and have put many Arab American and British organizations in a bind. After many Arab organizations refused to publicly condemn violence being committed by Syria and Russia, many pro-democracy Syrians reported feeling betrayed and abandoned by their former allies. The effects of home-country conflicts and intra-regional struggles on pan-Arab, Asian, African, and Latinx mobilization, among others, remains a fruitful topic, particularly when these coalitions are needed to contest white nativism and xenophobia.

More research is also needed on the relations between diaspora movements and non-foreign-born activists, particularly when it comes to fights over foreign policy (Grillo and Pupcenoks 2017; Zarnett 2015). During my fieldwork in 2012, for example, I observed white anti-war activists protesting with *pro*-Assad Syrian men and women in Los Angeles, holding "No Blood For Oil!" signs next to Syrians singing Assad's praises and threatening the lives of anti-Assad protesters in Arabic. So too did Libyans in Los Angeles and London report being forcefully kept out of anti-war meetings by white-majority socialist movements. As one of Raed Fares' banners from Kafrabel, Syria, read before he was killed for his peaceful activism, "Anti-war activists! Please support intervention. We are anti-war, we are against Assad killing our children." The ways in which the Arab Spring revolutions have exacerbated racial and ethnic exclusion by the Left deserves practitioners' attention for practical and moral reasons, not only academic ones. It has been shocking, alienating, and maddening for pro-democracy Syrians to see white anti-war activists and journalists *defend* the horrific atrocities committed by the Syrian and Russian regimes and *deny* Assad's chemical weapons attacks in the name of so-called anti-imperialism. This disturbing trend should haunt parts of the Left for years

---

[5] See, for example, Okamoto (2014) and Zepeda-Millán (2017) as examples of the utility of treating pan-ethnic and racial formation and solidarity as a dependent variable.

[6] See Zarnett (2015) for a fascinating study of the impact of diaspora mobilization on western solidarity given to Kurds and Palestinians.

to come (Munif 2020).[7] Far more attention is needed, therefore, to the ways in which diaspora activists are included or silenced by white activists who claim to know what is best for them and their home-country (Moss 2016a).

This study also highlights the utility of considering the varied political "positionalities" of diasporas and immigrants across host-countries in a comparative perspective (Koinova 2012). The access that diaspora activists have to great powers like the United States and Britain may grant them a disproportionate influence in political affairs when compared to kindred movements in less powerful host-country states (Quinsaat 2016, 2019). That said, more research is needed to compare host-country contexts, particularly as diaspora members become empowered to launch claims against home-country regimes from countries like Spain, Germany, and Sweden. As of 2017, for instance, a Spanish national court agreed to hear a case involving the murder of a delivery van driver in Syria. This was raised by the driver's sister, who accused top Syrian regime officials of state terrorism from her residence in Madrid. In 2020, Germany also opened cases against Syrian refugees accused of committing crimes against humanity in Syria (Amos 2020). Given the sway that authoritarian powers have over multilateral, rights-enforcing institutions, such as the United Nations Security Council and the International Criminal Court, host-countries without veto rights in the UN Security Council may provide new political opportunities for justice (Human Rights Watch 2017; Koinova 2014). This is particularly important when international institutions fail to fulfill their basic mandates of protecting human rights, as has been the case in Syria and elsewhere.

Diaspora activists in peripheral states also play an important role in rebellions when their host-country governments lend at least tacit geopolitical support to the cause (Betts and Jones 2016), as did Egypt, Tunisia, and Malta during the Libyan revolution. Aspiring powers – even ones that ban independent civic organizing – fuel diaspora activism when they see opportunities to advance their interests, as when Gulf monarchies permitted Syrians to remit resources during the Arab Spring (Dickinson 2015). This suggests the usefulness of attending to how different host-countries and the geopolitical dynamics in which they are embedded facilitate transnational activism beyond the cases investigated here.

Lastly, the question of how movements become transnational agents for change highlights the role of diaspora and immigrant activists in contesting the authoritarian practices of their democratic host-country governments (Quinsaat 2019). As mentioned above, the groups in this study have long been subjected to discrimination, racism, and systemic violence across the Western world for over a century (Bakalian and Bozorgmehr 2009; Cainkar 2009; Chaudhary 2015; Fadlalla 2019; Jamal and Naber 2008; Santoro and Azab

---

[7] See Yassir Munif's (2020) discussion on how these debates have also spread to academia.

2015; Tarrow 2015). This situation worsened during the US presidency of Donald Trump owing to his travel ban against these communities and many other marginalized nationalities. Yet, the Libyans, Syrians, and Yemenis who mobilized for the Arab Spring remain some of the strongest supporters of the principles that Western democratic governments claim to stand for. The cruel irony is that while transnational ties purportedly implicate diaspora actors as exporters of terrorism and culture clashes (Huntington 1997, 2004; Pupcenoks 2016), it is precisely Libyans, Syrians, and Yemenis who are *most* victimized by violence and who do the *most* to defend democracy and human rights in their homelands. Diaspora mobilization against authoritarianism should be protected and respected, rather than treated with suspicion. So too should their voices, which are as diverse as their identities, be listened to with care. They have a great deal to teach us about the perils and promises of activism in a globalized world.

Methodological Appendix

This book is based on research that compares six cases – three national groups (Libyan, Syrian, and Yemeni) across two host-countries (the United States and Britain) – using original, comparative evidence on the Arab Spring abroad. The unit of analysis is diaspora movement by national group (Libyan, Syrian, and Yemeni) and host-country (the United States and Britain); the units of observation are individual diaspora activists and movement groups. Initially, I justified this research design as providing what social scientists call a comparison based on "most similar" cases, since the Arab Spring gave new life to anti-regime activism, protest movements, and social movement organizations in each diaspora group. However, while the Arab Spring signified a new wave of mobilizations against authoritarian regimes, I came to discover that their collective actions varied in notable ways. This presented me with an ideal opportunity to explain this variation among the three national groups residing across two host-countries.

Before and upon arrival in each locale where interviews took place, which included Los Angeles, DC, New York, London, and Manchester, I used what social scientists call snowball and purposive sampling techniques in each community. These methods, which are common to case-based social movement research, allowed me to contact activists via referrals from their peers and to request interviews from specific organizations and groups, including women- and youth-run initiatives, in order to make the study as inclusive as possible. Snowball sampling provides access to relatively "hidden" populations and their "interactional units"; it also draws on the insider knowledge of those who know the relevant participants in a given "strategic action field" (Biernacki and Waldorf 1981: 141; Fligstein and McAdam 2012). This was especially important in my case since many organizations were dominated by older male elites (see also Chapters 2 and 4 on this point). I additionally used social movement websites, public Facebook pages, and media reports to identify participants and avoid sampling within insular networks. I made efforts to reach out to activists who had founded or led prominent diasporic pro-revolution organizations, as well as those who were identified by their peers as having contributed in a meaningful way to rebellion and relief efforts. What a "meaningful" contribution or being an "activist" in these contexts meant was intentionally kept open-ended so as not to prematurely assume or limit the kinds of activities that were undertaken and considered important by members. Interviewees often provided me with information and referrals across networks because they recognized that I did not just want to hear "one side" or about one type of experience. They often posited this as an invitation – talk to them and *they* will tell you! – as a way to affirm the veracity of their accounts, even if they did not agree with or get along personally with the referred-to individuals.

As described in the Introduction, this study is based on primary data that include interviews with 239 individuals (of which 231 were members of the three national groups studied); 30 ethnographic participant observations of diaspora-sponsored events, including fundraisers, concerts, and picnics; and secondary data such as electronic media (e.g., online newspapers, streaming news services, blogs, and social media such as Facebook and Twitter), think tank reports, documentary films, and scholarly books and memoirs published on the Arab Spring revolutions. Further information about the characteristics of my interviewees is listed in Table A.1. The ensuing dataset includes approximately three hundred hours of digital recordings and two thousand pages of single-spaced transcriptions and field notes. I sorted the data according to the principles of process tracing (George and Bennett 2004) and grounded methods (Charmaz 2006; Glaser 1965; Strauss and Corbin 1990), using a sample of the interviews to derive open codes denoting activists' experiences, such as "delivered aid to refugee camps" and "protested on the National Mall." I then grouped and refined the codes into focused categories, such as "volunteering on the front lines" and "broadcasting," using NVivo software, which helps qualitative researchers to lump and sort their data according to empirical patterns and emergent conceptual categories (Lofland et al. 2006[1971]).

Interviewees' preferences dictated where our conversations took place, which included Yemeni Community Associations, Syrian organization offices, cafes, restaurants, and in respondents' homes. In many cases, I was privy to what historian Sarah Gualtieri (2020: 14) calls "archival transactions"; during these transactions, the researcher is "shown material from family papers, given videos and photographs," and other material that supplements interviewees' oral histories and testimonials. In numerous cases, I was shown photographs of family members who had been imprisoned by regimes, grainy cell phone videos and photographs of anti-regime events, handmade flyers advertising events, typed catalogs and informational materials produced by activists on regime atrocities, PowerPoint presentations used to communicate claims to policy-makers and the media, and emails with respondents' contacts in the US government and NATO. While I was not "given" these materials to publish or own, these transactions provided important supplementary evidence of members' activities and illustrated the character of their mobilization dynamics and interactions in full color, so to speak.

This project illustrates the methodological promise of using a grounded approach (Charmaz 2006) to understand and analyze collective action dynamics among social groups. This is particularly important for the study of populations that remain largely invisible in social science research due to an iterative cycle of theoretical neglect and a lack of existing historical and survey data (see also my point on under-counted groups in the Conclusion). In this way, this study highlights the importance of substantiating community dynamics that are often subsumed under aggregated characteristics (such as "Arab," which excludes ethnic categories like Syrian Kurdish and Libyan Amazigh) through interview and ethnographic data-collection methods. The findings also emphasize the importance of taking respondents' accounts seriously. Such accounts can reveal perceptions and experiences that remain unaccounted for in other types of data sources, as I find in the case of transnational repression and conflict transmission. Furthermore, in contrast to predominant analytical tendencies in movement studies to focus narrowly on the emergence and frequency of protest events visible in major newspapers (Earl et al. 2004), the grounded approach used here sheds light on activists' fuller transnational tactical repertoires, including the ways they worked behind the scenes to facilitate rebellion and relief.

At the same time, this approach does not mean that investigators must rely solely on respondents' testimonials to understand their collective dynamics. Accounts should instead be used to formulate exploratory questions that can be investigated in depth and tested across cases. These accounts should also be triangulated with external data sources whenever possible, as I have done here, and grounded in comparisons that point to causal factors and processes (such as geopolitical support in the form of military and humanitarian intervention) (McAdam et al. 2001). This further emphasizes the usefulness of comparative case-study research in revealing patterns across cases in ways that defy prediction and insiders' beliefs (Bloemraad 2013; Ragin 2000, 2008; Ragin et al. 2004; Yin 2008). In its earliest inception, this study was designed as a binational comparison because reports by Yemeni activists attested that diaspora activism during the revolution had varied significantly between the US and British contexts in ways that warranted investigation. Through extensive, comparative fieldwork across the two countries, I discovered that in contrast to what many Yemeni respondents *believed* – that *other* diaspora communities had done a better job at mobilizing to help the revolution than they had – Yemeni activists across local and national contexts were instead impeded by a common set of challenges. Although the orienting assumptions that shaped the initial research design turned out to be unsupported by the data, the binational case comparison nevertheless revealed how the mobilization dynamics of diaspora groups across communities are shaped by a similar set of conditions.

TABLE A.1 *Characteristics of respondents by country of origin*

Descriptors		Libya	Syria	Yemen
Sex				
	Male	43 (67.2%)	59 (77.6%)	65 (71.4%)
	Female	21 (32.8%)	17 (22.4%)	26 (28.6%)
Immigrant generation				
	First[a]	46 (71.9%)	58 (76.3%)	68 (74.7%)
	Second	18 (28.1%)	17 (22.4%)	22 (24.2%)
	Third	0 (0.0%)	1 (1.3%)	1 (1.1%)
Age at revolution's onset				
	15–24[b]	12 (18.8%)	20 (26.3%)	22 (24.2%)
	25–34	24 (37.5%)	20 (26.3%)	37 (40.6%)
	35–44	14 (21.9%)	21 (27.7%)	18 (19.8%)
	45–54	13 (20.3%)	14 (18.4%)	10 (11.0%)
	55+	1 (1.5%)	1 (1.3%)	4 (4.4%)
Minority status				
	Ethnic minority	4 (6.3%)	7 (9.2%)	0 (0.0%)
	Religious minority	0 (0.0%)	3 (3.9%)	0 (0.0%)
	South Yemeni[c]	–	–	25 (27.5%)
	Total	4 (6.3%)	10 (13.1%)	25 (27.5%)
Host-country				
	United States	37 (57.8%)	49 (64.5%)	34 (37.4%)
	Britain	27 (42.2%)	25 (32.9%)	57 (62.6%)
	Both	0 (0.0%)	2 (2.6%)	0 (0.0%)
Active in collective efforts against regime before 2011		16 (25.0%)	16 (21.1%)	14 (15.4%)
Self/family forced to emigrate due to repression before 2011		32 (50.0%)	24 (31.6%)	7 (7.7%)
TOTAL		64 (100.0%)	76 (100.0%)	91 (100.0%)

[a] Not all first-generation participants emigrated from Libya, Syria, or Yemen directly.
[b] All participants were interviewed in accordance with Institutional Review Board protocols.
[c] South Yemeni is an important minority regional identity in Yemen.

It also suggested the importance of expanding the comparison to other national groups, which proceeded according to my description in the Introduction. In this way, the comparison revealed important information about similarities in the mobilization patterns of conationals across contexts, differences between the three national groups, and the mechanisms producing these findings.

References

ACADEMIC SOURCES, RESEARCH REPORTS, AND NONFICTION

Abdelrahman, M. (2011). The transnational and the local: Egyptian activists and transnational protest networks. *British Journal of Middle Eastern Studies*, 38(3), 407–24.

Aboueldahab, N. (2019). Reclaiming Yemen: The role of the Yemeni professional diaspora. Brookings Doha Center, Analysis Paper no. 26, pp. 1–31.

Abramson, Y. (2017). Making a homeland, constructing a diaspora: The case of Taglit-Birthright Israel. *Political Geography*, 58, 14–23.

Adamson, F. (2002). Mobilizing for the transformation of home: Politicized identities and transnational practices. In N. al-Ali and K. Koser, eds., *New Approaches to Migration? Transnational Communities and the Transformation of Home*. London: Routledge, pp. 155–68.

(2004). Displacement, diaspora mobilization, and transnational cycles of political violence. In J. Tirman, ed., *The Maze of Fear: Security and Migration after 9/11*. New York: New Press, pp. 45–58.

(2005). Globalisation, transnational political mobilisation, and networks of violence. *Cambridge Review of International Affairs*, 18(1), 35–53.

(2006). International terrorism, nonstate actors, and transnational political mobilization: A perspective from international relations. In T. Biersteker, P. Spiro, V. Raffo, and C. Sriram, eds., *International Law and International Relations: Bridging Theory and Practice*. New York: Routledge, pp. 79–92.

(2013). Mechanisms of diaspora mobilization and the transnationalization of civil war. In J. Checkel, ed., *Transnational Dynamics of Civil War*. Cambridge: Cambridge University Press, pp. 63–88.

(2016). The growing importance of diaspora politics. *Current History*, 115(784), 291–97.

(2019). Non-state authoritarianism and diaspora politics. *Global Networks*, 20(1), 150–69.

Adamson, F. and Demetriou, M. (2007). Remapping the boundaries of "state" and "national identity": Incorporating diasporas into IR theorizing. *European Journal of International Relations*, 13(4), 489–526.

Adamson, F. and Tsourapas, G. (2020). At home and abroad: Coercion-by-proxy as a tool of transnational repression. Freedom House Special Report 2020, December 15. https://freedomhouse.org/report/special-report/2020/home-and-abroad-coercion-proxy-tool-transnational-repression.

Adler, G., Jr. (2019). *Empathy beyond US Borders: The Challenges of Transnational Civic Engagement*. New York: Cambridge University Press.

Ahmida, A. A. (2006). When the subaltern speak: Memory of genocide in colonial Libya, 1929 to 1933. *Italian Studies*, 61(2), 175–90.

Al-Ali, N. and Koser, K. (2002). *New Approaches to Migration? Transnational Communities and the Transformation of Home*. New York: Routledge.

Al-Haj Saleh, Y. (2017). *The Impossible Revolution: Making Sense of the Syrian Tragedy*. Chicago: Haymarket Books.

Al-Jizawi, N., Anstis, S., Chan, S., Senft, A., and Deibert, R. (2020). Annotation bibliography: Transnational digital repression. The Citizen Lab, November 15. https://citizenlab.ca/2020/11/annotated-bibliography-transnational-digital-repression/.

Al-Rumi, A. (2009). Libyan Berbers struggle to assert their identity online. *Arab Media & Society*, May 6. www.arabmediasociety.com/libyan-berbers-struggle-to-assert-their-identity-online/.

Alloush, B. (2018). *Syrians in the USA: Solidarity despite Political Rifts*. Paris: Arab Reform Initiative, pp. 1–16.

Alunni, A. (2019). Long-distance nationalism and belonging in the Libyan diaspora (1969–2011). *British Journal of Middle Eastern Studies*, 46(2), 242–58.

  (2020). National Belonging and Everyday Nationhood in the Age of Globalization: An Account of Global Flows in Libya. PhD thesis, Durham University.

Amarsaringham, A. (2015). *Pain, Pride, and Politics: Social Movement Activism and the Sri Lankan Diaspora in Canada*. Athens: University of Georgia Press.

Ambrosio, T. (2002). *Ethnic Identity Groups and U.S. Foreign Policy*. Westport, CT: Praeger.

Amenta, E. (2006). *When Movements Matter: The Townsend Plan and the Rise of Social Security*. Princeton: Princeton University Press.

Amnesty International. (2011). The long reach of the *Mukhabaraat*: Violence and harassment against Syrians abroad and their relatives back home. Amnesty International, October 3. www.amnesty.org/en/documents/MDE24/057/2011/en/.

Andén-Papadopoulos, K. and Pantti, M. (2013). The media work of Syrian diaspora activists: Brokering between the protest and mainstream media. *International Journal of Communication*, 7, 2185–206.

Anderson, B. (1998). *The Spectre of Comparisons: Nationalism, Southeast Asia, and the World*. New York: Verso.

  (2006[1983]). *Imagined Communities*, 2nd ed. New York: Verso.

Andrews, K. (2004). *Freedom Is a Constant Struggle: The Mississippi Civil Rights Movement and Its Legacy*. Chicago: University of Chicago Press.

Anthias, F. (1998). Evaluating "diaspora": Beyond ethnicity? *Sociology*, 32(3), 557–80.

Appadurai, A. (1997). *Modernity at Large*. Minneapolis: University of Minnesota Press.

Appiah, K. (1997). Cosmopolitan patriots. *Critical Inquiry*, 23(3), 617–39.

Ayoub, P. (2013). Cooperative transnationalism in contemporary Europe: Europeanization and political opportunities for LGBT mobilization in the European Union. *European Political Science Review*, 5(2), 279–310.

(2016). *When States Come Out: Europe's Sexual Minorities and the Politics of Visibility*. New York: Cambridge University Press.

Bada, X. (2014). *Mexican Hometown Associations in Chicagoacán: From Local to Transnational Civic Engagement*. New Brunswick, NJ: Rutgers University Press.

Bakalian, A. and Bozorgmehr, M. (2009). *Backlash 9/11: Middle Eastern and Muslim Americans Respond*. Berkeley: University of California Press.

Bamyeh, M. (2014). Palestinians, diasporas, and US foreign policy. In R. Segura and J. DeWind, eds., *Diaspora Lobbies and the US Government: Convergence and Divergence in Making Foreign Policy*. New York: New York University Press, pp. 76–94.

Bamyeh, M. and Hanafi, S. (2015). Introduction to the special issue on Arab uprisings. *International Sociology*, 30(4), 343–47.

Basch, L., Glick Schiller, N., and Szanton Blanc, C. (1994). *Nations Unbound: Transnational Projects, Postcolonial Predicaments, and Deterritorialized Nation-States*. New York: Gordon & Breach.

Baser, B. (2015). *Diasporas and Homeland Conflicts: A Comparative Perspective*. New York: Routledge.

Baser, B. and Halperin, A. (2019). Diasporas from the Middle East: Displacement, transnational identities and homeland politics. *British Journal of Middle Eastern Studies*, 46(2), 215–21.

Baser, B. and Öztürk, A. (2020). Positive and negative diaspora governance in context: From public diplomacy to transnational authoritarianism. *Middle East Critique*, 29 (3), 1–16.

Baser, B. and Swain, A. (2011). Stateless diaspora groups and their repertoires of nationalist activism in host countries. *Journal of International Relations*, 8(1), 37–60.

Bassiouni, C. (2013). *Libya: From Repression to Revolution – A Record of Armed Conflict and International Law Violations, 2011–2013*. Boston: Brill–Nijhoff.

Bauböck, R. (2003). Towards a political theory of migrant transnationalism. *International Migration Review*, 37(3), 700–23.

(2008). Ties across borders: The growing salience of transnationalism and diaspora politics. *International Migration, Integration and Social Cohesion in Europe* [IMISCOE] *Policy Brief*, no. 13, 1–8.

Bauböck, R. and Faist, T., eds. (2010). *Diaspora and Transnationalism: Concepts, Theories and Methods*. Amsterdam: Amsterdam University Press.

Bayat, A. (2017). *Revolution without Revolutionaries: Making Sense of the Arab Spring*. Stanford, CA: Stanford University Press.

(2013). *Life as Politics: How Ordinary People Change the Middle East*, 2nd ed. Stanford, CA: Stanford University Press.

Beaugrand, C. and Geisser, V. (2016). Social mobilization and political participation in the diaspora during the "Arab Spring". *Journal of Immigrant & Refugee Studies*, 14(3), 239–43.

Beck, C. (2014). Reflections on the revolutionary wave in 2011. *Theory and Society*, 43(2), 197–223.

Beissinger, M. (2013). The semblance of democratic revolution: Coalitions in Ukraine's Orange Revolution. *American Political Science Review*, 107(3), 574–92.

Bell, J. (1972). Contemporary revolutionary organizations. In R. Keohane and J. Nye Jr., eds., *Transnational Relations and World Politics*. Cambridge, MA: Harvard University Press, pp. 153–68.

Benamer, H. (2012). The number of Libyan doctors in diaspora: Myths and facts. *Libyan Journal of Medicine*, 7(1), 1–2.

Benford, R. and Snow, D. (2000). Framing processes and social movements: An overview and assessment. *Annual Review of Sociology*, 26, 611–39.

Berberian, H. (2019). *Roving Revolutionaries: Armenians and the Connected Revolutions in the Russian, Iranian, and Ottoman Words*. Oakland: University of California Press.

Bermudez, A. (2010). The transnational political practices of Colombians in Spain and the United Kingdom. *Ethnic and Racial Studies*, 33(1), 75–91.

Bernal, V. (2014). *Nation as Network: Diaspora, Cyberspace, and Citizenship*. Chicago: University of Chicago Press.

Besteman, C. (2016). *Making Refuge: Somali Bantu Refugees and Lewiston, Maine*. Durham, NC: Duke University Press.

Betts, A. and Jones, W. (2016). *Mobilising the Diaspora: How Refugees Challenge Authoritarianism*. Cambridge: Cambridge University Press.

Biernacki, P. and Waldorf, D. (1981). Snowball sampling: Problems and techniques of chain referral sampling. *Sociological Methods & Research*, 10(2), 141–63.

Blanton, S. (1999). Instruments of security or tools of repression? Arms imports and human rights conditions in developing countries. *Journal of Peace Research*, 36(2), 233–44.

Blitz, B. (2009). Libyan nationals in the United Kingdom: Geo-political considerations and trends in asylum and return. *International Journal on Multicultural Societies*, 10(2), 106–27.

Bloemraad, I. (2006). *Becoming a Citizen: Incorporating Immigrants and Refugees in the United States and Canada*. Berkeley: University of California Press.

(2013). The promise and pitfalls of comparative research design in the study of migration. *Migration Studies*, 1(1), 27–46.

Bob, C. (2001). Marketing rebellion: Insurgent groups, international media, and NGO support. *International Politics*, 38(3), 311–34.

(2002). Political process theory and transnational movements: Dialectics of protest among Nigeria's Ogoni minority. *Social Problems*, 49(3), 395–415.

(2005). *The Marketing of Rebellion: Insurgents, Media, and International Activism*. New York: Cambridge University Press.

(2019). *Rights as Weapons: Instruments of Conflict, Tools of Power*. Princeton: Princeton University Press.

Boccagni, P., Lafleur, J.-M., and Levitt, P. (2016). Transnational politics as cultural circulation: Toward a conceptual understanding of migrant political participation on the move. *Mobilities*, 11(3), 444–63.

Boli, J. and Thomas, G. (1999). *Constructing World Culture: International Nongovernmental Organizations since 1875*. Stanford, CA: Stanford University Press.

Bozorgmehr, M., Der-Martirosian, C., and Sabagh, G. (1996). Middle Easterners: A new kind of immigrant. In R. Waldinger and M. Bozorgmehr, eds., *Ethnic Los Angeles*. New York: Russell Sage Foundation, pp. 345–78.

Bragdon, A. (1989). Early Arabic-speaking immigrant communities in Texas. *Arab Studies Quarterly*, 11(2/3), 83–101.

Brand, L. (2006). *Citizens Abroad: Emigration and the State in the Middle East and North Africa*. New York: Cambridge University Press.

Brighton, S. (2007). British Muslims, multiculturalism and UK foreign policy: "Integration" and "cohesion" in and beyond the state. *International Affairs*, 83 (1), 1–17.

Brinkerhoff, J. (2005). Digital diasporas and governance in semi-authoritarian states: the case of the Egyptian Copts. *Public Administration and Development*, 25(3), 193–204.

(2009). *Digital Diasporas: Identity and Transnational Engagement*. New York: Cambridge University Press.

(2011). Diasporas and conflict societies: Conflict entrepreneurs, competing interests or contributors to stability and development? *Conflict, Security & Development*, 11 (2), 115–43.

(2016). *Institutional Reform and Diaspora Entrepreneurs: The In-Between Advantage*. New York: Oxford University Press.

Brownlee, J., Masoud, T., and Reynolds, A. (2015). *The Arab Spring: Pathways of Repression and Reform*. Oxford: Oxford University Press.

Brubaker, R. (2004). *Ethnicity without Groups*. Cambridge, MA: Harvard University Press.

(2005). The "diaspora" diaspora. *Ethnic and Racial Studies*, 28(1), 1–19.

(2013). Categories of analysis and categories of practice: A note on the study of Muslims in European countries of immigration. *Ethnic and Racial Studies*, 36(1), 1–8.

(2015). *Grounds for Difference*. Cambridge, MA: Harvard University Press.

Brubaker, R. and Laitin, D. (1998). Ethnic and nationalist violence. *Annual Review of Sociology*, 24, 423–52.

Brysk, A. (2000). *From Tribal Village to Global Village*. Stanford, CA: Stanford University Press.

Butler, K. (2001). Defining diaspora, refining a discourse. *Diaspora: A Journal of Transnational Studies*, 10(2), 189–219.

Byman, D., Chalk, P., Hoffmann, B., Rosenau, W., and Brannan, D. (2001). *Trends in Outside Support for Insurgent Movements*. Santa Monica: RAND.

Cainkar, L. (2009). *Homeland Insecurity: The Arab American and Muslim American Experience after 9/11*. New York: Russell Sage Foundation.

(2013). Global Arab world migrations and diasporas. *Arab Studies Journal*, 21(1), 126–65.

(2018). Fluid terror threat: A genealogy of the racialization of Arab, Muslim, and South Asian Americans. *Amerasia Journal*, 44(1), 27–59.

Cannistraro, P. (1985). Luigi Antonini and the Italian anti-fascist movement in the United States, 1940–1943. *Journal of American Ethnic History*, 5(1), 21–40.

Carlson, E. and Williams, N., eds. (2020). *Comparative Demography of the Syrian Diaspora: European and Middle Eastern Destinations*. European Studies of Population, vol. 20. Switzerland: Springer.

Carpenter, C. (2010). Governing the global agenda: "Gatekeepers" and "issue adoption" in transnational advocacy networks. In D. Avant, M. Finnemore, and S. Sell, eds., *Who Governs the Globe?* New York: Cambridge University Press, pp. 202–37.

Carroll, P. (1994). *The Odyssey of the Abraham Lincoln Brigade: Americans in the Spanish Civil War.* Stanford, CA: Stanford University Press.

Cederman, L.-E., Girardin, L., and Gleditsch, K. (2009). Ethnonationalist triads: Assessing the influence of kin groups on civil wars. *World Politics,* 61(3), 403–37.

Chalk, P. (2008). The Tigers abroad: How the LTTE diaspora supports the conflict in Sri Lanka. *Georgetown Journal of International Affairs,* 9(2), 97–104.

Charmaz, K. (2006). *Constructing Grounded Theory: A Practical Guide through Qualitative Analysis.* London: Sage.

Chatty, D. (2010). *Displacement and Dispossession in the Modern Middle East.* New York: Cambridge University Press.

(2018). *Syria: The Making and Unmaking of a Refugee State.* New York: Oxford University Press.

Chang, P. (2015). *Protest Dialectics: State Repression and South Korea's Democracy Movement, 1970–1979.* Stanford, CA: Stanford University Press.

Chaudhary, A. (2015). *Spoiled by War: How Government Policies, Community Characteristics and Stigma Shape the Pakistani Migrant Non-profit Sector in London, Toronto and New York City.* PhD dissertation, University of California, Davis.

(2021). Ascriptive organizational stigma and the constraining of Pakistani immigrant organizations. *International Migration Review,* 55(1), 84–107. https://doi.org/10.1177/0197918320920563.

Chaudhary, A. and Moss, D. (2019). Suppressing transnationalism: Bringing constraints into the study of transnational political action. *Comparative Migration Studies,* 7 (9), 1–22.

Clifford, J. (1994). Diasporas. *Cultural Anthropology,* 9(3), 302–38.

Cochrane, F., Baser, B., and Swain, A. (2009). Home thoughts from abroad: Diasporas and peace-building in Northern Ireland and Sri Lanka. *Studies in Conflict and Terrorism,* 32(8), 681–704.

Cohen, R. (1996). Diasporas and the nation-state: From victims to challengers. *International Affairs,* 72(3), 507–20.

(2008[1997]). *Global Diasporas: An Introduction.* London: Routledge.

Collier, P. and Hoeffler, A. (2000). Greed and grievance in civil war. Policy Research Working Paper no. 2355. Washington, DC: World Bank.

Collier, P., Elliott, V., Hegre, H., Hoeffler, A., Reynal-Querol, M., and Sambanis, N. (2003). *Breaking the Conflict Trap: Civil War and Development Policy.* Washington, DC: World Bank and Oxford University Press.

Conduit, D. (2019). *The Muslim Brotherhood in Syria.* New York: Cambridge University Press.

Cooley, A. and Heathershaw, J. (2017). *Dictators without Borders: Power and Money in Central Asia.* New Haven, CT: Yale University Press.

Cress, D. and Snow, D. (2000). The outcomes of homeless mobilization: The influence of organization, disruption, political mediation, and framing. *American Journal of Sociology,* 105(4), 1063–104.

Curtis, R., Jr. and Zurcher, L., Jr. (1973). Stable resources of protest movements: The multi-organizational field. *Social Forces,* 52(1), 53–61.

Dalmasso, E., Del Sordi, A., Glasius, M., Hirt, N., Michaelsen, M., Mohammad, A., and Moss, D. (2017). Intervention: Extraterritorial authoritarian power. *Political Geography*, 64, 95–104.

Davis, D. and Moore, W. (1997). Ethnicity matters: Transnational ethnic alliances and foreign policy behavior. *International Studies Quarterly*, 41(1), 171–84.

Day, S. W. (2012). *Regionalism and Rebellion in Yemen: A Troubled National Union*. New York: Cambridge University Press.

Délano, A. and Gamlen, A. (2014). Comparing and theorizing state-diaspora relations. *Political Geography*, 41, 43–53.

Della Porta, D. and Tarrow, S., eds. (2005). *Transnational Protest and Global Activism*. Lanham, MD: Rowman & Littlefield.

DeWind, J. and Segura, R., eds. (2014). *Diaspora Lobbies and the US Government: Convergence and Divergence in Making Foreign Policy*. New York: New York University Press.

Dickinson, E. (2015). Godfathers and thieves. Deca. www.decastories.com/godfathers/.

Duquette-Rury, L. (2016). Migrant transnational participation: How citizen inclusion and government engagement matter for local democratic development in Mexico. *American Sociological Review*, 81(4), 771–99.

(2020). *Exit and Voice: The Paradox of Cross-border Politics in Mexico*. Oakland: University of California Press.

Dyssegaard Kallick, D., Roldan, C., and Mathema, S. (2016). Syrian immigrants in the United States: A receiving community for today's refugees. Center for American Progress. www.americanprogress.org/issues/immigration/reports/2016/12/13/294851/syrian-immigrants-in-the-united-states-a-receiving-community-for-todays-refugees/.

Earl, J., Martin, A., McCarthy, J., and Soule, S. (2004). The use of newspaper data in the study of collective action. *Annual Review of Sociology*, 30(1), 65–80.

Eccarius-Kelly, V. (2002). Political movements and leverage points: Kurdish activism in the European diaspora. *Journal of Muslim Minority Affairs*, 22(1), 91–118.

Eckstein, S. (2009). *The Immigrant Divide: How Cuban Americans Changed the US and Their Homeland*. New York: Routledge.

Edwards, B. and McCarthy, J. (2004). Resources and social movement mobilization. In D. Snow, S. Soule, and H. Kriesi, eds., *The Blackwell Companion to Social Movements*. Malden, MA: Blackwell, pp. 116–52.

Eid, K. and di Giovanni, J. (2018). *My Country: A Syrian Memoir*. New York: Bloomsbury.

Eisinger, P. (1973). The conditions of protest behavior in American cities. *American Political Science Review*, 67(1), 11–28.

El-Abani, S., Jacobs, S., Chadwick, K., and Arun, S. (2020). Migration and attitudes towards domestic violence against women: A case study of Libyan migrants in the UK. *Migration and Development*, 9(1), 111–30.

Fadlalla, A. H. (2019). *Branding Humanity: Competing Narratives of Rights, Violence, and Global Citizenship*. Stanford, CA: Stanford University Press.

Fahrenthold, S. (2013). Transnational modes and media: The Syrian press in the *Mahjar* and emigrant activism during World War I. *Mashriq & Mahjar*, 1(1), 30–54.

(2019). *Between the Ottomans and the Entente: The First World War in the Syrian and Lebanese Diaspora, 1908–1925*. New York: Oxford University Press.

Fair, C. (2005). Diaspora involvement in insurgencies: Insights from the Khalistan and Tamil Eelam movements. *Nationalism and Ethnic Politics*, 11(1), 125–56.

(2007). The Sri Lankan Tamil diaspora: Sustaining conflict and pushing for peace. In H. Smith and P. Stares, eds., *Diasporas in Conflict: Peace-Makers or Peace-Wreckers?* New York: United Nations University Press, pp. 172–95.

Faist, T. (2000). Transnationalization in international migration: Implications for the study of citizenship and culture. *Ethnic and Racial Studies*, 23(2), 189–222.

Field, J., Jr. (1971). Transnationalism and the new tribe. *International Organization*, 25 (3), 353–72.

Finn, M. and Momani, B. (2017). Established and emergent political subjectivities in circular human geographies: Transnational Arab activists. *Citizenship Studies*, 21 (1), 22–43.

Fligstein, N. and McAdam, D. (2012). *A Theory of Fields*. New York: Oxford University Press.

Foner, N. (1997). What's new about transnationalism? New York immigrants today and at the turn of the century. *Diaspora: A Journal of Transnational Studies*, 6(3), 355–75.

Friedlander, J., ed. (1988). *Sojourners and Settlers: The Yemeni Immigrant Experience*. Salt Lake City: University of Utah Press.

Gamlen, A. (2014). Diaspora institutions and diaspora governance. *International Migration Review*, 48(1), 180–217.

Gamlen, A., Cummings, M., and Vaaler, P. (2017). Explaining the rise of diaspora institutions. *Journal of Ethnic and Migration Studies*, 45(4), 492–516.

Gamson, W. and Wolfsfeld, G. (1993). Movements and media as interacting systems. *Annals of the American Academy of Political and Social Science*, 528, 114–25.

Gazzini, Claudia. (2007). Talking back: Exiled Libyans use the web to push for change. *Arab Media & Society*, March 2. www.arabmediasociety.com/talking-back-exiled-libyans-use-the-web-to-push-for-change/.

Gerges, Fawaz A., ed. (2015). *Contentious Politics in the Middle East: Popular Resistance and Marginalized Activism beyond the Arab Uprisings*. New York: Palgrave Macmillan.

George, A. and Bennett, A. (2004). *Case Studies and Theory Development in the Social Sciences*. Cambridge, MA: MIT Press.

Glaser, B. (1965). The constant comparative method of qualitative analysis. *Social Problems*, 12(4), 436–45.

Glasius, M. (2018). Extraterritorial authoritarian practices: A framework. *Globalizations*, 15(2), 179–97.

Glick Schiller, N. and Fouron, G. (2001). *Georges Woke Up Laughing: Long-Distance Nationalism and the Search for Home*. Durham, NC: Duke University Press.

Godwin, M. (2018). Winning, Westminster-style: Tamil diaspora interest group mobilisation in Canada and the UK. *Journal of Ethnic and Migration Studies*, 44(8), 1325–40.

Goldring, L. (2004). Family and collective remittances to Mexico: A multi-dimensional typology. *Development and Change*, 35(4), 799–840.

Goodwin, J. (2001). *No Other Way Out: States and Revolutionary Movements, 1945–1991*. New York: Cambridge University Press.

Goodwin, J., Jasper, J., and Polletta, F., eds. (2001). *Passionate Politics: Emotions and Social Movements*. Chicago: University of Chicago Press.

Gordon, P. (1987). The killing machine: Britain and the international repression trade. *Race & Class*, 29(2), 31–52.

Gordon, S. and El Taraboulsi-McCarthy, S. (2018). Counter-terrorism, bank de-risking and humanitarian response: A path forward. Humanitarian Policy Group, Policy Brief 72, May 28, 2021. https://odi.org/en/publications/counter-terrorism-bank-de-risking-and-humanitarian-response-a-path-forward/.

Green, N. and Waldinger, R., eds. (2016). *A Century of Transnationalism: Immigrants and Their Homeland Connections*. Urbana: University of Illinois Press.

Grillo, M. C. and Pupcenoks, J. (2017). Let's intervene! But only if they're like us: The effects of group dynamics and emotion on the willingness to support humanitarian intervention. *International Interactions*, 43(2), 349–74.

Gualtieri, S. (2009). *Between Arab and White: Race and Ethnicity in the Early Syrian American Diaspora*. Berkeley: University of California Press.

(2020). *Arab Routes: Pathways to Syrian California*. Stanford, CA: Stanford University Press.

Guarnizo, L., Sanchez, A., and Roach, E. (1999). Mistrust, fragmented solidarity, and transnational migration: Colombians in New York City and Los Angeles. *Ethnic and Racial Studies*, 22(2), 367–96.

Guarnizo, L. and Díaz, L. (1999). Transnational migration: A view from Colombia. *Ethnic and Racial Studies*, 22(2), 397–421.

Guarnizo, L., Portes, A., and Haller, W. (2003). Assimilation and transnationalism: Determinants of transnational political action among contemporary migrants. *American Journal of Sociology*, 108(6), 1211–48.

Hafner-Burton, E. and Tsutsui, K. (2007). Justice lost! The failure of international human rights law to matter where needed most. *Journal of Peace Research*, 44(4), 407–25.

Hall, Stuart. (2016[2000]). Diaspora or the logic of cultural translation. *MATRIZes*, 10(3), 47–58.

Halliday, F. (2010[1992]). *Britain's First Muslims: Portrait of an Arab Community*, 2nd ed. New York: I. B. Tauris.

Haney, P. and Vanderbush, W. (1999). The role of ethnic interest groups in U.S. foreign policy: The case of the Cuban American National Foundation. *International Studies Quarterly*, 43(2), 341–61.

Harpaz, Y. (2019). *Citizenship 2.0: Dual Nationality as a Global Asset*. Princeton: Princeton University Press.

He, R. (2014). *Tiananmen Exiles: Voices of the Struggle for Democracy in China*. New York: Palgrave Macmillan.

Hechter, M., Pfaff, S., and Underwood, P. (2016). Grievances and the genesis of rebellion: Mutiny in the Royal Navy, 1740 to 1820. *American Sociological Review*, 81(1), 165–89.

Hess, D. and Martin, B. (2006). Repression, backfire, and the theory of transformative events. *Mobilization*, 11(2), 249–67.

Hess, J. (2009). *Immigrant Ambassadors: Citizenship and Belonging in the Tibetan Diaspora*. Stanford, CA: Stanford University Press.

Hess, M. and Korf, B. (2014). Tamil diaspora and the political spaces of second-generation activism in Switzerland. *Global Networks*, 14(4), 419–37.

Heydemann, S. (1999). *Authoritarianism in Syria: Institutions and Social Conflict, 1946–1970*. Ithaca, NY: Cornell University Press.

Hilsum, L. (2012). *Sandstorm: Libya in the Time of Revolution*. New York: Penguin.

Hironaka, A. (2005). *Neverending Wars: The International Community, Weak States, and the Perpetuation of Civil War*. Cambridge, MA: Harvard University Press.

Hirsch, E. (1990). Sacrifice for the cause: Group processes, recruitment, and commitment in a student social movement. *American Sociological Review*, 55(2), 243–54.

Hirschman, A. (1970). *Exit, Voice, and Loyalty: Responses to Decline in Firms, Organizations, and States*. Cambridge, MA: Harvard University Press.

(1978). Exit, voice, and the state. *World Politics*, 31(1), 90–107.

(1986). Exit and voice: An expanding sphere of influence. In A. Hirschman, ed., *Rival Views of Market Society and Other Recent Essays*. New York: Penguin Books, pp. 77–101.

(1993). Exit, voice, and the fate of the German Democratic Republic: An essay in conceptual history. *World Politics*, 45(2), 173–202.

Hirt, N. (2014). The Eritrean diaspora and its impact on regime stability: Responses to UN sanctions. *African Affairs*, 114(454), 115–35.

Hockenos, P. (2003). *Homeland Calling: Exile Patriotism and the Balkan Wars*. Ithaca, NY: Cornell University Press.

Hoffmann, B. (2010). Bringing Hirschman back in: "Exit", "voice", and "loyalty" in the politics of transnational migration. *The Latin Americanist*, 54(2), 57–73.

Holmes, A. (2019). *Coups and Revolutions: Mass Mobilization, the Egyptian Military, and the United States from Mubarak to Sisi*. New York: Oxford University Press.

Hooglund, E. (1987). *Crossing the Waters: Arabic-Speaking Immigrants to the United States before 1940*. Washington, DC: Smithsonian Institution Press.

Horst, C. (2008a). A monopoly on assistance: International aid to refugee camps and the neglected role of the Somali diaspora. *Africa Spectrum*, 43(1), 121–31.

(2008b). The transnational political engagements of refugees: Remittance sending practices amongst Somalis in Norway. *Conflict, Security & Development*, 8(3), 317–39.

(2008c). The role of remittances in the transnational livelihood strategies of Somalis. In T. van Naerssen, E. Spaan, and A. Zoomers, eds., *Global Migration and Development*. New York: Routledge, pp. 91–107.

Horst, C. and van Hear, N. (2002). Counting the cost: Refugees, remittances and the "war against terrorism". *Forced Migration Review*, 14, 32–34.

Howell, S. and Shryock, A. (2003). Cracking down on diaspora: Arab Detroit and America's "War on Terror". *Anthropological Quarterly*, 76(3), 443–62.

Human Rights Watch. (1996). Syria: The silenced Kurds. *Human Rights Watch*, 8(4). www.hrw.org/reports/1996/Syria.htm.

(2011a). Days of bloodshed in Aden. Human Rights Watch, March 9. www.hrw.org/report/2011/03/09/days-bloodshed-aden.

(2011b). US/UK: Documents reveal Libya rendition details. Human Rights Watch, September 8. www.hrw.org/news/2011/09/08/us/uk-documents-reveal-libya-rendition-details.

(2017). "These are the crimes we are fleeing": Justice for Syria in Swedish and German courts. Human Rights Watch, October 3. www.hrw.org/report/2017/10/04/these-are-crimes-we-are-fleeing/justice-syria-swedish-and-german-courts#.

Huntington, S. (1997). The erosion of American national interests. *Foreign Affairs*, 76 (5), 28–49.

(2004). *Who Are We? The Challenges to America's National Identity*. New York: Simon & Schuster.

Huynh, J. and Yiu, J. (2015). Breaking blocked transnationalism: Intergenerational change in homeland ties. In A. Portes and P. Fernández-Kelly, eds., *The State and the Grassroots: Immigrant Transnational Organizations in Four Continents*. New York: Berghahn Books, pp. 160–88.

International Crisis Group. (2011a). Popular protest in North Africa and the Middle East (VI): The Syrian People's Slow-Motion Revolution. *Middle East/North Africa Report*, no. 108, July 6. www.crisisgroup.org/middle-east-north-africa/eastern-mediterranean/syria/popular-protest-north-africa-and-middle-east-vi-syrian-people-s-slow-motion-revolution.

(2011b). Popular protest in North Africa and the Middle East (VII): The Syrian Regime's Slow-Motion Suicide. *Middle East/North Africa Report*, no. 109, July 13. www.crisisgroup.org/middle-east-north-africa/eastern-mediterranean/syria/popular-protest-north-africa-and-middle-east-vii-syrian-regime-s-slow-motion-suicide.

(2011c). Uncharted waters: Thinking through Syria's dynamics. *Middle East Briefing*, no. 31, November 24. www.crisisgroup.org/middle-east-north-africa/eastern-mediterranean/syria/uncharted-waters-thinking-through-syria-s-dynamics.

(2011d). Yemen between reform and revolution. *Middle East/North Africa Report*, no. 102, March 14. www.crisisgroup.org/middle-east-north-africa/gulf-and-arabian-peninsula/yemen/yemen-between-reform-and-revolution.

(2011e). Breaking point? Yemen's southern question. *Middle East Report*, no. 114, October 20. www.crisisgroup.org/middle-east-north-africa/gulf-and-arabian-peninsula/yemen/breaking-point-yemen-s-southern-question.

Jacobs, L. (2015). *Strangers in the West: The Syrian Colony of New York City, 1880–1900*. New York: Kalimah Press.

Jamal, A. and Naber, N., eds. (2008). *Race and Arab Americans before and after 9/11: From Invisible Citizens to Visible Subjects*. Syracuse, NY: Syracuse University Press.

Jasper, J. (1998). The emotions of protest: Affective and reactive emotions in and around social movements. *Sociological Forum*, 13(3), 397–424.

(2018). *The Emotions of Protest*. Chicago: University of Chicago Press.

Jenkins, J. and Eckert, C. (1986). Channeling Black insurgency: Elite patronage and professional social movement organizations in the development of the Black Movement. *American Sociological Review*, 51(6), 812–29.

Jörum, E. (2015). Repression across borders: Homeland response to anti-regime mobilization among Syrians in Sweden. *Diaspora Studies*, 8(2), 104–19.

Kapur, D. (2010). *Diaspora, Development, and Democracy: The Domestic Impact of International Migration from India*. Princeton: Princeton University Press.

Kay, T. (2011). *NAFTA and the Politics of Labor Transnationalism*. New York: Cambridge University Press.

Keck, M. (1995). Social equity and environmental politics in Brazil: Lessons from the rubber tappers of Acre. *Comparative Politics*, 27(4), 409–24.

Keck, M. and Sikkink, K. (1998). *Activists beyond Borders: Advocacy Networks in International Politics*. Ithaca, NY: Cornell University Press.

Kennedy, G. (2019). Diaspora incorporation mechanisms: Sustained and episodic mobilisation among the British-Egyptian diaspora after the Arab Spring. *Journal of Ethnic and Migration Studies*. https://doi.org/10.1080/1369183X.2019.1693887.

Keohane, R. and Nye, J., Jr., eds. (1972). *Transnational Relations and World Politics*. Cambridge, MA: Harvard University Press.

Ketchley, Neil. (2017). *Egypt in a Time of Revolution: Contentious Politics and the Arab Spring*. Cambridge: Cambridge University Press.

Kitschelt, H. (1986). Political opportunity structures and political protest: Anti-nuclear movements in four democracies. *British Journal of Political Science*, 16(1), 57–85.

Kitts, J. (2000). Mobilizing in black boxes: Social networks and participation in social movement organizations. *Mobilization*, 5(2), 241–57.

Koinova, M. (2010a). Diasporas and international politics: Utilising the universalistic creed of liberalism for particularistic and nationalist purposes. In R. Bauböck and T. Faist, eds., *Diaspora and Transnationalism: Concepts, Theories and Methods*. Amsterdam: Amsterdam University Press, pp. 149–66.

(2010b). Unintended consequences of diaspora entrepreneurship during post-conflict reconstruction. *International Affairs Forum*, 153–58.

(2011). Diasporas and secessionist conflicts: The mobilization of the Armenian, Albanian and Chechen diasporas. *Ethnic and Racial Studies*, 34(2), 333–56.

(2012). Autonomy and positionality in diaspora politics. *International Political Sociology*, 6(1), 99–103.

(2013). Four types of diaspora mobilization: Albanian diaspora activism for Kosovo independence in the US and the UK. *Foreign Policy Analysis*, 9(4), 433–53.

(2014). Why do conflict-generated diasporas pursue sovereignty-based claims through state-based or transnational channels? Armenian, Albanian and Palestinian diasporas in the UK compared. *European Journal of International Relations*, 20(4), 1043–71.

(2018). Critical junctures and transformative events in diaspora mobilisation for Kosovo and Palestinian statehood. *Journal of Ethnic and Migration Studies*, 44(8), 1289–308.

Koinova, M. and Tsourapas, G. (2018). How do countries of origin engage migrants and diasporas? Multiple actors and comparative perspectives. *International Political Science Review*, 39(3), 311–21.

Koopmans, R. and Statham, P. (1999). Challenging the liberal nation-state? Postnationalism, multiculturalism, and the collective claims making of migrants and ethnic minorities in Britain and Germany. *American Journal of Sociology*, 105(3), 652–96.

Kurzman, C. (2004). *The Unthinkable Revolution in Iran*. Cambridge, MA: Harvard University Press.

Laakso, L. and Hautaniemi, P., eds. (2014). *Diasporas, Development and Peacemaking in the Horn of Africa*. London: Zed Books.

Lacroix, T., Levitt, P., and Vari-Lavoisier, I. (2016). Social remittances and the changing transnational political landscape. *Comparative Migration Studies*, 4(16), 1–5.

Lainer-Vos, D. (2013). *Sinews of the Nation: Constructing Irish and Zionist Bonds in the United States*. Malden, MA: Polity Press.

Lawson, G. (2019). *Anatomies of Revolution*. Cambridge: Cambridge University Press.

Lee, L.-T., ed. (1987). *The 1911 Revolution: The Chinese in British and Dutch Southeast Asia*. Singapore: Heinemann Asia.

Lefèvre, R. (2013). *Ashes of Hama: The Muslim Brotherhood in Syria*. New York: Oxford University Press.

Lemon, E. (2019). Weaponizing interpol. *Journal of Democracy*, 30(2), 15–29.

Levitt, P. (1998). Social remittances: Migration driven local-level forms of cultural diffusion. *International Migration Review*, 32(4), 926–48.

(2001). *The Transnational Villagers*. Berkeley: University of California Press.

(2003). Keeping feet in both worlds: Transnational practices and immigrant incorporation in the United States. In C. Jopke and E. Morowska, eds., *Toward Assimilation and Citizenship: Immigrants in Liberal Nation-States*. London: Palgrave Macmillan, pp. 177–94.

Levitt, P. and Glick Schiller, N. (2004). Conceptualizing simultaneity: A transnational social field perspective on society. *International Migration Review*, 38(3), 1002–39.

Lewis, D. (2015). "Illiberal spaces": Uzbekistan's extraterritorial security practices and the spatial politics of contemporary authoritarianism. *Nationalities Papers*, 43(1), 140–59.

Lindsley, L. (1943). *War Is People*. Boston: Houghton Mifflin.

Lipsky, M. (1968). Protest as a political resource. *American Political Science Review*, 62(4), 1144–58.

Lofland, J., Snow, D., Anderson, L., and Lofland, L. (2006[1971]). *Analyzing Social Settings: A Guide to Qualitative Observation and Analysis*. Belmont, CA: Wadsworth.

Lynch, M. (2016). *The New Arab Wars: Uprisings and Anarchy in the Middle East*. New York: PublicAffairs.

Lyons, T., and Mandaville, P. (2012). *Politics from Afar: Transnational Diasporas and Networks*. New York: Columbia University Press.

Ma, L. (1990). *Revolutionaries, Monarchists, and Chinatowns: Chinese Politics in the Americas and the 1911 Revolution*. Honolulu: University of Hawaii Press.

Ma, S.-Y. (1993). The exit, voice, and struggle to return of Chinese political exiles. *Pacific Affairs*, 66(3), 368–85.

Maghbouleh, N. (2017). *The Limits of Whiteness: Iranian Americans and the Everyday Politics of Race*. Stanford, CA: Stanford University Press.

Maghur, A. (2010). *Highly-Skilled Migration (Libya): Legal Aspects*. CARIM Analytic and Synthetic Notes, 2010/31. Fiesole, Italy: Robert Schuman Centre for Advanced Studies, European University Institute.

Maney, G. (2000). Transnational mobilization and civil rights in Northern Ireland. *Social Problems*, 47(2), 153–79.

Mann, M. (1984). The autonomous power of the state: Its origins, mechanisms and results. *European Journal of Sociology*, 25(2), 185–213.

(2005). *The Dark Side of Democracy: Explaining Ethnic Cleansing*. New York: Cambridge University Press.

Marx, K. (1978[1872]). Manifesto of the communist party. In R. Tucker, ed., *The Marx-Engels Reader*, 2nd ed. New York: W. W. Norton & Company, pp. 469–500.

Masud-Piloto, F. (1996). *From Welcomed Exiles to Illegal Immigrants: Cuban Migration to the U.S., 1959–1995*. Lanham, MD: Rowman & Littlefield.

Matar, H. (2016). *The Return: Fathers, Sons and the Land in Between*. New York: Random House.

McAdam, D. (1986). Recruitment to high-risk activism: The case of Freedom Summer. *American Journal of Sociology*, 92(1), 64–90.

(1988). *Freedom Summer*. New York: Oxford University Press.

(1996). Conceptual origins, current problems, future directions. In D. McAdam, J. McCarthy, and M. Zald, eds., *Comparative Perspectives on Social Movements: Political Opportunities, Mobilizing Structures, and Cultural Framings*. Cambridge: Cambridge University Press, pp. 23–40.

(1998). On the international origins of domestic political opportunities. In A. Costain and A. McFarland, eds., *Social Movements and American Political Institutions*. Lanham, MD: Rowman & Littlefield, pp. 251–67.

(1999[1982]). *Political Process and the Development of Black Insurgency, 1930–1970*, 2nd ed. Chicago: University of Chicago Press.

McAdam, D. and Boudet, H. (2012). *Putting Social Movements in Their Place: Explaining Opposition to Energy Projects in the United States, 2000–2005*. New York: Cambridge University Press.

McAdam, D., McCarthy, J., and Zald, M., eds. (1996). *Comparative Perspectives on Social Movements: Political Opportunities, Mobilizing Structures, and Cultural Framings*. Cambridge: Cambridge University Press.

McAdam, D., Tarrow, S., and Tilly, C. (2001). *Dynamics of Contention*. Cambridge: Cambridge University Press.

McCarthy, J. (1997). The globalization of social movement theory. In J. Smith, C. Chatfield, and R. Pagnucco, eds., *Transnational Social Movements and Global Politics: Solidarity beyond the State*. Syracuse, NY: Syracuse University Press, pp. 243–57.

McCarthy, J. and Zald, M. (1977). Resource mobilization and social movements: A partial theory. *American Journal of Sociology*, 82(6), 1212–41.

Mearsheimer, J. and Walt, S. (2007). *The Israel Lobby and U.S. Foreign Policy*. New York: Farrar, Straus and Giroux.

Meyer, D. (2004). Protest and political opportunities. *Annual Review of Sociology*, 30, 125–45.

Meyer, D. and Corrigall-Brown, C. (2005). Coalitions and political context: U.S. movements against wars in Iraq. *Mobilization*, 10(3), 327–44.

Michaelsen, M. (2017). Far away, so close: Transnational activism, digital surveillance and authoritarian control in Iran. *Surveillance & Society*, 15(3/4), 465–70.

(2018). Exit and voice in a digital age: Iran's exiled activists and the authoritarian state. *Globalizations*, 15(2), 248–64.

Miller, M. (1981). *Foreign Workers in Western Europe: An Emerging Political Force*. New York: Praeger.

Missbach, A. (2011). *Separatist Conflict in Indonesia. The Long-Distance Politics of the Acehnese Diaspora*. London: Routledge.

Moss, D. (2014). Repression, response, and contained escalation under "liberalized" authoritarianism in Jordan. *Mobilization: An International Quarterly*, 19(3), 489–514.

(2016a). Diaspora mobilization for western military intervention during the Arab Spring. *Journal of Immigrant & Refugee Studies*, 14(3), 277–97.

(2016b). Transnational repression, diaspora mobilization, and the case of the Arab Spring. *Social Problems*, 63(4), 480–98.

(2018). The ties that bind: Internet communication technologies, networked authoritarianism, and "voice" in the Syrian diaspora. *Globalizations*, 15(2), 265–82.

(2020). Voice after exit: Explaining diaspora mobilization for the Arab Spring. *Social Forces*, 98(4), 1669–94.

Moya, J. (2005). Immigrants and associations: A global and historical perspective. *Journal of Ethnic and Migration Studies*, 31(5), 833–64.

Mueller, C. M. (1992). Building social movement theory. In A. D. Morris and C. M. Mueller, eds., *Frontiers in Social Movement Theory*. New Haven, CT: Yale University Press, pp. 3–25.

(1999). Escape from the GDR, 1961–1989: Hybrid exit repertoires in a disintegrating Leninist regime. *American Journal of Sociology*, 105(3), 697–35.

Munif, Y. (2020). *The Syrian Revolution: Between the Politics of Life and the Geopolitics of Death*. London: Pluto Press.

Naber, N. (2006). The rules of forced engagement: Race, gender, and the culture of fear among Arab immigrants in San Francisco post-9/11. *Cultural Dynamics*, 18(3), 235–67.

(2012). *Arab America: Gender, Cultural Politics, and Activism*. New York: New York University Press.

(2014). Imperial whiteness and the diasporas of empire. *American Quarterly*, 66(4), 1107–115.

Nagel, C. (2002). Geopolitics by another name: Immigration and the politics of assimilation. *Political Geography*, 21(8), 971–87.

Nahlawi, Y. (2019). *The Responsibility to Protect in Libya and Syria: Mass Atrocities, Human Protection, and International Law*. New York: Routledge.

Nepstad, S. and Smith, C. (2001). The social structure of moral outrage in recruitment to the U.S. Central America Peace Movement. In J. Goodwin, J. Jasper, and F. Polletta, eds., *Passionate Politics: Emotions and Social Movements*. Chicago: University of Chicago Press, pp. 158–74.

Newland, K. (2010). *Voice after Exit: Diaspora Advocacy*. Washington, DC: Migration Policy Institute.

Noueihed, L. and Warren, A. (2012). *The Battle for the Arab Spring: Revolution, Counter-Revolution and the Making of a New Era*. New Haven, CT: Yale University Press.

Nye, J., Jr. and Keohane, R. (1971). Transnational relations and world politics: An introduction. *International Organization*, 25(3), 329–49.

O'Donnell, G. (1986). On the fruitful convergences of Hirschman's *Exit, Voice, and Loyalty* and *Shifting Involvements*: Reflections from the recent Argentine experience. In A. Foxley, M. McPherson, and G. O'Donnell, eds., *Development, Democracy, and the Art of Trespassing: Essays in the Honor of Albert O. Hirschman*. Notre Dame, IN: University of Notre Dame Press, pp. 249–68.

Ögelman, N., Money, J., and Martin, P. (2002). Immigrant cohesion and political access in influencing host country foreign policy. *SAIS Review*, 22(2), 145–65.

Okamoto, D. (2014). *Redefining Race: Asian American Panethnicity and Shifting Ethnic Boundaries*. New York: Russell Sage Foundation.

Orjuela, C. (2008). Distant warriors, distant peace workers? Multiple diaspora roles in Sri Lanka's violent conflict. *Global Networks*, 8(4), 436–52.

(2018). Mobilising diasporas for justice: Opportunity structures and the presencing of a violent past. *Journal of Ethnic and Migration Studies*, 44(8), 1357–73.

Orwell, G. (2015[1952]). *Homage to Catalonia*. Boston: Mariner Books.

Østergaard-Nielsen, E. (2001). Diasporas in world politics. In D. Josselin and W. Wallace, eds., *Non-state Actors in World Politics*. New York: Palgrave, pp. 217–35.

(2003). *Transnational Politics: Turks and Kurds in Germany*. New York: Routledge.

Othman, M. (2011). *Language Maintenance in the Arabic–Speaking Community in Manchester, Britain: A Sociolinguistic Investigation*. PhD thesis, University of Manchester, UK.

Pargeter, A. (2008). Qadhafi and political Islam in Libya. In D. Vandewalle, ed., *Libya since 1969: Qadhafi's Revolution Revisited*. New York: Palgrave Macmillan, pp. 83–104.

(2012). *Libya: The Rise and Fall of Qaddafi*. New Haven, CT: Yale University Press.

Paul, J. (1990). *Human Rights in Syria*. New York: Human Rights Watch.

Pearlman, W. (2014). Competing for Lebanon's diaspora: Transnationalism and domestic struggles in a weak state. *International Migration Review*, 48(1), 34–75.

(2016). Narratives of fear in Syria. *Perspectives on Politics*, 14(1), 21–37.

(2017). *We Crossed a Bridge and It Trembled: Voices from Syria*. New York: HarperCollins.

Pedraza, S. (2007). *Political Disaffection in Cuba's Revolution and Exodus*. Cambridge: Cambridge University Press.

Pedraza-Bailey, S. 1985. Cuba's exiles: Portrait of a refugee migration. *International Migration Review*, 19(1), 4–34.

Pennock, P. (2017). *The Rise of the Arab American Left: Activists, Allies, and Their Fight against Imperialism and Racism, 1960s–1980s*. Chapel Hill: University of North Carolina Press.

Pérez-Armendáriz, C. and Duquette-Rury, L. (2021). The 3x1 Program for migrants and vigilante groups in contemporary Mexico. *Journal of Ethnic and Migration Studies*, 47(6), 1414–1433. https://doi.org/10.1080/1369183X.2019.1623345.

Pfaff, S. (2006). *Exit-Voice Dynamics and the Collapse of East Germany: The Crisis of Leninism and the Revolution of 1989*. Durham, NC: Duke University Press.

Pfaff, S. and Kim, H. (2003). Exit-voice dynamics in collective action: An analysis of emigration and protest in the East German Revolution. *American Journal of Sociology*, 109(2), 401–44.

Polletta, F. and Jasper, J. (2001). Collective identity and social movements. *Annual Review of Sociology*, 27, 283–305.

Portes, A. (2000). The two meanings of social capital. *Sociological Forum*, 15(1), 1–12.

Portes, A. and Fernández-Kelly, P., eds. (2015). *The State and the Grassroots: Immigrant Transnational Organizations in Four Continents*. Oxford: Berghahn Books.

Pulcini, T. (1993). Trends in research on Arab Americans. *Journal of American Ethnic History*, 12(4), 27–60.

Pupcenoks, J. (2012). Religion or ethnicity?: Middle Eastern conflicts and American Arab-Muslim protest politics. *Nationalism and Ethnic Politics*, 18, 170–92.

(2016). *Western Muslims and Conflicts Abroad: Conflict Spillovers to Diasporas*. New York: Routledge.

Qayyum, M. (2011). *Syrian Diaspora: Cultivating a New Public Space Consciousness*. Policy Brief 35, August 2011. Washington, DC: Middle East Institute.

Quinsaat, S. (2013). Migrant mobilization for homeland politics: A social movement approach. *Sociology Compass*, 7(11), 952–64.

(2016). Diaspora activism in a non-traditional country of destination: The case of Filipinos in the Netherlands. *Ethnic and Racial Studies*, 39(6), 1014–33.

(2019). Linkages and strategies in Filipino diaspora mobilization for regime change. *Mobilization*, 24(2), 221–39.

Ragazzi, F. (2014). A comparative analysis of diaspora policies. *Political Geography*, 41, 74–89.

(2017). *Governing Diasporas in International Relations: The Transnational Politics of Croatia and Former Yugoslavia*. New York: Routledge.

Ragin, C. (2000). *Fuzzy-Set Social Science*. Chicago: University of Chicago Press.

(2008). *Redesigning Social Inquiry: Fuzzy Sets and Beyond*. Chicago: University of Chicago Press.

Ragin, C., Nagel, J., and White, P. (2004). *Workshop on Scientific Foundations of Qualitative Research*. Washington, DC: National Science Foundation.

Rasler, K. (1996). Concessions, repression, and political protest in the Iranian Revolution. *American Sociological Review*, 61(1), 132–52.

Ratha, D., De, S., Kim, E.-J., Plaza, S., Seshan, G., and Yameogo, N. (2019). Data release: Remittances to low- and middle-income countries on track to reach $551 billion in 2019 and $597 billion by 2021. World Bank Blog: People Move. https://blogs.worldbank.org/peoplemove/data-release-remittances-low-and-middle-income-countries-track-reach-551-billion-2019.

Rawlence, B. (2016). *City of Thorns: Nine Lives in the World's Largest Refugee Camp*. New York: Picador.

Repucci, S. (2020). Freedom in the world 2020: A leaderless struggle for democracy. Freedom House. https://freedomhouse.org/sites/default/files/2020-02/FIW_2020_REPORT_BOOKLET_Final.pdf

Richardson, R. (2015). *Comintern Army: The International Brigades and the Spanish Civil War*. Lexington: University Press of Kentucky.

Risse-Kappen, T., ed. (1995). *Bringing Transnational Relations Back In: Non-State Actors, Domestic Structures and International Institutions*. Cambridge: Cambridge University Press.

Risse, T., Ropp, S., and Sikkink, K. (2013). *The Persistent Power of Human Rights: From Commitment to Compliance*. Cambridge: Cambridge University Press.

Ron, J., Ramos, H., and Rodgers, K. (2005). Transnational information politics: NGO human rights reporting, 1986–2000. *International Studies Quarterly*, 49(3), 557–87.

Roston, A. (2008). *The Man Who Pushed America to War: The Extraordinary Life, Adventures, and Obsessions of Ahmad Chalabi*. New York: Nation Books.

Rucht, D. (2004). Movement allies, adversaries, and third parties. In D. Snow, S. Soule, and H. Kriesi, eds., *The Blackwell Companion to Social Movements*. Malden, MA: Blackwell, pp. 197–216.

Rudolph, S. and Piscatori, J., eds. (1997). *Transnational Religion and Fading States*. Boulder, CO: Westview Press.

Russo, C. (2018). *Solidarity in Practice: Moral Protest and the US Security State*. New York: Cambridge University Press.

Safran, W. (1991). Diasporas in modern societies: Myths of homeland and return. *Diaspora: A Journal of Transnational Studies*, 1(1), 83–99.

Said, A. (2020). The rise and fall of the Tahrir repertoire: Theorizing temporality, trajectory, and failure. *Social Problems*. https://doi.org/10.1093/socpro/spaa024.

Santoro, W. and Azab, M. (2015). Arab American protest in the terror decade: Macro- and micro-level response to post-9/11 repression. *Social Problems*, 62(2), 219–40.

Schattschneider, E. (1960). *The Semisovereign People: A Realist's View of Democracy in America.* New York: Thomson Learning.

Schwedler, J. (2006). *Faith in Moderation: Islamist Parties in Jordan and Yemen.* New York: Cambridge University Press.

Seddon, M. (2014). *The Last of the Lascars: Yemeni Muslims in Britain, 1836–2012.* Leicestershire: Kube.

Shain, Y. (1996). Arab-Americans at a crossroads. *Journal of Palestine Studies*, 25(3), 46–59.

(1999). *Marketing the American Creed Abroad: Diasporas in the U.S. and Their Homelands.* Cambridge: Cambridge University Press.

(2002). The role of diasporas in conflict perpetuation or resolution. *SAIS Review*, 22 (2), 115–44.

(2005[1989]). *The Frontier of Loyalty: Political Exiles in the Age of the Nation-State.* Ann Arbor: University of Michigan Press.

(2007). *Kinship and Diasporas in International Affairs.* Ann Arbor: University of Michigan Press.

Sheffer, G. (2003). *Diaspora Politics: At Home Abroad.* New York: Cambridge University Press.

Skrentny, J. (1998). The effects of the Cold War on African-American civil rights: America and the world audience, 1945–1968. *Theory and Society*, 27(2), 237–85.

Simes, J. (2021). *Punishing Places: The Geography of Mass Imprisonment in America.* Berkeley: University of California Press.

Smith, C. (1996). *Resisting Reagan: The U.S. Central America Peace Movement.* Chicago: University of Chicago Press.

Smith, H. and Stares, P. (2007). *Diasporas in Conflict: Peace-Makers or Peace-Wreckers?* New York: United Nations University Press.

Smith, J. (2004). Transnational processes and movements. In D. Snow, S. Soule, and H. Kriesi, eds., *The Blackwell Companion to Social Movements.* Malden, MA: Blackwell, pp. 311–53.

(2008). *Social Movements for Global Democracy.* Baltimore, MD: Johns Hopkins University Press.

Smith, J. and Johnston, H., eds., (2002). *Globalization and Resistance: Transnational Dimensions of Social Movements.* Lanham, MD: Rowman & Littlefield.

Smith, R. (2006). *Mexican New York: Transnational Lives of New Immigrants.* Berkeley: University of California Press.

Smith, T. (2000). *Foreign Attachments: The Power of Ethnic Groups in the Making of American Foreign Policy.* Cambridge, MA: Harvard University Press.

Snow, D. (2013). Identity dilemmas, discursive fields, identity work, and mobilization: Clarifying the identity-movement nexus. In J. van Stekelenburg, C. Roggeband, and B. Klandermans, eds., *The Future of Social Movement Research: Dynamics, Mechanisms, and Processes.* Minneapolis: University of Minnesota Press, pp. 263–80.

Snow, D. and Benford, R. (1988). Ideology, frame resonance, and participant mobiliza- tion. *International Social Movement Research*, 1(1), 197–218.

Snow, D. and Moss, D. (2014). Protest on the fly: Toward a theory of spontaneity in the dynamics of protest and social movements. *American Sociological Review*, 79(6), 1122–43.

Snow, D., Cress, D., Downey, L., and Jones, A. (1998). Disrupting the "quotidian": Reconceptualizing the relationship between breakdown and the emergence of collective action. *Mobilization*, 3(1), 1–22.

Sökefeld, M. (2006). Mobilizing in transnational space: A social movement approach to the formation of diaspora. *Global Networks*, 6(3), 265–84.

Soule, S. (2004). Diffusion processes within and across movements. In D. Snow, S. Soule, and H. Kriesi, eds., *The Blackwell Companion to Social Movements*. Malden, MA: Blackwell, pp. 294–310.

  (2013). Diffusion and scale shift. In D. Snow, D. Della Porta, B. Klandermans, and D. McAdam, eds., *The Wiley-Blackwell Encyclopedia of Social & Political Movements*, vol. 1. Malden, MA: Wiley-Blackwell, pp. 349–53.

St. John, R. B. (2017). *Libya: From Colony to Revolution*, 3rd ed. New York: Oneworld Publications.

Staeheli, L. and Nagel, C. (2008). Rethinking security: Perspectives from Arab-American and British Arab activists. *Antipode*, 40(5), 780–801.

Staggenborg, S. (1988). The consequences of professionalization and formalization in the pro-choice movement. *American Sociological Review*, 53(4), 585–605.

Strauss, A. and Corbin, J. (1990). *Basics of Qualitative Research: Grounded Theory Procedures and Techniques*. Thousand Oaks, CA: Sage.

Svoboda, E. and Pantuliano, S. (2015). International and local/diaspora actors in the Syria response: A diverging set of systems? Working Paper, Humanitarian Policy Group. London: Overseas Development Institute (ODI).

Tarrow, S. (1998). *Power in Movement: Social Movements and Contentious Politics*, 2nd ed. Cambridge: Cambridge University Press.

  (2001). Transnational politics: Contention and institutions in international politics. *Annual Review of Political Science*, 4(1), 1–20.

  (2005). *The New Transnational Activism*. New York: Cambridge University Press.

  (2011). *Power in Movement: Social Movements and Contentious Politics*, 3rd ed. New York: Cambridge University Press.

  (2015). *War, States, and Contention: A Comparative Historical Study*. Ithaca, NY: Cornell University Press.

Taylor, V. (1989). Social movement continuity: The women's movement in abeyance. *American Sociological Review*, 54(5), 761–75.

Tilly, C. (1976[1964]). *The Vendée*. Cambridge, MA: Harvard University Press.

  (1978). *From Mobilization to Revolution*. Reading, MA: Addison-Wesley.

  (2004). *Social Movements, 1768–2004*. Boulder, CO: Paradigm.

Tölölyan, K. (1996). Rethinking diaspora(s): Stateless power in the transnational moment. *Diaspora: A Journal of Transnational Studies*, 5(1), 3–36.

Tsourapas, G. (2020a). Global autocracies: Strategies of transnational repression, legitimation, and co-optation in world politics. *International Studies Review*. https://doi.org/10.1093/isr/viaa061.

  (2020b). The long arm of the Arab State. *Ethnic and Racial Studies*, 43(2), 351–70.

Tsutsui, K. (2004). Global civil society and ethnic social movements in the contemporary world. *Sociological Forum*, 19, 63–87.

  (2006). Redressing past human rights violations: Global dimensions of contemporary social movements. *Social Forces*, 85(1), 331–54.

(2018). *Rights Make Might: Global Human Rights and Minority Social Movements in Japan*. New York: Oxford University Press.

United States of America v. Mohamad Anas Haitham Soueid. (2011). U.S. District Court of Alexandria, VA, October. www.investigativeproject.org/documents/case_docs/1714.pdf.

van Hear, N. and Cohen, R. (2017). Diasporas and conflict: Distance, contiguity and spheres of engagement. *Oxford Development Studies*, 45(2), 171–84.

Vanderbush, W. (2014). The Iraqi diaspora and the US invasion of Iraq. In J. DeWind and R. Segura, eds., *Diaspora Lobbies and the US Government: Convergence and Divergence in Making Foreign Policy*. New York: New York University Press, pp. 211–35.

Vaughan, G. (2020). Storms spark activism among Turkmen diaspora. *The Diplomat*, June 19. https://thediplomat.com/2020/06/storms-spark-activism-among-turkmen-diaspora/.

Vertovec, S. (2004). Cheap calls: The social glue of migrant transnationalism. *Global Networks*, 4(2), 219–24.

(2005). The political importance of diasporas. Working Paper no. 13, Centre on Migration, Policy and Society. Oxford: University of Oxford.

von Bülow, M. (2010). *Building Transnational Networks: Civil Society Networks and the Politics of Trade in the Americas*. New York: Cambridge University Press.

Wald, K. (2008). Homeland interests, hostland politics: Politicized ethnic identity among Middle Eastern heritage groups in the United States. *International Migration Review*, 42(2), 273–301.

(2009). The diaspora project of Arab Americans: Assessing the magnitude and determinants of politicized ethnic identity. *Ethnic and Racial Studies*, 32(8), 1304–24.

Waldinger, R. (2008). Between "here" and "there": Immigrant cross-border activities and loyalties, *International Migration Review*, 42(1), 3–29.

(2015). *The Cross-Border Connection: Immigrants, Emigrants, and Their Homelands*. Cambridge, MA: Harvard University Press.

Waldinger, R. and Fitzgerald, D. (2004). Transnationalism in question. *American Journal of Sociology*, 109(5), 1177–95.

Warbrick, C. (2012). I. British policy and the National Transitional Council of Libya. *International & Comparative Law Quarterly*, 61(1), 247–64.

Wayland, S. (2004). Ethnonationalist networks and transnational opportunities: The Sri Lankan Tamil diaspora. *Review of International Studies*, 30(3), 405–26.

Weber, M. (1978). *Economy and Society: An Outline of Interpretive Sociology*. Edited by G. Roth and C. Wittich. Berkeley: University of California Press.

Wedeen, L. (2015[1999]). *Ambiguities of Domination: Politics, Rhetoric, and Symbols in Contemporary Syria*, 2nd ed. Chicago: University of Chicago Press.

Wehrey, F. (2017). Insecurity and governance challenges in southern Libya. Carnegie Endowment for International Peace, March 27. https://carnegieendowment.org/2017/03/30/insecurity-and-governance-challenges-in-southern-libya-pub-68451.

Wellman, E. (2021). Emigrant inclusion in home country elections: Theory and evidence from sub-Saharan Africa. *American Political Science Review*, 115(1), 82–96. https://doi.org/10.1017/S0003055420000866.

Wescott, C. and Brinkerhoff, J., eds. (2006). *Converting Migration Drains into Gains: Harnessing the Resources of Overseas Professionals*. Manilla, Philippines: Asian Development Bank.

White, R. (1989). From peaceful protest to guerrilla war: Micromobilization of the Provisional Irish Republican Army. *American Journal of Sociology*, 94(6), 1277–302.

Williamson, Hugh. (2015). Dispatches: Jailed in Azerbaijan for a protest in Berlin. Human Rights Watch, February 17. www.hrw.org/news/2015/02/17/dispatches-jailed-azerbaijan-protest-berlin.

Wimmer, A. (2013). *Ethnic Boundary Making: Institutions, Power, Networks*. New York: Oxford University Press.

Wimmer, A. and Glick Schiller, N. (2002). Methodological nationalism and beyond: Nation-state building, migration and the social sciences. *Global Networks*, 2(4), 301–34.

World Bank. (2018). Record high remittances to low- and middle-income countries in 2017. April 23. Washington, DC: World Bank. www.worldbank.org/en/news/press-release/2018/04/23/record-high-remittances-to-low-and-middle-income-countries-in-2017.

Wright, J. (2012). *A History of Libya*. New York: Columbia University Press.

Yadav, S. (2016). The ties that bind. *Middle East Research and Information Project*, 281 (Winter). https://merip.org/2017/05/the-ties-that-bind/.

Yassin-Kassab, R. and Al-Shami, L. (2018). *Burning Country: Syrians in Revolution and War*, 2nd ed. London: Pluto Press.

Yin, R. (2008). *Case Study Research: Design and Methods*, 4th ed. Thousand Oaks, CA: Sage.

Younis, A. (1995). *The Coming of the Arabic-Speaking People to the United States*. Edited by P. Kayal. New York: Center for Migration Studies.

Zarnett, D. (2015). Transnationalized domestic contention: Explaining the varying levels of western solidarity given to Kurds and Palestinians. In F. Gerges, ed., *Contentious Politics in the Middle East: Popular Resistance and Marginalized Activism beyond the Arab Uprisings*. New York: Palgrave Macmillan, pp. 197–228.

Zepeda-Millán, C. (2017). *Latino Mass Mobilization: Immigration, Racialization, and Activism*. New York: Cambridge University Press.

Ziadeh, R. (2011). *Power and Policy in Syria: Intelligence Services, Foreign Relations and Democracy in the Modern Middle East*. New York: I. B. Tauris.

DOCUMENTARY FILMS

Abdulhamid, A. (2011). Mutiny in the Syrian Army? *Al Jazeera English*, April 27. www.aljazeera.com/opinions/2011/4/27/mutiny-in-the-syrian-army

Germano, R. (2009). *The Other Side of Immigration*.

Ishaq, S. (2012). *Karama Has No Walls*.

Kalin, A. and Lukacs, O. (2014). *Red Lines*.

Omeish, A. (2011). *Libya 2011: Through the Fire*. www.aljazeera.com/program/featured-documentaries/2018/2/18/libya-2011-through-the-fire.

Piscatella, J. (2013). *#ChicagoGirl: The Social Network Takes on a Dictator*.

MEDIA ARTICLES AND WEBSITES

Al Jazeera English. (2011a). Gaddafi blames uprising on al-Qaeda. February 24. www .aljazeera.com/news/2011/2/24/gaddafi-blames-uprising-on-al-qaeda.

(2011b). UN rights body urges Libya action. February 25. www.aljazeera.com/news/ 2011/2/25/un-rights-body-urges-libya-action.

Amos, D. (2020). Syrian war crimes trial resumes in Germany. National Public Radio, Morning Edition, May 21. www.npr.org/2020/05/21/859991380/syrian-war-crimes-trial-resumes-in-germany.

Bachelor, L. (2014). HSBC accused of closing UK bank accounts held by Syrians. *Guardian*, August 8. http://www.theguardian.com/money/2014/aug/08/hsbc-accused-closing-bank-accounts-syrians.

Badran, T. (2018). "Ambassador Samantha Power lied to my face about Syria," by Kassem Eid. *The Tablet*, February 27. www.tabletmag.com/sections/israel-middle-east/articles/samantha-power-kassem-eid-syria.

Bittar, Y. (2013). Syria witness: "She refused to even look at me". *Middle East Voices*, February 18. http://middleeastvoices.voanews.com/2013/02/syria-witness-she-refused-to-even-look-at-me-94597/.

Black, I. (2011). Gaddafi threatens retaliation in Mediterranean as UN passes resolution. *Guardian*, March 17. http://www.theguardian.com/world/2011/mar/17/gaddafi-retaliation-mediterranean-libya-no-fly-zone.

Brand, L. (2014). The stakes and symbolism of voting from abroad. *Washington Post, Monkey Cage blog*, June 5. www.washingtonpost.com/news/monkey-cage/wp/2014/06/05/the-stakes-and-symbolism-of-voting-from-abroad/.

Bugaighis, M. and Buisier, M. (2003). Why the American Libyan Freedom Alliance (ALFA)? http://www.libya-watanona.com/letters/v2003b/v02nov3a.htm.

Carnegie Endowment for International Peace. (2013). Syria in Crisis: The Syrian National Council. Diwan Blog, Malcom H. Kerr Carnegie Middle Easter Center, September 25. http://carnegieendowment.org/syriaincrisis/?fa=48334.

Charbonneau, L. and Evans, D. (2012). Syria in civil war, U.N. official says. *Reuters*, June 12. www.reuters.com/article/us-syria/syria-in-civil-war-u-n-official-says-idUSBRE85B0DZ20120612.

Cornwell, S. (2013). U.S. providing some lethal aid to Syrian rebels: Opposition spokesman. *Reuters*, September 10. www.reuters.com/article/us-syria-crisis-usa-rebels/u-s-providing-some-lethal-aid-to-syrian-rebels-opposition-spokesman-idUSBRE9891EZ20130910.

Devi, S. (2012). Syrian diaspora laments opposition's disunity. *National*, October 14. http://www.thenational.ae/news/world/middle-east/syrian-diaspora-laments-oppositions-disunity.

Eid, K. (2017). I survived a sarin gas attack. *The New York Times*, April 7. www .nytimes.com/2017/04/07/opinion/what-its-like-to-survive-a-sarin-gas-attack.html.

Farooq, U. (2015). The hunted. *Foreign Policy*, April 2. http://foreignpolicy.com/2015/04/02/the-hunted-islam-karimov-assassination-istanbul-russia-putin-islamic-state-human-rights/.

Fisher, K. (2011). Protestors arrested for tearing down Qaddafi pictures at Libyan mission. WUSA 9 News, February 25. http://foggybottom.wusa9.com/news/news/protestors-arrested-tearing-down-qaddafi-pictures-libyan-mission/54432.

Gaylon, S. (2013). Raed and Razan, and on building functional citizens. Medium, December 30. https://medium.com/@shiyamg/raed-and-razan-and-on-building-func tional-citizens-61dfo8b5a2a4.

Hastings, R. (2012). Neighbours from hell: How Syria's war hit an Acton street. *Independent*, March 19. http://www.independent.co.uk/news/uk/home-news/neigh bours-from-hell-how-syrias-war-hit-an-acton-street-7576814.html.

Hill, E. (2011). Libyans in US allege coercion. Al Jazeera English, February 17. www .aljazeera.com/features/2011/2/17/libyans-in-us-allege-coercion.

Hollersen, W. (2012). Syrian in Berlin channels aid to embattled countrymen. *Spiegel Online*, March 16. http://www.spiegel.de/international/world/syrian-in-berlin-chan nels-aid-to-embattled-countrymen-a-821853.html.

Ighneiwa, I. Libya: Our home. http://www.libya-watanona.com/libya/.

Knickmeyer, E. Yemen's double game. (2010). *Foreign Policy*, December 7. https:// foreignpolicy.com/2010/12/07/yemens-double-game-2/.

Kofman, J. (2011). Resistance in Tripoli: Risking life with covert acts of defiance. *ABC News*, June 2. https://abcnews.go.com/International/anti-gadhafi-activists-move ment-libya-underground/story?id=13746119.

Kossaify, E. (2020). Caesar Act sends Syria's Bashar Assad a stark reality check. *Arab News*, June 16. www.arabnews.com/node/1690791/middle-east.

MacFarquhar, N. (2013). A very busy man behind the Syrian civil war's casualty count. *The New York Times*, April 9. www.nytimes.com/2013/04/10/world/middleeast/ the-man-behind-the-casualty-figures-in-syria.html.

Malek, A. (2013). From Houston AC repairman to Syrian border camp mayor. *Al Jazeera America*, September 12. http://america.aljazeera.com/articles/2013/9/12/ the-mayor-of-thesyrianidpcamp.html.

McKenzie, D. (2011). From deep inside Tripoli, displays of defiance. *CNN*, July 12. http://edition.cnn.com/2011/WORLD/africa/07/07/libya.tripoli.rebel/.

Meek, J., Bas, E., Christie, M., and Madden, P. (2017). FBI probes murder of Syrian-American journalist who sought to expose Assad regime abuses. *ABC News* (November 28). https://abcnews.go.com/International/fbi-probing-murder-syrian-american-journalist-mother-turkey/story?id=51436199.

Moss, D. M. (2017). Why so many syrians living abroad support U.S. intervention. Monkey Cage blog, *The Washington Post*, April 19. www.washingtonpost.com/ news/monkey-cage/wp/2017/04/19/why-so-many-syrians-living-abroad-support-u-s-intervention/.

Myers, S. (2011). U.S. and allies say Syria leader must step down. *New York Times*, August 18. www.nytimes.com/2011/08/19/world/middleeast/19diplo.html.

National Public Radio. (2011). Libyan Americans work to maintain ties to homeland. Talk of the Nation, March 3. www.npr.org/2011/03/03/134235473/Libyan-Americans-Work-To-Maintain-Ties-To-Homeland.

(2013). Syrian activist seeks support from Syrian-Americans. All Things Considered, December 22. www.npr.org/2013/12/22/256351915/syrian-activist-seeks-support-from-syrian-americans.

Nordheimer, J. (1984). Libyan exiles in Britain live in fear of Qaddafi assassins. *New York Times*, April 26. www.nytimes.com/1984/04/26/world/libyan-exiles-in-brit ain-live-in-fear-of-qaddafi-assassins.html.

O'Bagy, E. (2012). Disorganized like a fox. *Foreign Policy*, June 29. http://foreignpolicy
.com/2012/06/29/disorganized-like-a-fox/.

O'Grady, S. (2014). Holocaust Museum Displays Echoes of Nazi Era in Syria War
Photos. *Foreign Policy*, October 16. https://foreignpolicy.com/2014/10/16/holo
caust-museum-displays-echoes-of-nazi-era-in-syria-war-photos/.

Office of the Press Secretary. (2011). Remarks by President Obama and Prime Minister
Cameron of the United Kingdom in joint press conference in London, United
Kingdom. The White House, May 25. https://obamawhitehouse.archives.gov/the-
press-office/2011/05/25/remarks-president-obama-and-prime-minister-cameron-
united-kingdom-joint-.

Parvaz, D. (2011). Expats join Syrian revolution from afar. Al Jazeera English,
September 8. www.aljazeera.com/features/2011/9/8/expats-join-syrian-revolution-
from-afar.

Public Broadcasting Service. (2012). Are Syrian spies keeping tabs on opposition activists in U.S.? PBS NewsHour, January 3. http://www.pbs.org/newshour/bb/world-
jan-june12-syria_01-03/.

Railton, J. S. (2012). Can you get around an internet shutdown? July 27. www
.johnscottrailton.com/the-voices-feeds/.

Seale, P. (1982). Bloodbath at Hama reflects Paranoia of Syrian leadership. *Globe and
Mail*, May 11.

Sengupta, S. (2017). Loose definition of terrorism upends a Syrian asylum seeker's life.
New York Times, June 23. www.nytimes.com/2017/06/23/world/middleeast/immi
gration-asylum-syria-terrorism.html.

Siddique, H. and Borger, J. (2013). Family of British surgeon who died in Syria criticise
UK government. *The Guardian*, December 18. www.theguardian.com/politics/
2013/dec/18/family-surgeon-abbas-khan-syria-uk-government.

Simon, M. and Bolduan, K. (2019). He smuggled war crimes evidence and begged the US
for help. Now Congress is finally acting and set to sanction Syria. *CNN*, December
17, www.cnn.com/2019/12/17/politics/defense-caesar-syria-bill/index.html.

Ward, C. (2012). Doctor returns to Syria from U.S. to help rebels. CBS News, October
12. www.cbsnews.com/news/doctor-returns-to-syria-from-us-to-help-rebels/.

Yamin, B., Moubayed, S., Barq, M., and Stifo, G. (2017). Don't be fooled: Assad is no
friend of Syria's Christian minorities. *The Hill*, May 11. https://thehill.com/blogs/
pundits-blog/religion/332938-dont-be-fooled-assad-is-no-friend-of-syrias-christian-
minorities.

Index

Books in the Series (continued from p. iii)

CPSIA information can be obtained
at www.ICGtesting.com
Printed in the USA
BVHW031743120422
634087BV00002B/16